The
FOOTBALL ASSOCIATION YEARBOOK 1988–1989

GW00684868

The Football Association

Patron

HER MAJESTY THE QUEEN

President

HRH THE DUKE OF KENT KG

The
FOOTBALL ASSOCIATION YEARBOOK 1988–1989

LONDON

PELHAM BOOKS

PELHAM BOOKS

Published by the Penguin Group
27 Wrights Lane, London W8 5TZ, England
Viking Penguin Inc., 40 West 23rd Street, New York, New York 10010, USA
Penguin Books Australia Ltd, Ringwood, Victoria, Australia
Penguin Books Canada Ltd, 2801 John Street, Markham, Ontario, Canada L3R 1B4
Penguin Books (NZ) Ltd, 182-190 Wairau Road, Auckland 10, New Zealand

Penguin Books Ltd, Registered Offices: Harmondsworth, Middlesex, England
First published 1988

Made and printed in Great Britain by
Richard Clay Limited, Bungay, Suffolk
Typeset by Rowland Phototypesetting (London) Ltd.

ISBN 07207 1818 X

A CIP catalogue record for this book is available from the British Library

Photo credits
All the photographs used in this book are by Bob Thomas with the following
exceptions: pages 14, 16, 35, 141: the photograph on page 137 is by Harry
Ormesher.

The sale of advertisements in this
publication was carried out by
AIM Publications Ltd, London W1.

Contents

Cover picture: Peter Beardsley attempts to evade Colin Foster's tackle in the
Cup semi-final at Hillsbrough. *(Colorsport)*

Wimbledon's Dave Beasant holds the precious Cup aloft.

"The grounds are safer"

says Ted Croker

For many years Britain's three major pools companies – Littlewoods, Vernons and Zetters – have contributed large sums of money to British football in the form of "copyright" payments to the football authorities for the use of their fixtures on the pools coupons. In 1975 the Pool Promoters Association began to donate a significant proportion of the turnover from their "Spotting-the-Ball" competition to Football League clubs to meet the large expenditure made necessary by the provisions of the Safety of Sports Grounds Act.

The Football Trust was founded by the P.P.A. in 1979 and, with the money made available from "Spotting-the-Ball", it was empowered to provide funds for the benefit of football in general, but with particular emphasis on tackling any associated social problems. The main purposes for which the Trust has used its money have been as follows:

1 League club grounds – safety and improvements;
2 Football and the Community schemes;
3 Aid to football's grass roots: (a) more and improved playing pitches and changing facilities and (b) hard surface play areas;
4 Activities such as sponsoring conferences and reports, awarding grants to bodies like the National Playing Fields Association and the Disabled Sports Foundation;
5 Specific anti-hooligan measures including grants for police charges and the installation of closed-circuit television.

The work of The Football Trust in connection with the improvement of security in and around football grounds continues to be appreciated by the clubs, the police and the vast majority of spectators. It is a great pity that "football hooliganism" received such an unprecedented amount of media coverage during the period of England's participation in the European Championship Finals in West Germany. This was totally detrimental to the image of English football and in particular its "supporters" (a misnomer if you like).

By contrast, our domestic season had finished in May on a high note to confirm football's continued rise in popularity. Attendances at Barclays League matches had gone up to 18 million, as against 17.4 million in the previous season when there were more First Division matches, with the overall average reaching the highest level for four years.

With the help of The Football Trust, England's football grounds last season became safer, proving that police intelligence and closed-circuit surveillance really were working. There were more arrests admittedly, but that was a sign that the battle was being won in the grounds, not lost. It is in the city streets at home and abroad where we so often look to be losing the fight, and this is a problem that the Government must tackle. (The Football Trust is playing its part in setting aside a substantial sum each year to assist with transport improvements.) The football authorities are tired of being held responsible for the excesses of some members of a society in which violence and drunkenness have become endemic.

THE COCA-COLA FOOTBALL ASSOCIATION SOCCER ST★R SCHEME

"If you play or watch football – we'll make you a Soccer Star."

The Football Association has developed a Soccer Education programme – the Soccer Star Scheme – which will be launched in September 1988. Teachers, Coaches and Youth Leaders wishing to be eligible to examine the Soccer Star Tests must attend a workshop. For details of workshops in your area please write to The Soccer Star Office, 22/24A The Broadway, Darkes Lane, Potters Bar, Herts EN6 2HH (or telephone 0707 50057).

What is The Soccer Star Scheme?
The Scheme involves the essential soccer techniques of dribbling, running with the ball, shooting, heading, changing direction with and without the ball. As part of the Scheme, six simple tests have been devised after extensive research with over 5,000 children. Six grades or "Stars" are available to be awarded on the basis of the test scores of the child and the "norms" for the child at that age.

Who is the Scheme for?
Boys and girls aged between 6 and 16 of different abilities. All young players can be challenged within the Scheme as competition is geared towards improving on previous scores whatever level the child is working at. Above all the tests are *enjoyable – Football for Fun.*

How does the Scheme operate?
Teachers and coaches are recommended to conduct an assessment test. A course of instruction follows as outlined in the Scheme booklet which is distributed *free* to all tea-

chers and coaches registered. On completion of the course the children are tested for their awards.

What knowledge of results does the child receive?
On completion of the tests, the teacher or coach completes a record form card and sends this form to the Award Office at Potters Bar. On receipt of the record form the results are entered into a computer and a pack prepared for each child consisting of the following: a letter from Bobby Robson; an individual progress report; a certificate; a cloth badge; a lapel sticker; a pennant/bag sticker.

What feedback is available for the coach?
The coach or teacher will receive: a letter from the National Coach/General Secretary; a read out of the children's performance; a read out of the group's previous performances.

The Scheme is invaluable to the coach or teacher in order to: evaluate the teacher's or the coach's own performance; profile and record children's progress; develop ability groups; identify potentially gifted players. All teachers and coaches registering in the Scheme will receive: commission on tests conducted; a free Soccer Star booklet; a 30% discount to purchase the Soccer Star video.

What back up material is available?
The Scheme is fully integrated to incorporate: the 64-page Soccer Star booklet (£2.95) and the one-hour Soccer Star video (£9.99).

World Cup Winners 1930-86

Year	Winners		Runners-up		Venue
1930	Uruguay	4	Argentina	2	Montevideo
1934	*Italy	2	Czechoslovakia	1	Rome
1938	Italy	4	Hungary	2	Paris
1950	Uruguay	2	Brazil	1	Rio de Janeiro
1954	West Germany	3	Hungary	2	Berne
1958	Brazil	5	Sweden	2	Stockholm
1962	Brazil	3	Czechoslovakia	1	Santiago
1966	*England	4	West Germany	2	London
1970	Brazil	4	Italy	1	Mexico City
1974	West Germany	2	Holland	1	Munich
1978	*Argentina	3	Holland	1	Buenos Aires
1982	Italy	3	West Germany	1	Madrid
1986	Argentina	3	West Germany	2	Mexico City

*After extra time

European Football Championship
Henri Delaunay Cup Winners 1960-88

(formerly EUROPEAN NATIONS CUP)

Year	Winners		Runners-up		Venue
1960	U.S.S.R.	2	Yugoslavia	1	Paris
1964	Spain	2	U.S.S.R.	1	Madrid
1968	Italy	2	Yugoslavia	0	Rome
			(After 1-1 draw)		
1972	West Germany	3	U.S.S.R.	0	Brussels
1976	*Czechoslovakia	2	West Germany	2	Belgrade
1980	West Germany	2	Belgium	1	Rome
1984	France	2	Spain	0	Paris
1988	Holland	2	U.S.S.R.	0	Munich

*Won on penalty-kicks.

UEFA Competition for Under-23 Teams
Winners 1972-76

(AGGREGATE SCORES)

Year	Winners		Runners-up	
1972	Czechoslovakia	5	U.S.S.R.	3
1974	Hungary	6	German Dem Rep.	3
1976	U.S.S.R.	3	Hungary	2

UEFA Competition for Under-21 Teams
Winners 1976-88

(AGGREGATE SCORES)

Year	Winners		Runners-up	
1978	Yugoslavia	5	German Dem. Rep.	4
1980	U.S.S.R.	1	German Dem. Rep.	0
1982	England	5	West Germany	4
1984	England	3	Spain	0
1986	*Spain	3	Italy	3
1988	France		Greece	

*Won on penalty-kicks.

European Champion Clubs' Cup Winners 1956-88

Year	Winners		Runners-up		Venue
1956	Real Madrid	4	Stade de Rheims	3	Paris
1957	Real Madrid	2	A.C. Fiorentina	0	Madrid
1958	Real Madrid	3	A.C. Milan	2	Brussels
1959	Real Madrid	2	Stade de Rheims	0	Stuttgart
1960	Real Madrid	7	Eintracht Frankfurt	3	Glasgow
1961	Benfica	3	Barcelona	2	Berne
1962	Benfica	5	Real Madrid	3	Amsterdam
1963	A.C. Milan	2	Benfica	1	London
1964	Inter-Milan	3	Real Madrid	1	Vienna
1965	Inter-Milan	1	Benfica	0	Milan
1966	Real Madrid	2	Partizan Belgrade	1	Brussels
1967	Celtic	2	Inter-Milan	1	Lisbon
1968	Manchester United	4	Benfica	1	London
1969	A.C. Milan	4	Ajax Amsterdam	1	Madrid
1970	Feyenoord	2	Celtic	1	Milan
1971	Ajax Amsterdam	2	Panathinaikos	0	London
1972	Ajax Amsterdam	2	Inter-Milan	0	Rotterdam
1973	Ajax Amsterdam	1	Juventus	0	Belgrade
1974	Bayern Munich	4	Atletico Madrid	0	Brussels
		(After 1-1 draw in Brussels)			
1975	Bayern Munich	2	Leeds United	0	Paris
1976	Bayern Munich	1	St. Etienne	0	Glasgow
1977	Liverpool	3	Borussia Mönchengladbach	1	Rome
1978	Liverpool	1	Bruges	0	London
1979	Nottingham Forest	1	Malmo	0	Munich
1980	Nottingham Forest	1	S.V. Hamburg	0	Madrid
1981	Liverpool	1	Real Madrid	0	Paris
1982	Aston Villa	1	Bayern Munich	0	Rotterdam
1983	S.V. Hamburg	1	Juventus	0	Athens
1984	*Liverpool	1	Roma	1	Rome
1985	Juventus	1	Liverpool	0	Brussels
1986	*Steaua Bucharest	0	Barcelona	0	Seville
1987	Porto	2	Bayern Munich	1	Vienna
1988	*P.S.V. Eindhoven	0	Benfica	0	Stuttgart

*Won on penalty-kicks

European Fairs' Cup Winners 1958-71

(formerly INTER-CITIES FAIRS' CUP)
(AGGREGATE SCORES)

Year	Winners		Runners-up		Venue
1958	Barcelona	8	London	2	
1960	Barcelona	4	Birmingham City	1	
1961	A.S. Roma	4	Birmingham City	2	
1962	Valencia	7	Barcelona	3	
1963	Valencia	4	Dynamo Zagreb	1	
1964	*Real Zaragoza	2	Valencia	1	Barcelona
1965	*Ferencvaros	1	Juventus	0	Turin
1966	Barcelona	4	Real Zaragoza	3	
1967	Dynamo Zagreb	2	Leeds United	0	
1968	Leeds United	1	Ferencvaros	0	
1969	Newcastle United	6	Ujpest Dozsa	2	
1970	Arsenal	4	Anderlecht	3	
1971	†Leeds United	3	Juventus	3	

*One leg only   †Won on away goals.

European Cup Winners' Cup
Winners 1961-88

Year	Winners	Runners-up	Venue
1961	*A.C. Fiorentina...................... 4	Glasgow Rangers...................... 1	
1962	Atletico Madrid...................... 3	A.C. Fiorentina...................... 0	Stuttgart
	(After 1-1 draw in Glasgow)		
1963	Tottenham Hotspur.................. 5	Atletico Madrid...................... 1	Rotterdam
1964	Sporting Club, Lisbon................ 1	M.T.K. Budapest 0	Antwerp
	(After 3-3 draw in Brussels)		
1965	West Ham United 2	T.S.V. Munich 0	London
1966	Borussia Dortmund.................. 2	Liverpool............................... 1	Glasgow
1967	Bayern Munich 1	Glasgow Rangers...................... 0	Nuremberg
1968	A.C. Milan.............................. 2	S.V. Hamburg 0	Rotterdam
1969	Slovan Bratislava 3	Barcelona 2	Basle
1970	Manchester City 2	Gornik Zabrze 1	Vienna
1971	Chelsea 2	Real Madrid 1	Athens
	(After 1-1 draw in Athens)		
1972	Glasgow Rangers...................... 3	Moscow Dynamo...................... 2	Barcelona
1973	A.C. Milan.............................. 1	Leeds United 0	Salonika
1974	Magdeburg.............................. 2	A.C. Milan.............................. 0	Rotterdam
1975	Dinamo Kiev 3	Ferencvaros............................ 0	Basle
1976	Anderlecht 4	West Ham United 2	Brussels
1977	S.V. Hamburg 2	Anderlecht.............................. 0	Amsterdam
1978	Anderlecht.............................. 4	Austria Vienna......................... 0	Paris
1979	Barcelona 4	Fortuna Düsseldorf 3	Basle
1980	†Valencia 0	Arsenal 0	Brussels
1981	Dinamo Tbilisi 2	Carl Zeiss Jena 1	Düsseldorf
1982	Barcelona 2	Standard Liege........................ 1	Barcelona
1983	Aberdeen 2	Real Madrid 1	Gothenburg
1984	Juventus 2	Porto 1	Basle
1985	Everton 3	Rapid Vienna 1	Rotterdam
1986	Dinamo Kiev 3	Atletico Madrid........................ 0	Lyon
1987	Ajax Amsterdam...................... 1	Lokomotiv Leipzig.................... 0	Athens
1988	Mechelen 1	Ajax Amsterdam...................... 0	Strasbourg

*Aggregate scores   †Won on penalty-kicks.

UEFA Cup Winners 1972-88

(AGGREGATE SCORES)

Year	Winners	Runners-up
1972	Tottenham Hotspur.................. 3	Wolverhampton Wanderers 2
1973	Liverpool............................... 3	Borussia Mönchengladbach 2
1974	Feyenoord 4	Tottenham Hotspur................... 2
1975	Borussia Mönchengladbach 5	Twente Enschede 1
1976	Liverpool............................... 4	F.C. Bruges............................ 3
1977	†Juventus 2	Atletico Bilbao........................ 2
1978	P.S.V. Eindhoven 3	Bastia................................... 0
1979	Borussia Mönchengladbach 2	Red Star Belgrade 1
1980	†Eintracht Frankfurt.................. 3	Borussia Mönchengladbach 3
1981	Ipswich Town.......................... 5	AZ 67 Alkmaar 4
1982	I.F.K. Gothenburg 4	S.V. Hamburg 0
1983	Anderlecht............................. 2	Benfica 1
1984	*Tottenham Hotspur.................. 2	Anderlecht............................. 2
1985	Real Madrid 3	Videoton 1
1986	Real Madrid 5	Cologne................................ 3
1987	Gothenburg............................ 2	Dundee United 1
1988	*Bayer Leverkusen.................... 3	Español 3

†Won on away goals.   *Won on penalty-kicks

11

FIFA World Cup

Finals in Italy, 9th June to 8th July 1990

Preliminary Competition

EUROPE

Group 1

Denmark, Bulgaria, Rumania, Greece

19.10.88	Greece v Denmark
	Bulgaria v Rumania
2.11.88	Rumania v Greece
	Denmark v Bulgaria
26.4.89	Greece v Rumania
	Bulgaria v Denmark
17.5.89	Rumania v Bulgaria
	Denmark v Greece
11.10.89	Bulgaria v Greece
	Denmark v Rumania
15.11.89	Greece v Bulgaria
	Rumania v Denmark

Group 2

England, Poland, Sweden, Albania

19.10.88	England v Sweden
	Poland v Albania
5.11.88	Albania v Sweden
8.3.89	Albania v Sweden
26.4.89	England v Albania
7.5.89	Sweden v Poland
3.6.89	England v Poland
6.9.89	Sweden v England
8.10.89	Sweden v Albania
11.10.89	Poland v England
25.10.89	Poland v Sweden
15.11.89	Albania v Poland

Group 3

USSR, German Democratic Republic (GDR), Austria, Iceland, Turkey

31.8.88	Iceland v USSR
12.10.88	Turkey v Iceland
19.10.88	USSR v Austria
	GDR v Iceland
2.11.88	Austria v Turkey
30.11.88	Turkey v GDR
12.4.89	GDR v Turkey
26.4.89	USSR v GDR
10.5.89	Turkey v USSR
17.5.89	GDR v Austria
31.5.89	USSR v Iceland
14.6.89	Iceland v Austria
23.8.89	Austria v Iceland

6.9.89	Austria v USSR
	Iceland v GDR
20.9.89	Iceland v Turkey
7./8.10.89	GDR v USSR
25.10.89	Turkey v Austria
8.11.89	USSR v Turkey
15.11.89	Austria v GDR

Group 4

Germany FR, Netherlands, Wales, Finland

31.8.88	Finland v Germany FR
14.9.88	Netherlands v Wales
19.10.88	Wales v Finland
	Germany FR v Netherlands
26.4.89	Netherlands v Germany FR
31.5.89	Wales v Germany FR
	Finland v Netherlands
6.9.89	Finland v Wales
4.10.89	Germany FR v Finland
11.10.89	Wales v Netherlands
15.11.89	Germany FR v Wales
	Netherlands v Finland

Group 5

France, Scotland, Yugoslavia, Norway, Cyprus

14.9.88	Norway v Scotland
28.9.88	France v Norway
19.10.88	Scotland v Yugoslavia
22.10.88	Cyprus v France
2.11.88	Cyprus v Norway
19.11.88	Yugoslavia v France
11.12.88	Yugoslavia v Cyprus
8.2.89	Cyprus v Scotland
8.3.89	Scotland v France
25.4.89	Scotland v Cyprus
29.4.89	France v Yugoslavia
16.5.89	Norway v Cyprus
14.6.89	Norway v Yugoslavia
5.9.89	Norway v France
6.9.89	Yugoslavia v Scotland
11.10.89	Yugoslavia v Norway
	France v Scotland
28.10.89	Cyprus v Yugoslavia
15.11.89	Scotland v Norway
18.11.89	France v Cyprus

Group 6

Spain, Hungary, Northern Ireland, Ireland Republic, Malta

21.5.88	Northern Ireland v Malta
14.9.88	Northern Ireland v Ireland Republic
19.10.88	Hungary v Northern Ireland
16.11.88	Spain v Ireland Republic
11.12.88	Malta v Hungary
21.12.88	Spain v Northern Ireland
22.1.89	Malta v Spain
8.2.89	Northern Ireland v Spain
8.3.89	Hungary v Ireland Republic
22.3.89	Spain v Malta
12.4.89	Hungary v Malta
26.4.89	Malta v Northern Ireland
	Ireland Republic v Spain
28.5.89	Ireland Republic v Malta
4.6.89	Ireland Republic v Hungary
6.6.89	Northern Ireland v Hungary
11.10.89	Hungary v Spain
	Ireland Republic v Northern Ireland
15.11.89	Spain v Hungary
	Malta v Ireland Republic

Group 7

Belgium, Portugal, Czechoslovakia, Switzerland, Luxembourg

21.9.88	Luxembourg v Switzerland
19.10.88	Belgium v Switzerland
	Luxembourg v Czechoslovakia
16.11.88	Czechoslovakia v Belgium
	Portugal v Luxembourg
15.2.89	Portugal v Belgium
25./26.4.89	Portugal v Switzerland
30.4.89	Belgium v Czechoslovakia
10.5.89	Czechoslovakia v Luxembourg
31.5./1.6.89	Luxembourg v Belgium
7.6.89	Switzerland v Czechoslovakia
6.9.89	Belgium v Portugal
20.9.89	Switzerland v Portugal
6.10.89	Czechoslovakia v Portugal
11.10.89	Luxembourg v Portugal
	Switzerland v Belgium
25.10.89	Czechoslovakia v Switzerland
	Belgium v Luxembourg
15.11.89	Portugal v Czechoslovakia
	Switzerland v Luxembourg

The Football Association Celebrates its 125th Anniversary

In the nineteenth century the great public schools adopted football as a form of physical recreation ideally suited to the development of the Victorian ideals of manhood, loyalty, courage and discipline. Each school developed its own particular form of the game, with its own rules, size of pitch and number of players. Largely conditioned by the nature of the pitch available, football became either a "handling" or "hacking" game in country schools playing on the soft turf meadows, and became a dribbling and passing game in the narrow confines of the stone-flagged playgrounds of the London schools.

At the universities, players from the different schools found it difficult to continue to enjoy the game which they had grown up with, because there was no agreed set of rules by which all teams could play. In 1848, at Cambridge, a meeting was held to attempt to draw up some rules by which football would be played at that University. These "Cambridge Rules", however, were little observed, and another meeting in 1862 which attempted the same task was likewise unsuccessful. Meanwhile, football outside the schools and universities was becoming popular, with clubs starting at Sheffield (1855), Blackheath and Hallamshire (1857), and Forest and Wanderers (1860).

The Football Association came into being on 26th October 1863, when a meeting of members of the chief clubs and schools playing football decided to form an Association for the purpose of framing a set of

The Freemason's Tavern in London, where The Football Association was formed at a meeting in 1863.

official laws under which all clubs could play the game. Apart from a number of independent persons interested in the scheme, the following clubs were represented at the meeting: Barnes, Blackheath, Charterhouse, Perceval House, Kensington School, War Office, Crystal Palace, Blackheath Proprietary School, The Crusaders, Forest and No Names (Kilburn). There was a considerable difference of opinion among the original members as to the Laws of the Game. These were not passed until the fifth meeting.

The move which probably did most to broaden the outlook of The Football Association and spread its influence over a wider field was made on 20th July 1871, when it was proposed that a Challenge Cup be established for competition among its members. After this, membership increased by leaps and bounds, until in 1881 clubs and associations under the wing of The Association numbered 128.

The competition began in the 1871-72 season with fifteen entries, and Wanderers defeated Royal Engineers 1-0 before a 2,000 crowd at Kennington Oval to become the first Cup winners. The first Final at Wembley Stadium, in 1923, created so much interest that thousands of spectators broke into the ground and swarmed all over the stadium. Since then, all Finals have been all-ticket and The Association has kept a strict control of the distribution.

Memories of past Finals invariably centre on individuals – Mutch's dramatic last-minute penalty winner for Preston North End in 1938, Matthews' dazzling wing-play tormenting the Bolton Wanderers defence in 1953, or Montgomery's miraculous save from Lorimer's thunderous shot

virtually winning the Cup for Second Division Sunderland in 1973. The Football Association Challenge Cup is known worldwide as the principle competition of its kind. Interest in the results extends far from these shores, and the Cup Final, with its special tradition, is now watched by several hundred million on television.

The first international football matches were those played between England and Scotland in the 1870s. The series owed its beginning to the enterprise of Charles Alcock, Honorary Secretary of The Football Association, whose letter in *The Sportsman* on 5th February 1870 announced that a match between "the leading representatives of the Scotch and English sections" was to be played under the auspices of The Association and invited players to submit their names for selection. The first of the series to be played North of the Border – at the ground of the West of Scotland Cricket Club at Partick, near Glasgow, on 30th November 1872 – is now accepted as being the first official international.

Within a decade Wales and Ireland had joined the football family, and the first Home International series was instigated in 1884 with Scotland the first winners. In 1908 England met their first non-British opposition at full international level, when a European tour included matches against Austria, Hungary and Bohemia. England's first home defeat, outside the British Championship, was not registered until Eire won 2-0 at Goodison Park in 1949, but the belief that England were the best in the world persisted until the "Magical Magyars" gave England a football lesson at Wembley in 1953. Thirteen years later England *were* the best, as the team managed by Alf Ramsey

England in the 1890s. Steve Bloomer and G. O. Smith, both legendary goalscorers, are in the front row.

won the FIFA World Cup on home soil.

Since its foundation in 1863, The Football Association has built a reputation as the world's senior football administration and over the years has added enormously to its activities. Those activities now encompass a very wide range of educational projects. The Coca-Cola FA Education and Coaching Scheme provides for a pyramid of football education, with Coaching Centres and Funweeks at the base, Centres of Excellence at the next level, and the General Motors FA National School at the apex, where the country's best young players prepare for a career in professional football. With the aid of The Sports Council and The Football Trust, The Football Association has also established a National Rehabilitation and Sports Injury Centre at Lilleshall and has recently announced the opening of a Human Performance Department.

It is doubtful whether the representatives of the eleven clubs who assembled in London 125 years ago, visionaries though they must have been, could have foreseen the proportions and splendour of the edifice that was to grow up as a result of that meeting. But from those humble beginnings sprang The Football Association and the game that it now played in more than 150 countries and commands the affection of so many millions of people.

European Championship 1986-88

Qualifying Competition

GROUP 1: Spain, Rumania, Austria and Albania

10.9.86	Rumania	4	Austria	0
15.10.86	Austria	3	Albania	0
12.11.86	Spain	1	Rumania	0
3.12.86	Albania	1	Spain	2
25.3.87	Rumania	5	Albania	1
1.4.87	Austria	2	Spain	3
29.4.87	Albania	0	Austria	1
29.4.87	Rumania	3	Spain	1
14.10.87	Spain	2	Austria	0
28.10.87	Albania	0	Rumania	1
18.11.87	Spain	5	Albania	0
18.11.87	Austria	0	Rumania	0

	P	W	D	L	F	A	Pts
SPAIN	6	5	0	1	14	6	10
Rumania	6	4	1	1	13	3	9
Austria	6	2	1	3	6	9	5
Albania	6	0	0	6	2	17	0

GROUP 2: Portugal, Sweden, Switzerland, Italy and Malta

24.9.86	Sweden	2	Switzerland	0
12.10.86	Portugal	1	Sweden	1
29.10.86	Switzerland	1	Portugal	1
15.11.86	Italy	3	Switzerland	2
16.11.86	Malta	0	Sweden	5
6.12.86	Malta	0	Italy	2
24.1.87	Italy	5	Malta	0
14.2.87	Portugal	0	Italy	1
29.3.87	Portugal	2	Malta	2
15.4.87	Switzerland	4	Malta	1
24.5.87	Sweden	1	Malta	0
3.6.87	Sweden	1	Italy	0
17.6.87	Switzerland	1	Sweden	1
23.9.87	Sweden	0	Portugal	1
17.10.87	Switzerland	0	Italy	0
11.11.87	Portugal	0	Switzerland	0
14.11.87	Italy	2	Sweden	1
15.11.87	Malta	1	Switzerland	1
5.12.87	Italy	3	Portugal	0
20.12.87	Malta	0	Portugal	1

	P	W	D	L	F	A	Pts
ITALY	8	6	1	1	16	4	13
Sweden	8	4	2	2	12	5	10
Portugal	8	2	4	2	6	8	8
Switzerland	8	1	5	2	9	9	7
Malta	8	0	2	6	4	21	2

GROUP 3: France, U.S.S.R., East Germany, Norway and Iceland

10.9.86	Iceland	0	France	0
24.9.86	Iceland	1	U.S.S.R.	1
24.9.86	Norway	0	East Germany	0
11.10.86	France	0	U.S.S.R.	2
29.10.86	U.S.S.R.	4	Norway	0

29.10.86	East Germany	2	Iceland	0
19.11.86	East Germany	0	France	0
29.4.87	France	2	Iceland	0
29.4.87	U.S.S.R.	2	East Germany	0
3.6.87	Norway	0	U.S.S.R.	1
3.6.87	Iceland	0	East Germany	6
16.6.87	Norway	2	France	0
9.9.87	U.S.S.R.	1	France	1
9.9.87	Iceland	2	Norway	1
23.9.87	Norway	0	Iceland	1
10.10.87	East Germany	1	U.S.S.R.	1
14.10.87	France	1	Norway	1
28.10.87	East Germany	3	Norway	1
28.10.87	U.S.S.R.	2	Iceland	0
18.11.87	France	0	East Germany	1

	P	W	D	L	F	A	Pts
U.S.S.R.	8	5	3	0	14	3	13
East Germany	8	4	3	1	13	4	11
France	8	1	4	3	4	7	6
Iceland	8	2	2	4	4	14	6
Norway	8	1	2	5	5	12	4

GROUP 4: England, Northern Ireland, Turkey and Yugoslavia

15.10.86	England	3	Northern Ireland	0
29.10.86	Yugoslavia	4	Turkey	0
12.11.86	England	2	Yugoslavia	0
12.11.86	Turkey	0	Northern Ireland	0
1.4.87	Northern Ireland	0	England	2
29.4.87	Northern Ireland	1	Yugoslavia	2
29.4.87	Turkey	0	England	0
14.10.87	Yugoslavia	3	Northern Ireland	0
14.10.87	England	8	Turkey	0
11.11.87	Yugoslavia	1	England	4
11.11.87	Northern Ireland	1	Turkey	0
16.12.87	Turkey	2	Yugoslavia	3

	P	W	D	L	F	A	Pts
ENGLAND	6	5	1	0	19	1	11
Yugoslavia	6	4	0	2	13	9	8
Northern Ireland	6	1	1	4	2	10	3
Turkey	6	0	2	4	2	16	2

GROUP 5: Holland, Hungary, Poland, Greece and Cyprus

15.10.86	Hungary	0	Holland	1
15.10.86	Poland	2	Greece	1
12.11.86	Greece	2	Hungary	1
19.11.86	Holland	0	Poland	0
3.12.86	Cyprus	2	Greece	4
21.12.86	Cyprus	0	Holland	2
14.1.87	Greece	3	Cyprus	1
8.2.87	Cyprus	0	Hungary	1
25.3.87	Holland	1	Greece	1
12.4.87	Poland	0	Cyprus	0
29.4.87	Greece	1	Poland	0
29.4.87	Holland	2	Hungary	0
17.5.87	Hungary	5	Poland	3
23.9.87	Poland	3	Hungary	2
14.10.87	Hungary	3	Greece	0
14.10.87	Poland	0	Holland	2
11.11.87	Cyprus	0	Poland	1

2.12.87	Hungary	1	Cyprus	0
9.12.87	Holland	4	Cyprus	0
16.12.87	Greece	0	Holland	3

	P	W	D	L	F	A	Pts
HOLLAND	8	6	2	0	15	1	14
Greece	8	4	1	3	12	13	9
Poland	8	3	2	3	9	11	8
Hungary	8	4	0	4	13	11	8
Cyprus	8	0	1	7	3	16	1

GROUP 6: Denmark, Wales, Czechoslovakia and Finland

10.9.86	Finland	1	Wales	1
15.10.86	Czechoslovakia	3	Finland	0
29.10.86	Denmark	1	Finland	0
12.11.86	Czechoslovakia	0	Denmark	0
1.4.87	Wales	4	Finland	0
29.4.87	Finland	0	Denmark	1
29.4.87	Wales	1	Czechoslovakia	1
3.6.87	Denmark	1	Czechoslovakia	1
9.9.87	Wales	1	Denmark	0
9.9.87	Finland	3	Czechoslovakia	0
14.10.87	Denmark	1	Wales	0
11.11.87	Czechoslovakia	2	Wales	0

	P	W	D	L	F	A	Pts
DENMARK	6	3	2	1	4	2	8
Czechoslovakia	6	2	3	1	7	5	7
Wales	6	2	2	2	7	5	6
Finland	6	1	1	4	4	10	3

GROUP 7: Belgium, Bulgaria, Republic of Ireland, Scotland and Luxembourg

10.9.86	Scotland	0	Bulgaria	0
10.9.86	Belgium	2	Rep. of Ireland	2
14.10.86	Luxembourg	0	Belgium	6
15.10.86	Rep. of Ireland	0	Scotland	0
12.11.86	Scotland	3	Luxembourg	0
19.11.86	Belgium	1	Bulgaria	1
18.2.87	Scotland	0	Rep. of Ireland	1
1.4.87	Bulgaria	2	Rep. of Ireland	1
1.4.87	Belgium	4	Scotland	1
29.4.87	Rep. of Ireland	0	Belgium	0
30.4.87	Luxembourg	1	Bulgaria	4
20.5.87	Bulgaria	3	Luxembourg	0
28.5.87	Luxembourg	0	Rep. of Ireland	2
9.9.87	Rep. of Ireland	2	Luxembourg	1
23.9.87	Bulgaria	2	Belgium	0
14.10.87	Scotland	2	Belgium	0
14.10.87	Rep. of Ireland	2	Bulgaria	0
11.11.87	Belgium	3	Luxembourg	0
11.11.87	Bulgaria	0	Scotland	1
2.12.87	Luxembourg	0	Scotland	0

	P	W	D	L	F	A	Pts
REP. OF IRELAND	8	4	3	1	10	5	11
Bulgaria	8	4	2	2	12	6	10
Belgium	8	3	3	2	16	8	9
Scotland	8	3	3	2	7	5	9
Luxembourg	8	0	1	7	2	23	1

Finals

Group 1

10.6.88	West Germany	1	Italy	1
11.6.88	Denmark	2	Spain	3
14.6.88	West Germany	2	Denmark	0
14.6.88	Italy	1	Spain	0
17.6.88	West Germany	2	Spain	0
17.6.88	Italy	2	Denmark	0

	P	W	D	L	F	A	Pts
WEST GERMANY	3	2	1	0	5	1	5
ITALY	3	2	1	0	4	1	5
Spain	3	1	0	2	3	5	2
Denmark	3	0	0	3	2	7	0

Group 2

12.6.88	England	0	Rep. of Ireland	1
12.6.88	Holland	0	U.S.S.R.	1
15.6.88	England	1	Holland	3
15.6.88	Rep. of Ireland	1	U.S.S.R.	1
18.6.88	England	1	U.S.S.R.	3
18.6.88	Rep. of Ireland	0	Holland	1

	P	W	D	L	F	A	Pts
U.S.S.R.	3	2	1	0	5	2	5
HOLLAND	3	2	0	1	4	2	4
Rep. of Ireland	3	1	1	1	2	2	3
England	3	0	0	3	2	7	0

Semi-Finals

21.6.88	West Germany	1	Holland	2
22.6.88	U.S.S.R.	2	Italy	0

Final

25.6.88	Holland	2	U.S.S.R.	0

European Champion Clubs' Cup 1987-88

First Round		Second Round		Quarter-Final		Semi-Final		Final	
PSV Eindhoven	3:0	PSV Eindhoven	2:2						
Galatasaray	0:2			PSV Eindhoven	1:0*				
Rapid Vienna	6:1	Rapid Vienna	1:0						
Hamrun Spartans	0:0					PSV Eindhoven	1:0*		
Lillestrom	1:4	Lillestrom	0:0						
Linfield	1:2			Bordeaux	1:0				
Bordeaux	2:2	Bordeaux	0:1						
Dynamo Berlin	0:0							PSV Eindhoven	0†
Neuchatel Xamax	5:1	Neuchatel Xamax	2:0						
Kuusysi Lahti	0:2			Bayern Munich	3:0				
Bayern Munich	4:1	Bayern Munich	1:2						
CSKA Sofia	0:0					Real Madrid	1:0		
Real Madrid	2:1	Real Madrid	2:2						
Naples	0:1			Real Madrid	2:2				
Porto	3:3	Porto	1:1						
Vardar Skoplje	0:0							In Stuttgart	
Steaua Bucharest	4:0	Steaua Bucharest	3:2						
MTK Budapest	0:2			Steaua Bucharest	2:1				
Shamrock Rovers	0:0	Omonia Nicosia	1:0						
Omonia Nicosia	1:0					Steaua Bucharest	0:0		
Dinamo Kiev	1:0	Glasgow Rangers	3:1						
Glasgow Rangers	0:2			Glasgow Rangers	0:2				
Olympiakos	1:1	Gornik Zabrze	1:1						
Gornik Zabrze	1:2							Benfica	0
Fram Reykjavik	0:0	Sparta Prague	1:0						
Sparta Prague	2:8			Anderlecht	0:1				
Malmo	0:1	Anderlecht	2:1						
Anderlecht	1:1					Benfica	0:2		
Aarhus	4:0	Aarhus	0:0						
Jeunesse d'Esch	1:1			Benfica	2:0				
Partizan Tirana	0:–	Benfica	0:1						
Benfica	4:–								

*Won on away goals rule   †Won on penalty-kicks

P.S.V. Eindhoven prior to the Final in Stuttgart.

European Cup Winners' Cup 1987-88

First Round		Second Round		Quarter-Final		Semi-Final		Final	
Mechelen	1:2	Mechelen	0:2						
Dinamo Bucharest	0:0			Mechelen	1:1				
St Mirren	1:0	St Mirren	0:0						
Tromso	0:0					Mechelen	2:2		
Real San Sebastian	0:2	Real San Sebastian	1:0						
Slask Wroclaw	0:0			Dinamo Minsk	0:1				
Dinamo Minsk	2:2	Dinamo Minsk	1:0*						
Genclerbirligi	0:1							Mechelen	1
Vitocha Sofia	1:1	OFI Crete	1:0						
OFI Crete	0:3			Atalanta	2:1				
Merthyr Tydfil	2:0	Atalanta	0:2						
Atalanta	1:2					Atalanta	1:1		
Akranes	0:0	Kalmar	1:0						
Kalmar	0:1			Sporting Club	0:1				
Sporting Club	4:2	Sporting Club	0:5						
Swarowski Tirol	0:4							In Strasbourg	
Vllaznia Shkoder	2:4	Vllaznia Shkoder	0:0						
Sliema Wand.	0:0			Rovaniemen	0:0				
Rovaniemen	0:1*	Rovaniemen	1:1						
Glentoran	0:1					Olympic Marseilles	0:2		
Lokomotiv Leipzig	0:0	Olympic Marseilles	4:0						
Olympic Marseilles	0:1			Olympic Marseilles	1:3				
Aalborg	1:0	Hadjuk Split	0:2						
Hajduk Split	0:1†							Ajax Amsterdam	0
Ujpesti Dozsa	1:1	Den Haag	2:0						
Den Haag	0:3			Young Boys	0:1				
Dunajska Streda	2:1	Young Boys	1:1*						
Young Boys	1:3					Ajax Amsterdam	3:1		
Avenir Beggen	0:0	Hamburg	0:0						
Hamburg	5:3			Ajax Amsterdam	1:0†				
Dundalk	0:0	Ajax Amsterdam	1:2						
Ajax Amsterdam	4:2								

*Won on away goals rule   †Won on penalty-kicks

Mechelen celebrate after their victory in Strasbourg.

22

UEFA Cup 1987-88

First Round

Team	Score	Team	Score	Team	Score
Bohemians Dublin	0:0	Honved	1:0	Larnaca	0:0
Aberdeen	0:1	Lokeren	0:0	Victoria Bucharest	1:3
Barcelona	2:0	Coleraine	0:1	Flamurtari Vlora	2:1
Belenenses	0:1	Dundee United	1:3	Partizan Belgrade	0:2
Wismut Aue	0:1*	Spartak Moscow	3:0	Sporting Gijon	1:0
Valur	0:1	Dynamo Dresden	0:1	AC Milan	0:3
LASK Linz	0:0	Vitkovice Ostrava	1:2	Valletta	0:0
Utrecht	0:2	Solna	1:0	Juventus	4:3
Beveren	2:0	Turun PS	0:2	Univ. Craiova	3:1
Bohemians Prague	0:1	Admira Wacker	1:0	Chaves	2:2*
Borussia M'gladbach	0:1	Brondby	2:0	Red Star Belgrade	3:2
Espanol	1:4	Gothenburg	1:0	Trakia Plovdiv	0:2
Feyenoord	5:5	Zenit Leningrad	2:0	Toulouse	5:1
Spora Luxembourg	0:2	Bruges	0:5	Panionios	1:0
Tatabanyai Banyasz	1:0	Mjondalen	0:1	Besiktas	0:1
Vitoria Guimaraes	1:1	Werder Bremen	5:0	Internazionale	0:3
Grasshoppers	0:0	Sportul Studentesc	1:2	Austria Memphis	0:1
Dynamo Moscow	4:1	Katowice	0:1	Bayer Leverkusen	0:5
Celtic	2:0	Panathinaikos	2:2	Lokomotiv Sofia	3:0
Borussia Dortmund	1:2	Auxerre	0:3	Dynamo Tbilisi	1:3
Pogon Szczecin	1:1			Velez Mostar	5:0
Verona	1:3			Sion	0:3

Second Round		Third Round		Quarter-Final		Semi-Final		Final	
Bayer Leverkusen	1:1								
Toulouse	1:0	Bayer Leverkusen	2:1						
Aberdeen	2:0			Bayer Leverkusen	0:1				
Feyenoord	1:1*	Feyenoord	2:0						
Barcelona	2:0					Bayer Leverkusen	1:0		
Dinamo Moscow	0:0	Barcelona	4:0						
Wismut Aue	1:0			Barcelona	0:0				
Flamurtari	0:2	Flamurtari	1:1						
Utrecht	1:1							Bayer Leverkusen	0:3†
Verona	1:2	Verona	3:1						
Brondby	3:0			Verona	0:1				
Sportul Studentesc	0:3†	Sportul Studentesc	1:0						
Spartak Moscow	4:2					Werder Bremen	0:0		
Werder Bremen	1:6	Werder Bremen	2:1						
Victoria Bucharest	1:0			Werder Bremen	1:1				
Dinamo Tbilisi	2:0	Dinamo Tbilisi	1:1					First leg	
Chaves	1:1							at Espanol	
Honved	2:3	Honved	5:1					Second leg	
Panathinaikos	1:2*			Panathinaikos	2:0			in Leverkusen	
Juventus	0:3	Panathinaikos	2:5						
Borussia Dortmund	2:1					Bruges	2:0		
Velez Mostar	0:2	Borussia Dortmund	3:0						
Red Star Belgrade	3:0			Bruges	2:1				
Bruges	1:4	Bruges	0:5						
Vitoria Guimaraes	1:0†							Espanol	3:0
Beveren	0:1	Vitoria Guimaraes	2:0						
Dundee United	1:1			Vitkovice	0:0				
Vitkovice	2:1	Vitkovice	0:2†						
Internazionale	0:2					Espanol	0:3		
Turun PS	1:0	Internazionale	1:0						
AC Milan	0:0			Espanol	2:0				
Espanol	2:0	Espanol	1:1						

*Won on away goals   † Won on penalty-kicks

23

England's Full International Record 1872–1988

(Up to and including 18 June 1988)

	HOME				Goals		AWAY				Goals	
	P	W	D	L	For	Agst	P	W	D	L	For	Agst
Argentina	4	3	1	0	8	4	5	1	2	2	5	5
Australia	—	—	—	—	—	—	4	2	2	0	4	2
Austria	5	3	1	1	18	9	10	5	2	3	36	16
Belgium	4	3	1	0	17	3	13	9	3	1	49	21
Bohemia	—	—	—	—	—	—	1	1	0	0	4	0
Brazil	5	1	3	1	7	6	9	1	2	6	5	14
Bulgaria	2	1	1	0	3	1	3	2	1	0	4	0
Canada	—	—	—	—	—	—	1	1	0	0	1	0
Chile	—	—	—	—	—	—	3	2	1	0	4	1
Colombia	1	0	1	0	1	1	1	1	0	0	4	0
Cyprus	1	1	0	0	5	0	1	1	0	0	1	0
Czechoslovakia	4	3	1	0	9	4	6	3	1	2	10	7
Denmark	3	2	0	1	6	3	6	4	2	0	17	7
Ecuador	—	—	—	—	—	—	1	1	0	0	2	0
Egypt	—	—	—	—	—	—	1	1	0	0	4	0
F.I.F.A.	1	0	1	0	4	4	—	—	—	—	—	—
Finland	2	2	0	0	7	1	6	5	1	0	25	4
France	7	5	2	0	21	4	13	9	0	4	39	23
Germany, East	2	2	0	0	4	1	2	1	1	0	3	2
Germany, West	7	5	0	2	15	8	11	4	3	4	20	16
Greece	2	1	1	0	3	0	2	2	0	0	5	0
Holland	5	2	2	1	12	6	4	2	1	1	4	4
Hungary	6	5	0	1	17	9	10	5	1	4	28	18
Iceland	—	—	—	—	—	—	1	0	1	0	1	1
Ireland, Northern	49	40	6	3	169	36	47	34	10	3	150	44
Ireland, Republic of	5	3	1	1	10	5	5	2	2	1	6	4
Israel	—	—	—	—	—	—	2	1	1	0	2	1
Italy	5	3	1	1	9	5	10	3	3	4	15	15
Kuwait	—	—	—	—	—	—	1	1	0	0	1	0
Luxembourg	3	3	0	0	18	1	4	4	0	0	20	2
Malta	1	1	0	0	5	0	1	1	0	0	1	0
Mexico	2	2	0	0	10	0	4	1	1	2	4	3
Morocco	—	—	—	—	—	—	1	0	1	0	0	0
Norway	2	2	0	0	8	0	4	3	0	1	17	4
Paraguay	—	—	—	—	—	—	1	1	0	0	3	0
Peru	—	—	—	—	—	—	2	1	0	1	5	4
Poland	2	0	2	0	2	2	3	2	0	1	4	2
Portugal	6	5	1	0	12	4	9	3	4	2	23	13
Rest of Europe	1	1	0	0	3	0	—	—	—	—	—	—
Rest of the World	1	1	0	0	2	1	—	—	—	—	—	—
Rumania	3	0	3	0	2	2	5	2	2	1	4	2
Scotland	53	25	11	17	115	87	53	17	13	23	71	81
Spain	6	5	0	1	19	6	10	5	2	3	16	13
Sweden	3	2	0	1	9	6	8	4	2	2	14	8
Switzerland	5	3	2	0	12	3	10	7	0	3	25	9
Turkey	2	2	0	0	13	0	2	1	1	0	8	0
U.S.A.	—	—	—	—	—	—	5	4	0	1	29	5
U.S.S.R	3	1	1	1	7	4	7	3	2	2	9	8
Uruguay	2	1	1	0	2	1	5	1	1	3	5	9
Wales	49	32	9	8	126	46	48	30	12	6	113	44
Yugoslavia	6	3	3	0	13	6	7	1	2	4	8	13
TOTAL	270	174	56	40	723	279	368	195	83	90	828	425

GRAND TOTAL

				Goals	
Played	Won	Drawn	Lost	For	Against
638	369	139	130	1551	704

England's Full International Goalscorers 1946-88

(Up to and including 18 June 1988)

Charlton, R....	49	Coppell	7	Grainger	3	Astall	1
Greaves	44	Paine	7	Kennedy, R....	3	Beattie..........	1
Finney	30	Barnes, J.	6	McDermott....	3	Bowles..........	1
Lofthouse	30	Charlton, J.....	6	Matthews, S. ..	3	Bradford	1
Lineker	26	Johnson	6	Morris	3	Bridges	1
Hurst............	24	Macdonald.....	6	O'Grady........	3	Chamberlain ..	1
Mortensen	23	Mullen	6	Peacock	3	Crawford.......	1
Robson, B.	22	Rowley	6	Ramsey.........	3	Goddard	1
Channon	21	Atyeo	5	Sewell..........	3	Hughes, E.	1
Keegan	21	Baily	5	Steven	3	Kay..............	1
Peters	20	Beardsley	5	Wilkins	3	Kidd.............	1
Haynes	18	Brooking.......	5	Wright, W......	3	Langton	1
Hunt, R.	18	Carter..........	5	Allen, R.	2	Lawler	1
Lawton	16	Edwards........	5	Anderson	2	Lee, J.	1
Taylor, T.	16	Hitchens........	5	Bradley.........	2	Mabbutt	1
Woodcock	16	Latchford	5	Broadbent	2	Marsh...........	1
Chivers	13	Neal	5	Brooks..........	2	Medley	1
Mariner.........	13	Pearson, Stan	5	Cowans.........	2	Melia............	1
Smith, R........	13	Pearson, Stuart	5	Eastham........	2	Mullery	1
Francis, T.	12	Pickering, F. ..	5	Froggatt, J.	2	Nicholls.........	1
Douglas	11	Barnes, P.......	4	Froggatt, R. ...	2	Nicholson	1
Mannion	11	Dixon	4	Haines	2	Parry	1
Clarke, A.	10	Hassall.........	4	Hancocks	2	Sansom	1
Flowers.........	10	Revie...........	4	Hunter..........	2	Shackleton.....	1
Lee, F...........	10	Robson, R.	4	Lee, S.	2	Stiles	1
Milburn.........	10	Waddle	4	Moore	2	Summerbee....	1
Wilshaw	10	Watson, D.	4	Perry	2	Tambling.......	1
Bell..............	9	Adams.	3	Pointer..........	2	Thompson, Phil	1
Bentley	9	Baker	3	Royle	2	Viollet	1
Hateley	9	Blissett.........	3	Taylor, P.	2	Wallace	1
Ball..............	8	Butcher.........	3	Tueart	2	Walsh	1
Broadis	8	Currie..........	3	Wignall	2	Webb	1
Byrne, J.	8	Elliott..........	3	Worthington ..	2	Weller...........	1
Hoddle	8	Francis, G......	3	A'Court	1	Withe	1
Kevan...........	8						
Connelly	7						

England's Full International Caps 1946–88

(Up to and including 18 June 1988)
*Does not include pre-war caps

Player	Caps	Player	Caps
A'Court, A. (Liverpool)	5	*Broadis, I. (Manchester C. and*	
Adams. T. (Arsenal)	14	Newcastle)	14
Allen, A. (Stoke)	3	Brooking, T. (West Ham)	47
Allen, C. (Q.P.R. and Tottenham)	5	Brooks, J. (Tottenham)	3
Allen, R. (W.B.A)	5	Brown, A. (W.B.A.)	1
Anderson, S. (Sunderland)	2	Brown, K. (West Ham)	1
Anderson, V. (Nottm For., Arsenal		Butcher, T. (Ipswich and	
and Manchester United)	30	Glasgow Rangers)	54
Angus, J. (Burnley)	1	Byrne, G. (Liverpool)	2
Armfield, J. (Blackpool)	43	Byrne, J. (Crystal Palace and	
Armstrong, D. (Middlesbrough and		West Ham)	11
Southampton)	3	Byrne, R. (Manchester U.)	33
Armstrong, K. (Chelsea)	1		
Astall, G. (Birmingham)	2	Callaghan, I. (Liverpool)	4
Astle, J. (W.B.A.)	5	Carter, H. (Derby)	*7
Aston, J. (Manchester U.)	17	Chamberlain, M. (Stoke)	8
Atyeo, J. (Bristol C.)	6	Channon, M. (Southampton and	
		Manchester C.)	46
Bailey, G. (Manchester U.)	2	Charlton, J. (Leeds)	35
Bailey, M. (Charlton)	2	Charlton, R. (Manchester U.)	106
Baily, E. (Tottenham)	9	Charnley, R. (Blackpool)	1
Baker, J. (Hibernian and Arsenal)	8	Cherry, T. (Leeds)	27
Ball, A. (Blackpool, Everton and		Chilton, A. (Manchester U.)	2 ·
Arsenal)	72	Chivers, M. (Tottenham)	24
Banks, G. (Leicester and Stoke)	73	Clamp, E. (Wolves)	4
Banks, T. (Bolton)	6	Clapton, D. (Arsenal)	1
Barham, M. (Norwich City)	2	Clarke, A. (Leeds)	19
Barlow, R. (W.B.A.)	1	Clarke, H. (Tottenham)	1
Barnes, J. (Watford and Liverpool)	42	Clayton, R. (Blackburn)	35
Barnes, P. (Manchester C., W.B.A.		Clemence, R. (Liverpool and	
and Leeds)	22	Tottenham)	61
Barrass, M. (Bolton)	3	Clement, D. (Q.P.R.)	5
Baynham, R. (Luton)	3	Clough, B. (Middlesbrough)	2
Beardsley, P. (Newcastle and		Coates, R. (Burnley and	
Liverpool)	26	Tottenham)	4
Beattie, K. (Ipswich)	9	Cockburn, H. (Manchester U.)	13
Bell, C. (Manchester C.)	48	Cohen, G. (Fulham)	37
Bentley, R. (Chelsea)	12	Compton, L. (Arsenal)	2
Berry, J. (Manchester U.)	4	Connelly, J. (Burnley and Man-	
Birtles, G. (Nottingham For. and		chester U.)	20
Manchester U.)	3	Cooper, T. (Leeds)	20
Blissett, L. (Watford and		Coppell, S. (Manchester U.)	42
AC Milan)	14	Corrigan, J. (Manchester C.)	9
Blockley, J. (Arsenal)	1	Cottee, T. (West Ham)	3
Blunstone, F. (Chelsea)	5	Cowans, G. (Aston Villa and Bari)	9
Bonetti, P. (Chelsea)	7	Crawford, R. (Ipswich)	2
Bowles, S. (Q.P.R.)	5	Crowe, C. (Wolves)	1
Boyer, P. (Norwich)	1	Cunningham, L. (W.B.A. and Real	
Brabrook, P. (Chelsea)	3	Madrid)	6
Bracewell, P. (Everton)	3	Currie, A. (Sheffield U. and Leeds)	17
Bradford. G. (Bristol R.)	1		
Bradley, W. (Manchester U.)	3	Davenport, P. (Nottingham For.)	1
Bridges, B. (Chelsea)	4	Deeley, N. (Wolves)	2
Broadbent, P. (Wolves)	7	Devonshire, A. (West Ham)	8

Player	Caps
Dickinson, J. (Portsmouth)	48
Ditchburn, E. (Tottenham)	6
Dixon, K. (Chelsea)	8
Dobson, M. (Burnley and Everton)	5
Douglas, B. (Blackburn)	36
Doyle, M. (Manchester C.)	5
Duxbury, M. (Manchester U.)	10
Eastham, G. (Arsenal)	19
Eckersley, W. (Blackburn)	17
Edwards, D. (Manchester U.)	18
Ellerington, W. (Southampton)	2
Elliott, W. (Burnley)	5
Fantham, J. (Sheffield W.)	1
Fenwick, T. (Q.P.R. and Tottenham)	20
Finney, T. (Preston)	76
Flowers, R. (Wolves)	49
Foster, S. (Brighton)	3
Foulkes, W. (Manchester U.)	1
Francis, G. (Q.P.R.)	12
Francis, T. (Birmingham, Nottingham Forest, Manchester City and Sampdoria)	52
Franklin, N. (Stoke)	27
Froggatt, J. (Portsmouth)	13
Froggatt, R. (Sheffield W.)	4
Garrett, T. (Blackpool)	3
Gates, E. (Ipswich)	2
George, C. (Derby County)	1
Gidman, J. (Aston Villa)	1
Gillard, I. (Q.P.R.)	3
Goddard, P. (West Ham)	1
Grainger, C. (Sheffield United and Sunderland)	7
Greaves, J. (Chelsea and Tottenham)	57
Greenhoff, B. (Manchester U. and Leeds)	18
Gregory, J. (Q.P.R.)	6
Hagan, J. (Sheffield U.)	1
Haines, J. (W.B.A.)	1
Hall, J. (Birmingham)	17
Hancocks, J. (Wolves)	3
Hardwick, G. (Middlesbrough)	13
Harford, M. (Luton Town)	1
Harris, G. (Burnley)	1
Harris, P. (Portsmouth)	2
Harvey, C. (Everton)	1
Hassall, H. (Huddersfield and Bolton)	5
Hateley, M. (Portsmouth, AC Milan and Monaco)	31
Haynes, J. (Fulham)	56
Hector, K. (Derby)	2
Hellawell, M. (Birmingham)	2

Player	Caps
Henry, R. (Tottenham)	1
Hill, F. (Bolton)	2
Hill, G. (Manchester U.)	6
Hill, R. (Luton)	3
Hinton, A. (Wolves and N. Forest)	3
Hitchens, G. (Aston Villa and Internazionale Milan)	7
Hoddle, G. (Tottenham and Monaco)	53
Hodge, S. (Aston Villa and Tottenham)	15
Hodgkinson, A. (Sheffield U.)	5
Holden, D. (Bolton)	5
Holliday, E. (Middlesbrough)	3
Hollins, J. (Chelsea)	1
Hopkinson, E. (Bolton)	14
Howe, D. (W.B.A)	23
Howe, J. (Derby)	3
Hudson, A. (Stoke)	2
Hughes, E. (Liverpool and Wolves)	62
Hughes, L. (Liverpool)	3
Hunt, R. (Liverpool)	34
Hunt, S. (W.B.A.)	2
Hunter, N. (Leeds)	28
Hurst, G. (West Ham)	49
Jezzard, B. (Fulham)	2
Johnson, D. (Ipswich and Liverpool)	8
Johnston, H. (Blackpool)	10
Jones, M. (Sheffield U. and Leeds)	3
Jones, W. H. (Liverpool)	2
Kay, A. (Everton)	1
Keegan, K. (Liverpool, S.V. Hamburg and Southampton)	63
Kennedy, A. (Liverpool)	2
Kennedy, R. (Liverpool)	17
Kevan, D. (W.B.A.)	14
Kidd, B. (Manchester U.)	2
Knowles, C. (Tottenham)	4
Labone, B. (Everton)	26
Lampard, F. (West Ham)	2
Langley, J. (Fulham)	3
Langton, R. (Blackburn, Preston and Bolton)	11
Latchford, R. (Everton)	12
Lawler, C. (Liverpool)	4
Lawton, T. (Chelsea and Notts. County)	*15
Lee, F. (Manchester C.)	27
Lee, J. (Derby)	1
Lee, S. (Liverpool)	14
Lindsay, A. (Liverpool)	4
Lineker, G. (Leicester, Everton and Barcelona)	35
Little, B. (Aston Villa)	1

27

Player	Caps	Player	Caps
Lloyd, L. (Liverpool)	4	Peacock, A. (Middlesbrough and Leeds)	6
Lofthouse, N. (Bolton)	33	Pearce, S. (Nottingham Forest)	5
Lowe, E. (Aston Villa)	3	Pearson, Stanley (Manchester U.)	8
		Pearson, Stuart (Manchester U.)	15
Mabbutt, G. (Tottenham)	13	Pegg, D. (Manchester U.)	1
MacDonald, M. (Newcastle)	14	Pejic, M. (Stoke)	4
Madeley, P. (Leeds)	24	Perry, W. (Blackpool)	3
Mannion, W. (Middlesbrough)	26	Perryman, S. (Tottenham)	1
Mariner, P. (Ipswich and Arsenal)	35	Peters, M. (West Ham and Tottenham)	67
Marsh, R. (Q.P.R. and Manchester C.)	9	Phillips, L. (Portsmouth)	3
Martin, A. (West Ham)	17	Pickering, F. (Everton)	3
Matthews, R. (Coventry)	5	Pickering, N. (Sunderland)	1
Matthews, S. (Stoke and Blackpool)	*37	Pilkington, B. (Burnley)	1
McDermott, T. (Liverpool)	25	Pointer, R. (Burnley)	3
McDonald, C. (Burnley)	8	Pye, J. (Wolves)	1
McFarland, R. (Derby)	28		
McGarry, W. (Huddersfield)	4	Quixall, A. (Sheffield W.)	5
McGuinness, W. (Manchester U.)	2		
McMahon, S. (Liverpool)	4	Radford, J. (Arsenal)	2
McNab, R. (Arsenal)	4	Ramsey, A. (Southampton and Tottenham)	32
McNeil, M. (Middlesbrough)	9	Reaney, P. (Leeds)	3
Meadows, J. (Manchester C.)	1	Reeves, K. (Norwich and Manchester C.)	2
Medley, L. (Tottenham)	6	Regis, C. (W.B.A. and Coventry)	5
Melia, J. (Liverpool)	2	Reid, P. (Everton)	13
Merrick, G. (Birmingham)	23	Revie, D. (Manchester C.)	6
Metcalfe, V. (Huddersfield)	2	Richards, J. (Wolves)	1
Milburn, J. (Newcastle)	13	Rickaby, S. (W.B.A.)	1
Miller, B. (Burnley)	1	Rimmer, J. (Arsenal)	1
Mills, M. (Ipswich)	42	Rix, G. (Arsenal)	17
Milne, G. (Liverpool)	14	Robb, G. (Tottenham)	1
Milton, A. (Arsenal)	1	Roberts, G. (Tottenham)	6
Moore, R. (West Ham)	108	Robson, B. (W.B.A. and Manchester United)	69
Morley, A. (Aston Villa)	6	Robson, R. (W.B.A.)	20
Morris, J. (Derby)	3	Rowley, J. (Manchester U.)	6
Mortensen, S. (Blackpool)	25	Royle, J. (Everton and Manchester City)	6
Mozley, B. (Derby)	3		
Mullen, J. (Wolves)	12	Sadler, D. (Manchester U.)	4
Mullery, A. (Tottenham)	35	Sansom, K. (Crystal Palace and Arsenal)	86
Neal, P. (Liverpool)	50	Scott, L. (Arsenal)	17
Newton, K. (Blackburn and Everton)	27	Sewell, J. (Sheffield W.)	6
		Shackleton, L. (Sunderland)	5
Nicholls, J. (W.B.A.)	2	Shaw, G. (Sheffield U.)	5
Nicholson, W. (Tottenham)	1	Shellito, K. (Chelsea)	1
Nish, D. (Derby)	5	Shilton, P. (Leicester, Stoke, Nottingham For., Southampton and Derby County)	100
Norman, M. (Tottenham)	23		
O'Grady, M. (Huddersfield and Leeds)	2	Shimwell, E. (Blackpool)	1
Osgood, P. (Chelsea)	4	Sillett, P. (Chelsea)	3
Osman, R. (Ipswich)	11	Slater, W. (Wolves)	12
Owen, S. (Luton)	3	Smith, L. (Arsenal)	6
Paine, T. (Southampton)	19	Smith, R. (Tottenham)	15
Pallister, G. (Middlesbrough)	1		
Parkes, P. (Q.P.R.)	1		
Parry, R. (Bolton)	2		

28

Player	Caps	Player	Caps
Smith, T. (Liverpool)	1	Waddle, C. (Newcastle U. and Tottenham)	36
Smith, T. (Birmingham)	2	Waiters, A. (Blackpool)	5
Spink, N. (Aston Villa)	1	Wallace, D. (Southampton)	1
Springett, R. (Sheffield W.)	33	Walsh, P. (Luton)	5
Staniforth, R. (Huddersfield)	8	Ward, P. (Brighton)	1
Statham, D. (W.B.A.)	3	Ward, T. (Derby)	2
Stein, B. (Luton)	1	Watson, D. (Sunderland, Manchester C., Werder Bremen, Southampton and Stoke)	65
Stepney, A. (Manchester U.)	1		
Steven, T. (Everton)	24		
Stevens, G. (Tottenham)	7	Watson, D. (Norwich City and Everton)	12
Stevens, G. (Everton)	26		
Stiles, N. (Manchester U.)	28	Watson, W. (Sunderland)	4
Storey, P. (Arsenal)	19	Webb, N. (Nottingham Forest)	9
Storey-Moore, I. (Nottingham For.)	1	Weller, K. (Leicester)	4
Streten, B. (Luton)	1	West, G. (Everton)	3
Summerbee, M. (Manchester C.) ...	8	Wheeler, J. (Bolton)	1
Sunderland, A. (Arsenal)	1	Whitworth, S. (Leicester)	7
Swan, P. (Sheffield W.)	19	Whymark, T. (Ipswich)	1
Swift, F. (Manchester C.)	19	Wignall, F. (Nottingham For.)	2
		Wilkins, R. (Chelsea, Manchester U. and AC Milan)	84
Talbot, B. (Ipswich)	6		
Tambling, R. (Chelsea)	3	Williams, B. (Wolves)	24
Taylor, E. (Blackpool)	1	Williams, S. (Southampton)	6
Taylor, J. (Fulham)	2	Willis, A. (Tottenham)	1
Taylor, P. (Liverpool)	3	Wilshaw, D. (Wolves)	12
Taylor, P. (Crystal Palace)	4	Wilson, R. (Huddersfield and Everton)	63
Taylor, T. (Manchester U.)	19		
Temple, D. (Everton)	1	Withe, P. (Aston Villa)	11
Thomas, D. (Coventry City)	2	Wood, R. (Manchester U.)	3
Thomas, D. (Q.P.R.)	8	Woodcock, T. (Nottingham For., Cologne and Arsenal)	42
Thompson, Peter (Liverpool)	16		
Thompson, Phil (Liverpool)	42	Woods, C. (Norwich and Glasgow Rangers)	13
Thompson, T. (Aston Villa and Preston)	2		
		Worthington, F. (Leicester)	8
Thomson, R. (Wolves)	8	Wright, M. (Southampton and Derby County)	22
Todd, C. (Derby)	27		
Towers, A. (Sunderland)	3	Wright, T. (Everton)	11
Tueart, D. (Manchester City)	6	Wright, W. (Wolves)	105
Ufton, D. (Charlton)	1	Young. G. (Sheffield W.)	1
Venables, T. (Chelsea)	2		
Viljoen, C. (Ipswich)	2		
Viollet, D. (Manchester U.)	2		

England Senior Caps 1987-88

	West Germany	Turkey	Yugoslavia	Israel	Holland	Hungary	Scotland	Colombia	Switzerland	Rep. of Ireland	Holland	U.S.S.R.
P. Shilton (Derby County)	1	1	1		1		1	1	1	1	1	
V. Anderson (Manchester United)	2					2		2				
K. Sansom (Arsenal)..................	3	3	3		3		3	3	3	3	3	3
G. Hoddle (Monaco)	4	*4	*8		*8	*11		*8		*4	4	4
T. Adams (Arsenal)...................	5	5	5		5	5	6	6	6	6	6	6
G. Mabbutt (Tottenham Hotspur)	6											
P. Reid (Everton)......................	7		*7						*7			
J. Barnes (Liverpool)	8	11	11	10	11		11	11	11	11	11	11
P. Beardsley (Liverpool).............	9	9	9	9	9	9	9	9	9	9	9	
G. Lineker (Barcelona)	10	10	10		10	10	10	10	10	10	10	10
C. Waddle (Tottenham Hotspur) ..	11			11		11	*8	8	*8	8	*8	
S. Pearce (Nottingham Forest)	*3			3		3						
N. Webb (Nottingham Forest)	*4	8	8	4	8		4		4	4		*9
M. Hateley (Monaco).................	*11				*9	*9		*9		*9	*9	*10
G. Stevens (Everton)		2	2	2	2	*3	2		2	2	2	2
T. Steven (Everton)		4	4		4	4	8		8		8	8
T. Butcher (Glasgow Rangers).....		6	6									
B. Robson (Manchester United)...		7	7		7	7	7	7	7	7	7	7
C. Regis (Coventry City)		*9										
C. Woods (Glasgow Rangers)				1		1			*1			1
D. Watson (Everton)				5	6		5		*6			5
M. Wright (Derby County)..........				6	*6			5	5	5	5	
C. Allen (Tottenham Hotspur)				7								
S. McMahon (Liverpool)				8		8		4				9
T. Fenwick (Tottenham Hotspur)..				*6								
M. Harford (Luton Town)...........				*7								
G. Pallister (Middlesbrough)						6						
T. Cottee (West Ham United)						*10						

*Substitute

European Championship for Under-21 Teams 1986-88

Qualifying Competition

GROUP 1: Spain, Rumania, Austria and Albania

9.9.86	Rumania 1	Austria 0
14.10.86	Austria 1	Albania........................... 0
12.11.86	Spain............................. 1	Rumania 0
2.12.86	Albania.......................... 0	Spain.............................. 0
24.3.87	Rumania 3	Albania........................... 2
31.3.87	Austria 1	Spain.............................. 1
28.4.87	Albania.......................... 1	Austria 1
29.4.87	Rumania 0	Spain.............................. 1
14.10.87	Spain............................. 3	Austria 0
27.10.87	Albania.......................... 1	Rumania 2
17.11.87	Austria 2	Rumania 1
18.11.87	Spain............................. 3	Albania........................... 0

	P	W	D	L	F	A	Pts
SPAIN	6	4	2	0	9	1	10
Rumania	6	3	0	3	7	7	6
Austria	6	2	2	2	5	7	6
Albania	6	0	2	4	4	10	2

GROUP 2: Portugal, Sweden, Switzerland and Italy

23.9.86	Sweden........................... 0	Switzerland...................... 0
11.10.86	Portugal.......................... 2	Sweden 0
28.10.86	Switzerland...................... 3	Portugal.......................... 1
19.11.86	Italy 1	Switzerland...................... 1
11.2.87	Portugal.......................... 1	Italy 2
4.6.87	Sweden........................... 2	Italy 2
16.6.87	Switzerland...................... 0	Sweden 0
22.9.87	Sweden 4	Portugal.......................... 2
16.10.87	Switzerland...................... 0	Italy 3
10.11.87	Portugal.......................... 2	Switzerland...................... 0
12.11.87	Italy 0	Sweden 0
2.12.87	Italy 6	Portugal.......................... 0

	P	W	D	L	F	A	Pts
ITALY	6	3	3	0	14	4	9
Sweden	6	2	3	1	6	6	6
Switzerland	6	1	3	2	4	7	5
Portugal	6	2	0	4	8	15	4

GROUP 3: France, U.S.S.R., East Germany and Norway

23.9.86	Norway........................... 0	East Germany 0
10.10.86	France 2	U.S.S.R........................... 1
28.10.86	U.S.S.R........................... 1	Norway........................... 0
18.11.86	East Germany 1	France 0
28.4.87	U.S.S.R........................... 2	East Germany 1
2.6.87	Norway........................... 0	U.S.S.R........................... 2
15.6.87	Norway........................... 1	France 2
8.9.87	U.S.S.R........................... 0	France 1
9.10.87	East Germany 5	U.S.S.R........................... 1
13.10.87	France 1	Norway........................... 1
27.10.87	East Germany 1	Norway........................... 1
17.11.87	France 2	East Germany 2

	P	W	D	L	F	A	Pts
FRANCE	6	3	2	1	8	6	8
East Germany	6	2	3	1	10	6	7
U.S.S.R.	6	3	0	3	7	9	6
Norway	6	0	3	3	3	7	3

GROUP 4: England, Yugoslavia and Turkey

28.10.86	Yugoslavia	3	Turkey	0
11.11.86	England	1	Yugoslavia	1
28.4.87	Turkey	0	England	0
13.10.87	England	1	Turkey	1
10.11.87	Yugoslavia	1	England	5
15.12.87	Turkey	3	Yugoslavia	2

	P	W	D	L	F	A	Pts
ENGLAND	4	1	3	0	7	3	5
Turkey	4	1	2	1	4	6	4
Yugoslavia	4	1	1	2	7	9	3

GROUP 5: Hungary, Poland, Greece and Cyprus

14.10.86	Poland	1	Greece	0
11.11.86	Greece	2	Hungary	1
2.12.86	Cyprus	0	Greece	4
13.1.87	Greece	5	Cyprus	1
7.2.87	Cyprus	2	Hungary	1
11.4.87	Poland	3	Cyprus	0
28.4.87	Greece	2	Poland	0
16.5.87	Hungary	3	Poland	0
22.9.87	Poland	0	Hungary	1
13.10.87	Hungary	2	Greece	2
10.11.87	Cyprus	0	Poland	1
1.12.87	Hungary	4	Cyprus	1

	P	W	D	L	F	A	Pts
GREECE	6	4	1	1	15	5	9
Hungary	6	3	1	2	12	7	7
Poland	6	3	0	3	5	6	6
Cyprus	6	1	0	5	4	18	2

GROUP 6: Denmark, Czechoslovakia, Finland and Iceland

4.9.86	Finland	2	Iceland	0
25.9.86	Iceland	0	Czechoslovakia	4
14.10.86	Czechoslovakia	2	Finland	0
28.10.86	Denmark	4	Finland	1
11.11.86	Czechoslovakia	1	Denmark	1
28.4.87	Finland	0	Denmark	1
2.6.87	Denmark	0	Czechoslovakia	1
24.6.87	Iceland	0	Denmark	0
5.8.87	Iceland	2	Finland	2
26.8.87	Denmark	1	Iceland	3
8.9.87	Finland	3	Czechoslovakia	2
14.10.87	Czechoslovakia	4	Iceland	4

	P	W	D	L	F	A	Pts
CZECHOSLOVAKIA	6	3	2	1	14	8	8
Denmark	6	2	2	2	7	6	6
Finland	6	2	1	3	8	11	5
Iceland	6	1	3	2	9	13	5

GROUP 7: Belgium, Republic of Ireland and Scotland

9.9.86	Belgium 0	Rep. of Ireland 0
14.10.86	Rep. of Ireland 1	Scotland 2
17.2.87	Scotland 4	Rep. of Ireland 1
31.3.87	Belgium 0	Scotland 0
28.4.87	Rep. of Ireland 3	Belgium 0
13.10.87	Scotland 1	Belgium 0

	P	W	D	L	F	A	Pts
SCOTLAND	4	3	1	0	7	2	7
Rep. of Ireland	4	1	1	2	5	6	3
Belgium	4	0	2	2	0	4	2

GROUP 8: West Germany, Holland, Bulgaria and Luxembourg

29.10.86	West Germany 2	Bulgaria 0
19.11.86	Bulgaria 1	Holland 0
3.12.86	Luxembourg 0	Holland 2
24.3.87	West Germany 4	Luxembourg 1
31.3.87	Bulgaria 1	Luxembourg 0
28.4.87	Holland 3	West Germany 1
29.4.87	Luxembourg 0	Bulgaria 1
13.10.87	Holland 1	Luxembourg 0
28.10.87	Luxembourg 1	West Germany 4
17.11.87	West Germany 0	Holland 2
2.12.87	Bulgaria 2	West Germany 1
15.12.87	Holland 4	Bulgaria 3

	P	W	D	L	F	A	Pts
HOLLAND	6	5	0	1	12	5	10
Bulgaria	6	4	0	2	8	7	8
West Germany	6	3	0	3	12	9	6
Luxembourg	6	0	0	6	2	13	0

QUARTER-FINALS

First Legs

16.2.88	Scotland 0	England 1
24.2.88	Spain 0	Holland 1
2.3.88	Greece 1	Czechoslovakia 1
16.3.88	France 2	Italy 1

Second Legs

22.3.88	England 1	Scotland 0
23.3.88	Italy 2	France 2
23.3.88	Holland 2	Spain 1
23.3.88	Czechoslovakia 2	Greece 2*

SEMI-FINALS

First Legs

13.4.88	France 4	England 2
13.4.88	Greece 5	Holland 0

Second Legs

27.4.88	England 2	France 2
27.4.88	Holland 2	Greece 0

FINAL

First Leg

24.5.88	Greece 0	France 0
12.10.88	France	Greece ....

*Won on away goals rule

33

Under-21 International Matches 1976-88

EC European Under-21 Championship

ENGLAND v. BULGARIA

				Goals	
Year	Date		Venue	Eng	Bulg
EC1979	June	5	Pernik	3	1
EC1979	Nov.	20	Leicester	5	0

ENGLAND v. DENMARK

				Eng	Den
EC1978	Sep.	19	Hvidovre	2	1
EC1979	Sep.	11	Watford	1	0
EC1982	Sep.	21	Hvidovre	4	1
EC1983	Sep.	20	Norwich	4	1
EC1986	Mar.	12	Copenhagen	1	0
EC1986	Mar.	26	Manchester City	1	1

ENGLAND v. FINLAND

				Eng	Fin
EC1977	May	26	Helsinki	1	0
EC1977	Oct.	12	Hull	8	1
EC1984	Oct.	16	Southampton	2	0
EC1985	May	21	Mikkeli	1	3

ENGLAND v. FRANCE

				Eng	Fra
EC1984	Feb.	28	Sheffield Weds.	6	1
EC1984	Mar.	28	Rouen	1	0
1987	June	11	Toulon	0	2
EC1988	Apr.	13	Besancon	2	4
EC1988	Apr.	27	Highbury	2	2
1988	June	12	Toulon	2	4

ENGLAND v. GERMANY D.R.

				Eng	GDR
EC1980	April	16	Sheffield United	1	2
EC1980	April	23	Jena	0	1

ENGLAND v. GERMANY F.R.

				Eng	GFR
EC1982	Sep.	21	Sheffield United	3	1
EC1982	Oct.	12	Bremen	2	3
1987	Sep.	8	Lüdenscheid	0	2

ENGLAND v. GREECE

				Eng	Gre
EC1982	Nov.	16	Piraeus	0	1
EC1983	Mar.	29	Portsmouth	2	1

ENGLAND v. HUNGARY

				Eng	Hun
EC1981	June	5	Keszthely	2	1
EC1981	Nov.	17	Nottingham Forest	2	0
EC1983	April	26	Newcastle	1	0
EC1983	Oct.	11	Nyiregyhaza	2	0

ENGLAND v. ISRAEL

				Eng	Isr
1985	Feb.	27	Tel Aviv	2	1

ENGLAND v. ITALY

				Goals	
Year	Date		Venue	Eng	Italy
EC1978	Mar.	8	Manchester City	2	1
EC1978	April	5	Rome	0	0
EC1984	April	18	Manchester City	3	1
EC1984	May	2	Florence	0	1
EC1986	April	9	Pisa	0	2
EC1986	April	23	Swindon	1	1

ENGLAND v. MEXICO

				Eng	Mex
1988	June	5	Toulon	2	1

ENGLAND v. MOROCCO

				Eng	Mor
1987	June	7	Toulon	2	0
1988	June	9	Toulon	1	0

ENGLAND v. NORWAY

				Eng	Nor
EC1977	June	1	Bergen	2	1
EC1977	Sep.	6	Brighton	6	0
1980	Sep.	9	Southampton	3	0
1981	Sep.	8	Drammen	0	0

ENGLAND v. POLAND

				Eng	Pol
EC1982	Mar.	17	Warsaw	2	1
EC1982	April	7	West Ham	2	2

ENGLAND v. PORTUGAL

				Eng	Por
1987	June	13	Sollies-Pont	0	0

ENGLAND v. REPUBLIC OF IRELAND

				Eng	Rep of Ire
1981	Feb.	25	Liverpool	1	0
1985	Mar.	25	Portsmouth	3	2

ENGLAND v. RUMANIA

				Eng	Rum
EC1980	Oct.	14	Ploesti	0	4
EC1981	April	28	Swindon	3	0
EC1985	April	30	Brasov	0	0
EC1985	Sep.	9	Ipswich	3	0

ENGLAND v. SCOTLAND

				Eng	Scot
1977	April	27	Sheffield United	1	0
EC1980	Feb.	12	Coventry	2	1
EC1980	Mar.	4	Aberdeen	0	0
EC1982	April	19	Glasgow	1	0
EC1982	April	28	Manchester City	1	1
EC1988	Feb.	16	Aberdeen	1	0
EC1988	Mar.	22	Nottingham	1	0

<table>
</table>

ENGLAND v. SPAIN

Year	Date		Venue	Eng	Goals Spa
EC1984	May	17	Seville	1	0
EC1984	May	24	Sheffield United	2	0
1987	Feb.	18	Burgos	2	1

ENGLAND v. SWEDEN

Year	Date		Venue	Eng	Swe
1979	June	9	Vasteras	2	1
1986	Sep.	9	Oestersund	1	1

ENGLAND v. SWITZERLAND

				Eng	Swit
EC1980	Nov.	18	Ipswich	5	0
EC1981	May	31	Neuenburg	0	0
1988	May	28	Lausanne	1	1

ENGLAND v. TURKEY

				Eng	Turk
EC1984	Nov.	13	Bursa	0	0
EC1985	Oct.	15	Bristol City	3	0
EC1987	April	28	Izmir	0	0
EC1987	Oct.	13	Sheffield	1	1

ENGLAND v. U.S.S.R.

Year	Date		Venue	Eng	Goals USSR
1987	June	9	La Ciotat	0	0
1988	June	7	Six-Fours	1	0

ENGLAND v. WALES

				Eng	Wales
1976	Dec.	15	Wolverhampton	0	0
1979	Feb.	6	Swansea	1	0

ENGLAND v. YUGOSLAVIA

				Eng	Yugo
EC1978	April	19	Novi Sad...................	1	2
EC1978	May	2	Manchester City..........	1	1
EC1986	Nov.	11	Peterborough	1	1
EC1987	Nov.	10	Zemun	5	1

The England Under-21 team in Toulon.

England (Under-21) Caps 1987-88

	West Germany	Turkey	Yugoslavia	Scotland	Scotland	France	France	Switzerland	Mexico	U.S.S.R.	Morocco	France
G. Walsh (Manchester United)	1		1									
N. McDonald (Newcastle United)	2		*9									
T. Dorigo (Chelsea)	3		3	3	3							
D. Walker (Nottingham Forest)	4	6		6	6							
G. Rodger (Coventry City)	5											
P. Davis (Arsenal)	6	4	4				4					
D. Rocastle (Arsenal)	7	8	10	10	10		10		10	10	10	10
P. Gascoigne (Newcastle United)	8		8	8	8		8	8	8	*11	8	8
N. Clough (Nottingham Forest)	9	9	9	9	9				9		9	9
T. Cottee (West Ham United)	10											
P. Beagrie (Sheffield United)	11	11										
T. Flowers (Southampton)	*1											
A. Thorn (Wimbledon)	*5		6		5	6		5				
S. Parkin (Stoke City)	*8	3		*2	2	2						
F. Carr (Nottingham Forest)	*11	7	7				7					
F. Digby (Swindon Town)		1										
N. Gibbs (Watford)		2										
M. Keown (Aston Villa)		5		5		5	6					
D. Coney (Queens Park Rangers)		10										
G. Porter (Watford)		*11	11	11	11		11	10				
M. Thomas (Arsenal)		2	2				2		4	4	4	4
C. Fairclough (Tottenham Hotspur)			5			5						
M. Allen (Queens Park Rangers)			*8									
P. Suckling (Crystal Palace)				1	1	1	1	1				
S. Robson (West Ham United)				4				4				
D. White (Manchester City)				7	7	7				7		
A. Gray (Aston Villa)						4	4					
S. Sellars (Blackburn Rovers)					*8	11		11				
C. Cooper (Middlesbrough)						3			2	3	2	2
S. Redmond (Manchester City)						*6	*6		5	5	5	5
S. Sedgley (Coventry City)						8						
P. Stewart (Manchester City)						9						
G. Parker (Nottingham Forest)						10						
G. Ablett (Liverpool)								3				
D. Lowe (Ipswich Town)						9	*9					
M. Hayes (Arsenal)							*11					
B. Statham (Tottenham Hotspur)								2				
M. Forsyth (Derby County)								3				
A. McLeary (Millwall)								6				
D. Wise (Wimbledon)								7				
T. Sheringham (Millwall)								9				
N. Martyn (Bristol Rovers)								*1	1	1	1	1
J. Dicks (West Ham United)								*2	3		3	3
D. Batty (Leeds United)								*7				
V. Samways (Tottenham Hotspur)								*11		11		11
S. Chettle (Nottingham Forest)									6	6	6	6
D. Platt (Aston Villa)									7		7	7
D. Smith (Coventry City)									11	*7	11	
C. Beeston (Stoke City)										2		
S. Ripley (Middlesbrough)										8		*7
D. Hirst (Sheffield Wednesday)										9		*2
A. Miller (Arsenal)											*1	

*Substitute

England Under-21 Caps 1976-88

(Up to and including 12th June 1988)

Player	*Caps*
Ablett, G. (Liverpool)	1
Adams, N. (Everton)...................	1
Adams, T. (Arsenal)	5
Allen, C. (Q.P.R. and C. Palace) ...	3
Allen, M. (Queens Park Rangers) ..	2
Allen, P. (West Ham and Tottenham)	3
Anderson, V. (Nottingham For.)....	1
Andrews, I. (Leicester City)..........	1
Bailey, G. (Manchester United)	14
Baker, G. (Southampton).............	2
Bannister, G. (Sheffield Wed.).......	1
Barker, S. (Blackburn Rovers).......	4
Barnes, J. (Watford)...................	3
Barnes, P. (Manchester City).........	9
Batty, D. (Leeds United)..............	1
Beagrie, P. (Sheffield United)........	2
Beeston, C. (Stoke City)	1
Bertschin, K. (Birmingham City)....	3
Birtles, G. (Nottingham Forest)	2
Blissett, L. (Watford)	4
Bracewell, P. (Stoke, Sunderland and Everton)	13
Bradshaw, P. (Wolverhampton)	4
Breacker, T. (Luton Town)	2
Brennan, M. (Ipswich Town).........	5
Brock, K. (Oxford United)	4
Butcher, T. (Ipswich Town)	7
Butterworth, I. (Coventry and Nottingham Forest)....................	8
Caesar, G. (Arsenal)	3
Callaghan, N. (Watford)..............	9
Carr, C. (Fulham)	1
Carr, F. (Nottingham Forest)........	9
Caton, T. (Man. C. and Arsenal)....	14
Chamberlain, M. (Stoke City)	4
Chapman, L. (Stoke City)............	1
Chettle, S. (Nottingham Forest)	4
Clough, N. (Nottingham Forest)	15
Coney, D. (Fulham)	4
Connor, T. (Brighton & H.A.)	1
Cooke, R. (Tottenham Hotspur)	1
Cooper, C. (Middlesbrough)	5
Corrigan, J. (Manchester City)	3
Cottee, T. (West Ham United).......	10
Cowans, G. (Aston Villa)	5

Player	*Caps*
Cranson, I. (Ipswich Town)..........	5
Crooks, G. (Stoke City)	4
Cunningham, L. (W.B.A.)............	6
Curbishley, A. (Birmingham City)	1
Daniel, P. (Hull City).................	7
Davis, P. (Arsenal).....................	11
D'Avray, M. (Ipswich Town)	2
Deehan, J. (Aston Villa)	7
Dennis, M. (Birmingham City)	3
Dickens, A. (West Ham United)	1
Digby, F. (Swindon Town)...........	4
Dillon, K. (Birmingham City).......	1
Dixon, K. (Chelsea)	1
Donowa, L. (Norwich City)	3
Dorigo, T. (Aston Villa and Chelsea)	11
Dozzell, J. (Ipswich Town)	6
Duxbury, M. (Manchester United)..	7
Dyson, P. (Coventry City)............	4
Elliott, P. (Luton and Aston Villa)	3
Fairclough, C. (Nottingham Forest and Tottenham)	7
Fairclough, D. (Liverpool)...........	1
Fashanu, J. (Norwich and Nottm. Forest)	11
Fenwick, T. (Queen's Park Rangers)................................	11
Fereday, W. (Q.P.R.)	5
Flowers, T. (Southampton)	3
Forsyth, M. (Derby County)	1
Foster, S. (Brighton & H.A.)........	1
Futcher, P. (Luton and Man. C.)	11
Gale, A. (Fulham)	1
Gascoigne, P. (Newcastle United)	13
Gayle, H. (Birmingham City)	3
Gernon, I. (Ipswich Town)...........	1
Gibbs, N. (Watford)...................	5
Gibson, C. (Aston Villa)	1
Gilbert, W. (Crystal Palace)	11
Goddard, P. (West Ham United)	8
Gordon, D. (Norwich City)..........	4
Gray, A. (Aston Villa).................	2
Haigh, P. (Hull City)	1
Hardyman, P. (Portsmouth)..........	2

Player	Caps
Hateley, M. (Coventry and Portsmouth)	10
Hayes, M. (Arsenal)	3
Hazell, R. (Wolverhampton)	1
Heath, A. (Stoke City)	8
Hesford, I. (Blackpool)	7
Hilaire, V. (Crystal Palace)	9
Hinshelwood, P. (Crystal Palace)	2
Hirst, D. (Sheffield Wednesday)	2
Hoddle, G. (Tottenham Hotspur)	12
Hodge, S. (Nottingham F. and Aston Villa)	8
Hodgson, D. (Middlesbrough and Liverpool)	7
Hucker, P. (Queens Park Rangers)	2
Johnston, C. (Middlesbrough)	2
Jones, C. (Tottenham Hotspur)	1
Jones, D. (Everton)	1
Keegan, G. (Oldham Athletic)	1
Keown, M. (Aston Villa)	8
Kerslake, D. (Queen's Park Rangers)	1
Kilcline, B. (Notts. County)	2
King, A. (Everton)	2
Knight, A. (Portsmouth)	2
Knight, I. (Sheffield Wednesday)	2
Langley, T. (Chelsea)	1
Lee, R. (Charlton Athletic)	2
Lee, S. (Liverpool)	6
Lowe, D. (Ipswich Town)	2
Lukic, J. (Leeds United)	7
Lund, G. (Grimsby Town)	1
McCall, S. (Ipswich Town)	6
McDonald, N. (Newcastle United)	5
McGrath, L. (Coventry City)	1
McLeary, A. (Millwall)	1
McMahon, S. (Everton and Aston Villa)	6
Mabbutt, G. (Bristol R. and Tottenham)	6
Mackenzie, S. (W.B.A.)	3
Martyn, N. (Bristol Rovers)	5
May, A. (Manchester City)	1
Middleton, J. (Nottingham Forest and Derby County)	3
Miller, A. (Arsenal)	1
Mills, G. (Nottingham Forest)	2
Mimms, R. (Rotherham and Everton)	3

Player	Caps
Moran, S. (Southampton)	2
Morgan, S. (Leicester City)	2
Mountfield, D. (Everton)	1
Moses, R. (W.B.A. and Man. U.)	8
Newell, M. (Luton Town)	4
Osman, R. (Ipswich Town)	7
Owen, G. (Man. C. and W.B.A.)	22
Painter, I. (Stoke City)	1
Parker, G. (Hull City and Nottingham Forest)	6
Parker, P. (Fulham)	8
Parkes, P. (Q.P.R.)	1
Parkin, S. (Stoke City)	6
Peach, D. (Southampton)	8
Peake, A. (Leicester City)	1
Pearce, S. (Nottingham Forest)	1
Pickering, N. (Sunderland and Coventry)	15
Platt, D. (Aston Villa)	3
Porter, G. (Watford)	12
Proctor, M. (Middlesbrough and Nottm. Forest)	5
Ranson, R. (Manchester City)	11
Redmond, S. (Manchester City)	6
Reeves, K. (Norwich and Man. C.)	10
Regis, C. (W.B.A.)	6
Reid, N. (Manchester City)	6
Reid, P. (Bolton Wanderers)	6
Richards, J. (Wolverhampton)	2
Rideout, P. (Aston Villa and Bari)	6
Ripley, S. (Middlesbrough)	2
Ritchie, A. (Brighton & H.A.)	1
Rix, G. (Arsenal)	7
Robson, B. (W.B.A.)	7
Robson, S. (Arsenal and West Ham United)	8
Rocastle, D. (Arsenal)	14
Rodger, G. (Coventry City)	4
Rosario, R. (Norwich City)	4
Rowell, G. (Sunderland)	1
Ryan, J. (Oldham Athletic)	1
Samways, V. (Tottenham Hotspur)	3
Sansom, K. (Crystal Palace)	8
Seaman, D. (Birmingham City)	10
Sedgley, S. (Coventry City)	4
Sellars, S. (Blackburn Rovers)	3
Shaw, G. (Aston Villa)	7

Player	Caps
Shelton, G. (Sheffield Wednesday)	1
Sheringham, T. (Millwall)............	1
Simpson, P. (Manchester City)	5
Sims, S. (Leicester City)...............	10
Sinnott, L. (Watford)..................	1
Smith, D. (Coventry City)	3
Smith, M. (Sheffield Wednesday) ...	5
Snodin, I. (Doncaster Rovers and Leeds United)	4
Statham, B. (Tottenham Hotspur)	1
Statham, D. (W.B.A.)	6
Stein, B. (Luton Town)	3
Sterland, M. (Sheffield Wednesday)	7
Steven, T. (Everton)...................	2
Stevens, G. (Everton).................	1
Stevens, G. (Brighton & H.A. and Tottenham)	7
Stewart, P. (Manchester City)........	1
Suckling, P. (Coventry, Man. City and Crystal Palace)	10
Sunderland, A. (Wolverhampton)	1
Swindlehurst, D. (Crystal Palace)...	1
Talbot, B. (Ipswich Town)	1
Thomas, D. (Coventry and Tottenham)....................................	7
Thomas, M. (Arsenal)	7
Thomas, M. (Luton Town)...........	3
Thompson, G. (Coventry City)	6

Player	Caps
Thorn, A. (Wimbledon)...............	5
Venison, B. (Sunderland)	10
Waddle, C. (Newcastle United)......	1
Walker, D. (Nottingham Forest)	7
Wallace, D. (Southampton)	14
Walsh, G. (Manchester United)	2
Walsh, P. (Luton Town)	7
Walters, M. (Aston Villa)	9
Ward, P. (Brighton & H.A.).........	2
Watson, D. (Norwich City)	7
Webb, N. (Portsmouth and Nottm. Forest)	3
White, D. (Manchester City).........	4
Whyte, C. (Arsenal)...................	4
Wicks, S. (Q.P.R.).....................	1
Wilkins, R. (Chelsea)	1
Wilkinson, P. (Grimsby Town and Everton)................................	4
Williams, S. (Southampton)	14
Winterburn, N. (Wimbledon)........	1
Wise, D. (Wimbledon).................	1
Woodcock, A. (Nottingham Forest)	2
Woods, C. (Nottm. Forest, Q.P.R. and Norwich)..........................	6
Wright, M. (Southampton)	4
Wright, W. (Everton)	6

England 'B' Caps 1978-88

(Up to and including 14th October 1987)

Player	Caps
Anderson, V. (Nottingham Forest)	7
Armstrong, D. (Middlesbrough)	2
Bailey, G. (Manchester United)	2
Bailey, J. (Everton)	1
Barnes, P. (W.B.A.)	1
Batson, B. (W.B.A.)	3
Birtles, G. (Nottingham Forest)	1
Blissett, L. (Watford)	1
Bond, K. (Norwich City and Manchester City)	2
Brock, K. (Q.P.R.)	1
Bruce, S. (Norwich City)	1
Butcher, T. (Ipswich Town)	1
Callaghan, N. (Watford)	1
Corrigan, J. (Manchester City)	10
Cowans, G. (Aston Villa)	1
Crook, I. (Norwich City)	1
Cunningham, L. (W.B.A.)	1
Daley, S. (Wolves)	6
Davenport, P. (Nottingham For.)	1
Devonshire, A. (West Ham United)	1
Elliott, S. (Sunderland)	3
Eves, M. (Wolves)	3
Fairclough, C. (Tottenham)	1
Fairclough, D. (Liverpool)	1
Fashanu, J. (Nottingham For.)	1
Flanagan, M. (Charlton and Crystal Palace)	3
Gallagher, J. (Birmingham)	1
Geddis, D. (Ipswich)	1
Gibson, C. (Aston Villa)	1
Gidman, J. (Aston Vila)	2
Goddard, P. (West Ham United)	1
Greenhoff, B. (Manchester United)	1
Harford, M. (Luton Town)	1
Hazell, R. (Wolverhampton)	1
Heath, A. (Everton)	1
Hilaire, V. (Crystal Palace)	1
Hill, G. (Manchester United and Derby County)	6
Hoddle, G. (Tottenham Hotspur)	2
Hodge, S. (Nottingham For.	1
Hollins, J. (Q.P.R.)	5
Johnston, C. (Liverpool)	1
Kennedy, A. (Liverpool)	7

Player	Caps
Langley, T. (Chelsea)	3
Lineker, G. (Leicester City)	1
Lyons, M. (Everton)	1
McCall, S. (Ipswich Town)	1
McDermott, T. (Liverpool)	1
McMahon, S. (Aston Villa and Liverpool)	2
Mabbutt, G. (Tottenham)	1
Mackenzie, S. (Manchester City)	1
Mariner, P. (Ipswich Town)	7
Martin, A. (West Ham United)	2
Money, R. (Liverpool)	1
Morley, T. (Aston Villa)	2
Mortimer, D. (Aston Villa)	3
Mountfield, D. (Everton)	1
Needham, D. (Nottingham For.)	6
Osman, R. (Ipswich Town)	2
Owen, G. (Manchester City)	7
Parker, P. (Q.P.R.)	1
Parkes, P. (West Ham United)	1
Peach, D. (Southampton)	1
Power, P. (Manchester City)	1
Reeves, K. (Manchester City)	3
Regis, C. (W.B.A.)	3
Richards, J. (Wolverhampton)	3
Rix, G. (Arsenal)	3
Roberts, G. (Tottenham Hotspur)	1
Robson, B. (W.B.A.)	2
Roeder, G. (Orient and Q.P.R.)	6
Sansom, K. (Crystal Palace)	2
Seaman, D. (Q.P.R.)	1
Sims, S. (Leicester City)	1
Snodin, I. (Everton)	1
Speight, M. (Sheffield United)	4
Statham, D. (W.B.A.)	2
Sterland, M. (Sheffield Wednesday)	1
Stevens, G. (Everton)	1
Sunderland, A. (Arsenal)	7
Talbot, B. (Ipswich and Arsenal)	8
Thomas, M. (Tottenham Hotspur)	1
Thompson, P. (Liverpool)	1
Waldron, M. (Southampton)	1
Ward, P. (Nottingham For.)	2
Williams, S. (Southampton)	4
Woodcock, T. (Cologne)	1
Woods, C. (Norwich City)	1
Wright, B. (Everton)	2

England's International Matches 1987-88

West Germany 2   England 0
(Under-21)
8th September 1987, Lüdenscheid

On a generally gloomy evening for Dave Sexton's Under-21s, winners just twice in their last 12 matches, a more skilful and imaginative West German side achieved a comprehensive victory and England full cap Tony Cottee was dismissed on the hour for retaliating against some rough treatment from right-back Zanter.

Ludwig Kogl, the outstanding Bayern Munich winger, played a major part in the Germans' success, combining well with Schwabl to continually outwit England's defence on the left. Labbadia gave the home side the lead midway through the first half, forcing the ball in after Kreuzer's looping header had come back off a post.

Gary Walsh, the Manchester United goalkeeper, had experienced some difficulty in dealing with crosses and gave way to Tim Flowers, successor to Shilton at Southampton, for the second half. Virtually his first act was to pick the ball out of the net after Riedle's diving header from Schwabl's centre had flashed past him to put the Germans 2-0 up.

England wasted several opportunities, with Nigel Clough the chief culprit, and the scoresheet remained depressingly blank for the fourth successive Under-21 match.

West Germany: Reck, Zanter, Kutowski (Binz), Kreuzer, Sauer, Neun, Riedle (Kirchhoff), Foda, Labbadia (Glesius), Schwabl, Kogl.

England: Walsh (Flowers), McDonald, Dorigo, Walker, Rodger (Thorn), Davis, Rocastle, Gascoigne (Parkin), Clough, Cottee, Beagrie (Carr).

West Germany 3   England 1
9th September 1987, Düsseldorf

West Germany, with only three remnants from the side that reached the World Cup Final in Mexico, were being rebuilt by Franz Beckenbauer, and his new team reduced England to a state of bewilderment in an opening 35 minutes in which they showed the kind of determination that could help them to win the European Championship on home soil.

With Steve Hodge failing to recover from a virus, Bobby Robson resurrected an adventurous experiment that he had only used once since the summer of 1984, bringing back John Barnes and Chris Waddle to operate down each flank. But England, rather than expanding their own attacking ideas, found themselves having to concentrate on defence as the Germans began with a sharpness that suggested they were intent on finishing the match as a contest as soon as possible.

England's Tony Adams was in for a torrid time throughout against a striker of Völler's quality, and Littbarski proved as difficult to control on 24 minutes as he capitalised on the yard of space offered him by the

Viv Anderson (on ground) clears from Frontzek in Düsseldorf.

young Arsenal defender to curl a memorable 20-yarder past England captain Peter Shilton. Eleven minutes later Sansom and Anderson at the near post succeeded only in nudging Littbarski's inswinging corner past Shilton's outstretched hands.

England, two down and seemingly out, then came back into the picture with a typical example of Gary Lineker opportunism a couple of minutes before half-time. But German substitute Wuttke, understudy to the impressive Völler whom he replaced, added a third goal six minutes from the end with an explosive shot to complete a disappointing evening for the England team, so often on the receiving end in these early-season internationals.

West Germany: Immel, Brehme (Reuter), Frontzek, Kohler, Herget, Buchwald, Littbarski, Dorfner, Völler (Wuttke), Thon, Allofs.

England: Shilton, Anderson, Sansom (Pearce), Hoddle (Webb), Adams, Mabbutt, Reid, Barnes, Beardsley, Lineker, Waddle (Hateley).

Referee: Casarin (Italy).

England 1   Turkey 1
(Under-21)
13th October 1987, Sheffield

England had their hopes of reaching the European Championship quarter-finals seriously threatened when they failed to defeat a skilful and well-organised Turkish team at Bramall Lane in the penultimate match in Group 4. They now faced the prospect of having to win in Yugoslavia to qualify.

The Under-21 team's main problem had been an inability to score enough goals, having managed just six in their last nine matches. Manager Dave Sexton's attempt at finding a solution involved the pairing of Dean Coney and Nigel Clough as strikers and bringing in two recognised wingers in Franz Carr and Peter

Beagrie, but as it turned out only midfielder Paul Davis found the net this time.

Turkey's passing was generally more accurate than the home side's, and they managed to string about a dozen together before Unal cut across in front of Parkin and beat Digby with a low cross-shot from 25 yards, the first goal scored by a Turkish team against England at either full or Under-21 level. England should really have levelled this sixth-minute effort immediately as Clough broke down the left to play a perfect ball into Coney's path, but the Rangers player failed from close in with only Okan in the Turkish goal to beat.

England's often undermanned midfield were frequently overrun by Turkey's quick, precise breaks, and only Digby's desperate save at Zeki's feet prevented a further score before half-time. Gary Porter's introduction for the injured Beagrie tended to balance the forces, and England pressed forward with increasing urgency until Paul Davis headed home from Porter's cross in the 57th minute.

England: Digby, Gibbs, Parkin, Davis, Keown, Walker, Carr, Rocastle, Clough, Coney, Beagrie (Porter).

Turkey: Okan, Recep, Selami, Gokhan G., Hasan, Hami (Durmus), Gokhan K., Unal, Zeki (Mustafa), Yucel, Hamdi.

Malta 0   England "B" 2
14th October 1987, Ta'Qali

Earlier in the year the Maltese minnows had held Portugal, the team that had beaten Bobby Robson's seniors in the World Cup in Mexico,

to a surprise 2-2 away draw, but they were totally outclassed by an England "B" team managed by Graham Taylor in a near-deserted Ta'Qali Stadium.

A slightly unbalanced England side, with no left-footer and no one wide who could dribble and cross, played the ball around accurately and confidently on a rock-hard pitch. The first goal came when Craig Johnston's free-kick in the 34th minute was only cleared as far as Mel Sterland, and the Sheffield Wednesday full-back scored with a stunning right-foot volley from about 25 yards. Mick Harford of Luton, dangerous throughout, stabbed in a low shot off a post from Adrian Heath's first-time pass for the second goal on 58 minutes.

England's defence, well marshalled by skipper Steve Bruce, limited the Maltese part-timers to a couple of goal attempts and neither of these had worried David Seaman unduly.

Malta: Cluett, Camilleri, Micallef, Laferia, Scicluna, Buttigieg, Basuttil, Vella, Mizzi, Gregory, Degiorgio.

England: Seaman, Sterland, Thomas, McMahon (Crook), Bruce, Fairclough (Parker), Johnston, Heath, Harford, Snodin, Brock.

England 8   Turkey 0
14th October 1987, Wembley

Turkey, humiliated 8-0 in their own country by England in a World Cup qualifying match in 1984, suffered the same unpleasant fate at Wembley in the European Championship. England, utterly transformed from the team beaten in West Germany, ran riot to punish the Turks for their

Peter Beardsley beats Semih to a cross to head England's sixth against the Turks.

obvious tactical shortcomings. The plan to render sweeper Erhan's presence irrelevant by probing the space down the flanks worked spectacularly well.

The onslaught was started by John Barnes after only two minutes, Liverpool's new acquisition showing commendable composure to shoot home left-footed after Neil Webb's cross had curled away from Fatih in the Turkish goal. Gary Lineker added a second in the 10th minute and then, three missed chances later, Peter Beardsley swerved away from two challenges to set up Barnes who made it 3-0 on the half-hour.

Lineker's initial shot from Beardsley's instant pass was blocked on the line by a defender, but his follow-up attempt was more successful and had the Turks suffering the indignity to returning to the dressing room at half-time 4-0 down.

Bryan Robson was credited with the fifth, a deflection of Webb's shot, and Beardsley nodded in Hoddle's

measured chip for the sixth, his own first at Wembley. Lineker, put through by his captain, tucked in the seventh to complete his fourth England hat-trick, and the promising Webb finished the spree a minute from the end with a volley for his first international goal.

England: Shilton, Stevens, Sansom, Steven (Hoddle), Adams, Butcher, Robson, Webb, Beardsley (Regis), Lineker, Barnes.

Turkey: Fatih, Riza, Semih, Ali Coban, Erhan, Ali Gultiken (Savas), Ugur, Muhammet, Kayhan, Erdal, Iskender.

Referee: Thomas (Holland).

Yugoslavia 1   England 5
(Under-21)
10th November 1987, Zemun

England's Under-21s romped to an astonishing victory in the final group match of the European Championship, achieving the best away result since matches at Under-21 level were introduced in 1976. It left Yugoslavia, surely favourites to top the group after their draw at Peterborough a year earlier, needing a 5-0 win in Turkey in December to deny England a quarter-final place.

Nigel Clough, the Nottingham Forest forward, opened England's account after seven minutes with his first Under-21 goal in 10 appearances. It followed a Gary Porter corner and encouraged England to take control, in front of Bobby Robson's senior team watching from the stand, against a side that included six of Yugoslavia's World Youth Cup-winning team.

Newcastle's Paul Gascoigne put the issue beyond any reasonable doubt with a burst of two goals in two minutes that gave England a 3-0 lead after only 25 minutes. His first was a thumping left-foot volley and his second a simple prod past Lekovic, and though he was immediately withdrawn after collecting a yellow card in the 75th minute, his contribution had been a highly significant one.

Pancev raised Yugoslav hopes when he held off Fairclough to pull a goal back on 33 minutes, but England finished them off with another purple patch on the hour as first David Rocastle, sweeping past two defenders to score with a tremendous solo effort, then Franz Carr, knocking in the rebound after Clough had hit a post, gave the scoreline a slightly unreal look.

Yugoslavia: Lekovic, Brnovic B., Brnovic D., Prosinecki, Janovsky, Pavlicic, Boban, Savicevic, Pancev, Stevenovic, Suker.

England: Walsh, Thomas, Dorigo, Davis, Fairclough, Thorn, Carr, Gascoigne (Allen), Clough (McDonald), Rocastle, Porter.

Yugoslavia 1   England 4
11th November 1987, Belgrade

England's final European Championship group match in Belgrade, described beforehand by Bobby Robson as "the most important game since we lost to Argentina in the quarter-finals of the World Cup 18 months ago", produced a dazzling England victory that clinched a deserved place in the Finals in West Germany.

Even though a draw would have guaranteed qualification, England began the match in such a committed and purposeful way that they found themselves a scarcely credible four goals to the good within a mere 24 minutes. For only the third of 60 fixtures in his five-year spell as England manager, Bobby Robson had been able to name an unchanged side, and for only the second time had he been allowed to spend more than just a couple of days preparing his squad for an international.

There have always been question marks concerning the frailty of the Yugoslav spirit when it comes to a match of crucial importance and, in reality, the contest was over as soon as Peter Beardsley had punished the first Yugoslav defensive error after just two minutes and 44 seconds. Hadzibegic's imaginative back-header dropped between sweeper Elsner and goalkeeper Ravnic and, with both lingering over the possibilities, Beardsley stretched out a leg to hook the ball over the line.

After that, the demoralised Yugoslavs were almost unrecognisable as the team which had caused so

Bryan Robson shoots home England's third in Belgrade as Bazdarevic's tackle comes too late.

many problems at Wembley. Barnes, Robson and Adams piled in the goals, and Katanec's consolation header 10 minutes from time was as meaningless as Yugoslavia's last match in Turkey would now be.

Yugoslavia: Ravnic (Radaca), Zoran Vujovic, Baljic, Katanec, Elsner (Jankovic), Hadzibegic, Stojkovic, Mlinaric, Vokri, Bazdarevic, Zlatko Vujovic.

England: Shilton, Stevens, Sansom, Steven, Adams, Butcher, Robson (Reid), Webb (Hoddle), Beardsley, Lineker, Barnes.

Referee: Vautrot (France).

Scotland 0   England 1
(Under-21)
16th February 1988, Aberdeen

England, who had beaten their arch-rivals in both of their previous meet-ings at this level, would probably have settled for a goalless stalemate in the first leg at Pittodrie. Such an outcome looked more and more likely, particularly after Gary Por-ter's close-range strike had been ruled out for offside.

David White, making his Under-21 debut, missed England's only first-half chance by heading over from a Dorigo cross, and at the other end Durrant, Rangers' equally accom-plished midfielder who could easily have travelled with the seniors to Saudi Arabia, should have done better with two good chances that came his way midway through the second period.

The only goal of an unexceptional match owed everything to the enter-prise of Nigel Clough who produced a flash of skill when it mattered most. With just five minutes left he presssed confidently down the right wing, long after most players would have relea-sed the ball inside, and crossed

46

accurately behind the Scottish defence for Porter to steady himself before shotting precisely into the far corner. So once again England were poised to eliminate the Scots from the European Championship, the home side having arguably been the moral victors on this occasion.

Scotland: Geddes, Shannon, Robertson, Whyte, Hegarty, Grant, Ferguson D., Gallacher, Fleck, Durrant, Wilson (Ferguson I.).

England: Suckling, Thomas (Parkin), Dorigo, Robson, Keown, Walker, White, Gascoigne, Clough, Rocastle, Porter.

Israel 0 England 0
17th February 1988, Tel Aviv

For Bobby Robson, England's second Friendly International in the Ramat Gan Stadium in three years provided the first of six chances to evaluate the ability of fringe players like Stuart Pearce, Dave Watson and Clive Allen, and finalise his party of 20 players for West Germany in the summer. For Liverpool midfielder Steve McMahon it was a priceless opportunity to further his international ambitions and at least prove that he could be an able understudy for Bryan Robson, missing this time through injury.

Far from being the gentle stroll in the winter sun envisaged by the manager, England were very nearly embarrassed as the match developed into a slog over a rain-soaked surface. McMahon had an impressive debut as possibly England's most effective player in the trying conditions, and it was unfortunate that his only error almost presented Israel with a goal.

Taking advantage of the slip, Brailovsky raced towards goal with only Woods to beat but panicked and sent in a shot which brushed the top of the crossbar.

It would have been a travesty if England had lost, because they had created a lot more chances. John Barnes was the man who had the skill to win the match and he engineered the best opening for this inexperienced England team, captained for the first time by Peter Beardsley, in the 81st minute. He controlled Stevens' cross on his chest, waited for the ball to drop and then delivered a stinging volley that brought the best out of Ginzburg.

The Israeli goalkeeper had failed to get anywhere near Barnes' other notable effort on 37 minutes, when a free-kick awarded for Ginzburg's handling outside the penalty-area was curled expertly over the defensive wall and against the face of the bar.

Israel: Ginzburg, Avraham Cohen, E. Cohen, Klinger, Avi Cohen, Shimonov, Alon, Malmillian, Driekes (Eizenberg), Ivanir (Ovadia), Tikva (Brailovsky).

England: Woods, Stevens, Pearce, Webb, Watson, Wright (Fenwick), Allen (Harford), McMahon, Beardsley, Barnes, Waddle.

Referee: Constantin (Belgium).

England 1 Scotland 0
(Under-21)
22nd March 1988, Nottingham

In steady, depressing rain David White's late goal at the City Ground added to Gary Porter's in Aberdeen to ensure England's place in the semi-finals of the European Under-

21 Championship for the sixth time in as many attempts. Scotland seemed to be threatening the goal that would have meant a further half-hour of aquatics, when Clough and Rocastle exchanged passes at speed to allow White in to blast a shot past Main.

England would possibly have made a quicker impact if Paul Gascoigne, clutching his left side, had not had to leave the action in the 23rd minute to be replaced by the more subtle but less powerful Sellars. One of the Newcastle midfielder's last contributions was to put White through for a low skimmer that Main did well to hold under pressure from a menacing group of white shirts.

Nigel Clough, who had been left to battle away up front virtually on his own in the first leg, was always in the thick of things on his home ground and, in tandem with Rocastle, threatened the Scottish goal on numerous occasions. Clough had already been robbed of a goal when White preferred a hurried shot to a more sensible sideways pass, but he could have made up for that when Robertson's back-pass had Rocastle driving past Main for Clough, poaching on the far side, to ram his shot against an upright. But all was forgiven eight minutes from time as White, the Manchester City forward, put the tie beyond Scotland's reach.

England: Suckling, Parkin, Dorigo, Gray, Thorn, Walker, White, Gascoigne (Sellars), Clough, Rocastle, Porter.

Scotland: Main, Shannon (Hunter), Robertson, Hegarty, Whyte, Grant, Wilson, McCall, Fleck, Collins, Gallacher (Miller).

England 2   Holland 2
23rd March 1988, Wembley

The Wembley dress rehearsal for a more significant encounter in Düsseldorf three months ahead ended with the honours shared. England had started and finished strongly, and the Dutch, inspired by the charismatic Ruud Gullit, controlled things in between with a classic exhibition of "the Continental game" – lengthy pauses punctuated with sudden explosions of movement.

In a scintillating first 20 minutes for England, John Barnes' header prompted a spectacular leaping save from Van Breukelen, formerly of Nottingham Forest, Tony Adams volleyed Sansom's free-kick home on 13 minutes but the point was disallowed for offside and then, a minute later, Gary Lineker sprinted onto Stevens' 40-yard pass and guided the ball past the goalkeeper with some degree of nonchalance.

The Dutch immediately slowed the pace of the game down, patiently retaining possession and giving Gullit every opportunity to drag defenders out of position and create space for colleagues to exploit. Every time the ball came near him, something extraordinary would invariably happen. He oozed class.

Koeman, with a typically direct pass, released Wouters on the right in the 21st minute and his low cross towards the far post was deflected past a bemused Shilton by Adams for the equaliser. Seven minutes on, Gullit, aware as ever, knocked the ball down for Van Aerle and the ball was destined for the back of the net as soon as the latter's instant cross found Bosman's head.

After Wouters has wasted a clear chance to make it 3-1 from Gullit's

Gary Lineker shakes off Dutch defender Silooy to put England in front.

delicate chip, England responded to the escape and, shortly after the hour, were rewarded with a goal that tied things up at 2-2. No sooner had Gullit limped to the touchline with a calf strain than Adams atoned for his previous error by heading sweetly in from Stevens' free-kick.

England:: Shilton, Stevens, Sansom, Steven, Adams, Watson (Wright), Robson, Webb (Hoddle), Beardsley (Hateley), Lineker, Barnes.

Holland: Van Breukelen, Troost, Silooy, Koeman, Van Aerle, Wouters, Vanenburg, Muhren, Bosman, Gullit (Kruzen), Van't Schip (Koot).

Referee: Prokop (East Germany).

France 4   England 2
(Under-21)
13th April 1988, Besancon

England, without nine first-choice players, courageously took the fight to France and, with eight minutes remaining, were clinging on to an honourable 3-2 defeat which would have given them genuine hope of reaching their third Under-21 final.

Then a back-heel by Cantona, one of several full internationals in the French team, put Paille through to score a fourth and suddenly the odds appeared stacked against England. Dave Sexton would certainly have a stronger squad available for the return leg, the match being played during a designated international week, but the French would fancy their chances now with a two-goal cushion.

A 20,000 crowd in the packed Leo Legrange Stadium, former home of the defunct Besancon club, saw France move ahead in the 22nd minute when Angloma received a perfectly weighted pass from Paille and lobbed the ball with great panache over Suckling's head before running round behind him to score. But England's response was immediate, Gary Parker following up to score from a difficult angle after Gray's free-kick had bounced away off a defender.

The play continued at a cut-and-thrust pace with England doing supremely well to match their opponents who, on paper at least, were far superior. As if to underline that point, Cantona dissected the visitors' defence with a thrilling 40-yard run and finish three minutes after half-time. But, again, England refused to lie down, and Paul Stewart equalised from a 75th-minute penalty given for a foul on Sellars. Then came those two late goals from Dogon and Paille which changed the character of the tie.

France: Barrabe, Reuzeau, Pauk, Buisine, Silvestre, Roche (Dogon), Angloma, Despeyroux, Paille, Guerin, Cantona.

England: Suckling, Parkin, Cooper, Gray, Keown, Thorn (Redmond), White, Sedgley, Stewart, Parker, Sellars.

Hungary 0　England 0
27th April 1988, Budapest

An experimental team in the Nep Stadium which included Gary Pallister, the tall and dominating centre-half plucked from Second Division Middlesbrough, completed a hat-trick of England draws in European Championship warm-up matches.

It was the England captain, man-of-the-match Bryan Robson, who protected Pallister during the first 30 minutes when Hungary, and Lajos Detari in particular, threatened to embarrass England's young defence and inflict considerable damage to the England cause. Pallister himself,

relaxed and confident, had an encouraging debut, while Tony Adams looked slightly vulnerable at the start and poor Stuart Pearce lasted only one half before retiring with a knee injury that was to keep him out of the European finals.

The occasionally prolific striking pair of Beardsley and Lineker had an afternoon of limited opportunities and general frustration, though the latter should certainly have earned a penalty in the 13th minute when goalkeeper Szendrei hauled him down, and both were eventually substituted – a rare sight indeed.

Gradually Steve McMahon got to grips with the effective Detari, the subject of a £1 million bid from Juventus, and England, through a Pallister header and a couple of rasping Robson shots, almost snatched victory. As it was they had to settle for the first-ever draw between the two countries, England having won 10 and lost five of the previous 15 Internationals.

Hungary: Szendrei, Kozma, Pinter, Sass, Balog, Roth (Varga), Kiprich (Kovacs), Garaba, Fitos, Detari, Vincze.

England: Woods, Anderson, Pearce (Stevens), Steven, Adams, Pallister, Robson, McMahon, Beardsley (Hateley), Lineker (Cottee), Waddle (Hoddle).

Referee: Tritschler (West Germany).

England 2　France 2
(Under-21)
27th April 1988, Highbury

Strengthened by the retun of nine First Division players, England put up a brave fight against a lively

Garaba's foot is slightly higher than Tony Adams' in this clash in Budapest.

French side, going ahead twice but eventually having to settle for a draw which unfortunately meant elimination.

Persistent rain for three hours before the start, which at one stage looked like causing a postponement, was always going to make it a difficult night for defenders, and this was illustrated as early as the third minute when England had a miraculous double let-off. First Perry Suckling palmed Paille's downward header against his right-hand post and then, as new cap Gary Ablett tried to clear Guerin's pass back into the goalmouth, the ball again smacked against the woodwork.

France must have been wondering if it was going to be one of those nights when England stole the lead a minute later – just the start the home team needed with a two-goal deficit to make up. Davis chipped a long ball

forward and Gascoigne was onto it in a flash to rifle a right-footer past Barrabe.

David Lowe's 33rd-minute "goal" was mysteriously disallowed, presumably for offside, and the first half ended in controversy following the award of a throw-in to France, as Rocastle accidentally kicked the ball against Silvestre and a fracas ensured which involved most of the players.

Cantona made it 1-1 on the night in the 55th minute, but when Silvestre turned Franz Carr's cross-shot into his own net three minutes later, an aggregate victory was still within England's sights. Then, 12 minutes from time, Sauzee's pass released Cantona and he went on to beat Suckling and restore France's two-goal advantage in the tie.

England: Suckling, Thomas, Ablett, Davis, Fairclough, Keown

(Redmond), Carr, Gascoigne, Lowe, Rocastle, Porter (Hayes).

France: Barrabe, Reuzeau, Galtier, Silvestre, Roche, Despeyroux, Dogon, Sauzee, Paille, Guerin, Cantona.

England 1   Scotland 0
21st May 1988, Wembley

Following the goalless draw between Scotland and Colombia at Hampden four days earlier, England beat the Scots in the second match of the Rous Cup series with Peter Beardsley's clever goal after 11 minutes. England had demonstrated their superiority in class after a slightly shaky first few minutes during which Watson saw yellow for clattering into the back of the dangerous Johnston, but the fact that they only registered a single goal for all that was down to some indifferent finishing and some inspired goalkeeping from Leighton.

England looked the only winners after Beardsley's goal. He chipped the ball delicately over the advancing Leighton, from much the same position as his disallowed effort in the F.A. Cup Final, after Stevens and Barnes had helped him to ghost through to the edge of the six-yard box. Scotland appeared to pin most of their hopes on a quick breakthrough, all the more surprising because the fit McClair had been left out on a matter of principle, but they never looked as busy again as they had in the opening few minutes.

Many Scotland goalkeepers have received criticism in the past, none more so than poor Frank Haffey who conceded nine at Wembley in 1961, but Manchester United's Jim Leighton were certainly above that. His one-man show began with a straightforward save from Webb,

Scottish defender Willie Miller succeeds in blocking this Chris Waddle effort.

continued with a superb double stop to deny Lineker and Beardsley and then included a flying leap to turn Sansom's chip away for a corner. He probably deserved his lucky moment in the 79th minute, when a weak fisted clearance from Waddle's centre was headed onto the top of the bar by Barnes.

Apart from scoring the match-winning goal, Beardsley had a good match throughout, with his cunning footwork and nimble brain posing a constant problem to the Scottish defence. The renewed midfield partnership of Bryan Robson and Neil Webb was another success.

England: Shilton, Stevens, Sansom, Webb, Watson, Adams, Robson, Steven (Waddle), Beardsley, Lineker, Barnes.

Scotland: Leighton, Gough, Nicol, Aitken, McLeish, Miller, Simpson (Burns), McStay, McCoist (Gallacher), MacLeod, Johnston.

Referee: Quiniou (France).

England 1   Colombia 1
24th May 1988, Wembley

England duly collected the Rous Cup trophy for the second time in the four years of the competition with a Wembley draw against skilful Colombia, making their first-ever visit to these shores, but a crowd of only 25,756 was present to give England a European Championship send-off.

An evening that had begun with a flourish for Bobby Robson's team, with another Gary Lineker goal on 22 minutes, ended with something like a sigh of relief. The Colombians, placed third in the recent South American Championship (higher than Brazil and Argentina), showed all the delicate ball skills and improvisation

Neil Webb gets between Scotland's McStay and Johnston to make a forward pass.

Gary Lineker gets in a header and the ball is on its way into the Colombian net.

expected of South Americans, and in Carlos Valderrama they possessed a genuinely world-class performer.

The bushy-haired Valderrama, a South American version of Holland's Gullit, mesmerised the England defence as he set up countless intricate passing movements with his colleagues. Their display was rewarded with an equaliser in the 67th minute, the unmarked Escobar heading in from a corner, and it was probably the least they deserved.

Attired in the same yellow and blue strip that has come to be associated with the Brazilians, Colombia were a lot more lively and threatening than they had been in the tight goalless draw at Hampden a week earlier. Valderrama was the major influence as expected – he will undoubtedly serve Monpellier well, the French club that he was about to join in a $4

million deal – but forwards Redin and Iguaran were no less impressive over the 90 minutes.

The eccentric penalty-taking Colombian goalkeeper, Higuita, was not averse to racing out of his goal to chest down long passes or slide in for tackles, but he was beaten just once. Seconds after McMahon's drive had been turned round a post, Waddle curled in a cross towards the forehead of the predatory Lineker and with a deft glance he registered his 25th England goal.

England: Shilton, Anderson, Sansom, McMahon, Wright, Adams, Robson, Waddle (Hoddle), Beardsley (Hateley), Lineker, Barnes.

Colombia: Higuita, Escobar, Herrera, Hoyos, Arango (Trellez), Garcia, Valderrama C., Redin,

Alvarez, Perea, Iguaran (Valder-rama A.).

Referee: Assenmacher (West Germany).

Rous Cup Table

	P	W	D	L	F	A	Pts
ENGLAND	2	1	1	0	2	1	3
Colombia	2	0	2	0	1	1	2
Scotland	2	0	1	1	0	1	1

Switzerland 0   England 1
28th May 1988, Lausanne

England's final warm-up International prior to the European Championship in West Germany produced a narrow victory and Gary Lineker's 26th goal in 28 England starts. Lineker, who dovetailed perfectly with striking partner Peter Beardsley, had the Swiss defence on the run from the very first minute when his powerful shot was blocked by Corminboeuf in goal.

England continued to look considerably the more incisive team and were very close to scoring again on two occasions in the first half. Corminboeuf had saved acrobatically from Barnes' drive before excelling himself with a block from Adams' strong header. Then the Swiss goalkeeper almost let his team-mates down by making a mess of dealing with Lineker's high cross from the right; fortunately Weber was on the spot to effect a clearance from near the goal-line.

Switzerland looked a shade more determined as they began the second half, and midfielder Hermann did enterprising work on both flanks. Just when it appeared that England had lost control of the match they got the vital breakthrough in the 59th minute. It was a borderline affair, with the Swiss vainly appealing for offside as Beardsley was sent clear on the left by Robson's clever pass, and he delivered a perfectly-weighted ball to the far post for Lineker to thump it high into the net.

In the closing stages Lineker might have netted a couple more. He ran unchallenged from the halfway-line onto another Beardsley through-ball only to fluff the chance by shooting wide, and then, following a brilliant Barnes run that took the Liverpool player from one end of the field to the other, Lineker rather spoilt things by missing the target once again.

Three minutes from time, confusion between Watson and Sansom presented Andermatt with a chance that he put over the bar. So England held onto their lead, and despite being less of a dominant force in the second half, they were worth a victory that preserved an unbeaten sequence stretching back eight matches.

England Under-21s drew 1-1 with their Swiss counterparts in a curtain-raiser to the main match. Paul Gascoigne equalising Wyss's long-range effort from a free-kick after 63 minutes.

Switzerland: Corminboeuf, Geiger, Schallibaum, Tschuppert, Weber, Bickel (Mottiez), Bonvin (Turkiyimaz), Perret (Andermatt), Hermann, Sutter, Zwicker.

England: Shilton (Woods), Stevens, Sansom, Webb, Wright, Adams (Watson), Robson (Reid), Steven (Waddle), Beardsley, Lineker, Barnes.

Referee: Agnolin (Italy).

Bryan Robson looks to have lost this tussle for the ball with Tschuppert in Lausanne.

England 2   Mexico 1
(Under-21)
5th June 1988, Toulon

The England Under-21 team won their opening game of the Toulon International Tournament but at the cost of having West Ham full-back Julian Dicks sent off for a second bookable offence three minutes from the end. Dicks would now have to miss the following match against the Soviet Union.

Nigel Clough, Nottingham Forest's leading scorer who had initially struggled to find the net in Under-21 Internationals, notched a brace of goals in the first half to clinch victory for England. He had only just returned from a club tour of Australia, but there was no evident lack of sharpness as he opened his account with a crisp right-foot volley from Rocastle's cross on 19 minutes.

Paul Gascoigne came very close to immediately increasing England's lead with a chip over Campos' head that flicked off the top of the crossbar, and then missed a relatively simple chance near to half-time when his hurried bicycle kick at the far post went well wide of the target.

England were well on top during the first half, showing much more composure on the ball than their Central American opponents, and Bristol Rovers goalkeeper Martyn was barely tested at all. All matches in the tournament were scheduled to last only 40 minutes each way, and it was in the final moments of an entertaining first half that England went two goals up. Rocastle, the captain, was blatantly pulled back by Diaz and Clough stroked home the spot-kick.

Thomas missed a good early chance in the second period, shooting over the top after another telling Smith cross had put him clear, and in the 17th minute of the half Mexico pulled a goal back through Medina.

England: Martyn, Cooper, Dicks, Thomas, Redmond, Chettle, Platt, Gascoigne, Clough, Rocastle, Smith.

Mexico: Campos, Torres, Morales, Pernes, Diaz, Salas M., Salas A., Raya, Medina, Gonzalez, Sanchez.

England 1   U.S.S.R. 0
(Under-21)
7th June 1988, Six-Fours

Bobby Robson's senior side were due to meet the Soviet Union in the European Championship Finals in the following week and the England youngsters beat the Russian Under-21s with Vinny Samways' goal to offer their seniors the perfect fillip. The win meant that England were favourites to reach their second Final in three years of participating in the Toulon tournament.

Manager Sexton made five changes from the team which had faced Mexico. Dicks was automatically suspended after his indiscretion in the opening match and an Under-21 debut was given to Stoke defender Carl Beeston, who had only been brought into the squad a few days before their departure for France. Ripley, White, Hirst and Samways were the other players brought in, but it was goalkeeper Martyn who contributed most to England's victory with a string of excellent saves.

England survived a scare after 11 minutes when the Russian centre-forward, Shalimov, raced clear of the English back line and seemed certain to score until Martyn expertly blocked his eventual shot with his legs. The all-important goal came eight minutes before half-time as 19-year-old Tottenham midfielder Samways, making his first full appearance for the Under-21s, struck a left-footed half-volley home from a difficult angle.

Throughout the first half the Russians had repeatedly out-thought the English offside manoeuvre and only Martyn's inspired goalkeeping ensured that Samways' strike proved decisive. Gascoigne replaced the scorer in the closing stages, but England managed to hold out against increasing pressure.

England: Martyn, Beeston, Cooper, Thomas, Redmond, Chettle, White (Smith), Ripley, Hirst, Rocastle, Samways (Gascoigne).

U.S.S.R.: Kalinauskas, Chugunov, Gerashenko, Kuznetsov, Soloutsov, Smertin, Piatnitski, Revischivilli, Kasumov (Shugzhda), Shalimov, Pisarev.

England 1   Morocco 0
(Under-21)
9th June 1988, Toulon

England required only a draw from their last match in Group A, against Morocco in the Mayol Stadium, to confirm their place in the Final against either France or Bulgaria. Manager Sexton reverted to the team which had beaten Mexico in the opening match, recalling Dicks, the West Ham defender, after his one-match ban.

Newcastle's Paul Gascoigne fired in a left-foot volley following a cross by Coventry's David Smith after 19 minutes and this ultimately proved to be sufficient to preserve England's 100% record in the tournament. Thomas and Gascoigne had goals disallowed for offside, defender Cooper hit a post from 30 yards and Clough also went close as England overcame some intimidatory Moroccan tactics.

As the foul count increased markedly after the interval, Morroco had Zouhir sent off when he was penalised for a second bookable offence in the 50th minute, thereby becoming the fourth player to be dismissed in the tournament. The tough-tackling Africans continued to keep Martyn busy in goal, despite their handicap, and it was only in the last couple of minutes that Sexton felt it appropriate to give Arsenal's Miller some brief international experience between the posts.

England: Martyn (Miller), Cooper, Dicks, Thomas, Redmond, Chettle, Platt, Gascoigne, Clough, Rocastle, Smith.

Morocco: Deghay, Hamdouch, Areski (Gurichate), Masbahi, Belghitti, Zouhir, M'tioui, Ameur, Meziane, Loumari (Jabrane), Zerouali.

England 0   Rep. of Ireland 1
12th June 1988, Stuttgart

England began their bid for the European Championship in Stuttgart's Neckar Stadium in much the same depressing way as their bid for the World Cup in Monterrey two years earlier – with a shock 1-0 defeat. Their unlikely conquerors this time were the Republic of Ireland, managed by one of England's

Gary Lineker holds off a determined Mick McCarthy in Stuttgart.

World Cup heroes of 1966 and put on the road to victory by a player with a noticeably Glaswegian accent.

England, second favourites behind West Germany prior to kick-off, had the worst possible start to the match when a series of defensive howlers let in Liverpool's Ray Houghton to score with a header after six minutes. Wright and Stevens both went up to deal with Moran's mammoth free-kick into the danger area and only succeeded in knocking the ball down for Galvin, lurking just inside the penalty-area. His lob across the face of the goal was inexplicably kicked over his own head by Sansom, Aldridge easily beat Adams to the dropping ball and Houghton was perfectly placed to nod it over Shilton.

As the massive Irish contingent in the 53,000 crowd celebrated in and around the ground after the final whistle, England were left to reflect on a series of disastrous missed chances in the second half. The early Irish goal had had such a demoralising effect that England had struggled to regain their composure to a sufficient degree to have been able to engineer some scoring opportunities, but after the break Gary Lineker frequently got clear of his markers only to be thwarted by the brilliance, and occasionally luck, of Bonner in the Irish goal.

Bonner. as much a hero as Houghton, had an outstanding match. His most memorable save came in the dying seconds, as the Irish hordes on the terracing were howling at the East German referee to conclude the proceedings. Substi-

59

tute Mark Hateley soared to flick Hoddle's curling free-kick goalwards and Bonner's acrobatics barely turned the ball round his right-hand post.

With that chance went England's last hope of salvaging anything from a desperately disappointing first match of the tournament. They now faced the prospect of needing victories against both Holland and U.S.S.R. in order to clinch a semi-final place.

England: Shilton, Stevens, Sansom, Webb (Hoddle), Wright, Adams, Robson, Waddle, Beardsley (Hateley), Lineker, Barnes.

Rep. of Ireland: Bonner, Morris, Hughton, McCarthy, Moran, Whelan, McGrath, Houghton, Aldridge, Stapleton (Quinn), Galvin (Sheedy).

Referee: Kirschen (East Germany).

France 4   England 2
(Under-21)
12th June 1988, Toulon

To complete a disappointing day for England teams, Dave Sexton's youngsters twice surrendered the lead before finally succumbing to France in the Toulon tournament final. Michael Thomas, the Arsenal midfielder, twice put England in control, but a late equaliser from Zitelli, his second goal, took the match into extra time and England then conceded two further goals. To add to their dismay, England lost Cooper, the Middlesbrough fullback, on the stroke of full-time when he was taken away for a precautionary X-ray on a damaged ankle.

Thomas gave England the lead

after 28 minutes, converting Gascoigne's long pass, only for Zitelli to equalise by completing a flowing move with his fifth goal of the tournament. Thomas's second, on 47 minutes, put England into a commanding position that they preserved until 17 minutes from the end of normal time, when Zitelli, undoubtedly the pick of the French strikers, beat Dicks to a centre and sent a looping shot over the unfortunate Martyn.

The heat took its toll in extra time with both teams looking weary, but French captain Dogon still had enough energy left to run through and score after 91 minutes to give France the lead for the first time in the match. There was a suspicion of offside about this goal, but no doubts at all about Ginola's clinching fourth goal three minutes from the end.

Michael Thomas was voted player of the tournament and Bristol Rovers goalkeeper Nigel Martyn was voted goalkeeper of the tournament.

France: Foret, Lhoste, Dogon, Leclerc, Bonalair, Deschamps, Metais, Eyraud (Depesch), Avenet (Pavon), Ginola, Zitelli.

England: Martyn, Cooper (Hirst), Dicks, Thomas, Redmond, Chettle, Platt (Ripley), Gascoigne, Clough, Rocastle, Samways.

England 1   Holland 3
15th June 1988, Düsseldorf

England's dreams of winning the European Championship were shattered in the Rheinstadion by Holland's Milan-based Marco Van Basten, who had missed most of the "Serie A" season with a damaged

Bryan Robson bravely lifts the ball over Van Breukelen for England's equaliser against the Dutch.

ankle and had begun the finals as third-choice central striker behind Kieft and Bosman. Van Basten's hat-trick was the first registered against England in a full international since Seminario's for Peru back in 1959.

England began optimistically and looked a well-balanced outfit with Glenn Hoddle starting his first international since England had been beaten 3-1 in the same stadium nine months earlier. He linked up well with Bryan Robson in midfield and it was the England captain who carved out a clear-cut chance for Gary Lineker after nine minutes. Koeman's attempt to cut out Robson's pass only diverted the ball beyond his

goalkeeper and the Barcelona striker, albeit from a sharp angle, shot against the near post with the goal at his mercy.

In the 40th minute Hoddle curled a brilliant free-kick against the same post, thereby indicating again the kind of Championship England were having, but Van Basten took centre stage after that with a performance that outshone anything seen in the finals so far. His first strike, at two minutes before half-time the perfect psychological moment to break through, came when he turned superbly onto Gullit's cross to leave Adams floundering and then drove a shot past Shilton's left hand into the corner.

Robson battled bravely through the Dutch rearguard to get on the end of Lineker's flick into the box and force the ball over the line an instant before Van Breukelen crashed into him on 54 minutes, and for a while an England victory looked feasible. But Van Basten and Gullit were to have the final say, combining twice in four minutes to score the goals that ended England's interest in the competition. Peter Shilton, winning his 100th cap, had little chance with either effort.

England: Shilton, Stevens, Sansom, Hoddle, Wright, Adams, Robson, Steven (Waddle), Beardsley (Hateley), Lineker, Barnes.

Holland: Van Breukelen, Van Tiggelen, Rijkaard, Koeman R., Van Aerle, Wouters, Vanenburg (Kieft), Muhren, Van Basten (Suvrijn), Gullit, Koeman E..

Referee: Casarin (Italy).

England 1   U.S.S.R. 3
18th June 1988, Frankfurt

Manager Bobby Robson had hoped that his much-criticised team would go out of the European Championship on a high note by beating the Russians in the Waldstadion, but it was not to be – the match was too important for opponents who wanted to be sure of topping the group and avoiding West Germany in the semi-finals.

England had an awful start, conceding a goal after only two minutes when Aleinikov dispossessed Glenn Hoddle and found his progress towards England's goal scarcely impeded at all as he went on to easily beat the unprotected Chris Woods.

The agony piled on for England as Belanov chipped narrowly over and the second of two good Protasov efforts rebounded from the inside of the far post. Then, almost incredibly, England not only equalised with Tony Adams' glancing header from Hoddle's free-kick in the 15th minute but came within a whisker of going 2-1 up when Trevor Steven's downward header bounced up against the bar.

The Russians regained the lead on 29 minutes, when Michailichenko stole in for a header from Rats' precise cross. There was a brief moment of hope that England might salvage something with Bryan Robson's close-range header which Dassayev saved well in the 63rd minute, but Woods had no chance as Pasulko wrapped it all up 16 minutes from time to complete a sad and sorry afternoon for Robson's men.

England: Woods, Stevens, Sansom, Hoddle, Watson, Adams, Robson, Steven, McMahon (Webb), Lineker (Hateley), Barnes.

U.S.S.R.: Dassayev, Bessonov, Khidiyatulin, Kuznetsov, Aleinikov, Rats, Litovchenko, Zavarov (Gotsmanov), Belanov (Pasulko), Michailichenko, Protasov.

Referee: Rosa Dos Santos (Portugal).

England's Full International Teams 1946–88

(Up to and including 18th June 1988)

*Captain † Own goal

Columns 3–4: Small numerals goals scored · Columns 5–7: Number after sub. player replaced

versus	Result	1	2	3	4	5	6	7	8	9	10	11	Substitutes
Season 1946–47													
Ireland	7-2	Swift	Scott	Hardwick*	Wright, W.	Franklin	Cockburn	Finney[1]	Carter[1]	Lawton[1]	Mannion[3]	Langton[1]	
Republic of Ireland	1-0	Swift	Scott	Hardwick*	Wright, W.	Franklin	Cockburn	Finney[1]	Carter	Lawton	Mannion[1]	Langton	
Wales	3-0	Swift	Scott	Hardwick*	Wright, W.	Franklin	Cockburn	Finney[1]	Carter	Lawton[1]	Mannion[2]	Langton	
Netherlands	8-2	Swift	Scott	Hardwick*	Wright, W.	Franklin	Johnston	Finney[1]	Carter[2]	Lawton[4]	Mannion[1]	Langton	
Scotland	1-1	Swift	Scott	Hardwick*	Wright, W.	Franklin	Johnston	Matthews, S.	Carter[1]	Lawton	Mannion[1]	Mullen	
France	3-0	Swift	Scott	Hardwick*	Wright, W.	Franklin	Lowe	Finney[1]	Carter[1]	Lawton	Mannion[1]	Langton	
Switzerland	0-1	Swift	Scott	Hardwick*	Wright, W.	Franklin	Lowe	Matthews, S.	Carter	Lawton	Mannion	Langton	
Portugal	10-0	Swift	Scott	Hardwick*	Wright, W.	Franklin	Lowe	Matthews, S.[1]	Mortensen[4]	Lawton[4]	Mannion	Finney[1]	Mullen (7)[1]
1947–48													
Belgium	5-2	Swift	Scott	Hardwick*	Ward	Franklin	Wright, W.	Matthews, S.	Mortensen[1]	Lawton[2]	Mannion	Finney[2]	
Wales	3-0	Swift	Scott	Hardwick*	Taylor, P.	Franklin	Wright, W.	Matthews, S.	Mortensen[1]	Lawton[1]	Mannion	Finney[1]	
Ireland	2-2	Swift	Scott	Hardwick*	Taylor, P.	Franklin	Wright, W.	Matthews, S.	Mortensen[1]	Lawton[1]	Mannion[1]	Finney	
Sweden	4-2	Swift	Scott	Hardwick*	Ward	Franklin	Wright, W.	Finney	Mortensen[3]	Lawton[1]	Mannion	Langton	
Scotland	2-0	Swift	Scott	Hardwick*	Wright, W.	Franklin	Cockburn	Matthews, S.	Mortensen[1]	Lawton[1]	Pearson	Finney[1]	
Italy	4-0	Swift*	Scott	Howe, J.	Wright, W.	Franklin	Cockburn	Matthews, S.	Mortensen[1]	Lawton[1]	Mannion	Finney[2]	
1948–49													
Denmark	0-0	Swift*	Scott	Aston	Wright, W.	Franklin	Cockburn	Matthews, S.	Hagan	Lawton	Shackleton	Lawton	
Ireland	6-2	Swift*	Scott	Howe, J.	Wright, W.[1]	Franklin	Cockburn	Matthews, S.[1]	Mortensen[3]	Milburn	Pearson[1]	Finney	
Wales	1-0	Swift	Scott	Aston	Ward	Franklin	Wright, W.*	Matthews, S.	Mortensen	Milburn[1]	Shackleton	Finney	
Switzerland	6-0	Swift	Ramsey	Aston	Wright, W.*	Franklin	Cockburn	Wright, W.*[1]	Rowley, J.[1]	Milburn[1]	Haines[2]	Hancocks[2]	†
Scotland	1-3	Swift	Aston	Howe, J.	Wright, W.*	Franklin	Cockburn	Matthews, S.	Mortensen	Milburn[1]	Pearson	Finney	
Sweden	1-3	Ditchburn	Shimwell	Aston	Wright, W.*	Jones, W. H.	Cockburn	Finney[1]	Mortensen	Bentley	Rowley, J.	Langton	
Norway	4-1	Swift	Ellerington	Aston	Wright, W.*[1]	Franklin	Dickinson	Finney[1]	Morris[1]	Mortensen	Mortensen	Mullen[1]	
France	3-1	Williams	Ellerington	Aston	Wright, W.*	Franklin	Dickinson	Finney	Morris[2]	Rowley, J.	Mannion	Mullen	
1949–50													
Republic of Ireland	0-2	Williams	Mozley	Aston	Wright, W.*	Franklin	Dickinson	Harris, P.	Morris	Pye	Mannion	Finney	
Wales	4-1	Williams	Mozley	Aston	Wright, W.*[1]	Franklin	Dickinson	Finney	Mortensen[2]	Milburn[3]	Shackleton	Hancocks	
Ireland	9-2	Streten	Mozley	Aston	Watson, W.	Franklin	Wright, W.*[1]	Finney	Mortensen[2]	Rowley, J.[4]	Pearson[2]	Froggatt, J.[1]	
Italy	2-0	Williams	Ramsey	Aston	Watson, W.	Franklin	Wright, W.*	Finney	Mortensen	Rowley, J.[1]	Pearson	Froggatt, J.	
Scotland	1-0	Williams	Ramsey	Aston	Wright, W.*	Franklin	Dickinson	Finney	Mannion	Mortensen	Bentley[1]	Langton	
Portugal	5-3	Williams	Ramsey	Aston	Wright, W.*[1]	Jones, W. H.	Dickinson	Milburn	Mortensen[1]	Bentley[1]	Mannion[1]	Finney[4]	
Belgium	4-1	Williams	Ramsey	Aston	Wright, W.*	Jones, W. H.	Dickinson	Milburn	Mortensen[1]	Bentley[1]	Mannion[1]	Finney[1]	
Chile	2-0	Williams	Ramsey	Aston	Wright, W.*	Hughes, L.	Dickinson	Finney	Mannion[1]	Bentley	Mortensen[1]	Mullen	
U.S.A.	0-1	Williams	Ramsey	Aston	Wright, W.*	Hughes, L.	Dickinson	Finney	Mannion	Bentley	Mortensen	Mullen	
Spain	0-1	Williams	Ramsey	Eckersley	Wright, W.*	Hughes, L.	Dickinson	Matthews, S.	Mortensen	Milburn	Baily, E.	Finney	
1950–51													
Ireland	4-1	Williams	Ramsey	Aston	Wright, W.*[1]	Chilton	Dickinson	Matthews, S.	Mannion	Lee, J.[1]	Baily, E.[2]	Langton	
Wales	4-2	Williams	Ramsey*	Smith, L.	Watson, W.	Compton, L.	Dickinson	Finney	Mannion[1]	Milburn[1]	Baily, E.[2]	Medley	
Yugoslavia	2-2	Williams	Ramsey*	Eckersley	Watson, W.	Compton, L.	Dickinson	Hancocks	Mannion	Lofthouse[1]	Baily, E.[1]	Medley	
Scotland	2-3	Williams	Ramsey	Eckersley	Johnston	Froggatt, J.	Dickinson	Matthews, S.	Mannion	Mortensen	Hassall[1]	Finney[1]	
Argentina	2-1	Williams	Ramsey	Eckersley	Wright, W.*[1]	Taylor, J.	Cockburn	Finney[1]	Mortensen	Milburn[2]	Hassall	Metcalfe	
Portugal	5-2	Williams	Ramsey*	Eckersley	Nicholson[1]	Taylor, J.	Cockburn	Finney[1]	Pearson	Milburn[2]	Hassall[1]	Metcalfe	

ENGLAND'S FULL INTERNATIONAL TEAMS 1946–88 (contd)

versus	Result	1	2	3	4	5	6	7	8	9	10	11	Substitutes
1951–52													
France	2-2	Williams	Ramsey	Willis	Wright. W.*	Chilton	Cockburn	Finney	Mannion	Milburn	Hassall	Medley[1]	†
Wales	1-1	Williams	Ramsey	Smith. L.	Wright. W.*	Barrass	Dickinson	Finney	Thompson. T	Lofthouse[2]	Baily. E.[1]	Medley[1]	
Ireland	2-0	Merrick	Ramsey	Smith. L.	Wright. W.*	Barrass	Dickinson	Finney	Sewell	Lofthouse[1]	Phillips	Medley	
Austria	2-2	Merrick	Ramsey[1]	Eckersley	Wright. W.*	Froggatt. J.	Dickinson	Milton	Broads	Lofthouse[1]	Baily. E.	Medley	
Scotland	2-1	Merrick	Ramsey	Garrett	Wright. W.*	Froggatt. J.	Dickinson	Finney	Broads	Lofthouse	Pearson[2]	Rowley. J.	
Italy	1-1	Merrick	Ramsey	Garrett	Wright. W.*	Froggatt. J.	Dickinson	Finney	Broads[1]	Lofthouse[1]	Pearson	Elliott	
Austria	3-2	Merrick	Ramsey	Eckersley	Wright. W.*	Froggatt. J.	Dickinson	Finney	Sewell[1]	Lofthouse[2]	Baily. E.	Elliott	
Switzerland	3-0	Merrick	Ramsey	Eckersley	Wright. W.*	Froggatt. J.	Dickinson	Allen. R.	Sewell[1]	Lofthouse[2]	Baily. E.	Finney	
Ireland	2-2	Merrick	Ramsey	Eckersley	Wright. W.*	Froggatt. J.[1]	Dickinson	Finney	Sewell	Lofthouse[1]	Baily. E.	Elliott[1]	
Wales	5-2	Merrick	Ramsey	Smith. L.	Wright. W.*	Froggatt. J.[1]	Dickinson	Finney[1]	Froggatt. R.	Lofthouse[2]	Bentley[1]	Elliott	
Belgium	5-0	Merrick	Ramsey	Smith. L.	Wright. W.*	Froggatt. J.[1]	Dickinson	Finney	Bentley[1]	Lofthouse[2]	Froggatt. R.[1]	Elliott[2]	
Scotland	2-2	Merrick	Ramsey	Smith. L.	Wright. W.*	Barrass	Dickinson	Finney	Broads[2]	Lofthouse	Froggatt. R.	Froggatt. J.	
Argentina	0-0	Merrick	Ramsey	Eckersley	Wright. W.*	Johnston	Dickinson	Finney	Broads	Lofthouse[1]	Taylor. T.[1]	Berry	
Chile	2-1	Merrick	Ramsey	Eckersley	Wright. W.*	Johnston	Dickinson	Finney	Broads	Lofthouse[1]	Taylor. T.[1]	Berry	
Uruguay	1-2	Merrick	Ramsey	Eckersley	Wright. W.*	Johnston	Dickinson	Finney	Broads	Lofthouse	Taylor. T.[1]	Berry	
U.S.A.	6-3	Ditchburn	Ramsey	Eckersley	Wright. W.*	Johnston	Dickinson	Finney[2]	Broads[1]	Lofthouse[2]	Froggatt. R.[1]	Froggatt. J.	
1953–54													
Wales	4-1	Merrick	Garrett	Eckersley	Wright. W.*	Johnston	Dickinson	Finney	Quixall	Lofthouse[2]	Wilshaw[2]	Mullen	
F.I.F.A.	4-4	Merrick	Ramsey[1]	Eckersley	Wright. W.*	Ufton	Dickinson	Matthews. S.	Mortensen	Lofthouse[2]	Quixall	Mullen[2]	
Ireland	3-1	Merrick	Rickaby	Eckersley	Wright. W.*	Johnston	Dickinson	Matthews. S.	Quixall	Lofthouse[1]	Hassall[2]	Mullen	
Hungary	3-6	Merrick	Ramsey[1]	Eckersley	Wright. W.*	Johnston	Dickinson	Matthews. S.	Taylor. E.	Lofthouse[1]	Sewell[1]	Robb	
Scotland	4-2	Merrick	Staniforth	Byrne. R.	Wright. W.*	Clarke. H.	Dickinson	Finney	Broads[1]	Nicholls[1]	Mullen[1]	Allen. R.[1]	
Yugoslavia	0-1	Merrick	Staniforth	Byrne. R.	Wright. W.*	Owen	Dickinson	Finney	Broads	Allen. R.	Nicholls	Mullen	
Hungary	1-7	Merrick	Staniforth	Byrne. R.	Wright. W.*	Owen	Dickinson	Harris. P.	Sewell	Jezzard	Broads[1]	Finney	
Belgium	4-4	Merrick	Staniforth	Byrne. R.	Wright. W.*	Owen	Dickinson	Matthews. S.	Broads[2]	Lofthouse[2]	Taylor. T.[1]	Finney[1]	
Switzerland	2-0	Merrick	Staniforth	Byrne. R.	McGarry	Wright. W.*	Dickinson	Finney	Broads	Taylor. T.	Wilshaw[1]	Mullen[1]	
Uruguay	2-4	Merrick	Staniforth	Byrne. R.	McGarry	Wright. W.*	Dickinson	Matthews. S.	Broads	Lofthouse[1]	Wilshaw	Finney[1]	
1954–55													
Ireland	2-0	Wood	Foulkes	Byrne. R.	Wheeler	Wright. W.*	Barlow	Matthews. S.	Revie[1]	Lofthouse	Haynes[1]	Pilkington	
Wales	3-2	Wood	Staniforth	Byrne. R.	Phillips	Wright. W.*	Slater	Matthews. S.	Bentley[3]	Allen. R.	Shackleton	Blunstone	
West Germany	3-1	Williams	Staniforth	Byrne. R.	Phillips	Wright. W.*	Slater	Matthews. S.	Bentley[1]	Allen. R.[1]	Shackleton	Finney	
Scotland	7-2	Williams	Meadows	Byrne. R.	Armstrong	Wright. W.*	Edwards	Matthews. S.	Revie[1]	Lofthouse[2]	Wilshaw[4]	Blunstone	
France	0-1	Williams	Sillett. P.	Byrne. R.	Flowers	Wright. W.*	Edwards	Matthews. S.	Revie	Lofthouse	Wilshaw	Blunstone	
Spain	1-1	Williams	Sillett. P.	Byrne. R.	Dickinson	Wright. W.*	Edwards	Matthews. S.	Bentley[1]	Lofthouse	Quixall	Wilshaw	Quixall (9)
Portugal	1-3	Williams	Sillett. P.	Byrne. R.	Dickinson	Wright. W.*	Edwards	Matthews. S.	Bentley[1]	Lofthouse	Wilshaw	Blunstone	
1955–56													
Denmark	5-1	Baynham	Hall	Byrne. R.	McGarry	Wright. W.*	Dickinson	Milburn	Revie[2]	Lofthouse[2]	Bradford[1]	Finney	†
Wales	1-2	Williams	Hall	Byrne. R.	McGarry	Wright. W.*	Dickinson	Matthews. S.	Revie	Lofthouse	Wilshaw	Finney	
Ireland	3-0	Baynham	Hall	Byrne. R.	Clayton	Wright. W.*	Dickinson	Finney[1]	Haynes	Jezzard	Wilshaw[2]	Perry	
Spain	4-1	Baynham	Hall	Byrne. R.	Clayton	Wright. W.*	Dickinson	Finney[1]	Atyeo[1]	Lofthouse	Haynes	Perry[2]	
Scotland	1-1	Matthews. R.	Hall	Byrne. R.	Dickinson	Wright. W.*	Edwards	Finney	Taylor. T.	Lofthouse	Haynes[1]	Perry	
Brazil	4-2	Matthews. R.	Hall	Byrne. R.	Clayton	Wright. W.*	Edwards	Matthews. S.	Atyeo	Taylor. T.[2]	Haynes	Grainger[2]	Lofthouse (9)[2]
Sweden	0-0	Matthews. R.	Hall	Byrne. R.	Clayton	Wright. W.*	Edwards	Berry	Atyeo	Taylor. T.	Haynes	Grainger	
Finland	5-1	Wood	Hall	Byrne. R.	Clayton	Wright. W.*	Edwards	Astall[1]	Haynes[1]	Taylor. T.	Wilshaw[1]	Grainger	

Margin notes (top right): Taylor. T. (10)[2]   +   Flowers (6) Bradley (7)

Opponents	Score											
West Germany 1956-7	3-1	Matthews. R.	Hall	Byrne. R.	Clayton	Wright. W.*	Edwards[1]	Astall	Haynes[1]	Taylor. T.	Wilshaw	Grainger[1]
Ireland 1956-7 (contd)	1-1	Matthews. R.	Hall	Byrne. R.	Clayton	Wright. W.*	Edwards	Matthews. S.[1]	Revie	Taylor. T.	Wilshaw	Grainger
Wales	3-1	Ditchburn	Hall	Byrne. R.	Clayton	Wright. W.*	Dickinson	Matthews. S.	Brooks[1]	Taylor. T.	Haynes[1]	Grainger
Yugoslavia	3-0	Ditchburn	Hall	Byrne. R.	Clayton	Wright. W.*	Dickinson	Matthews. S.	Brooks	Taylor. T.	Haynes[1]	Blunstone
Denmark	5-2	Ditchburn	Hall	Byrne. R.	Clayton	Wright. W.*	Dickinson	Matthews. S.	Brooks	Taylor. T.	Edwards[2]	Finney
Scotland	2-1	Hodgkinson	Hall	Byrne. R.	Clayton	Wright. W.*	Edwards	Matthews. S.	Thompson. T.[1]	Taylor. T.	Haynes[1]	Grainger
Republic of Ireland	5-1	Hodgkinson	Hall	Byrne. R.	Clayton	Wright. W.*	Edwards	Matthews. S.	Atyeo[2]	Taylor. T.	Haynes	Finney
Denmark	4-1	Hodgkinson	Hall	Byrne. R.	Clayton	Wright. W.*	Edwards	Matthews. S.	Atyeo[1]	Taylor. T.	Haynes	Finney
Republic of Ireland	1-1	Hodgkinson	Hall	Byrne. R.	Clayton	Wright. W.*	Edwards	Finney	Atyeo[1]	Taylor. T.	Haynes	Pegg
1957-58												
Wales	4-0	Hopkinson	Howe. D.	Byrne. R.	Clayton	Wright. W.*	Edwards	Douglas	Kevan	Taylor. T.	Haynes[2]	Finney[1]
Ireland	2-3	Hopkinson	Howe. D.	Byrne. R.	Clayton	Wright. W.*	Edwards	Douglas	Kevan	Taylor. T.	Haynes	A'Court[1]
France	4-0	Hopkinson	Howe. D.	Byrne. R.	Clayton	Wright. W.*	Edwards	Douglas	Robson. R.[2]	Taylor. T.	Haynes	Finney
Scotland	4-0	Hopkinson	Howe. D.	Langley	Clayton	Wright. W.*	Slater	Douglas	Charlton. R.[1]	Kevan	Haynes	Finney
Portugal	2-1	Hopkinson	Howe. D.	Langley	Clayton	Wright. W.*	Slater	Douglas	Charlton. R.	Kevan	Haynes	Finney
Yugoslavia	0-5	Hopkinson	Howe. D.	Langley	Clayton	Wright. W.*	Slater	Douglas	Charlton. R.	Kevan	Haynes	Finney
U.S.S.R.	1-1	McDonald	Howe. D.	Banks. T.	Clayton	Wright. W.*	Slater	Douglas	Robson. R.	Kevan	Haynes	Finney
U.S.S.R.	2-2	McDonald	Howe. D.	Banks. T.	Clamp	Wright. W.*	Slater	Douglas	Robson. R.	Kevan	Haynes	Finney[1]
Brazil	0-0	McDonald	Howe. D.	Banks. T.	Clamp	Wright. W.*	Slater	Douglas	Robson. R.	Kevan	Haynes[1]	A'Court
Austria	2-2	McDonald	Howe. D.	Banks. T.	Clamp	Wright. W.*	Slater	Douglas	Robson. R.	Kevan	Haynes	A'Court
U.S.S.R.	0-1	McDonald	Howe. D.	Banks. T.	Clayton	Wright. W.*	Slater	Brabrook	Broadbent	Kevan	Haynes	A'Court
1958-59												
Ireland	3-3	McDonald	Howe. D.	Banks. T.	Clayton	Wright. W.*	McGuinness	Brabrook	Charlton. R.[1]	Lofthouse	Haynes[1]	Finney[1]
U.S.S.R.	5-0	McDonald	Howe. D.	Shaw. G.	Clayton	Wright. W.*	Slater	Clapton	Charlton. R.[1]	Lofthouse	Haynes[3]	Finney
Wales	1-0	McDonald	Howe. D.	Shaw. G.	Clayton	Wright. W.*	Flowers	Douglas	Broadbent	Charlton. R.	Haynes	A'Court
Scotland	1-0	Hopkinson	Howe. D.	Shaw. G.	Clayton*	Wright. W.*	Flowers	Bradley[1]	Broadbent	Charlton. R.	Haynes	Holden
Italy	2-2	Hopkinson	Howe. D.	Shaw. G.	Clayton*	Wright. W.*	Flowers	Deeley	Broadbent	Charlton. R.	Haynes	Holden
Brazil	0-2	Hopkinson	Howe. D.	Allen. A.	Clayton*	Wright. W.*	Flowers	Deeley	Greaves	Charlton. R.	Haynes	Holden
Peru	1-4	Hopkinson	Howe. D.	Allen. A.	Clayton*	Wright. W.*	Flowers	Holden	Greaves	Charlton. R.	Haynes	Holden
Mexico	1-2	Hopkinson	Howe. D.	Allen. A.	Clayton*	Wright. W.*	McGuinness	Bradley[1]	Greaves	Kevan	Haynes[1]	Charlton. R.
U.S.A.	8-1	Hopkinson	Howe. D.	Allen. A.	Robson. R.	Wright. W.*	Flowers[2]	Brabrook	Greaves	Kevan	Haynes	Charlton. R.
1959-60												
Wales	1-1	Hopkinson	Howe. D.	Shaw. G.	Robson. R.	Smith. T.	Flowers	Connelly[1]	Greaves[1]	Clough	Charlton. R.[1]	Holliday
Sweden	2-3	Hopkinson	Howe. D.	Shaw. G.	Robson. R.	Smith. T.	Flowers	Connelly[1]	Greaves	Clough	Charlton. R.[1]	Holliday
Ireland	2-1	Springett. R.	Howe. D.	Shaw. G.	Clayton	Brown. K.	Flowers	Connelly	Haynes	Baker	Parry[1]	Holliday
Scotland	1-1	Springett. R.	Armfield	Wilson	Robson. R.	Slater	Flowers	Connelly[1]	Broadbent	Baker	Greaves[1]	Charlton. R.[1]
Yugoslavia	3-3	Springett. R.	Armfield	Wilson	Robson. R.	Swan	Flowers	Douglas[1]	Haynes*	Baker	Greaves	Charlton. R.
Spain	0-3	Springett. R.	Armfield	Wilson	Robson. R.[1]	Swan	Flowers	Brabrook	Haynes*	Baker	Viollet	Charlton. R.
Hungary	0-2	Springett. R.	Armfield	McNeil	Robson. R.[1]	Swan	Flowers	Douglas	Haynes*	Baker	Greaves	Charlton. R.
1960-61												
Ireland	5-2	Springett. R.	Armfield	McNeil	Robson. R.	Swan	Flowers	Douglas[1]	Greaves[2]	Smith. R.[1]	Haynes*[1]	Charlton. R.[1]
Luxembourg	9-0	Springett. R.	Armfield	McNeil	Robson. R.	Swan	Flowers	Douglas[1]	Greaves[3]	Smith. R.[2]	Haynes*[1]	Charlton. R.[3]
Spain	4-2	Hodgkinson	Armfield	McNeil	Robson. R.	Swan	Flowers	Douglas[1]	Greaves[2]	Smith. R.[1]	Haynes*[1]	Charlton. R.[1]
Wales	5-1	Springett. R.	Armfield	McNeil	Robson. R.[1]	Swan	Flowers	Douglas[1]	Greaves[3]	Smith. R.[1]	Haynes*[1]	Charlton. R.
Scotland	9-3	Springett. R.	Armfield	McNeil	Robson. R.[1]	Swan	Flowers[1]	Douglas[2]	Kevan	Smith. R.[2]	Haynes*[2]	Charlton. R.[3]
Mexico	8-0	Springett. R.	Armfield	McNeil	Robson. R.[1]	Swan	Flowers[1]	Douglas	Greaves	Smith. R.[1]	Haynes*	Charlton. R.
Portugal	1-1	Springett. R.	Armfield	McNeil	Robson. R.	Swan	Flowers[1]	Douglas	Greaves[1]	Hitchens[1]	Haynes*	Charlton. R.
Italy	3-2	Springett. R.	Armfield	McNeil	Robson. R.	Swan	Flowers	Douglas	Greaves	Hitchens[2]	Haynes*[2]	Charlton. R.

ENGLAND'S FULL INTERNATIONAL TEAMS 1946–88 (contd)

versus	Result	1	2	3	4	5	6	7	8	9	10	11	Substitutes
1961–62													
Austria	1–3	Springett, R.	Armfield*	Angus	Miller	Swan	Flowers	Douglas	Greaves[1]	Hitchens	Haynes*	Charlton, R.	
Luxembourg	4–1	Springett, R.	Armfield	McNeil	Robson, R.	Swan	Flowers	Douglas	Fantham	Pointer[1]	Violet[1]	Charlton, R.[2]	
Wales	1–1	Springett, R.	Armfield	Wilson	Robson, R.	Swan	Flowers	Connelly[1]	Douglas[1]	Pointer[1]	Haynes*	Charlton, R.	
Portugal	2–0	Springett, R.	Armfield	Wilson	Robson, R.	Swan	Flowers	Connelly[1]	Douglas	Pointer[1]	Haynes*	Charlton, R.	
Ireland	1–1	Springett, R.	Armfield	Wilson	Anderson	Swan	Flowers[1]	Douglas	Byrne, J.	Crawford	Haynes*	Charlton, R.[1]	
Austria	3–1	Springett, R.	Armfield	Wilson	Anderson	Swan	Flowers[1]	Connelly	Hunt[1]	Crawford[1]	Haynes*	Charlton, R.	
Scotland	0–2	Springett, R.	Armfield	Wilson	Robson, R.	Swan	Flowers[1]	Douglas	Greaves	Smith, R.[1]	Haynes*	Charlton, R.	
Switzerland	3–1	Springett, R.	Armfield	Wilson	Moore	Norman	Flowers[1]	Connelly[1]	Greaves[1]	Hitchens[1]	Haynes*	Charlton, R.	
Peru	4–0	Springett, R.	Armfield	Wilson	Moore	Norman	Flowers[1]	Douglas	Greaves[3]	Hitchens	Haynes*	Charlton, R.	
Hungary	1–2	Springett, R.	Armfield	Wilson	Moore	Norman	Flowers[1]	Douglas	Greaves[1]	Hitchens	Haynes*	Charlton, R.	
Argentina	3–1	Springett, R.	Armfield	Wilson	Moore	Norman	Flowers[1]	Douglas	Greaves[1]	Peacock	Haynes*	Charlton, R.	
Bulgaria	0–0	Springett, R.	Armfield	Wilson	Moore	Norman	Flowers	Douglas	Greaves	Peacock	Haynes*	Charlton, R.	
Brazil	1–3	Springett, R.	Armfield	Wilson	Moore	Norman	Flowers	Douglas	Greaves	Hitchens	Haynes*	Charlton, R.	
1962–63													
France	1–1	Springett, R.	Armfield*	Wilson	Moore	Norman	Flowers[1]	Hellawell	Crowe	Charnley	Greaves	Hinton, A.	
Ireland	3–1	Springett, R.	Armfield*	Wilson	Moore	Labone	Flowers	Hellawell	Hill, F.	Peacock[2]	Greaves[1]	O'Grady[2]	
Wales	4–0	Springett, R.	Armfield*	Shaw, G.	Moore	Labone	Flowers	Connelly[1]	Hill, F.	Peacock[2]	Greaves[1]	Tambling	
France	2–5	Springett, R.	Armfield*	Henry	Moore	Labone	Flowers	Connelly	Tambling[1]	Smith, R.[1]	Greaves	Charlton, R.	
Scotland	1–2	Banks, G.	Armfield*	Byrne, G.	Milne	Norman	Moore	Douglas[1]	Greaves	Smith, R.	Melia	Charlton, R.	
Brazil	1–1	Banks, G.	Armfield*	Wilson	Milne	Norman	Moore	Douglas[1]	Greaves[2]	Smith, R.	Eastham	Charlton, R.	
Czechoslovakia	4–2	Banks, G.	Shelito	Wilson	Milne	Norman	Moore*	Paine	Greaves[2]	Smith, R.	Eastham	Charlton, R.[1]	
German D. R.	2–1	Banks, G.	Armfield*	Wilson	Milne	Norman	Moore*	Paine	Hunt[1]	Smith, R.[1]	Eastham	Charlton, R.[1]	
Switzerland	8–1	Springett, R.	Armfield*	Wilson	Kay[1]	Moore	Moore*	Douglas[1]	Greaves	Byrne, J.[2]	Melia[1]	Charlton, R.[3]	
1963–64													
Wales	4–0	Banks, G.	Armfield*	Wilson	Milne	Norman	Moore	Paine	Greaves[1]	Smith, R.[2]	Eastham	Charlton, R.[1]	
Rest of the World	2–1	Banks, G.	Armfield*	Wilson	Milne	Norman	Moore	Paine[1]	Greaves[1]	Smith, R.[1]	Eastham	Charlton, R.	
Ireland	8–3	Banks, G.	Armfield*	Thomson, R.	Milne	Norman	Moore	Paine[3]	Greaves[4]	Smith, R.[1]	Eastham	Charlton, R.	
Scotland	0–1	Banks, G.	Armfield*	Wilson	Milne	Norman	Moore	Paine	Hunt	Byrne, J.	Eastham	Charlton, R.	
Uruguay	2–1	Banks, G.	Cohen	Wilson	Milne	Norman	Moore*	Paine	Greaves	Byrne, J.[2]	Eastham	Charlton, R.	
Portugal	4–3	Banks, G.	Cohen	Wilson	Milne	Norman	Moore*	Thompson, P.	Greaves	Byrne, J.[3]	Eastham	Charlton, R.[1]	
Republic of Ireland	3–1	Waiters	Cohen	Wilson	Milne	Flowers	Moore*	Thompson, P.	Greaves	Byrne, J.[1]	Eastham[1]	Charlton, R.[1]	
U.S.A.	10–0	Banks, G.	Cohen	Thomson, R.	Bailey, M.	Norman	Flowers*	Paine[2]	Hunt[4]	Pickering[3]	Eastham	Thompson, P.	Charlton, R. (10)[1]
Brazil	1–5	Waiters	Cohen	Wilson	Bailey, M.	Norman	Flowers*	Thompson, P.	Hunt[1]	Byrne, J.	Eastham	Charlton, R.	
Portugal	1–1	Banks, G.	Thomson, R.	Wilson	Flowers	Norman	Moore*	Paine	Greaves	Byrne, J.	Hunt[1]	Thompson, P.	
Argentina	0–1	Banks, G.	Thomson, R.	Wilson	Milne	Moore	Moore*	Thompson, P.	Greaves	Byrne, J.	Eastham	Charlton, R.	
1964–65													
Ireland	4–3	Banks, G.	Cohen	Thomson, R.	Milne	Norman	Moore*	Paine	Greaves[3]	Pickering[1]	Charlton, R.	Thompson, P.	
Belgium	2–2	Waiters	Cohen	Thomson, R.	Milne	Norman	Moore*	Thompson, P.	Greaves	Pickering	Venables	Hinton, A.	†
Wales	2–1	Waiters	Cohen	Thomson, R.	Bailey, M.	Flowers*	Young	Thompson, P.	Hunt	Wignall[2]	Byrne, J.	Hinton, A.	
Netherlands	1–1	Waiters	Cohen	Thomson, R.	Mullery	Norman	Flowers*	Thompson, P.	Hunt	Wignall	Venables	Charlton, R.	
Scotland	2–2	Banks, G.	Cohen	Wilson	Stiles	Charlton, J.	Moore*	Thompson, P.	Greaves[1]	Bridges	Byrne, J.[1]	Charlton, R.[1]	
Hungary	1–0	Banks, G.	Cohen	Wilson	Stiles	Charlton, J.	Moore*	Paine	Greaves[1]	Bridges	Eastham	Connelly	
Yugoslavia	1–1	Banks, G.	Cohen	Wilson	Stiles	Charlton, J.	Moore*	Paine[1]	Greaves[1]	Bridges[1]	Ball	Connelly	
West Germany	1–0	Banks, G.	Cohen	Wilson	Flowers	Charlton, J.	Moore*	Paine[1]	Ball	Jones, M.	Eastham	Temple	

Sweden	2–1	Banks, G.	Cohen	Wilson	Stiles	Charlton, J.	Moore*	Paine	Ball[1]	Jones, M.	Eastham	Connelly[1]	
1965–66													
Wales	0–0	Springett, R.	Cohen	Wilson	Stiles	Charlton, J.	Moore*	Paine	Greaves	Peacock	Charlton, R.	Connelly	
Austria	2–3	Springett, R.	Cohen	Wilson	Stiles	Charlton, J.	Moore*	Paine	Greaves	Bridges	Charlton, R.[1]	Connelly[1]	
Ireland	2–1	Banks, G.	Cohen	Wilson	Stiles	Charlton, J.	Moore*	Thompson, P.	Baker[1]	Peacock[1]	Charlton, R.	Connelly	
Spain	2–0	Banks, G.	Cohen	Wilson	Stiles	Charlton, J.	Moore*	Ball	Hunt[1]	Baker[1]	Eastham	Charlton, R.	Hunter (9)
Poland	1–1	Banks, G.	Cohen	Wilson	Stiles	Charlton, J.	Moore*[1]	Ball	Hunt	Baker	Eastham	Harris, G.	
West Germany	1–0	Banks, G.	Cohen	Newton, K.	Moore*	Charlton, J.	Hunter	Ball	Hunt	Stiles[1]	Hurst, G.	Charlton, R.	Wilson (3)
Scotland	4–3	Banks, G.	Cohen	Newton, K.	Stiles	Charlton, J.	Moore*	Ball	Hunt[2]	Charlton, R.[1]	Hurst, G.[1]	Connelly	
Yugoslavia	2–0	Banks, G.	Armfield*	Wilson	Peters	Charlton, J.	Hunter	Paine	Greaves[1]	Charlton, R.[1]	Hurst, G.	Tambling	
Finland	3–0	Banks, G.	Armfield*	Wilson	Peters[1]	Charlton, J.[1]	Hunter	Callaghan	Hunt[1]	Charlton, R.	Hurst, G.	Ball	
Norway	6–1	Springett, R.	Cohen	Byrne, G.	Stiles	Flowers	Moore*[1]	Paine	Greaves[4]	Charlton, R.	Hunt	Connelly[1]	
Denmark	2–0	Bonetti	Cohen	Wilson	Stiles	Charlton, J.[1]	Moore*	Ball	Greaves	Hurst, G.	Eastham[1]	Connelly	
Poland	1–0	Banks, G.	Cohen	Wilson	Stiles	Charlton, J.	Moore*	Ball	Greaves	Charlton, R.	Hunt[1]	Peters	
Uruguay	0–0	Banks, G.	Cohen	Wilson	Stiles	Charlton, J.	Moore*	Ball	Greaves	Charlton, R.	Hunt	Connelly	
Mexico	2–0	Banks, G.	Cohen	Wilson	Stiles	Charlton, J.	Moore*	Paine	Greaves	Charlton, R.[1]	Hunt[1]	Peters	
France	2–0	Banks, G.	Cohen	Wilson	Stiles	Charlton, J.	Moore*	Callaghan	Greaves	Charlton, R.	Hunt[2]	Peters	
Argentina	1–0	Banks, G.	Cohen	Wilson	Stiles	Charlton, J.	Moore*	Ball	Hurst, G.[1]	Charlton, R.	Hunt	Peters	
Portugal	2–1	Banks, G.	Cohen	Wilson	Stiles	Charlton, J.	Moore*	Ball	Hurst, G.	Charlton, R.[2]	Hunt	Peters	
West Germany	4–2	Banks, G.	Cohen	Wilson	Stiles	Charlton, J.	Moore*	Ball	Hurst, G.[3]	Charlton, R.	Hunt	Peters[1]	
1966–67													
Ireland	2–0	Banks, G.	Cohen	Wilson	Stiles	Charlton, J.	Moore*	Ball	Hurst, G.	Charlton, R.	Hunt[1]	Peters[1]	
Czechoslovakia	0–0	Banks, G.	Cohen	Wilson	Stiles	Charlton, J.	Moore*	Ball	Hurst, G.	Charlton, R.	Hunt	Peters	
Wales	5–1	Banks, G.	Cohen	Wilson	Stiles	Charlton, J.[1]	Moore*	Ball	Hurst, G.[2]	Charlton, R.[1]	Hunt	Peters	†
Scotland	2–3	Banks, G.	Cohen	Wilson	Stiles	Charlton, J.[1]	Moore*	Ball	Greaves	Charlton, R.	Hurst, G.[1]	Peters	
Spain	2–0	Bonetti	Cohen	Newton, K.	Mullery	Labone	Moore*	Ball	Greaves[1]	Hurst, G.	Hunt[1]	Hollins	
Austria	1–0	Bonetti	Newton, K.	Wilson	Mullery	Labone	Moore*	Ball[1]	Greaves	Hurst, G.	Hunt	Hunter	
1967–68													
Wales	3–0	Banks, G.	Cohen	Newton, K.	Mullery	Charlton, J.	Moore*	Ball[1]	Hunt	Charlton, R.[1]	Hurst, G.	Peters[1]	
Ireland	2–0	Banks, G.	Cohen	Wilson	Mullery	Sadler	Moore*	Thompson, P.	Hunt	Charlton, R.[1]	Hurst, G.[1]	Peters	
U.S.S.R.	2–2	Banks, G.	Knowles, C.	Wilson	Mullery	Sadler	Moore*	Ball[1]	Hunt	Charlton, R.	Hurst, G.	Peters[1]	
Scotland	1–1	Banks, G.	Newton, K.	Wilson	Mullery	Labone	Moore*	Ball	Hurst, G.	Summerbee	Charlton, R.	Peters[1]	
Spain	1–0	Banks, G.	Knowles, C.	Wilson	Mullery	Charlton, J.	Moore*	Ball	Hunt	Summerbee	Charlton, R.[1]	Peters	
Spain	2–1	Bonetti	Newton, K.	Wilson	Mullery	Labone	Moore*	Ball	Peters[1]	Charlton, R.	Hunt	Hunter[1]	
Sweden	3–1	Stepney	Newton, K.	Knowles, C.	Mullery	Labone	Moore*	Bell	Peters[1]	Charlton, R.[1]	Hunt[1]	Hunter	Hurst, G. (9)
West Germany	0–1	Banks, G.	Newton, K.	Knowles, C.	Hunter	Labone	Moore*	Ball	Bell	Summerbee	Hurst, G.	Thompson, P.	
Yugoslavia	0–1	Banks, G.	Newton, K.	Wilson	Mullery	Labone	Moore*	Ball	Peters	Charlton, R.	Hunt	Hunter	
U.S.S.R.	2–0	Banks, G.	Wright, T.	Wilson	Stiles	Labone	Moore*	Hunter	Hunt	Charlton, R.[1]	Hurst, G.[1]	Peters	
1968–69													
Rumania	0–0	Banks, G.	Wright, T.	Newton, K.	Mullery	Labone	Moore*	Ball	Hunt	Charlton, R.	Hurst, G.	Peters	McNab (2)
Bulgaria	1–1	West	Newton, K.	McNab	Mullery	Labone	Moore*	Lee, F.	Bell	Charlton, R.	Hurst, G.[1]	Peters	Reaney (2)
Rumania	1–1	Banks, G.	Wright, T.	McNab	Stiles	Charlton, J.[1]	Hunter	Radford	Hunt	Charlton, R.*	Hurst, G.	Ball	
France	5–0	Banks, G.	Newton, K.	Cooper	Mullery	Charlton, J.	Moore*	Lee, F.[1]	Bell	Hurst, G.[3]	Peters	O'Grady[1]	
Ireland	3–1	Banks, G.	Newton, K.	McNab	Mullery	Labone	Moore*	Ball	Lee, F.[1]	Charlton, R.	Hurst, G.[1]	Peters[1]	
Wales	2–1	West	Newton, K.	Cooper	Moore*	Charlton, J.	Hunter	Lee, F.[1]	Bell	Astle	Charlton, R.[1]	Ball	
Scotland	4–1	Banks, G.	Newton, K.	Cooper	Mullery	Labone	Moore*	Lee, F.	Ball	Charlton, R.	Hurst, G.[2]	Peters[2]	
Mexico	0–0	West	Newton, K.	Cooper	Mullery	Labone	Moore*	Lee, F.	Ball	Charlton, R.	Hurst, G.	Peters	Wright, T. (2)
Uruguay	2–1	Banks, G.	Wright, T.	Newton, K.	Mullery	Labone	Moore*	Lee, F.[1]	Bell	Hurst, G.[1]	Ball	Peters	
Brazil	1–2	Banks, G.	Wright, T.	Newton, K.	Mullery	Labone	Moore*	Ball	Bell[1]	Charlton, R.	Hurst, G.	Peters	

ENGLAND'S FULL INTERNATIONAL TEAMS 1946–88 (contd)

versus	Result	1	2	3	4	5	6	7	8	9	10	11	Substitutes
1969–70													
Netherlands	1–0	Bonetti	Wright, T.	Hughes, E.	Mullery	Charlton, J.	Moore*	Lee, F.	Bell[1]	Charlton, R.	Hurst, G.	Peters	Thompson, P. (7)
Portugal	1–0	Bonetti	Reaney	Cooper	Mullery	Charlton, J.[1]	Moore*	Lee, F.	Bell	Astle	Charlton, R.	Ball	Peters (8)
Netherlands	0–0	Banks, G.	Newton, K.	Cooper	Peters	Charlton, J.	Hunter	Lee, F.	Bell	Jones, M.	Charlton, R.*	Storey-Moore	Mullery (7) Hurst, G. (9)
Belgium	3–1	Banks, G.	Wright, T.	Cooper	Moore*	Labone	Hughes, E.	Lee, F.[1]	Bell[1]	Osgood	Hurst, G.	Peters	
Wales	1–1	Banks, G.	Wright, T.	Hughes, E.	Mullery	Labone	Moore*	Lee, F.[1]	Ball[2]	Charlton, R.[1]	Hurst, G.	Peters[1]	Bell (2)
Ireland	3–1	Banks, G.	Newton, K.	Hughes, E.	Mullery	Labone	Moore*	Coates	Ball	Charlton, R.[1]	Hurst, G.	Peters[1]	Mullery (7)
Scotland	0–0	Banks, G.	Newton, K.	Cooper	Stiles	Moore*	Thompson, P.	Lee, F.[1]	Kidd	Astle	Hurst, G.	Peters	
Columbia	4–0	Banks, G.	Newton, K.	Cooper	Mullery	Labone	Moore*	Lee, F.	Ball[1]	Charlton, R.[1]	Hurst, G.	Peters[2]	Kidd (7)[1] Sadler (9)
Ecuador	2–0	Banks, G.	Newton, K.	Cooper	Mullery	Labone	Moore*	Lee, F.[1]	Ball	Charlton, R.	Hurst, G.[1]	Peters[1]	Wright, T. (2) Osgood (7)
Rumania	1–0	Banks, G.	Newton, K.	Cooper	Mullery	Labone	Moore*	Lee, F.	Ball	Charlton, R.	Hurst, G.[1]	Peters[1]	Astle (7) Bell (9)
Brazil	0–1	Banks, G.	Wright, T.	Cooper	Mullery	Labone	Moore*	Lee, F.	Ball	Charlton, R.	Hurst, G.	Peters[1]	Ball (8) Osgood (9)
Czechoslovakia	1–0	Banks, G.	Newton, K.	Cooper	Mullery	Charlton, J.	Moore*	Bell	Charlton, R.	Astle	Clarke, A.[1]	Peters[1]	Bell (9) Hunter (11)
West Germany	2–3	Bonetti	Newton, K.	Cooper	Mullery[1]	Labone	Moore*	Lee, F.	Ball	Charlton, R.	Hurst, G.	Peters[1]	
1970–71													
German D. R.	3–1	Banks, G.	Hughes, E.	Cooper	Mullery	Sadler	Moore*	Lee, F.[1]	Bell	Hurst, G.	Clarke, A.[1]	Peters[1]	
Malta	1–0	Banks, G.	Reaney	Hughes, E.	Mullery*	McFarland	Hunter	Ball	Chivers	Royle	Harvey	Peters[1]	
Greece	3–0	Banks, G.	Storey	Hughes, E.	Mullery	McFarland	Moore*	Lee, F.[1]	Ball	Chivers[2]	Hurst, G.[1]	Peter	Coates (8)
Malta	5–0	Banks, G.	Lawler[1]	Cooper	Moore*	McFarland	Hughes, E.	Lee, F.[1]	Coates	Chivers	Clarke, A.[1]	Peters	Ball (11)
Ireland	0–0	Shilton	Lawler	Cooper	Storey	McFarland	Moore*	Lee, F.	Ball	Chivers	Clarke, A.[1]	Peters*	
Wales	0–0	Shilton	Lawler	Cooper	Smith, T.	Lloyd	Hughes, E.	Lee, F.	Brown, A.	Hurst, G.	Coates	Peters[1]	Clarke, A. (8)
Scotland	3–1	Banks, G.	Lawler	Cooper	Storey	McFarland	Moore*	Lee, F.	Ball	Chivers[2]	Hurst, G.	Peters[1]	Clarke, A. (7)
1971–72													
Switzerland	3–2	Banks, G.	Lawler	Cooper	Mullery	Lloyd	Moore*	Lee, F.	Madeley	Chivers[1]	Hurst, G.[1]	Peters	Radford (10)
Switzerland	1–1	Shilton	Madeley	Cooper	Storey	Lloyd	Moore*	Summerbee[1]	Ball	Hurst, G.	Lee, F.	Hughes, E.	Chivers (7) Marsh (10)
Greece	2–0	Banks, G.	Madeley	Hughes, E.	Bell	McFarland	Hunter	Lee, F.[1]	Ball	Chivers[1]	Hurst, G.[1]	Peters	Marsh (10)
West Germany	1–3	Banks, G.	Madeley	Hughes, E.	Bell	McFarland	Moore*	Lee, F.[1]	Ball	Chivers	Marsh	Hunter	Summerbee (10) Peters (11)
West Germany	0–0	Banks, G.	Madeley	Hughes, E.	Bell	McFarland	Moore*	Lee, F.	Ball	MacDonald	Marsh	Hunter	Peters (11) Chivers (9)
Wales	3–0	Banks, G.	Madeley	Hughes, E.	Storey	McFarland	Moore*	Ball	Bell	Chivers	Marsh	Currie	MacDonald (10)
Ireland	0–1	Banks, G.	Madeley	Hughes, E.	Storey	Lloyd	Hunter	Summerbee	Bell*	Chivers	Marsh	Peters	
Scotland	1–0	Banks, G.	Madeley	Hughes, E.	Storey	McFarland	Moore*	Ball[1]	Bell	Chivers	Marsh	Hunter	
1972–73													
Yugoslavia	1–1	Shilton	Mills, M.	Lampard	Storey	Blockley	Moore*	Ball	Channon	Royle[1]	Bell	Marsh	
Wales	1–1	Clemence	Storey	Hughes, E.	Hunter	McFarland	Moore*	Keegan	Bell[1]	Chivers	Marsh	Ball	
Wales	1–1	Clemence	Storey	Hughes, E.	Hunter[1]	McFarland	Moore*	Keegan	Bell	Chivers	Marsh	Ball	
Scotland	5–0	Shilton	Madeley	Hughes, E.	Bell	Madeley	Hunter	Ball	Channon[1]	Chivers[2]	Clarke, A.[2]	Peters	
Ireland	2–1	Shilton	Storey	Nish	Bell	McFarland	Moore*	Ball	Channon	Chivers	Richards	Peters[1]	
Wales	3–0	Shilton	Storey	Hughes, E.	Bell	McFarland	Moore*	Ball	Channon	Chivers	Clarke, A.	Peters[1]	
Scotland	1–1	Shilton	Madeley	Storey	Bell	McFarland	Moore*	Ball	Channon	Chivers	Clarke, A.[1]	Peters	
Czechoslovakia	1–1	Shilton	Madeley	Hughes, E.	Bell	McFarland	Moore*	Ball	Channon	Chivers	Clarke, A.[1]	Peters[1]	
Poland	0–2	Shilton	Madeley	Hughes, E.	Storey	McFarland	Moore*	Ball	Bell	Chivers	Clarke, A.	Peters	MacDonald (10) Hunter (11)
U.S.S.R.	2–1	Shilton	Madeley	Hughes, E.	Storey	McFarland	Moore*	Currie	Channon	Chivers[1]	Clarke, A.	Peters†	Summerbee (8)
Italy	0–2	Shilton	Madeley	Hughes, E.	Storey	McFarland	Moore*	Currie	Channon	Chivers	Clarke, A.	Peters	
1973–74													
Austria	7–0	Shilton	Madeley	Hughes, E.	Bell[1]	McFarland	Hunter	Currie[1]	Channon[2]	Chivers[1]	Clarke, A.[2]	Peters*	
Poland	1–1	Shilton	Madeley	Hughes, E.	Bell	McFarland	Hunter	Currie	Channon	Chivers	Clarke, A.[1]	Peters*	Hector (9)

Opponent	Score											Substitutes
Italy	0-1	Shilton	Madeley	Hughes, E.	Bell	McFarland	Moore*	Currie	Channon	Osgood	Clarke, A.	Peters	Hector (10)
Portugal	0-0	Parkes	Nish	Pejic	Dobson	Watson	Todd	Bowles	Channon	MacDonald	Brooking	Peters*	Ball (9)
Wales	2-0	Shilton	Nish	Pejic	Hughes, E.*	McFarland	Todd	Keegan	Channon	Worthington	Weller[1]	Bowles[1]	Hunter (5) Worthington (11)
Ireland	1-0	Shilton	Nish	Pejic	Hughes, E.*	McFarland	Todd	Keegan	Channon	Worthington	Weller	Bowles[1]	Watson (5) MacDonald (9)
Scotland	0-2	Shilton	Hughes, E.*	Hughes, E.*	Hughes, E.*	Hunter	Bell	Keegan	Channon	Worthington	Weller	Peters	
Argentina	2-2	Shilton	Hughes, E.*	Hughes, E.*	Todd	Watson	Dobson	Keegan	Channon	Worthington	Bell	Brooking	MacDonald (9)
German D.R.	1-1	Clemence	Hughes, E.*	Lindsay	Todd	Watson	Dobson	Keegan	Channon	Worthington	Bell	Brooking	
Bulgaria	1-0	Clemence	Hughes, E.*	Lindsay	Todd	Watson	Dobson	Keegan	Channon	Worthington	Bell	Brooking	
Yugoslavia	2-2	Clemence	Hughes, E.*	Lindsay	Todd	Watson	Dobson	Keegan	Channon	Worthington	Keegan	Brooking	
1974-75													
Czechoslovakia	3-0	Clemence	Madeley	Dobson	Dobson	Watson	Hunter	Bell[2]	Channon	Francis, G.	Keegan	Francis, G.	Brooking (4) Thomas (9)
Portugal	0-0	Clemence	Madeley	Cooper	Brooking	Watson	Bell	Bell	Channon	MacDonald	Clarke, A.	Thomas	Todd (3) Worthington (10)
West Germany	2-0	Clemence	Whitworth	Gillard	Bell	Watson	Todd	Ball*	Channon	MacDonald	Hudson	Keegan	Thomas (8)
Cyprus	5-0	Shilton	Madeley	Beattie	Bell	Watson	Todd	Ball*	Channon	MacDonald	Hudson	Thomas	Hughes, E. (3) Tueart (11)
Cyprus	1-0	Clemence	Whitworth	Beattie	Bell	Watson	Todd	Ball*	Channon	MacDonald	Keegan	Thomas	Channon (9)
Ireland	0-0	Clemence	Whitworth	Hughes, E.	Bell	Watson	Todd	Ball*	Channon	MacDonald	Keegan	Tueart	Little (8)
Wales	2-2	Clemence	Whitworth	Gillard	Bell	Watson	Todd	Keegan	Channon	Johnson	Keegan	Thomas	Thomas (11)
Scotland	5-1	Clemence	Whitworth	Beattie[1]	Bell[1]	Watson	Todd	Keegan	Channon	Johnson	Keegan	Thomas	
1975-76													
Switzerland	2-1	Clemence	Beattie	Gillard	Francis, G.*	Watson	Todd	Keegan*	Channon	Johnson	Clarke, A.	Bell	MacDonald (9)
Czechoslovakia	1-2	Clemence	Madeley	Gillard	Francis, G.*	McFarland	Todd	Keegan	Channon	MacDonald	Clarke, A.	Bell	Watson (5) Thomas (8)
Portugal	1-1	Clemence	Whitworth	Beattie	Madeley	Watson	Mills, M.	Keegan*	Channon	MacDonald	Francis, G.[2]	Brooking	Clarke, A. (9) Thomas (4)
Wales	2-1	Clemence	Cherry	Neal	Doyle	Thompson, P.	Mills, M.	Keegan	Channon	Boyer	Taylor, P.	Taylor, P.[1]	Clement (2) Taylor, P. (8)[1]
Wales	1-0	Clemence	Clement	Mills, M.	Thompson, P.	Greenhoff, B.	Kennedy, R.	Keegan	Channon	Pearson, S.	Towers	Taylor, P.	
N. Ireland	4-0	Clemence	Todd	Mills, M.	Thompson, P.	Greenhoff, B.	Kennedy, R.	Keegan*	Channon	Pearson, S.	Tueart	Taylor, P.	Towers (11) Royle (7)
Scotland	1-2	Clemence	Todd	Mills, M.	Thompson, P.	McFarland	Kennedy, R.	Keegan	Channon	Pearson, S.	Francis, G.*	Brooking	Cherry (9) Doyle (5)
Italy	3-2	Rimmer	Clement	Mills, M.	Thompson, P.[1]	Doyle	Mills, M.	Keegan	Channon	Pearson, S.	Brooking	Brooking	
Finland	4-1	Clemence	Todd	Mills, M.	Thompson, P.	Doyle	Towers	Keegan[2]	Channon	Pearson, S.[1]	Brooking	George	Corrigan (1) Mills, M. (3)
1976-77													
Republic of Ireland	1-1	Clemence	Todd	Cherry	Greenhoff, B.	McFarland	Mills, M.	Keegan*	Wilkins	Royle	Brooking	Tueart[1]	
Finland	2-1	Clemence	Clement	Beattie	Thompson, P.	Greenhoff, B.	Mills, M.	Keegan*	Channon	Pearson, S.	Brooking	Brooking	Hill, G. (11)
Italy	0-2	Clemence	Clement	Cherry	Greenhoff, B.	McFarland	Mills, M.	Keegan*	Channon	Pearson, S.	Brooking	Hill, G.	Mills, M. (10) Hill, G. (11)
Netherlands	0-2	Clemence	Gidman	Cherry	Kennedy, R.[1]	Watson	Madeley	Wilkins	Francis, T.	Mariner	Tueart	Tueart[1]	Beattie (2)
Luxembourg	5-0	Shilton	Cherry	Neal	Greenhoff, B.	Watson	Wilkins	Keegan*	Channon*	Pearson, S.	Brooking	Brooking	Todd (9) Pearson, S. (6)
N. Ireland	2-1	Shilton	Shilton	Neal	Greenhoff, B.	Watson	Madeley	Keegan*	Channon*	Pearson, S.	Talbot	Talbot	Mariner (7)
Wales	0-1	Clemence	Neal	Neal	Mills, M.	Watson	Wilkins	Keegan*	Channon	Pearson, S.[1]	Talbot	Talbot	Talbot (7)
Scotland	1-2	Clemence	Neal	Cherry	Greenhoff, B.	Watson	Wilkins	Keegan*	Francis, T.	Pearson, S.	Kennedy, R.	Kennedy, R.	Tueart (10)
Brazil	0-0	Clemence	Neal	Cherry	Greenhoff, B.	Watson	Wilkins	Keegan*	Channon	Pearson, S.	Kennedy, R.	Kennedy, R.	Cherry (4) Tueart (11)
Argentina	1-1	Clemence	Neal	Cherry	Greenhoff, B.	Watson	Wilkins	Keegan*	Channon	Pearson, S.	Talbot	Talbot	Channon (9) Kennedy, R. (10)
Uruguay	0-0	Clemence	Neal	Cherry	Greenhoff, B.	Watson	Wilkins	Keegan*	Channon	Pearson, S.	Talbot	Talbot	Talbot
1977-78													
Switzerland	0-0	Clemence	Cherry	Mills, M.	Watson	McDermott	Callaghan	McDermott	Wilkins	Francis, T.	Wilkins	Francis, T.	Talbot
Luxembourg	2-0	Clemence	Neal	Cherry	Wilkins	Watson	Hughes, E.*	Keegan	Coppell	Mariner[1]	Brooking	Brooking	Hill, G. (8) Wilkins (11)
Italy	2-0	Clemence	Neal	Mills, M.	Wilkins	Watson	Currie	Keegan	Coppell	Pearson, S.	Brooking	Francis, T.	Whymark (7) Beattie (4)
West Germany	1-2	Corrigan	Mills, M.	Cherry	Greenhoff, B.	Greenhoff, B.	Wilkins	Keegan	Coppell	Latchford, R.	Francis, T.	Barnes[1]	Pearson, S. (9) Francis, T. (7)
Brazil	1-1	Shilton	Mills, M.*	Mills, M.*	Greenhoff, B.	Greenhoff, B.	Hughes, E.*	McDermott	Francis, T.	Latchford, R.	Brooking	Barnes[1]	Francis, T. (7)
Wales	3-1	Clemence	Mills, M.*	Cherry	Greenhoff, B.	Greenhoff, B.	Hughes, E.*	Keegan	Wilkins	Pearson, S.	Currie	Woodcock	Currie (3)[1] Mariner (9)

ENGLAND'S FULL INTERNATIONAL TEAMS 1946–88 (contd)

versus	Result	1	2	3	4	5	6	7	8	9	10	11	Substitutes
1978-79 (contd)													
Scotland	1-0	Clemence	Neal	Mills, M.	Wilkins	Watson	Hughes, E.*	Coppell[1]	Currie	Mariner	Francis, T.	Barnes[1]	Greenhoff, B. (6) Brooking (9)
Hungary	4-1	Shilton	Neal[1]	Mills, M.	Wilkins	Watson	Hughes, E.*	Keegan	Coppell	Francis, T.[1]	Brooking	Barnes[1]	Greenhoff, B. (5) Currie (8)[1]
1978-79													
Denmark	4-3	Clemence	Neal[1]	Mills, M.	Wilkins	Watson	Hughes, E.*	Keegan[2]	Coppell	Latchford, R.[1]	Brooking	Barnes	Thompson, P. (5) Woodcock (11)
Czechoslovakia	1-1	Clemence	Neal	Mills, M.	Wilkins	Watson	Wilkins	Keegan*	Coppell	Latchford, R.[1]	Currie	Barnes	Latchford, R. (9)
Republic of Ireland	1-0	Shilton	Anderson	Cherry	Currie	Watson[1]	Hughes, E.*	Keegan*	Coppell[1]	Woodcock	Currie	Barnes	
Northern Ireland	4-0	Clemence	Neal	Mills, M.	Thompson, P.	Watson[1]	Hughes, E.[1]	Keegan[1]	Coppell	Latchford, R.[1]	Brooking[2]	Barnes	
Northern Ireland	2-0	Clemence	Neal	Mills, M.*	Currie	Watson	Currie	Coppell[1]	Wilkins	Latchford, R.[1]	McDermott	Barnes	Coppell (9) Brooking (4)
Wales	0-0	Corrigan	Cherry	Sansom	Thompson, P.	Watson	Hughes, E.*	Keegan[1]	Coppell[1]	Latchford, R.	McDermott	Cunningham	
Scotland	3-1	Clemence	Neal	Mills, M.	Thompson, P.	Watson[1]	Wilkins	Keegan*[1]	Coppell	Latchford, R.	Brooking	Barnes[1]	Francis, T. (9) Woodcock (11)
Bulgaria	3-0	Clemence	Neal	Mills, M.	Thompson, P.	Watson[1]	Hughes, E.*	Keegan	Coppell	Latchford, R.	Currie	Cunningham	Wilkins, R. (4) Thompson, P. (5) Brooking (10)
Sweden	0-0	Shilton	Anderson	Cherry	McDermott	Watson	Wilkins[1]	Keegan*	Francis, T.	Woodcock	Currie	Barnes[1]	Clemence (1) Francis, T. (9) Cunningham (11)
Austria	3-4	Shilton	Neal	Mills, M.	Thompson, P.	Watson	Wilkins[1]	Keegan[1]	Coppell[1]	Latchford, R.[1]	Brooking	Barnes	Clemence (1) Francis, T. (9) Cunningham (11)
1979-80													
Denmark	1-0	Clemence	Neal	Mills, M.	Thompson, P.	Watson	Wilkins	Keegan[1]	Coppell	McDermott	Brooking	Barnes	McDermott (10)
Northern Ireland	5-1	Shilton	Neal	Mills, M.	Thompson, P.	Watson	Wilkins	Keegan*	Coppell	Francis[2]	Brooking	Woodcock[2]	
Bulgaria	2-0	Clemence	Cherry	Sansom	Thompson, P.*	Watson[1]	Wilkins	Keegan*[2]	Hoddle[1]	Francis	Kennedy, R.	Woodcock	Coppell (9)
Republic of Ireland	2-0	Clemence	Cherry	Sansom	Thompson, P.	Watson	Robson	Reeves	McDermott	Johnson	Woodcock	Cunningham	Hughes (2) Cunningham (9)
Spain	2-0	Shilton	Neal	Mills, M.	Thompson, P.	Watson	Wilkins	Keegan*	Coppell	Johnson	Kennedy, R.	Woodcock[1]	Cherry (2) Birtles (9)
Argentina	3-1	Clemence	Neal	Sansom	Thompson, P.	Watson	Wilkins	Keegan[1]	Coppell	Francis[1]	Woodcock	Kennedy, R.	Sansom (2) Wilkins (5)
Wales	1-4	Clemence	Cherry	Cherry	Brooking	Lloyd	Kennedy, R.	Keegan*	Hoddle	Johnson[2]	Brooking	Devonshire	Mariner (10)
Northern Ireland	1-1	Corrigan	Cherry	Sansom	Thompson, P.*	Watson	Hughes*	Coppell[1]	Wilkins	Mariner[1]	Reeves	Brooking[1]	Hughes (10)
Scotland	2-0	Clemence	Cherry	Sansom	Brooking	Watson	Wilkins	McDermott	McDermott	Johnson[1]	Mariner	Armstrong	Greenhoff (7) Ward (10) Devonshire (11)
Australia	2-1	Corrigan	Cherry*	Lampard	Talbot	Osman	Butcher	Coppell[1]	Hoddle[1]	Mariner[1]	Sunderland		McDermott (8) Kennedy, R. (9)
Belgium	1-1	Clemence	Neal	Sansom	Thompson, P.	Watson	Wilkins[1]	Robson	Coppell	Johnson	Brooking	Woodcock	Mariner (9)
Italy	0-1	Shilton	Neal	Sansom	Thompson, P.	Watson	Wilkins	Keegan*	Coppell	Birtles	Kennedy, R.[1]	Woodcock	Cherry (2) Mariner (8)
Spain	2-1	Clemence	Anderson	Mills, M.	Thompson, P.	Watson	Wilkins	Keegan*	Hoddle	McDermott	Brooking[1]	Woodcock[1]	
1980-81													
Norway	4-0	Shilton	Anderson	Sansom	Thompson*	Watson	Robson	Gates	McDermott[2]	Mariner[1]	Woodcock[2]	Rix	Cunningham (9) Coppell (11)
Rumania	1-2	Clemence	Neal	Sansom	Thompson*	Watson	Robson	Rix	McDermott	Birtles	Woodcock	Gates	Rix (10)
Switzerland	2-1	Clemence	Neal	Sansom	Robson	Osman	Mills*	Coppell	McDermott	Mariner[1]	Brooking	Woodcock†	Barnes (8) Wilkins (10)
Spain	1-2	Clemence	Neal	Sansom	Robson	Watson*	Butcher	Keegan*	Francis	McDermott	Brooking	Hoddle[1]	McDermott (10)
Rumania	0-0	Shilton	Anderson	Sansom	Robson	Martin	Osman	Coppell	Wilkins	Withe	Brooking	Woodcock	
Brazil	0-1	Clemence*	Anderson	Sansom	Robson	Watson*	Wilkins	Coppell	McDermott	Withe	Rix	McDermott	Woodcock (9)
Wales	0-0	Corrigan	Anderson	Sansom	Robson	Watson*	Wilkins	Coppell	Hoddle	Withe	Rix	Barnes	Martin (5) Francis (11)
Scotland	0-1	Corrigan	Anderson	Sansom	Wilkins	Watson	Robson	Coppell	Hoddle	Mariner	Rix	Woodcock	McDermott (11)[1] Barnes (5)
Switzerland	1-2	Clemence	Mills	Sansom	Wilkins	Watson	Osman	Keegan*[1]	Coppell	Mariner	Robson	Francis	Wilkins (10)
Hungary	3-1	Clemence	Neal	Mills	Thompson	Watson	Robson	Keegan*[1]	Coppell	Mariner	Brooking[2]	McDermott	
1981-82													
Norway	1-2	Clemence	Neal	Mills	Thompson	Osman	Robson[1]	Keegan*	Francis	Mariner[1]	Hoddle	McDermott	Withe (9) Barnes (10)
Hungary	1-0	Shilton	Neal	Mills	Thompson	Martin	Robson	Keegan*[1]	Coppell[1]	Mariner[1]	Brooking	McDermott	Morley (8)
Northern Ireland	4-0	Clemence	Anderson	Sansom	Wilkins[1]	Watson	Foster	Keegan*[1]	Robson[1]	Francis	Hoddle[1]	Morley	Regis (9) Woodcock (11)

Opponent	Score											
Wales	1-0	Corrigan*	Neal	Sansom	Thompson*	Butcher	Robson	Wilkins	Francis[1]	Withe	Morley	McDermott (8) Regis (10)
Holland	2-0	Shilton*	Neal	Sansom	Thompson	Foster	Robson	Wilkins	Devonshire	Mariner	Woodcock	Rix (8) Barnes (9)
Scotland	1-0	Shilton	Mills	Sansom	Thompson	Butcher	Robson	Wilkins	Coppell	Mariner	Wilkins	McDermott (7) Francis (10)
Iceland	1-1	Corrigan	Anderson	Neal*	Watson	Osman	McDermott	Hoddle	Devonshire	Mariner	Morley	Perryman (8) Goddard (10)[1]
Finland	4-1	Clemence	Mills	Sansom	Thompson	Martin	Robson[2]	Wilkins	Coppell	Withe	Wilkins	Woodcock (10)
France	3-1	Shilton*	Mills*	Sansom	Thompson	Butcher	Robson[2]	Wilkins	Francis[1]	Mariner	Coppell	Neal (3)
Czechoslovakia	2-0	Shilton	Mills*	Sansom	Thompson	Butcher	Hoddle	Coppell	Francis[1]	Mariner	Rix	Hoddle (6)
Kuwait	1-0	Shilton*	Neal	Mills*	Thompson	Foster	Robson	Hoddle	Francis	Mariner	Rix	
West Germany	0-0	Shilton*	Mills*	Sansom	Thompson	Butcher	Robson	Wilkins	Francis	Woodcock	Rix	Woodcock (8)
Spain	0-0	Shilton*	Mills*	Sansom	Thompson	Butcher	Robson	Rix	Francis	Woodcock	Wilkins	
1982-83												
Denmark	2-2	Shilton	Neal	Sansom	Wilkins*	Osman	Butcher	Robson[2]	Robson	Mariner	Morley	Brooking (7) Keegan (10)
West Germany	1-2	Shilton	Mabbutt	Sansom	Thompson	Butcher	Wilkins	Hoddle	Armstrong	Mariner	Woodcock[1]	
1983-84												
Greece	3-0	Shilton*	Neal	Sansom	Thompson	Martin	Robson*	Mabbutt	Mariner[1]	Woodcock[3]	Morley	Hill (7)
Luxembourg	9-0	Clemence	Neal[1]	Statham	Robson*	Martin	Butcher[1]	Lee	Blissett[3]	Woodcock[1]	Mabbutt†	Woodcock (8)[1] Blissett (9) Rix (10)
Wales	2-1	Shilton*	Neal	Sansom	Lee	Martin	Butcher	Mabbutt[1]	Coppell[1]	Mariner	Devonshire	Chamberlain (7)[1] Hoddle (11)[1]
Greece	0-0	Shilton*	Neal[1]	Sansom	Lee	Martin	Butcher[1]	Coppell	Blissett	Francis	Devonshire	Blissett (10) Rix (11)
Hungary	2-0	Shilton*	Neal	Sansom	Lee	Roberts	Butcher	Mabbutt	Francis[1]	Withe[1]	Cowans	Barnes J (10)
Northern Ireland	0-0	Shilton*	Neal	Sansom	Hoddle	Roberts	Butcher	Mabbutt	Coppell	Withe	Cowans	Mabbutt (7) Blissett (9)
Scotland	2-0	Shilton*	Neal	Statham	Lee	Osman	Butcher	Robson[4]	Mabbutt	Walsh[1]	Barnes	Barnes(3) Walsh(9)
Australia	1-0	Shilton*	Thomas	Statham	Williams	Osman	Butcher	Robson	Gregory	Walsh[1]	Cowans[1]	Williams(3)
Australia	0-0	Shilton*	Neal	Pickering	Barham	Osman	Butcher	Gregory	Barham	Walsh	Williams	Spink(1) Thomas(2) Blissett(9)
Australia	1-1	Shilton	Statham	Sansom	Lee	Osman	Butcher	Gregory	Gregory	Walsh	Barnes	Spink(1) Thomas(2) Blissett(9)
1983-84												
Denmark	0-1	Shilton	Neal	Sansom	Lee	Osman	Butcher	Gregory	Gregory	Mariner[1]	Francis[1]	Blissett(4) Chamberlain(11)
Hungary	3-0	Shilton	Gregory	Sansom	Lee	Martin	Butcher	Hoddle	Hoddle	Mariner[1]	Blissett	Withe(10)
Luxembourg	4-0	Clemence	Duxbury	Sansom	Lee	Martin	Butcher	Hoddle	Hoddle	Mariner[1]	Woodcock[1]	Barnes(10)
France	0-2	Shilton	Duxbury	Kennedy	Lee	Roberts	Butcher	Stein	Robson*	Withe[1]	Barnes	Barnes(4) Woodcock (8)
Northern Ireland	1-0	Shilton	Anderson	Kennedy	Lee	Roberts	Butcher	Wilkins	Robson*[2]	Walsh[1]	Mabbutt	Fenwick(5) Blissett(11)
Wales	0-1	Shilton	Duxbury	Anderson	Wilkins	Martin	Butcher	Wilkins	Robson*	Walsh	Barham	Hunt(7) Lineker(9)
Scotland	1-1	Shilton	Duxbury	Sansom	Wilkins	Wright	Butcher	Stein	Robson*[2]	Woodcock[1]	Gregory	Hateley(9) Hunt(11)
U.S.S.R.	0-2	Shilton	Duxbury	Sansom	Wilkins	Fenwick	Butcher	Gregory	Robson*	Woodcock[1]	Cowans	Allen (10)
Brazil	2-0	Shilton	Duxbury	Sansom	Wilkins	Fenwick	Butcher	Hoddle	Chamberlain	Hateley[1]	Barnes[1]	Woodcock (10)
Uruguay	0-2	Shilton	Duxbury	Sansom	Wilkins	Watson	Butcher	Hoddle	Chamberlain	Hateley[1]	Barnes[1]	Lee (8)
Chile	0-0	Shilton	Duxbury	Sansom	Wilkins	Watson	Butcher	Chamberlain	Chamberlain	Walsh[1]	Barnes	Hateley (9) Francis (10)
1984-85												
East Germany	1-0	Shilton	Duxbury	Sansom	Williams	Wright	Butcher	Wilkins*	Robson*[1]	Mariner	Woodcock*	Stevens (4) Chamberlain (7)
Finland	5-0	Shilton	Duxbury	Sansom	Williams	Wright	Butcher	Wilkins	Robson*[2]	Hateley[2]	Woodcock*[1]	Stevens (4) Francis (10)
Turkey	8-0	Shilton	Anderson[1]	Sansom	Williams	Martin	Butcher	Wilkins*	Robson*[3]	Withe	Woodcock*[2]	Francis (10)
Northern Ireland	1-0	Shilton	Anderson	Sansom	Steven[1]	Wright	Butcher	Wilkins*	Robson*	Hateley[1]	Waddle	Hoddle (7) Davenport (9)
Republic of Ireland	2-1	Bailey	Anderson	Sansom[1]	Steven[1]	Wright	Butcher	Wilkins*	Robson*	Hateley[1]	Barnes[1]	Lineker (9) Waddle (11)
Rumania	0-0	Shilton	Anderson	Sansom	Steven	Fenwick	Butcher	Wilkins*	Robson*	Mariner	Barnes	Waddle (4)
Finland	1-1	Shilton	Anderson	Sansom	Steven	Fenwick	Butcher	Wilkins*	Robson*	Hateley[1]	Barnes	Lineker (4) Waddle (11)
Scotland	0-1	Shilton	Anderson	Sansom	Hoddle	Fenwick	Butcher	Wilkins	Robson*	Hateley	Waddle	Barnes (11)
Italy	1-2	Shilton	Stevens	Sansom	Hoddle	Wright	Butcher	Wilkins	Francis[1]	Hateley[1]	Waddle	Dixon (4) Reid (8)
Mexico	0-1	Bailey	Anderson	Sansom	Hoddle	Fenwick	Watson	Wilkins	Reid	Hateley	Barnes	Waddle (11)
West Germany	3-0	Shilton	Stevens	Sansom	Hoddle	Wright	Butcher	Wilkins	Lineker	Dixon[2]	Waddle	Bracewell (7) Barnes (10)

71

ENGLAND'S FULL INTERNATIONAL TEAMS 1946-88 (*contd*)

versus	Result	1	2	3	4	5	6	7	8	9	10	11	Substitutes
1981-82 (contd)													
U.S.A.	5-0	Woods	Anderson	Sansom	Hoddle	Fenwick	Butcher	Robson*	Bracewell	Dixon[2]	Lineker[2]	Waddle	Watson (3) Steven (4)[1] Reid (7) Barnes (11)
1985-86													
Rumania	1-1	Shilton	Stevens	Sansom	Reid	Wright	Fenwick	Robson*	Hoddle[1]	Hateley	Lineker	Waddle[1]	Woodcock(10) Barnes(11)
Turkey	5-0	Shilton	Stevens	Sansom	Hoddle	Wright	Fenwick	Robson*[1]	Wilkins	Hateley	Lineker[3]	Waddle[1]	Steven(7) Woodcock(9)
Northern Ireland	0-0	Shilton	Stevens	Sansom	Hoddle	Wright	Fenwick	Bracewell	Wilkins*	Dixon	Lineker	Waddle	Woods(1) Hill(7)
Egypt	4-0	Shilton	Stevens	Sansom	Cowans[1]	Wright	Fenwick	Steven[1]	Wilkins*	Hateley	Lineker	Wallace[1]†	Beardsley(10)
Israel	2-1	Shilton	Stevens	Sansom	Hoddle	Martin	Butcher	Robson*[2]	Wilkins	Dixon	Beardsley	Waddle	Woods(1) Woodcock(9) Barnes(11)
U.S.S.R.	1-0	Shilton	Anderson	Sansom	Hoddle[1]	Wright	Butcher	Cowans	Wilkins*	Beardsley	Lineker	Waddle[1]	Hodge(7) Steven(11)
Scotland	2-1	Shilton	Stevens	Sansom	Hoddle[1]	Watson	Butcher[1]	Wilkins*	Francis	Hateley	Hodge	Waddle	Reid(7) Stevens(10)
Mexico	3-0	Shilton	Anderson	Sansom	Hoddle	Fenwick	Butcher	Robson*	Wilkins	Hateley[2]	Beardsley[1]	Waddle	Stevens(7) Steven(8) Dixon(9) Barnes(11)
Canada	1-0	Shilton	Stevens	Sansom	Hoddle	Martin	Butcher	Hodge	Wilkins*	Hateley[1]	Lineker	Waddle	Woods(1) Reid(8)
1986-87													
Portugal	0-1	Shilton	Stevens	Sansom	Hoddle	Fenwick	Butcher	Robson*	Wilkins	Hateley	Lineker	Waddle	Beardsley(10) Barnes(11)
Morocco	0-0	Shilton	Stevens	Sansom	Hoddle	Fenwick	Butcher	Robson*	Wilkins	Hateley	Lineker	Waddle	Hodge(7) Beardsley(11)
Poland	3-0	Shilton*	Stevens	Sansom	Hoddle	Fenwick	Butcher	Hodge	Reid	Beardsley	Lineker[3]	Steven	Hodge(7) Stevens(9)
Paraguay	3-0	Shilton*	Stevens	Sansom	Hoddle	Martin	Butcher	Hodge	Reid	Beardsley[1]	Lineker[2]	Steven	Waddle(9) Dixon(10)
Argentina	1-2	Shilton*	Stevens	Sansom	Hoddle	Fenwick	Butcher	Hodge	Reid	Beardsley	Lineker[1]	Steven	Stevens(8) Hateley (9) Waddle(8) Barnes(11)
Sweden	0-1	Shilton*	Anderson	Sansom	Hoddle	Martin	Butcher	Steven	Wilkins	Dixon	Hodge	Barnes	Cottee(7) Waddle(11)
Northern Ireland	3-0	Shilton	Anderson[1]	Sansom	Hoddle	Watson	Butcher*	Robson*[1]	Hodge	Beardsley	Lineker[2]	Waddle[1]	Cottee(9)
Yugoslavia	2-0	Shilton	Anderson[1]	Sansom	Hoddle	Wright	Butcher*	Mabbutt[1]	Hodge	Beardsley	Lineker[4]	Waddle	Wilkins(8) Steven(11)
Spain	4-2	Shilton	Anderson	Sansom	Hoddle	Adams	Butcher	Robson*[1]	Hodge	Beardsley	Lineker[4]	Waddle[1]	Woods(1) Steven(1)
Northern Ireland	2-0	Shilton	Anderson	Sansom	Mabbutt	Wright	Mabbutt	Robson*[1]	Hodge	Beardsley	Lineker	Waddle	Woods(1)
Turkey	0-0	Woods	Anderson	Sansom	Hoddle	Adams	Butcher	Robson*	Hodge	Allen	Lineker[1]	Waddle	Barnes(8) Hateley(9)
Brazil	1-1	Shilton	Stevens	Pearce	Reid	Adams	Butcher	Robson*	Barnes	Beardsley	Lineker[1]	Waddle	Hateley(10)
Scotland	0-0	Woods	Stevens	Pearce	Hoddle	Wright	Butcher	Robson*	Hodge	Beardsley	Hateley	Waddle	
1987-88													
West Germany	1-3	Shilton*	Anderson	Sansom	Hoddle	Adams	Mabbutt	Reid	Barnes	Beardsley	Lineker[1]	Waddle	Pearce(3) Webb(4) Hateley(11)
Turkey	8-0	Shilton	Stevens	Sansom	Steven	Adams	Butcher	Robson*[1]	Webb[2]	Beardsley[1]	Lineker[3]	Barnes[2]	Hoddle(4) Regis(9)
Yugoslavia	4-1	Shilton	Stevens	Sansom	Steven	Adams[1]	Butcher	Robson*[1]	Webb	Beardsley*	Lineker	Barnes[1]	Reid(7) Hoddle(8)
Israel	0-0	Woods	Stevens	Pearce	Webb	Watson[1]	Wright	Allen	McMahon	Beardsley*	Barnes	Waddle	Fenwick(6) Harford(7)
Holland	2-2	Shilton	Stevens	Sansom	Steven	Adams[1]	Pallister	Robson*	Webb	Beardsley	Lineker*	Barnes	Wright(6) Hoddle(8) Hateley(9)
Hungary	0-0	Woods	Anderson	Pearce	Steven	Adams	Wright	Robson*	McMahon	Beardsley	Lineker	Waddle	Stevens(3) Hateley(9) Cottee(10) Hoddle(11)
Scotland	1-0	Shilton	Stevens	Sansom	Webb	Watson	Adams	Robson*	Steven	Beardsley[1]	Lineker[1]	Barnes	Waddle(8)
Colombia	1-1	Shilton	Anderson	Sansom	McMahon	Wright	Adams	Robson*	Waddle	Beardsley	Lineker[1]	Barnes	Hoddle(8) Hateley(9)
Switzerland	1-0	Shilton	Stevens	Sansom	Webb	Wright	Adams	Robson*	Steven	Beardsley	Lineker[1]	Barnes	Woods(1) Watson(6) Reid (7) Waddle(8)
Rep. of Ireland	0-1	Shilton	Stevens	Sansom	Webb	Wright	Adams	Robson*[1]	Waddle	Beardsley	Lineker[1]	Barnes	Hoddle(4) Hateley(9)
Holland	1-3	Shilton	Stevens	Sansom	Hoddle	Wright	Adams[1]	Robson*	Steven	Beardsley	Lineker	Barnes	Waddle(8) Hateley(9)
U.S.S.R.	1-3	Woods	Stevens	Sansom	Hoddle	Watson	Adams[1]	Robson*	Steven	McMahon	Lineker	Barnes	Webb(9) Hateley(10)

International Matches 1872–1988

(*Up to and including 18th June 1988*)

wc World Cup   ENC European Nations' Cup   BJT Brazilian Jubilee Tournament
EC European Championship   SFAC Scottish F.A. Centenary   FAWC F.A. of Wales Centenary
USABCT United States of America Bi-Centenary Tournament   RC Rous Cup

ENGLAND v. ARGENTINA

				Goals	
Year	Date		Venue	Eng	Arg
1951	May	9	Wembley	2	1
wc1962	June	2	Rancagua...............	3	1
BJT1964	June	6	Rio de Janeiro.......	0	1
wc1966	July	23	Wembley	1	0
1974	May	22	Wembley	2	2
1977	June	12	Buenos Aires	1	1
1980	May	13	Wembley	3	1
wc1986	June	22	Mexico City............	1	2

ENGLAND v. AUSTRIA

				Eng	Aust
1908	June	6	Vienna	6	1
1908	June	8	Vienna	11	1
1909	June	1	Vienna	8	1
1930	May	14	Vienna	0	0
1932	Dec.	7	Chelsea..................	4	3
1936	May	6	Vienna	1	2
1951	Nov.	28	Wembley	2	2
1952	May	25	Vienna	3	2
wc1958	June	15	Boras	2	2
1961	May	27	Vienna	1	3
1962	April	4	Wembley	3	1
1965	Oct.	20	Wembley	2	3
1967	May	27	Vienna	1	0
1973	Sept.	26	Wembley	7	0
1979	June	13	Vienna	3	4

ENGLAND v. AUSTRALIA

				Eng	Aus
1980	May	31	Sydney	2	1
1983	June	12	Sydney	0	0
1983	June	15	Brisbane	1	0
1983	June	19	Melbourne	1	1

ENGLAND v. BELGIUM

				Eng	Belg
1921	May	21	Brussels	2	0
1923	Mar.	19	Highbury	6	1
1923	Nov.	1	Antwerp	2	2
1924	Dec.	8	West Bromwich.......	4	0
1926	May	24	Antwerp	5	3
1927	May	11	Brussels	9	1
1928	May	19	Antwerp	3	1
1929	May	11	Brussels	5	1
1931	May	16	Brussels	4	1
1936	May	9	Brussels	2	3
1947	Sept.	21	Brussels	5	2
1950	May	18	Brussels	4	1
1952	Nov.	26	Wembley	5	0
wc1954	June	17	Basle	4	4
1964	Oct.	21	Wembley	2	2
1970	Feb.	20	Brussels	3	1
EC1980	June	12	Turin.....................	1	1

ENGLAND v. BOHEMIA

				Eng	Boh
1908	June	13	Prague..................	4	0

ENGLAND v. BRAZIL

				Eng	Brazil
1956	May	9	Wembley	4	2
wc1958	June	11	Gothenburg...........	0	0
1959	May	13	Rio de Janeiro........	0	2
wc1962	June	10	Vina Del Mar.........	1	3
1963	May	8	Wembley	1	1
BJT1964	May	30	Rio de Janeiro........	1	5

ENGLAND v. BRAZIL (*contd*)

				Goals	
Year	Date		Venue	Eng	Brazil
1969	June	12	Rio de Janeiro........	1	2
wc1970	June	7	Guadalajara	0	1
USABCT1976	May	23	Los Angeles...........	0	1
1977	June	8	Rio de Janeiro........	0	0
1978	April	19	Wembley	1	1
1981	May	12	Wembley	0	1
1984	June	10	Rio de Janeiro........	2	0
RC1987	May	19	Wembley	1	1

ENGLAND v. BULGARIA

				Eng	Bulg
wc1962	June	7	Rancagua...............	0	0
1968	Dec.	11	Wembley	1	1
1974	June	1	Sofia......................	1	0
EC1979	June	6	Sofia......................	3	0
EC1979	Nov.	22	Wembley	2	0

ENGLAND v. CANADA

				Eng	Can
1986	May	24	Vancouver..............	1	0

ENGLAND v. CHILE

				Eng	Chile
wc1950	June	25	Rio de Janeiro........	2	0
1953	May	24	Santiago.................	2	1
1984	June	17	Santiago.................	0	0

ENGLAND v. COLOMBIA

				Eng	Col
1970	May	20	Bogota	4	0
RC1988	May	24	Wembley	1	1

ENGLAND v. CYPRUS

				Eng	Cyp
EC1975	April	16	Wembley	5	0
EC1975	May	11	Limassol	1	0

ENGLAND v. CZECHOSLOVAKIA

				Eng	Czech
1934	May	16	Prague...................	1	2
1937	Dec.	1	Tottenham	5	4
1963	May	29	Bratislava...............	4	2
1966	Nov.	2	Wembley	0	0
wc1970	June	11	Guadalajara	1	0
1973	May	27	Prague...................	1	1
EC1974	Oct.	30	Wembley	3	0
EC1975	Oct.	30	Bratislava...............	1	2
1978	Nov.	29	Wembley	1	0
wc1982	June	20	Bilbao	2	0

ENGLAND v. DENMARK

				Eng	Den
1948	Sept.	26	Copenhagen	0	0
1955	Oct.	2	Copenhagen	5	1
wc1956	Dec.	5	Wolverhampton	5	2
wc1957	May	15	Copenhagen	4	1
1966	July	3	Copenhagen	2	0
EC1978	Sept.	20	Copenhagen	4	3
EC1979	Sept.	12	Wembley	1	0
EC1982	Sept.	22	Copenhagen	2	2
EC1983	Sept.	21	Wembley	0	1

ENGLAND v. ECUADOR

Year	Date		Venue	Goals Eng	Ecua
1970	May	24	Quito	2	0

ENGLAND v. EGYPT

Year	Date		Venue	Eng	Egy
1986	Jan	29	Cairo	4	0

ENGLAND v. F.I.F.A.

Year	Date		Venue	Eng	FIFA
1953	Oct.	21	Wembley	4	4

ENGLAND v. FINLAND

Year	Date		Venue	Eng	Fin
1937	May	20	Helsinki	8	0
1956	May	20	Helsinki	5	1
1966	June	26	Helsinki	3	0
wc1976	June	13	Helsinki	4	1
wc1976	Oct.	13	Wembley	2	1
1982	June	3	Helsinki	4	1
wc1984	Oct.	17	Wembley	5	0
wc1985	May	22	Helsinki	1	1

ENGLAND v. FRANCE

Year	Date		Venue	Eng	Fr
1923	May	10	Paris	4	1
1924	May	17	Paris	3	1
1925	May	21	Paris	3	2
1927	May	26	Paris	6	0
1928	May	17	Paris	5	1
1929	May	9	Paris	4	1
1931	May	14	Paris	2	5
1933	Dec.	6	Tottenham	4	1
1938	May	26	Paris	4	2
1947	May	3	Highbury	3	0
1949	May	22	Paris	3	1
1951	Oct.	3	Highbury	2	2
1955	May	15	Paris	0	1
1957	Nov.	27	Wembley	4	0
ENC1962	Oct.	3	Sheffield	1	1
ENC1963	Feb.	27	Paris	2	5
wc1966	July	20	Wembley	2	0
1969	Mar.	12	Wembley	5	0
wc1982	June	16	Bilbao	3	1
1984	Feb.	29	Paris	0	2

ENGLAND v. GERMANY D.R.

Year	Date		Venue	Eng	D.R.
1963	June	2	Leipzig	2	1
1970	Nov.	25	Wembley	3	1
1974	May	29	Leipzig	1	1
1984	Sept.	12	Wembley	1	0

ENGLAND v. GERMANY F.R.

Year	Date		Venue	Eng	F.R.
1930	May	10	Berlin	3	3
1935	Dec.	4	Tottenham	3	0
1938	May	14	Berlin	6	3
1954	Dec.	1	Wembley	3	1
1956	May	26	Berlin	3	1
1965	May	12	Nuremberg	1	0
1966	Feb.	23	Wembley	1	0
wc1966	July	30	Wembley	4	2
1968	June	1	Hanover	0	1
wc1970	June	14	Leon	2	3
EC1972	April	29	Wembley	1	3
EC1972	May	13	Berlin	0	0
1975	Mar.	12	Wembley	2	0
1978	Feb.	22	Munich	1	2
wc1982	June	29	Madrid	0	0
1982	Oct.	13	Wembley	1	2
1985	June	12	Mexico City	3	0
1987	Sept.	9	Düsseldorf	1	3

ENGLAND v. GREECE

Year	Date		Venue	Goals Eng	Gr
EC1971	April	21	Wembley	3	0
EC1971	Dec.	1	Athens	2	0
EC1982	Nov.	17	Salonika	3	0
EC1983	Mar.	30	Wembley	0	0

ENGLAND v. HUNGARY

Year	Date		Venue	Eng	Hun
1908	June	10	Budapest	7	0
1909	May	29	Budapest	4	2
1909	May	31	Budapest	8	2
1934	May	10	Budapest	1	2
1936	Dec.	2	Highbury	6	2
1953	Nov.	25	Wembley	3	6
1954	May	23	Budapest	1	7
1960	May	22	Budapest	0	2
wc1962	May	31	Rancagua	1	2
1965	May	5	Wembley	1	0
1978	May	24	Wembley	4	1
wc1981	June	6	Budapest	3	1
wc1981	Nov.	18	Wembley	1	0
EC1983	Apr.	27	Wembley	2	0
EC1983	Oct.	12	Budapest	3	0
1988	Apr.	27	Budapest	0	0

ENGLAND v. ICELAND

Year	Date		Venue	Eng	Ice
1982	June	2	Reykjavik	1	1

ENGLAND v. IRELAND

Year	Date		Venue	Eng	Ire
1882	Feb.	18	Belfast	13	0
1883	Feb.	24	Liverpool	7	0
1884	Feb.	23	Belfast	8	1
1885	Feb.	28	Manchester	4	0
1886	Mar.	13	Belfast	6	1
1887	Feb.	5	Sheffield	7	0
1888	Mar.	31	Belfast	5	1
1889	Mar.	2	Everton	6	1
1890	Mar.	15	Belfast	9	1
1891	Mar.	7	Wolverhampton	6	1
1892	Mar.	5	Belfast	2	0
1893	Feb.	25	Birmingham	6	1
1894	Mar.	3	Belfast	2	2
1895	Mar.	9	Derby	9	0
1896	Mar.	7	Belfast	2	0
1897	Feb.	20	Nottingham	6	0
1898	Mar.	5	Belfast	3	2
1899	Feb.	18	Sunderland	13	2
1900	Mar.	17	Dublin	2	0
1901	Mar.	9	Southampton	3	0
1902	Mar.	22	Belfast	1	0
1903	Feb.	14	Wolverhampton	4	0
1904	Mar.	12	Belfast	3	1
1905	Feb.	25	Middlesborough	1	1
1906	Feb.	17	Belfast	5	0
1907	Feb.	16	Everton	1	0
1908	Feb.	15	Belfast	3	1
1909	Feb.	13	Bradford	4	0
1910	Feb.	12	Belfast	1	1
1911	Feb.	11	Derby	2	1
1912	Feb.	10	Dublin	6	1
1913	Feb.	15	Belfast	1	2
1914	Feb.	14	Middlesborough	0	3
1919	Oct.	25	Belfast	1	1
1920	Oct.	23	Sunderland	2	0
1921	Oct.	22	Belfast	1	1
1922	Oct.	21	West Bromwich	2	0
1923	Oct.	20	Belfast	1	2
1924	Oct.	22	Everton	3	1
1925	Oct.	24	Belfast	0	0
1926	Oct.	20	Liverpool	3	3
1927	Oct.	22	Belfast	0	2
1928	Oct.	22	Everton	2	1
1929	Oct.	19	Belfast	3	0
1930	Oct.	20	Sheffield	5	1

ENGLAND v. IRELAND (contd)

Year	Date		Venue	Eng	Ire
				Goals	
1931	Oct.	17	Belfast	6	2
1932	Oct.	17	Blackpool	1	0
1933	Oct.	14	Belfast	3	0
1935	Feb.	6	Everton	2	1
1935	Oct.	19	Belfast	3	1
1936	Nov.	18	Stoke	3	1
1937	Oct.	23	Belfast	5	1
1938	Nov.	16	Manchester	7	0
1946	Sept.	28	Belfast	7	2
1947	Nov.	5	Everton	2	2
1949	Oct.	9	Belfast	6	2
wc1949	Nov.	16	Manchester	9	2
1950	Oct.	7	Belfast	4	1
1951	Nov.	14	Aston Villa	2	0
1952	Oct.	4	Belfast	2	2
wc1953	Nov.	11	Liverpool	3	1
1954	Oct.	2	Belfast	2	0
1955	Nov.	2	Wembley	3	0
1956	Oct.	6	Belfast	1	1
1957	Nov.	6	Wembley	2	3
1958	Oct.	4	Belfast	3	3
1959	Nov.	18	Wembley	2	1
1960	Oct.	8	Belfast	5	2
1961	Nov.	22	Wembley	1	1
1962	Oct.	20	Belfast	3	1
1963	Nov.	20	Wembley	8	3
1964	Oct.	3	Belfast	4	3
1965	Nov.	10	Wembley	2	1
ec1966	Oct.	22	Belfast	2	0
ec1967	Nov.	22	Wembley	2	0
1969	May	3	Belfast	3	1
1970	April	21	Wembley	3	1
1971	May	15	Belfast	1	0
1972	May	23	Wembley	0	1
1973	May	12	Everton	2	1
1974	May	15	Wembley	1	0
1975	May	17	Belfast	0	0
1976	May	11	Wembley	4	0
1977	May	28	Belfast	2	1
1978	May	16	Wembley	1	0
ec1979	Feb.	7	Wembley	4	0
1979	May	19	Belfast	2	0
ec1979	Oct.	17	Belfast	5	1
1980	May	20	Wembley	1	1
1982	Feb.	23	Wembley	4	0
1983	May	28	Belfast	0	0
1984	April	4	Wembley	1	0
wc1985	Feb.	27	Belfast	1	0
wc1985	Nov.	13	Wembley	0	0
ec1986	Oct.	15	Wembley	3	0
ec1987	Apr.	1	Belfast	2	0

ENGLAND v. REPUBLIC OF IRELAND

				Eng	Rep of Ire
1946	Sept.	30	Dublin	1	0
1949	Sept.	21	Everton	0	2
wc1957	May	8	Wembley	5	1
wc1957	May	19	Dublin	1	1
1964	May	24	Dublin	3	1
1976	Sept.	8	Wembley	1	1
ec1978	Oct.	25	Dublin	1	1
ec1980	Feb.	6	Wembley	2	0
1985	Mar.	26	Wembley	2	1
ec1988	June	12	Stuttgart	0	1

ENGLAND v. ISRAEL

				Eng	Isr
1986	Feb.	26	Tel Aviv	2	1
1988	Feb.	17	Tel Aviv	0	0

ENGLAND v. ITALY

Year	Date		Venue	Eng	Italy
				Goals	
1933	May	13	Rome	1	1
1934	Nov.	14	Highbury	3	2
1939	May	13	Milan	2	2
1948	May	16	Turin	4	0
1949	Nov.	30	Tottenham	2	0
1952	May	18	Florence	1	1
1959	May	6	Wembley	2	2
1961	May	24	Rome	3	2
1973	June	14	Turin	0	2
1973	Nov.	14	Wembley	0	1
usabct1976	May	28	New York	3	2
wc1976	Nov.	17	Rome	0	2
wc1977	Nov.	16	Wembley	2	0
ec1980	June	15	Turin	0	1
1985	June	6	Mexico City	1	2

ENGLAND v. KUWAIT

				Eng	Kuw
wc1982	June	25	Bilbao	1	0

ENGLAND v. LUXEMBOURG

				Eng	Lux
1927	May	21	Luxembourg	5	2
wc1960	Oct.	19	Luxembourg	9	0
wc1961	Sept.	28	Highbury	4	1
wc1977	Mar.	30	Wembley	5	0
wc1977	Oct.	12	Luxembourg	2	0
ec1982	Dec.	15	Wembley	9	0
ec1983	Nov.	16	Luxembourg	4	0

ENGLAND v. MALTA

				Eng	Malta
ec1971	Feb.	3	Valletta	1	0
ec1971	May	12	Wembley	5	0

ENGLAND v. MEXICO

				Eng	Mex
1959	May	24	Mexico City	1	2
1961	May	10	Wembley	8	0
wc1966	July	16	Wembley	2	0
1969	June	1	Mexico City	0	0
1985	June	9	Mexico City	0	1
1986	May	17	Los Angeles	3	0

ENGLAND v. MOROCCO

				Eng	Mor
wc1986	June	6	Monterrey	0	0

ENGLAND v. NETHERLANDS

				Eng	Neth
1935	May	18	Amsterdam	1	0
1946	Nov.	27	Huddersfield	8	2
1964	Dec.	9	Amsterdam	1	1
1969	Nov.	5	Amsterdam	1	0
1970	Jan.	14	Wembley	0	0
1977	Feb.	9	Wembley	0	2
1982	May	25	Wembley	2	0
1988	Mar.	23	Wembley	2	2
ec1988	June	15	Düsseldorf	1	3

ENGLAND v. NORWAY

				Eng	Nor
1937	May	14	Oslo	6	0
1938	Nov.	9	Newcastle	4	0
1949	May	18	Oslo	4	1
1966	June	29	Oslo	6	1
wc1980	Sept.	10	Wembley	4	0
wc1981	Sept.	9	Oslo	1	2

ENGLAND v. PARAGUAY

				Goals	
Year	Date		Venue	Eng	Par
wc1986	June	18	Mexico City	3	0

ENGLAND v. PERU

				Eng	Peru
1959	May	17	Lima	1	4
1962	May	20	Lima	4	0

ENGLAND v. POLAND

				Goals	
Year	Date		Venue	Eng	Pol
1966	Jan	5	Everton	1	1
1966	July	5	Chorzow	1	0
wc1973	June	6	Chorzow	0	2
wc1973	Oct.	17	Wembley	1	1
wc1986	June	11	Monterrey	3	0

ENGLAND v. PORTUGAL

				Eng	Port
1947	May	25	Lisbon	10	0
1950	May	14	Lisbon	5	3
1951	May	19	Everton	5	2
1955	May	22	Oporto	1	3
1958	May	7	Wembley	2	1
wc1961	May	21	Lisbon	1	1
wc1961	Oct.	25	Wembley	2	0
1964	May	17	Lisbon	4	3
BJT1964	June	4	Sao Paulo	1	1
wc1966	July	26	Wembley	2	1
1969	Dec.	10	Wembley	1	0
1974	April	3	Lisbon	0	0
EC1974	Nov.	20	Wembley	0	0
EC1975	Nov.	19	Lisbon	1	1
wc1986	June	3	Monterrey	0	1

ENGLAND v. REST OF EUROPE

				Eng	RoE
1938	Oct.	26	Highbury	3	0

ENGLAND v. REST OF THE WORLD

				Eng	RoW
1963	Oct.	23	Wembley	2	1

ENGLAND v. RUMANIA

				Eng	Rum
1939	May	24	Bucharest	2	0
1968	Nov.	6	Bucharest	0	0
1969	Jan.	15	Wembley	1	1
wc1970	June	2	Guadalajara	1	0
wc1980	Oct.	15	Bucharest	1	2
wc1981	April	29	Wembley	0	0
wc1985	May	1	Bucharest	0	0
wc1985	Sept.	11	Wembley	1	1

ENGLAND v. SCOTLAND

				Eng	Scot
1872	Nov.	30	Glasgow	0	0
1873	Mar.	8	Kennington Oval	4	2
1874	Mar.	7	Glasgow	1	2
1875	Mar.	6	Kennington Oval	2	2
1876	Mar.	4	Glasgow	0	3
1877	Mar.	3	Kennington Oval	1	3
1878	Mar.	2	Glasgow	2	7
1879	April	5	Kennington Oval	5	4
1880	Mar.	13	Glasgow	4	5
1881	Mar.	12	Kennington Oval	1	6
1882	Mar.	11	Glasgow	1	5
1883	Mar.	10	Sheffield	2	3
1884	Mar.	15	Glasgow	0	1
1885	Mar.	21	Kennington Oval	1	1

ENGLAND v. SCOTLAND *(contd)*

				Goals	
Year	Date		Venue	Eng	Scot
1886	Mar.	31	Glasgow	1	1
1887	Mar.	19	Blackburn	2	3
1888	Mar.	17	Glasgow	5	0
1889	April	13	Kennington Oval	2	3
1890	April	5	Glasgow	1	1
1891	April	6	Blackburn	2	1
1892	April	2	Glasgow	4	1
1893	April	1	Richmond	5	2
1894	April	7	Glasgow	2	2
1895	April	6	Everton	3	0
1896	April	4	Glasgow	1	2
1897	April	3	Crystal Palace	1	2
1898	April	2	Glasgow	3	1
1899	April	8	Birmingham	2	1
1900	April	7	Glasgow	1	4
1901	Mar.	30	Crystal Palace	2	2
1902	Mar.	3	Birmingham	2	2
1903	April	4	Sheffield	1	2
1904	April	9	Glasgow	1	0
1905	April	1	Crystal Palace	1	0
1906	April	7	Glasgow	1	2
1907	April	6	Newcastle	1	1
1908	April	4	Glasgow	1	1
1909	April	3	Crystal Palace	2	0
1910	April	2	Glasgow	0	2
1911	April	1	Everton	1	1
1912	Mar.	23	Glasgow	1	1
1913	April	5	Chelsea	1	0
1914	April	14	Glasgow	1	3
1920	April	10	Sheffield	5	4
1921	April	9	Glasgow	0	3
1922	April	8	Aston Villa	0	1
1923	April	14	Glasgow	2	2
1924	April	12	Wembley	1	1
1925	April	4	Glasgow	0	2
1926	April	17	Manchester	0	1
1927	April	2	Glasgow	2	1
1928	Mar.	31	Wembley	1	5
1929	April	13	Glasgow	0	1
1930	April	5	Wembley	5	2
1931	Mar.	28	Glasgow	0	2
1932	April	9	Wembley	3	0
1933	April	1	Glasgow	1	2
1934	April	14	Wembley	3	0
1935	April	6	Glasgow	0	2
1936	April	4	Wembley	1	1
1937	April	17	Glasgow	1	3
1938	April	9	Wembley	0	1
1939	April	15	Glasgow	2	1
1947	April	12	Wembley	1	1
1948	April	10	Glasgow	2	0
1949	April	9	Wembley	1	3
wc1950	April	15	Glasgow	1	0
1951	April	14	Wembley	2	3
1952	April	5	Glasgow	2	1
1953	April	18	Wembley	2	2
wc1954	April	3	Glasgow	4	2
1955	April	2	Wembley	7	2
1956	April	14	Glasgow	1	1
1957	April	6	Wembley	2	1
1958	April	19	Glasgow	4	0
1959	April	11	Wembley	1	0
1960	April	9	Glasgow	1	1
1961	April	15	Wembley	9	3
1962	April	14	Glasgow	0	2
1963	April	6	Wembley	1	2
1964	April	11	Glasgow	0	1
1965	April	10	Wembley	2	2
1966	April	2	Glasgow	4	3
EC1967	April	15	Wembley	2	3
EC1968	Feb.	24	Glasgow	1	1
1969	May	10	Wembley	4	1
1970	April	25	Glasgow	0	0
1971	May	22	Wembley	3	1
1972	May	27	Glasgow	1	0
SFAC1973	Feb.	14	Glasgow	5	0
1973	May	19	Wembley	1	0

ENGLAND v. SCOTLAND *(contd)*

Year	Date		Venue	Eng	Scot
1974	May	18	Glasgow.................	0	2
1975	May	24	Wembley	5	1
1976	May	15	Glasgow.................	1	2
1977	June	4	Wembley	1	2
1978	May	20	Glasgow.................	1	0
1979	May	26	Wembley	3	1
1980	May	24	Glasgow.................	2	0
1981	May	23	Wembley	0	1
1982	May	29	Glasgow.................	1	0
1983	June	1	Wembley	2	0
1984	May	26	Glasgow.................	1	1
RC1985	May	25	Glasgow.................	0	1
RC1986	April	23	Wembley	2	1
RC1987	May	23	Glasgow.................	0	0
RC1988	May	21	Wembley	1	0

ENGLAND v. SPAIN

Year	Date		Venue	Eng	Spain
1929	May	15	Madrid	3	4
1931	Dec.	9	Highbury	7	1
WC1950	July	2	Rio de Janeiro.........	0	1
1955	May	18	Madrid	1	1
1955	Nov.	30	Wembley	4	1
1960	May	15	Madrid	0	3
1960	Oct.	26	Wembley	4	2
1965	Dec.	8	Madrid	2	0
1967	May	24	Wembley	2	0
EC1968	April	3	Wembley	1	0
EC1968	May	8	Madrid	2	1
1980	Mar.	26	Barcelona	2	0
EC1980	June	18	Naples	2	1
1981	Mar.	25	Wembley	1	2
WC1982	July	5	Madrid	0	0
1987	Feb.	18	Madrid	4	2

ENGLAND v. SWEDEN

Year	Date		Venue	Eng	Swe
1923	May	21	Stockholm..............	4	2
1923	May	24	Stockholm..............	3	1
1937	May	17	Stockholm..............	4	0
1947	Nov.	19	Highbury	4	2
1949	May	13	Stockholm..............	1	3
1956	May	16	Stockholm..............	0	0
1959	Oct.	28	Wembley	2	3
1965	May	16	Gothenburg............	2	1
1968	May	22	Wembley	3	1
1979	June	10	Stockholm..............	0	0
1986	Sept.	10	Stockholm..............	0	1

ENGLAND v. SWITZERLAND

Year	Date		Venue	Eng	Swit
1933	May	29	Berne	4	0
1938	May	21	Zurich	1	2
1947	May	18	Zurich	0	1
1948	Dec.	2	Highbury	6	0
1952	May	28	Zurich	3	0
WC1954	June	20	Berne	2	0
1962	May	9	Wembley	3	1
1963	June	5	Basle.....................	8	1
EC1971	Oct.	13	Basle.....................	3	2
EC1971	Nov.	10	Wembley	1	1
1975	Sept.	3	Basle.....................	2	1
1977	Sept.	7	Wembley	0	0
WC1980	Nov.	19	Wembley	2	1
WC1981	May	30	Basle.....................	1	2
1988	May	28	Lausanne	1	0

ENGLAND v. TURKEY

Year	Date		Venue	Eng	Turk
WC1984	Nov.	14	Istanbul	8	0
WC1985	Oct.	16	Wembley	5	0
EC1987	Apr.	29	Izmir.....................	0	0
EC1987	Oct.	14	Wembley	8	0

ENGLAND v. U.S.A.

Year	Date		Venue	Eng	USA
WC1950	June	20	Belo Horizonte	0	1
1953	June	8	New York	6	3
1959	May	28	Los Angeles............	8	1
1964	May	27	New York	10	0
1985	June	16	Los Angeles............	5	0

ENGLAND v. U.S.S.R.

Year	Date		Venue	Eng	USSR
1958	May	18	Moscow	1	1
WC1958	June	8	Gothenburg............	2	2
WC1958	June	17	Gothenburg............	0	1
1958	Oct.	22	Wembley	5	0
1967	Dec.	6	Wembley	2	2
EC1968	June	8	Rome	2	0
1973	June	10	Moscow	2	1
1984	June	2	Wembley	0	2
1986	Mar.	26	Tbilisi	1	0
EC1988	June	18	Frankfurt	1	3

ENGLAND v. URUGUAY

Year	Date		Venue	Eng	Uru
1953	May	31	Montevideo............	1	2
WC1954	June	26	Basle.....................	2	4
1964	May	6	Wembley	2	1
WC1966	July	11	Wembley	0	0
1969	June	8	Montevideo............	2	1
1977	June	15	Montevideo	0	0
1984	June	13	Montevideo	0	2

ENGLAND v. WALES

Year	Date		Venue	Eng	Wales
1879	Jan.	18	Kennington Oval	2	1
1880	Mar.	15	Wrexham	3	2
1881	Feb.	26	Blackburn	0	1
1882	Mar.	13	Wrexham	3	5
1883	Feb.	3	Kennington Oval	5	0
1884	Mar.	17	Wrexham	4	0
1885	Mar.	14	Blackburn	1	1
1886	Mar.	29	Wrexham	3	1
1887	Feb.	26	Kennington Oval	4	0
1888	Feb.	4	Crewe	5	1
1889	Feb.	23	Stoke	4	1
1890	Mar.	15	Wrexham	3	1
1891	Mar.	7	Sunderland..............	4	1
1892	Mar.	5	Wrexham	2	0
1893	Mar.	13	Stoke	6	0
1894	Mar.	12	Wrexham	5	1
1895	Mar.	18	Queen's Club, Kensington	1	1
1896	Mar.	16	Cardiff...................	9	1
1897	Mar.	29	Sheffield	4	0
1898	Mar.	28	Wrexham	3	0
1899	Mar.	20	Bristol	4	0
1900	Mar.	26	Cardiff...................	1	1
1901	Mar.	18	Newcastle	6	0
1902	Mar.	3	Wrexham	0	0
1903	Mar.	2	Portsmouth	2	1
1904	Feb.	29	Wrexham	2	2
1905	Mar.	27	Liverpool	3	1
1906	Mar.	19	Cardiff...................	1	0
1907	Mar.	18	Fulham	1	1
1908	Mar.	16	Wrexham	7	1
1909	Mar.	15	Nottingham	2	0
1910	Mar.	14	Cardiff...................	1	0
1911	Mar.	13	Millwall	3	0
1912	Mar.	11	Wrexham	2	0
1913	Mar.	17	Bristol	4	3
1914	Mar.	16	Cardiff...................	2	0
1920	Mar.	15	Highbury	1	2
1921	Mar.	14	Cardiff...................	0	0
1922	Mar.	13	Liverpool	1	0
1923	Mar.	5	Cardiff...................	2	2
1924	Mar.	3	Blackburn	1	2
1925	Feb.	28	Swansea.................	2	1
1926	Mar.	1	Crystal Palace	1	3

ENGLAND v. WALES *(contd)*

Year	Date		Venue	Eng	Wales
1927	Feb.	12	Wrexham	3	3
1927	Nov.	28	Burnley	1	2
1928	Nov.	17	Swansea	3	2
1929	Nov.	20	Chelsea	6	0
1930	Nov.	22	Wrexham	4	0
1931	Nov.	18	Liverpool	3	1
1932	Nov.	16	Wrexham	0	0
1933	Nov.	15	Newcastle	1	2
1934	Sept.	29	Cardiff	4	0
1936	Feb.	5	Wolverhampton	1	2
1936	Oct.	17	Cardiff	1	2
1937	Nov.	17	Middlesborough	2	1
1938	Oct.	22	Cardiff	2	4
1946	Nov.	13	Manchester	3	0
1947	Oct.	18	Cardiff	3	0
1948	Nov.	10	Aston Villa	1	0
wc1949	Oct.	15	Cardiff	4	1
1950	Nov.	15	Sunderland	4	2
1951	Oct.	20	Cardiff	1	1
1952	Nov.	12	Wembley	5	2
wc1953	Oct.	10	Cardiff	4	1
1954	Nov.	10	Wembley	3	2
1955	Oct.	22	Cardiff	1	2
1956	Nov.	14	Wembley	3	1
1957	Oct.	19	Cardiff	4	0
1958	Nov.	26	Aston Villa	2	2
1959	Oct.	17	Cardiff	1	1
1960	Nov.	23	Wembley	5	1
1961	Oct.	14	Cardiff	1	1
1962	Nov.	21	Wembley	4	0
1963	Oct.	12	Cardiff	4	0
1964	Nov.	18	Wembley	2	1
1965	Oct.	2	Cardiff	0	0
EC1966	Nov.	16	Wembley	5	1
EC1967	Oct.	21	Cardiff	3	0
1969	May	7	Wembley	2	1

ENGLAND v. WALES *(contd)*

Year	Date		Venue	Eng	Wales
1970	April	18	Cardiff	1	1
1971	May	19	Wembley	0	0
1972	May	20	Cardiff	3	0
wc1972	Nov.	15	Cardiff	1	0
wc1973	Jan.	24	Wembley	1	1
1973	May	15	Wembley	3	0
1974	May	11	Cardiff	2	0
1975	May	21	Wembley	2	2
FAWC1976	Mar.	24	Wrexham	2	1
1976	May	8	Cardiff	1	0
1977	May	31	Wembley	0	1
1978	May	13	Cardiff	3	1
1979	May	23	Wembley	0	0
1980	May	17	Wrexham	1	4
1981	May	20	Wembley	0	0
1982	April	27	Cardiff	1	0
1983	Feb.	23	Wembley	2	1
1984	May	2	Wrexham	0	1

ENGLAND v. YUGOSLAVIA

Year	Date		Venue	Eng	Yugo
1939	May	18	Belgrade	1	2
1950	Nov.	22	Highbury	2	2
1954	May	16	Belgrade	0	1
1956	Nov.	28	Wembley	3	0
1958	May	11	Belgrade	0	5
1960	May	11	Wembley	3	3
1965	May	9	Belgrade	1	1
1966	May	4	Wembley	2	0
EC1968	June	5	Florence	0	1
1972	Oct.	11	Wembley	1	1
1974	June	5	Belgrade	2	2
EC1986	Nov.	12	Wembley	2	0
EC1987	Nov.	11	Belgrade	4	1

"We'll be back"

says Bobby Robson

The day we lost to the Soviet Union in Frankfurt was one of the saddest of my life, and I don't mind admitting that our third European Championship defeat in a row left me feeling even more depressed than those earlier international losses against Wales, the Soviet Union at Wembley or Portugal in the Mexico World Cup. I didn't need reminding that this was the first time in any major finals that England had been beaten in all their matches. It has gone down in the record books now and it is something that the players and I will always have to live with.

I am the manager and it is my job to pick the team, decide on the way we play, motivate the players and make sure the preparations are right. But when the players walk onto the pitch, it is now in their hands and it is very much "their turn". Football has always been about players and it is players who win or lose matches in the end. But the responsibility for winning or losing, in football at least, tends to lie with the manager.

My squad in Germany was the best I have ever had, stronger than in Mexico two years ago, although we were always going to miss Terry Butcher at the heart of the defence. That is why I can hardly believe how badly things went for us. Several players didn't make the impression in the finals that we believed they would. Some appeared to be physically and mentally drained after a long season of chasing honours at home. But next season they will be back as good as ever. So will England.

I cannot honestly think of any player who should have been brought in for the Championship. We have a crop of good youngsters coming through the Under-21s at the moment – Cottee, Davis, Walker, Rocastle, Thomas of Arsenal, Gascoigne and Clough for example – but I do believe that a high-profile tournament like the European Championship would have been too much for them to handle. They are still young boys, after all, and we have got to rebuild the team gradually – not throw all these players in at the deep end.

We are due to take our first step towards the 1990 World Cup when we play Sweden, one of the best teams in Europe at the present time, at Wembley on 19th October. They didn't feature in the European finals, having finished second to Italy in their qualifying group, but they were very impressive when I saw them beat the Soviet Union to win the four-nation tournament in Berlin at Easter.

Our match with the Swedes at Wembley is absolutely vital. This is a match we cannot lose, otherwise qualification for the World Cup becomes difficult right away. It is up to me to decide which players to let go and which ones to keep. I will be loyal to those players who deserve it and, as always, will have to make decisions for the benefit of the country.

F.A. Charity Shield Winners 1908–87

Year	Winners	Runners-up	Score
1908	Manchester United	Queen's Park Rangers	4-0 after 1-1 draw
1909	Newcastle United	Northampton Town	2-0
1910	Brighton and Hove Albion	Aston Villa	1-0
1911	Manchester United	Swindon Town	8-4
1912	Blackburn Rovers	Queen's Park Rangers	2-1
1913	Professionals	Amateurs	7-2
1920	West Bromwich Albion	Tottenham Hotspur	2-0
1921	Tottenham Hotspur	Burnley	2-0
1922	Huddersfield Town	Liverpool	1-0
1923	Professionals	Amateurs	2-0
1924	Professionals	Amateurs	3-1
1925	Amateurs	Professionals	6-1
1926	Amateurs	Professionals	6-3
1927	Cardiff City	Corinthians	2-1
1928	Everton	Blackburn Rovers	2-1
1929	Professionals	Amateurs	3-0
1930	Arsenal	Sheffield Wednesday	2-1
1931	Arsenal	West Bromwich Albion	1-0
1932	Everton	Newcastle United	5-3
1933	Arsenal	Everton	3-0
1934	Arsenal	Manchester City	4-0
1935	Sheffield Wednesday	Arsenal	1-0
1936	Sunderland	Arsenal	2-1
1937	Manchester City	Sunderland	2-0
1938	Arsenal	Preston North End	2-1
1948	Arsenal	Manchester United	4-3
1949	Portsmouth	Wolverhampton Wanderers	1-1*
1950	World Cup Team	Canadian Touring Team	4-2
1951	Tottenham Hotspur	Newcastle United	2-1
1952	Manchester United	Newcastle United	4-2
1953	Arsenal	Blackpool	3-1
1954	Wolverhampton Wanderers	West Bromwich Albion	4-4*
1955	Chelsea	Newcastle United	3-0
1956	Manchester United	Manchester City	1-0
1957	Manchester United	Aston Villa	4-0
1958	Bolton Wanderers	Wolverhampton Wanderers	4-1
1959	Wolverhampton Wanderers	Nottingham Forest	3-1
1960	Burnley	Wolverhampton Wanderers	2-2*
1961	Tottenham Hotspur	F.A. XI	3-2
1962	Tottenham Hotspur	Ipswich Town	5-1
1963	Everton	Manchester United	4-0
1964	Liverpool	West Ham United	2-2*
1965	Manchester United	Liverpool	2-2*
1966	Liverpool	Everton	1-0
1967	Manchester United	Tottenham Hotspur	3-3*
1968	Manchester City	West Bromwich Albion	6-1
1969	Leeds United	Manchester City	2-1
1970	Everton	Chelsea	2-1
1971	Leicester City	Liverpool	1-0
1972	Manchester City	Aston Villa	1-0
1973	Burnley	Manchester City	1-0
1974	Liverpool	Leeds United	1-1†
1975	Derby County	West Ham United	2-0
1976	Liverpool	Southampton	1-0
1977	Liverpool	Manchester United	0-0*
1978	Nottingham Forest	Ipswich Town	5-0
1979	Liverpool	Arsenal	3-1
1980	Liverpool	West Ham United	1-0
1981	Aston Villa	Tottenham Hotspur	2-2*
1982	Liverpool	Tottenham Hotspur	1-0
1983	Manchester United	Liverpool	2-0
1984	Everton	Liverpool	1-0
1985	Everton	Manchester United	2-0
1986	Everton	Liverpool	1-1*
1987	Everton	Coventry City	1-0

* Each Club retained Shield for six months
† Liverpool won 6-5 on penalty-kicks

General Motors – F.A. Charity Shield 1987

Everton 1 Coventry City 0

The annual Charity Shield curtain-raiser to the season was played slightly earlier than usual, on 1st August, to accommodate the Football League's Centenary fixture against a Rest of the World XI a week later at the same stadium. As usual, Wembley was bathed in warm sunshine as the League champions, Everton, narrowly beat the previous season's romantic F.A. Cup winners, Coventry City, to win the Shield outright for the third time in four years.

Everton's strength in their Championship-winning season had been the quality of their "squad players" who had come into the side to replace injured stars. They had used 23 players in pursuit of a deserved title and now, at Wembley, they showed that the loss of five top players through injury – Southall, Stevens, Van den Hauwe, Bracewell and Snodin – was barely a handicap.

Some had thought that Coventry, back at Wembley for the second time in four months after a 104-year wait prior to that, would be hungrier to win the Shield and establish themselves as a "top club". The Cup holders did give a creditable account of themselves, but Everton's experience was decisive and their victory deserved.

It was Wayne Clarke, a £250,000 buy from Birmingham City in March, who scored the winning goal in the 43rd minute; 15 years ago brother Allan scored the Leeds winner in the F.A. Cup Final. A right-wing cross from the underestimated Harper eluded Peake and Clarke, loitering at the far post, swivelled to rifle the ball past Ogrizovic from 10 yards.

The Shield was presented at the finish by Eric Fountain, Director of Public Affairs at Vauxhall Motors.

Everton: Mimms, Harper, Power, Ratcliffe, Watson, Reid, Steven, Clarke, Sharp, Heath, Sheedy (Pointon).

Coventry City: Ogrizovic, Phillips, Downs, McGrath (Sedgley), Kilcline, Peake, Bennett, Gynn (Borrows), Speedie, Houchen, Pickering.

Referee: Lewis (Gt. Bookham).

Attendance: 88,000

81

F.A. Challenge Cup Winners 1872-1988

1872 & 1874-92	Kennington Oval
1873	Lillie Bridge
1893	Fallowfield, Manchester
1894	Everton
1895-1914	Crystal Palace
1915	Old Trafford, Manchester
1920-22	Stamford Bridge
1923 to date	Wembley

Year	Winners	Runners-up	Score
1872	Wanderers	Royal Engineers	1-0
1873	Wanderers	Oxford University	2-0
1874	Oxford University	Royal Engineers	2-0
1875	Royal Engineers	Old Etonians	2-0 after 1-1 draw
1876	Wanderers	Old Etonians	3-0 after 0-0 draw
1877	Wanderers	Oxford University	2-0 after extra time
1878	*Wanderers	Royal Engineers	3-1
1879	Old Etonians	Clapham Rovers	1-0
1880	Clapham Rovers	Oxford University	1-0
1881	Old Carthusians	Old Etonians	3-0
1882	Old Etonians	Blackburn Rovers	1-0
1883	Blackburn Olympic	Old Etonians	2-1 after extra time
1884	Blackburn Rovers	Queen's Park, Glasgow	2-1
1885	Blackburn Rovers	Queen's Park, Glasgow	2-0
1886	†Blackburn Rovers	West Bromwich Albion	2-0 after 0-0 draw
1887	Aston Villa	West Bromwich Albion	2-0
1888	West Bromwich Albion	Preston North End	2-1
1889	Preston North End	Wolverhampton Wanderers	3-0
1890	Blackburn Rovers	Sheffield Wednesday	6-1
1891	Blackburn Rovers	Notts. County	3-1
1892	West Bromwich Albion	Aston Villa	3-0
1893	Wolverhampton Wanderers	Everton	1-0
1894	Notts. County	Bolton Wanderers	4-1
1895	Aston Villa	West Bromwich Albion	1-0
1896	Sheffield Wednesday	Wolverhampton Wanderers	2-1
1897	Aston Villa	Everton	3-2
1898	Nottingham Forest	Derby County	3-1
1899	Sheffield United	Derby County	4-1
1900	Bury	Southampton	4-0
1901	Tottenham Hotspur	Sheffield United	3-1 after 2-2 draw
1902	Sheffield United	Southampton	2-1 after 1-1 draw
1903	Bury	Derby County	6-0
1904	Manchester City	Bolton Wanderers	1-0
1905	Aston Villa	Newcastle United	2-0
1906	Everton	Newcastle United	1-0
1907	Sheffield Wednesday	Everton	2-1
1908	Wolverhampton Wanderers	Newcastle United	3-1
1909	Manchester United	Bristol City	1-0
1910	Newcastle United	Barnsley	2-0 after 1-1 draw
1911	Bradford City	Newcastle United	1-0 after 0-0 draw
1912	Barnsley	West Bromwich Albion	1-0 after 0-0 draw
1913	Aston Villa	Sunderland	1-0
1914	Burnley	Liverpool	1-0
1915	Sheffield United	Chelsea	3-0
1920	Aston Villa	Huddersfield Town	1-0 after extra time
1921	Tottenham Hotspur	Wolverhampton Wanderers	1-0
1922	Huddersfield Town	Preston North End	1-0
1923	Bolton Wanderers	West Ham United	2-0
1924	Newcastle United	Aston Villa	2-0
1925	Sheffield United	Cardiff City	1-0
1926	Bolton Wanderers	Manchester City	1-0
1927	Cardiff City	Arsenal	1-0
1928	Blackburn Rovers	Huddersfield Town	3-1
1929	Bolton Wanderers	Portsmouth	2-0
1930	Arsenal	Huddersfield Town	2-0
1931	West Bromwich Albion	Birmingham	2-1
1932	Newcastle United	Arsenal	2-1
1933	Everton	Manchester City	3-0
1934	Manchester City	Portsmouth	2-1
1935	Sheffield Wednesday	West Bromwich Albion	4-2
1936	Arsenal	Sheffield United	1-0
1937	Sunderland	Preston North End	3-1
1938	Preston North End	Huddersfield Town	1-0 after extra time
1939	Portsmouth	Wolverhampton Wanderers	4-1
1946	Derby County	Charlton Athletic	4-1 after extra time
1947	Charlton Athletic	Burnley	1-0 after extra time
1948	Manchester United	Blackpool	4-2

Year	Winners	Runners-up	Score
1949	Wolverhampton Wanderers	Leicester City	3-1
1950	Arsenal	Liverpool	2-0
1951	Newcastle United	Blackpool	2-0
1952	Newcastle United	Arsenal	1-0
1953	Blackpool	Bolton Wanderers	4-3
1954	West Bromwich Albion	Preston North End	3-2
1955	Newcastle United	Manchester City	3-1
1956	Manchester City	Birmingham City	3-1
1957	Aston Villa	Manchester United	2-1
1958	Bolton Wanderers	Manchester United	2-0
1959	Nottingham Forest	Luton Town	2-1
1960	Wolverhampton Wanderers	Blackburn Rovers	3-0
1961	Tottenham Hotspur	Leicester City	2-0
1962	Tottenham Hotspur	Burnley	3-1
1963	Manchester United	Leicester City	3-1
1964	West Ham United	Preston North End	3-2
1965	Liverpool	Leeds United	2-1 after extra time
1966	Everton	Sheffield Wednesday	3-2
1967	Tottenham Hotspur	Chelsea	2-1
1968	West Bromwich Albion	Everton	1-0 after extra time
1969	Manchester City	Leicester City	1-0
1970	Chelsea	Leeds United	2-1 after 2-2 draw both games extra time
1971	Arsenal	Liverpool	2-1 after extra time
1972	Leeds United	Arsenal	1-0
1973	Sunderland	Leeds United	1-0
1974	Liverpool	Newcastle United	3-0
1975	West Ham United	Fulham	2-0
1976	Southampton	Manchester United	1-0
1977	Manchester United	Liverpool	2-1
1978	Ipswich Town	Arsenal	1-0
1979	Arsenal	Manchester United	3-2
1980	West Ham United	Arsenal	1-0
1981	Tottenham Hotspur	Manchester City	3-2 after 1-1 draw after extra time
1982	Tottenham Hotspur	Queen's Park Rangers	1-0 after 1-1 draw after extra time
1983	Manchester United	Brighton & Hove Albion	4-0 after 2-2 draw after extra time
1984	Everton	Watford	2-0
1985	Manchester United	Everton	1-0 after extra time
1986	Liverpool	Everton	3-1
1987	Coventry City	Tottenham Hotspur	3-2 after extra time
1988	Wimbledon	Liverpool	1-0

* Won outright, but restored to the Association
† A special trophy was awarded for third consecutive win

Wimbledon – F.A. Cup Winners.

F.A. Challenge Cup – Final Tie 1988

Wimbledon 1   Liverpool 0

Outsiders at 33-1 before the third round in January, Wimbledon turned the form book upside down to beat Liverpool, recently crowned League champions and one of the hottest favourites for years, in the 107th Challenge Cup Final before a shirt-sleeved 98,000 crowd in the Stadium and about 250 million television viewers worldwide.

It proved to be a day for unlikely heroes, and Wimbledon, a non-League club 11 years ago and playing in the Fourth Division just *five* years ago, had two outstanding performers in goalkeeper Dave Beasant and midfielder Lawrie Sanchez. Beasant, 6'4", was responsible for two F.A. Cup Final "firsts" as he became the first goalkeeper to receive the Cup (on this occasion from H.R.H. The Princess of Wales) and the first to save a penalty-kick at Wembley. In

fact no one had missed anywhere since Wallace for Sunderland in 1913.

Wimbledon had lived dangerously at times, but their luck looked to have run out in the 61st minute, when referee Hill pointed dramatically to the spot after John Aldridge had gone down as Goodyear came sliding in to deny the Liverpool striker a shooting opportunity. Beasant and his defence were adamant that the man had played the ball, but the controversy subsided after Beasant had brilliantly turned Aldridge's spot-kick round his left-hand post.

It was Aldridge's first failure in 12 penalties, and as he was substituted almost immediately, he must have looked back in frustration at another incident, in the first half, when Beasant had foiled him with a spec-tacular one-handed save from point-blank range. As the ball looped into

John Fashanu has both Steve Nicol and the linesman beaten for pace.

It's there! Lawrie Sanchez (second from left) has scored the goal that won the Cup for Wimbledon.

the air with the giant goalkeeper lying on his back on the goal-line, an upright John Barnes seemed certain to score, but somehow Beasant stretched up to palm the ball sideways for Jones to hack it away for a corner.

Liverpool felt mighty aggrieved in the 35th minute, when Peter Beardsley broke away from Thorn's illegal tackle on the edge of the penalty-area and proceeded to coolly chip the ball over Beasant's dive and gently into the net, only to be called back and given a meaningless free-kick instead. Within two minutes Wimbledon had got the vital goal that ultimately won the Cup for this unfashionable team from a quiet London suburb.

Full-back Terry Phelan was jostled by Nicol near to the corner flag out on the left, and when Dennis Wise's right-footer from the free-kick curled in towards the near post, Lawrie Sanchez – born in London with a father from Ecuador and an Irish mother – scored with a simple glancing header into the far corner. It was his first F.A. Cup goal and only his fifth all season.

Wimbledon might have snatched a second goal just before the interval, but Terry Gibson's left-foot shot from a difficult angle cleared the bar after the leaping Grobbelaar had allowed the ball to drop behind him. Liverpool, in the quest for a second "double" in three years, moved purposefully forward throughout the seond half, but only in rare moments did Beardsley and Barnes look like producing something to save the day.

Wimbledon: Beasant, Goodyear, Phelan, Jones, Young, Thorn, Gibson (Scales), Cork (Cunningham), Fashanu, Sanchez, Wise.

Liverpool: Grobbelaar, Gillespie, Ablett, Nicol, Spackman (Molby), Hansen, Beardsley, Aldridge (Johnston), Houghton, Barnes, McMahon.

Referee: Hill (Kettering).
Attendance: 98,203
Receipts: £1,422,814

F.A. Challenge Cup Competition 1987-88

Preliminary Round	Result				Attendance			
Saturday 29th August 1987	*1st Tie*	*1st Rep*	*2nd Rep*	*3rd Rep*	*1st Tie*	*1st Rep*	*2nd Rep*	*3rd Rep*
Clitheroe *v* Bridlington Trinity	4-0				212			
Harrogate Town *v* Esh Winning	2-1				258			
Seaham Red Star *v* Shildon	2-0				109			
Ossett Albion *v* Chester-le-Street Town...........	1-1				123			
Chester-le-Street Town *v* Ossett Albion...........		2-1				205		
Alnwick Town *v* Durham City	1-1				67			
Durham City *v* Alnwick Town		1-1				82		
Alnwick Town *v* Durham City			0-0				82	
Durham City *v* Alnwick Town				1-2				104
Bridlington Town *v* Accrington Stanley	1-0				148			
Ferryhill Athletic *v* Langley Park Welfare	3-0				30			
Annfield Plain *v* West Auckland Town	0-4				48			
Crook Town *v* Bedlington Terriers	2-1				59			
Penrith Town *v* Horden CW.........................	7-0				105			
Evenwood Town *v* Leyland Motors	0-2				37			
Ashington *v* Guiseley	3-1				87			
Lancaster City *v* Darwen	0-4				89			
Norton & Stockton Ancients *v* Farsley Celtic	4-5				44			
Shotton Comrades *v* Garforth Town	2-1				90			
Rossendale United *v* Northallerton Town	3-0				295			
Guisborough Town *v* Armthorpe Welfare	2-0				226			
Peterlee Newtown *v* Denaby United	1-3				101			
Burscough *v* Warrington Town	1-2				69			
Droylsden *v* Belper Town............................	4-2				214			
St Helens Town *v* Curzon Ashton	6-2				73			
Stalybridge Celtic *v* Congleton Town	2-0				314			
Glossop *v* Heanor Town..............................	2-3				170			
Ashton United *v* Kirkby Town......................	2-0				168			
Alfreton Town *v* Formby.............................	3-0				171			
Radcliffe Borough *v* Skelmersdale United........	1-0				144			
Colwyn Bay *v* Winsford United.....................	3-0				262			
Long Eaton United *v* Sutton Town	1-3				103			
Brigg Town *v* Oakham United	4-0				45			
Leek Town *v* GKN Sankey	3-3				180			
GKN Sankey *v* Leek Town		2-3				80		
Holbeach United *v* Walsall-Wood	1-4				72			
Moor Green *v* Tividale...............................	3-1				227			
Arnold *v* Hednesford Town	1-0				305			
Wisbech Town *v* Brackley Town	1-0				412			
Tamworth *v* Gresley Rovers........................	3-2				717			
Grantham *v* Chatteris Town.........................	2-2				462			
Chatteris Town *v* Grantham........................		1-0				279		
Wednesfield Social *v* Hinckley Athletic............	0-1				89			
Oldswinford *v* Racing Club Warwick..............	0-1				18			
Wolverton Town *v* Ashtree Highfield..............	0-2				128			
Wellingborough Town *v* Spalding United	3-2				66			
Baker Perkins *v* Rushall Olympic	2-2				105			
Rushall Olympic *v* Baker Perkins		3-0				170		
Hinckley Town *v* Bridgnorth Town.................	2-1				67			
Highgate United *v* Bilston Town	1-1				30			
Bilston Town *v* Highgate United		0-0				120		
Bilston Town *v* Highgate United			2-0					108
Northampton Spencer *v* Atherstone United......	2-5				120			
Chasetown *v* Evesham United	0-2				189			
Dudley Town *v* Rothwell Town.....................	1-1				107			
Rothwell Town *v* Dudley Town.....................		2-1				115		
Chalfont St Peter *v* Arlesey Town..................	1-1				79			
Arlesey Town *v* Chalfont St Peter..................		1-0				51		
Stamford *v* Vauxhall Motors	0-0				115			
Vauxhall Motors *v* Stamford		3-2				70		

Coventry Sporting v Barton Rovers	2-1		39		
Wootton Blue Cross v Berkhamsted Town	0-0		80		
Berkhamsted Town v Wootton Blue Cross		2-0		75	
Soham Town Rangers v Hemel Hempstead	0-0		78		
Hemel Hempstead v Soham Town Rangers		1-0		88	
Banbury United v Edgware	3-0		174		
Tiptree United v Aveley	0-4		76		
Gorleston v Chesham United	1-0		113		
Bourne Town v Milton Keynes Borough	1-4		71		
Uxbridge v Haringey Borough	2-2		104		
Haringey Borough v Uxbridge		2-3		75	
Baldock Town v Hampton	1-0		211		
Great Yarmouth Town v Tilbury	0-0		214		
Tilbury v Great Yarmouth Town		0-2		164	
Tring Town v Harlow Town	0-2		154		
Lowestoft Town v Kingsbury Town	0-1		192		
Felixstowe Town v Walthamstow Avenue	1-2		87		
Hoddesdon Town v Southall	2-0		40		
Watton United v Royston Town	0-1		85		
Newmarket Town v Dunstable	0-3		82		
Staines Town v Ware	0-0		129		
Ware v Staines Town		1-1		72	
Ware v Staines Town			4-2		144
Hertford Town v Potton United	1-1		65		
Potton United v Hertford Town		1-2		188	
Sudbury Town v Hounslow	1-1		280		
Hounslow v Sudbury Town		1-3		160	
Corinthian-Casuals v Camberley Town	1-1		16		
Camberley Town v Corinthian-Casuals		2-0		64	
Finchley v Kempston Rovers	1-0		50		
Basildon United v Cray Wanderers	1-3		117		
Feltham v Alma Swanley	5-0		28		
Darenth Heathside v Leatherhead	2-1		121		
Chatham Town v Collier Row	4-1		86		
Heybridge Swifts v Dorking	1-1		112		
Dorking v Heybridge Swifts		2-1		154	
Erith & Belvedere v Wivenhoe Town	0-0		125		
Wivenhoe Town v Erith & Belvedere		4-2		200	
Hornchurch v Horsham YMCA	7-0		76		
Flackwell Heath v Crockenhill	0-3		75		
Three Bridges v Gravesend & Northfleet	0-0		256		
Gravesend & Northfleet v Three Bridges		2-1		295	
Witham Town v Burgess Hill Town	1-0		321		
Rainham Town v Sittingbourne	1-1		43		
Sittingbourne v Rainham Town		2-3		180	
Petersfield United v Wick	1-1		125		
Wick v Petersfield United		4-3		131	
Thatcham Town v Worthing	0-3		100		
Maidenhead United v Tunbridge Wells	1-1		135		
Tunbridge Wells v Maidenhead United		4-3		116	
Sheppey United v Metropolitan Police	1-3		155		
Epsom & Ewell v Arundel	4-0		95		
Faversham Town v Shoreham	1-1		78		
Shoreham v Faversham Town		2-0		119	
Horsham v Whitehawk	0-0		121		
Whitehawk v Horsham		2-0		174	
Thanet United v Canterbury City	3-0		241		
Beckenham Town v Hailsham United	2-2		97		
Hailsham United v Beckenham Town		2-4		60	
Ringmer v Eastbourne United	1-5		113		
Tonbridge AFC v Folkestone	5-2		302		
Hastings Town v Lancing	0-1		283		
Bracknell Town v Peacehaven & Telscombe	1-0		76		
Egham Town v Portfield	1-1		78		
Portfield v Egham Town		1-3		47	
Haywards Heath v Steyning Town	4-0		84		
Melksham Town v Andover	2-0		120		
Abingdon United v Oxford City	1-1		275		
Oxford City v Abingdon United		3-0		327	

	Result				Attendance			
	1st Tie	1st Rep	2nd Rep	3rd Rep	1st Tie	1st Rep	2nd Rep	3rd Rep
Shortwood United v Waterlooville	1-6				124			
Frome Town v Poole Town	1-0				217			
Newbury Town v Welton Rovers	2-2				100			
Welton Rovers v Newbury Town		2-4				80		
Eastleigh v Swanage Town & Herston	1-1				72			
Swanage Town & Herston v Eastleigh		3-1				127		
Gloucester City v Westbury United	7-0				489			
Bridgend Town v Weston-super-Mare	1-3				75			
Hungerford Town v Yate Town	1-1				144			
Yate Town v Hungerford Town		1-0				165		
Salisbury v Barry Town	0-1				251			
Devizes Town v Paulton Rovers	0-0				82			
Paulton Rovers v Devizes Town		1-0				119		
Llanelli v Barnstaple Town	1-2				113			
Torrington v Glastonbury	3-0				120			
Taunton Town v Clandown	2-0				182			
Ottery St Mary v Chippenham Town	1-0				87			
St Blazey v Tiverton Town	4-4				122			
Tiverton Town v St Blazey		5-2				181		

First Round Qualifying

Saturday 12th September 1987

	Result				Attendance			
	1st Tie	1st Rep	2nd Rep	3rd Rep	1st Tie	1st Rep	2nd Rep	3rd Rep
Clitheroe v Whitley Bay	2-0				251			
Murton v Seaham Red Star	0-1				63			
Bishop Auckland v Workington	5-2				269			
Willington v Harrogate Town	0-3				111			
Chester-le-Street Town v Consett	2-1				103			
Billingham Town v Bridlington Town	0-3				50			
Blyth Spartans v Gateshead	2-1				730			
Billingham Synthonia v Alnwick Town	2-0				62			
Ferryhill Athletic v Gretna	1-2				53			
Netherfield v Crook Town	1-1				123			
Crook Town v Netherfield		2-1				126		
North Shields v Barrow	1-1				208			
Barrow v North Shields		3-0				485		
Fleetwood Town v West Auckland Town	3-2				194			
Penrith v Brandon United	2-1				117			
Ryhope CA v Ashington	1-1				24			
Ashington v Ryhope CA		1-2				124		
Newcastle Blue Star v Morecambe	1-0				177			
Easington Collieries v Leyland Motors	2-1				47			
Darwen v Tow Law Town	2-2				177			
Tow Law Town v Darwen		3-2				184		
Darlington CB v Shotton Comrades	2-0				96			
South Bank v Spennymoor United	1-0				155			
Wren Rovers v Farsley Celtic	1-2				75			
Rossendale United v Worksop Town	1-1				722			
Worksop Town v Rossendale United		2-4				382		
Stockton v Denaby United	1-0				44			
Emley v Southport	2-0				408			
Thackley v Guisborough Town	1-1				151			
Guisborough Town v Thackley		0-0				353		
Guisborough Town v Thackley			1-0				550	
Warrington Town v Northwich Victoria	1-1				415			
Northwich Victoria v Warrington Town		5-1				645		
Ilkeston Town v St Helens Town	1-1				106			
St Helens Town v Ilkeston Town		1-1				92		
Ilkeston Town v St Helens Town			1-4				44	
Horwich RMI v South Liverpool	1-1				192			
South Liverpool v Horwich RMI		3-4				170		
North Ferriby United v Droyslden	2-3				95			
Stalybridge Celtic v Macclesfield Town	1-1				750			
Macclesfield Town v Stalybridge Celtic		5-1				920		
Bootle v Ashton United	1-0				70			

88

Bangor City v Marine	2-2		350	
Marine v Bangor City		3-1		240
Chadderton v Heanor Town	1-0		30	
Alfreton Town v Witton Albion	4-2		198	
Prescot Cables v Colwyn Bay	0-1		86	
Buxton v Rhyl	6-3		240	
Irlam Town v Radcliffe Borough	1-0		88	
Sutton Town v Goole Town	1-2		128	
Eastwood Hanley v Leek Town	0-0		302	
Leek Town v Eatwood Hanley		2-0		689
Hyde United v Mossley	1-0		402	
Mile Oak Rovers & Youth v Brigg Town	1-2		106	
Walsall-Wood v Stafford Rangers	0-3		454	
Eastwood Town v Arnold	1-2		133	
Matlock Town v Gainsborough Trinity	3-3		330	
Gainsborough Trinity v Matlock Town		0-3		396
Halesowen Harriers v Moor Green	1-1		129	
Moor Green v Halesowen Harriers		2-1		316
Wisbech Town v Kettering Town	2-0		748	
Boldmere St Michaels v Chatteris Town	2-2		38	
Chatteris Town v Boldmere St Michaels		0-3		227
Shepshed Charterhouse v Stourbridge	2-0		233	
Paget Rangers v Tamworth	1-4		384	
Hinckley Athletic v Bedworth United	2-3		299	
Halesown Town v Ashtree Highfield	1-1		833	
Ashtree Highfield v Halesowen Town		0-1		596
Wellingborough Town v Leicester United	1-1		84	
Leicester United v Wellingborough Town		1-0		259
Desborough Town v Racing Club Warwick	2-2		77	
Racing Club Warwick v Desborough Town		4-0		103
Rushall Olympic v Oldbury United	0-2		74	
Friar Lane OB v Bilston Town	2-2		102	
Bilston Town v Friar Lane OB		3-2		151
Willenhall Town v Bromsgrove Rovers	3-2		248	
Sutton Coldfield Town v Hinckley Town	1-1		158	
Hinckley Town v Sutton Coldfield Town		2-1		89
Atherstone United v Malvern Town	1-1		301	
Malvern Town v Atherstone United		0-2		125
Rushden Town v Rothwell Town	1-4		128	
Alvechurch v Redditch United	1-1		434	
Redditch United v Alvechurch		1-3		475
Lye Town v Evesham United	1-0		142	
Arlesey Town v Buckingham Town	0-4		80	
Leamington v Coventry Sporting	2-1		189	
Corby Town v Worcester City	1-1		224	
Worcester City v Corby Town		3-1		1023
Boreham Wood v Vauxhall Motors	2-0		87	
Berkhamsted Town v Hitchin Town	3-1		161	
Irthlingborough Diamonds v Banbury United	3-1		98	
Witney Town v Barnet	0-3		442	
Ely City v Hemel Hempstead	1-1		54	
Hemel Hempstead v Ely City		2-1		124
Aveley v Bury Town	2-2		133	
Bury Town v Aveley		3-1		499
Haverhill Rovers v Milton Keynes Borough	1-1		89	
Milton Keynes Borough v Haverhill Rovers		0-4		74
Kings Lynn v March Town United	1-2		650	
Letchworth GC v Gorleston	1-0		79	
Uxbridge v Barking	4-1		147	
Clapton v Great Yarmouth Town	1-2		61	
Cambridge City v Harwich & Parkeston	2-0		300	
Canvey Island v Baldock Town	0-1		127	
Harlow Town v Woodford Town	1-0		46	
Histon v Walthamstow Avenue	2-1		100	
Leytonstone Ilford v St Albans City	2-0		170	
Billericay Town v Kingsbury Town	0-3		222	
Hoddesdon Town v Wembley	1-3		100	
Stowmarket Town v Dunstable	1-3		185	
Leyton-Wingate v Stevenage Borough	1-1		152	

Stevenage Borough v Leyton-Wingate	2-3		306
Ruislip Manor v Royston Town.....................	3-2	59	
Ware v Hendon..	0-1	185	
Braintree Town v Sudbury Town...................	0-4	353	
Aylesbury Athletic v Wycombe Wanderers	2-0	1530	
Grays Athletic v Hertford Town....................	1-3	155	
Camberley Town v Welling United	0-2	114	
Burnham v Cray Wanderers.........................	1-1	150	
Cray Wanderers v Burnham.........................	1-2		80
Harrow Borough v Yeading	2-0	412	
Walton & Hersham v Finchley	3-0	84	
Feltham v Hayes	1-3	128	
Crawley Town v Chatham Town	1-3	365	
Dorking v Fisher Athletic	0-2	210	
Rayners Lane v Darenth Heathside	1-2	58	
Wivenhoe Town v Sutton United	0-3	439	
Harefield United v Crockenhill.....................	3-1	80	
Bromley v Ashford Town	5-2	359	
Redhill v Hornchurch................................	3-3	102	
Hornchurch v Redhill.................................	1-3		149
Gravesend & Northfleet v Herne Bay	6-1	306	
Saffron Walden Town v Rainham Town...........	2-1	89	
Carshalton Athletic v Kingstonian.................	1-0	185	
Malden Vale v Witham Town	1-3	70	
Wick v Tooting & Mitcham United	1-1	156	
Tooting & Mitcham United v Wick	3-0		167
Marlow v Tunbridge Wells...........................	5-1	127	
Basingstoke Town v Dulwich Hamlet	3-0	415	
Pagham v Worthing	2-2	243	
Worthing v Pagham	0-2		431
Metropolitan Police v Dover Athletic.............	3-1	88	
Ramsgate v Shoreham	2-0	184	
Southwick v Croydon	1-3	115	
Molesey v Epsom & Ewell	1-2	62	
Whitehawk v Littlehampton Town	1-2	82	
Banstead Athletic v Beckenham Town	5-3	25	
Windsor & Eton v Woking...........................	0-0	360	
Woking v Windsor & Eton	6-3		394
Merstham v Thanet United	1-3	70	
Eastbourne United v Hythe Town	6-2	69	
Whyteleafe v Lancing................................	2-0	93	
Wokingham Town v Lewes..........................	3-0	314	
Horndean v Tonbridge AFC	0-2	82	
Bracknell Town v Abingdon Town	3-2	55	
Chertsey Town v Haywards Heath..................	3-1	105	
Newport IOW v AFC Totton.........................	2-0	138	
Chichester City v Egham Town	1-1	42	
Egham Town v Chichester City......................	0-2		110
Melksham Town v Wimborne Town	1-3	110	
Havant Town v Waterlooville........................	0-2	282	
Gosport Borough v Yeovil Town....................	0-1	387	
Calne Town v Oxford City	1-5	87	
Frome Town v Weymouth	2-2	410	
Weymouth v Frome Town	3-0		1567
Sholing Sports v Swanage Town & Herston.......	1-3	66	
Fareham Town v Trowbridge Town	1-0	129	
Radstock Town v Newbury Town	5-0	90	
Gloucester City v Ton Pentre	1-2	470	
Mangotsfield United v Yate Town	1-0	257	
Cheltenham Town v Dorchester Town	4-1	856	
Bristol Manor Farm v Weston-super-Mare	0-3	109	
Barry Town v Clevedon Town	5-1	175	
Minehead v Barnstaple Town	1-1	175	
Barnstaple Town v Minehead........................	1-0		182
Torrington v Forest Green Rovers..................	0-3	90	
Merthyr Tydfil v Paulton Rovers	2-0	1069	
Taunton Town v Saltash United	0-3	194	
Maesteg Park v Tiverton Town	0-1	63	

	Result				Attendance			
	1st Tie	1st Rep	2nd Rep	3rd Rep	1st Tie	1st Rep	2nd Rep	3rd Rep
Bideford v Exmouth Town	1-1				248			
Exmouth Town v Bideford		0-2				236		
Sharpness v Ottery St Mary	1-4				60			

Second Round Qualifying

Saturday 26th September 1987

	Result				Attendance			
	1st Tie	1st Rep	2nd Rep	3rd Rep	1st Tie	1st Rep	2nd Rep	3rd Rep
Clitheroe v Harrogate Town	0-0				377			
Harrogate Town v Clitheroe		2-1				603		
Seaham Red Star v Bishop Auckland	0-1				233			
Chester-le-Street Town v Billingham Synthonia	1-1				92			
Billingham Synthonia v Chester-le-Street Town		4-3				122		
Bridlington Town v Blyth Spartans	1-2				250			
Gretna v Fleetwood Town	1-2				87			
Crook Town v Barrow	0-1				112			
Penrith v Easington Collieries	1-2				142			
Ryhope CA v Newcastle Blue Star	0-2				98			
Tow Law Town v Farsley Celtic	2-1				161			
Darlington CB v South Bank	2-1				64			
Rossendale United v Guisborough Town	2-3				377			
Stockton v Emley	0-1				174			
Northwich Victoria v Droylsden	2-1				512			
St Helens Town v Horwich RMI	0-0				156			
Horwich RMI v St Helens Town		2-3				307		
Macclesfield Town v Chadderton	5-0				759			
Bootle v Marine	2-2				300			
Marine v Bootle		1-0				528		
Alfreton Town v Irlam Town	2-0				164			
Colwyn Bay v Buxton	2-2				382			
Buxton v Colwyn Bay		2-5				731		
Goole Town v Brigg Town	1-3				228			
Leek Town v Hyde United	2-1				409			
Stafford Rangers v Moor Green	2-3				845			
Arnold v Matlock Town	2-3				385			
Wisbech Town v Tamworth	2-3				792			
Boldmere St Michaels v Shepshed Charterhouse	1-2				136			
Bedworth United v Racing Club Warwick	1-2				209			
Halesowen Town v Leicester United	5-1				1068			
Oldbury Town v Hinckley Town	5-2				97			
Bilston Town v Willenhall Town	0-3				232			
Atherstone United v Lye Town	1-0				303			
Rothwell Town v Alvechurch	1-2				125			
Buckingham Town v Boreham Wood	0-0				136			
Boreham Wood v Buckingham Town		2-1				120		
Leamington v Worcester City	0-6				432			
Berkhamsted Town v Hemel Hempstead	3-3				173			
Hemel Hempstead v Berkhamsted Town		1-4				425		
Irthlingborough Diamonds v Barnet	0-4				642			
Bury Town v Letchworth GC	1-1				363			
Letchworth GC v Bury Town		3-1				170		
Haverhill Rovers v March Town United	0-1				135			
Uxbridge v Baldock Town	1-0				165			
Great Yarmouth Town v Cambridge City	3-1				187			
Harlow Town v Kingsbury Town	1-1				77			
Kingsbury Town v Harlow Town		2-2				135		
Kingsbury Town v Harlow Town			3-2				73	
Histon v Leytonstone Ilford	1-2				130			
Wembley v Ruislip Manor	1-1				119			
Ruislip Manor v Wembley		0-5				252		
Dunstable v Leyton-Wingate	0-1				101			
Hendon v Hertford Town	1-2				194			
Sudbury Town v Aylesbury United	1-1				626			
Aylesbury United v Sudbury Town		2-1				826		
Welling United v Walton & Hersham	2-1				612			
Burnham v Harrow Borough	2-1				144			

Match	Result 1st Tie	1st Rep	Att 1st Tie	Att 1st Rep
Hayes v Darenth Heathside	4-1		173	
Chatham Town v Fisher Athletic	0-3		181	
Sutton United v Redhill	3-1		559	
Harefield United v Bromley	2-3		110	
Gravesend & Northfleet v Witham Town	1-0		401	
Saffron Walden Town v Carshalton Athletic	1-5		126	
Tooting & Mitcham United v Pagham	0-0		192	
Pagham v Tooting & Mitcham United		3-4		510
Marlow v Basingstoke Town	1-1		270	
Basingstoke Town v Marlow		2-1		440
Metropolitan Police v Epsom & Ewell	3-0		104	
Ramsgate v Croydon	0-1		284	
Littlehampton Town v Thanet United	0-3		150	
Banstead Athletic v Woking	0-0		133	
Woking v Banstead Athletic		1-0		356
Eastbourne United v Tonbridge AFC	0-0		190	
Tonbridge AFC v Eastbourne United		3-1		384
Whyteleafe v Wokingham Town	3-3		176	
Wokingham Town v Whyteleafe		1-0		344
Bracknell Town v Chichester City	4-0		65	
Chertsey Town v Newport IOW	0-1		110	
Wimborne Town v Oxford City	2-1		151	
Waterlooville v Yeovil Town	1-1		278	
Yeovil Town v Waterlooville		3-2		1459
Weymouth v Radstock Town	3-0		1181	
Swanage Town & Herston v Fareham Town	0-2		186	
Ton Pentre v Weston-super-Mare	1-2		484	
Mangotsfield United v Cheltenham Town	1-1		703	
Cheltenham Town v Mangotsfield United		2-0		1334
Barry Town v Merthyr Tydfil	0-1		1389	
Barnstaple Town v Forest Green Rovers	1-2		218	
Saltash United v Ottery St Mary	7-1		134	
Tiverton Town v Bideford	4-2		232	

Third Round Qualifying	Result				Attendance			
Saturday 10th October 1987	1st Tie	1st Rep	2nd Rep	3rd Rep	1st Tie	1st Rep	2nd Rep	3rd Rep
Harrogate Town v Bishop Auckland	1-1				705			
Bishop Auckland v Harrogate Town		2-0				672		
Billingham Synthonia v Blyth Spartans	5-2				278			
Fleetwood Town v Barrow	0-0				882			
Barrow v Fleetwood Town		3-2				974		
Easington Collieries v Newcastle Blue Star	3-0				103			
Tow Law Town v Darlington CB	4-0				161			
Guisborough Town v Emley	3-2				408			
Northwich Victoria v St Helens Town	3-2				544			
Macclesfield Town v Marine	0-0				805			
Marine v Macclesfield Town		1-2				502		
Alfreton Town v Colwyn Bay	1-1				185			
Colwyn Bay v Alfreton Town		1-0				452		
Brigg Town v Leek Town	3-2				100			
Moor Green v Matlock Town	3-2				412			
Tamworth v Shepshed Charterhouse	3-2				819			
Racing Club Warwick v Halesowen Town	1-3				817			
Oldbury United v Willenhall Town	0-1				252			
Atherstone United v Alvechurch	4-3				401			
Boreham Wood v Worcester City	1-3				239			
Berkhamsted v Barnet	0-3				1163			
Letchworth GC v March Town United	2-2				196			
March Town United v Letchworth GC		2-3				380		
Uxbridge v Great Yarmouth Town	0-2				227			
Kingsbury Town v Leytonstone Ilford	0-1				120			
Wembley v Leyton-Wingate	2-2				125			
Leyton-Wingate v Wembley		5-1				204		
Hertford Town v Aylesbury United	0-4				454			
Welling United v Burnham	3-1				640			

	Result				Attendance			
Hayes v Fisher Athletic	2-0				331			
Sutton United v Bromley	0-0				697			
Bromley v Sutton United		1-2				897		
Gravesend & Northfleet v Carshalton Athletic	2-6				363			
Tooting & Mitcham United v Basingstoke Town	0-0				294			
Basingstoke Town v Tooting & Mitcham United		4-1				542		
Metropolitan Police v Croydon	0-1				109			
Thanet United v Woking	1-1				483			
Woking v Thanet United		0-2				367		
Tonbridge AFC v Wokingham Town	0-0				293			
Wokingham Town v Tonbridge AFC		2-1				488		
Bracknell Town v Newport IOW	4-1				101			
Wimborne Town v Yeovil Town	0-4				805			
Weymouth v Fareham Town	2-2				1475			
Fareham Town v Weymouth		1-2				455		
Weston-super-Mare v Cheltenham Town	1-2				692			
Merthyr Tydfil v Forest Green Rovers	3-1				1603			
Saltash United v Tiverton Town	3-0				233			

Fourth Round Qualifying   Result   Attendance

Saturday 24th October 1987

	1st Tie	1st Rep	2nd Rep	3rd Rep	1st Tie	1st Rep	2nd Rep	3rd Rep
Macclesfield Town v Whitby Town	3-1				946			
Colwyn Bay v Tow Law Town	2-1				703			
Northwich Victoria v Easington Collieries	3-0				687			
Caernarfon Town v Billingham Synthonia	0-2				424			
Guisborough Town v Bishop Auckland	1-2				956			
Runcorn v Barrow	2-1				1005			
Chorley v Frickley Athletic	2-0				670			
Brigg Town v Lincoln City	1-4				2023			
Leyton-Wingate v Atherstone United	0-0				282			
Atherstone United v Leyton-Wingate		4-2				1070		
Letchworth GC v Chelmsford City	0-1				663			
Boston United v Welling United	1-1				1345			
Welling United v Boston United		3-2				1070		
Great Yarmouth Town v Dagenham	0-2				993			
VS Rugby v Nuneaton Borough	3-0				1105			
Willenhall Town v Barnet	0-6				490			
Enfield v Aylesbury United	1-2				1065			
Hayes v Moor Green	2-0				531			
Halesowen Town v Bishops Stortford	1-0				1608			
Leytonstone Ilford v Worcester City	0-1				331			
Tamworth v Wealdstone	2-0				2078			
Carshalton Athletic v Wokingham Town	2-1				370			
Sutton United v Basingstoke Town	3-0				840			
Merthyr Tydfil v Croydon	3-0				2130			
Farnborough Town v Saltash United	4-2				513			
Bath City v Slough Town	3-1				821			
Thanet United v Bognor Regis Town	0-4				934			
Cheltenham Town v Bracknell Town	2-1				1304			
Weymouth v Yeovil Town	1-3				3522			
Maidstone United v Dartford	2-0				1308			

First Round Proper   Result   Attendance

Saturday 14th November 1987

	1st Tie	1st Rep	2nd Rep	3rd Rep	1st Tie	1st Rep	2nd Rep	3rd Rep
Lincoln City v Crewe Alexandra	2-1				4002			
Scunthorpe United v Bury	3-1				3151			
Burnley v Bolton Wanderers	0-1				10788			
Doncaster Rovers v Rotherham United	1-1				3359			
Rotherham United v Doncaster Rovers		2-0				4525		
Northwich Victoria v Colwyn Bay	1-0				1520			
Notts County v Chesterfield	3-3				4850			

Match	Result		Attendance	
Chesterfield v Nots County	0-1			4482
Sunderland v Darlington	2-0		16892	
Scarborough v Grimsby Town	1-2		3864	
York City v Burton Albion	0-0		3140	
Burton Albion v York City		1-2		4381
Chester City v Runcorn	0-1		3533	
Rochdale v Wrexham	0-2		1831	
Altrincham v Wigan Athletic	0-2		4057	
Billingham Synthonia v Halifax Town (at Hartlepool United FC)	2-4		1153	
Bishop Auckland v Blackpool	1-4		2462	
Macclesfield Town v Carlisle United	4-2		2671	
Telford United v Stockport County	1-1		2758	
Stockport County v Telford United		2-0		3083
Preston North End v Mansfield Town	1-1		7415	
Mansfield Town v Preston North End		4-2		4682
Chorley v Hartlepool United	0-2		2462	
Tranmere Rovers v Port Vale	2-2		4035	
Port Vale v Tranmere Rovers		3-1		4097
Bristol Rovers v Merthyr Tydfil	6-0		4635	
Bognor Regis Town v Torquay United	0-3		2539	
Gillingham v Fulham	2-1		4444	
Sutton United v Aldershot	3-0		3451	
Cambridge United v Farnborough Town	2-1		2200	
Welling United v Carshalton Athletic	3-2		2237	
Worcester City v Yeovil Town	1-1		3080	
Yeovil Town v Worcester City		1-0		3913
Northampton Town v Newport County	2-1		4581	
Colchester United v Tamworth	3-0		3215	
VS Rugby v Atherstone United	0-0		1511	
Atherstone United v VS Rugby		0-2		2816
Leyton Orient v Exeter City	2-0		3787	
Peterborough United v Cardiff City	2-1		4342	
Hayes v Swansea City	0-1		2553	
Dagenham v Maidstone United	0-2		1137	
Wolverhampton Wanderers v Cheltenham T.	5-1		10541	
Chelmsford City v Bath City	1-2		1721	
Barnet v Hereford United	0-0		2754	
Halesowen Town v Kidderminster Harriers	2-2		2932	
Kidderminster Harriers v Halesowen Town		4-0		4011
Southend United v Walsall	0-0		3035	
Walsall v Southend United		2-1		5162
Bristol City v Aylesbury United	1-0		8263	
Brentford v Brighton & Hove Albion	0-2		6358	

Second Round Proper

Saturday 5th December 1987	Result				Attendance			
	1st Tie	1st Rep	2nd Rep	3rd Rep	1st Tie	1st Rep	2nd Rep	3rd Rep
Macclesfield Town v Rotherham United	4-0				4500			
Wrexham v Bolton Wanderers	1-2				4703			
Runcorn v Stockport County	0-1				3012			
Grimsby Town v Halifax Town	0-0				3239			
Halifax Town v Grimsby Town		2-0				2633		
Northwich Victoria v Blackpool	0-2				2528			
Mansfield Town v Lincoln City	4-3				5671			
Wigan Athletic v Wolverhampton Wanderers	1-3				5879			
Port Vale v Notts County	2-0				5039			
Scunthorpe United v Sunderland	2-1				7178			
York City v Hartlepool United	1-1				3455			
Hartlepool United v York City		3-1				4057		
Bristol City v Torquay United	0-1				9027			
Maidstone United v Kidderminster Harriers	1-1				1657			
Kidderminster Harriers v Maidstone United		2-2				3018		
Kidderminster Harriers v Maidstone United			0-0				3008	
Maidstone United v Kidderminster Harriers				2-1				2052
Gillingham v Walsall	2-1				4915			
Northampton Town v Brighton & Hove Albion	1-2				6444			

Cambridge United *v* Yeovil Town	0-1				2588			
Leyton Orient *v* Swansea City	2-0				4668			
Peterborough United *v* Sutton United	1-3				4723			
VS Rugby *v* Bristol Rovers	1-1				3168			
Bristol Rovers *v* VS Rugby		4-0				2846		
Colchester United *v* Hereford United	3-2				2221			
Welling United *v* Bath City	0-1				2332			

Third Round Proper	Result				Attendance			
Saturday 9th January 1988	*1st Tie*	*1st Rep*	*2nd Rep*	*3rd Rep*	*1st Tie*	*1st Rep*	*2nd Rep*	*3rd Rep*
West Ham United *v* Charlton Athletic	2-0				22043			
Leeds United *v* Aston Villa	1-2				29124			
Gillingham *v* Birmingham City	0-3				9266			
Scunthorpe United *v* Blackpool	0-0				6217			
Blackpool *v* Scunthorpe United		1-0				6127		
Bradford City *v* Wolverhampton Wanderers	2-1				13334			
Barnsley *v* Bolton Wanderers	3-1				9667			
Sutton United *v* Middlesbrough	1-1				5955			
Middlesbrough *v* Sutton United		1-0				17932		
Shrewsbury Town *v* Bristol Rovers	2-1				6551			
Newcastle United *v* Crystal Palace	1-0				20415			
Mansfield Town *v* Bath City	4-0				5086			
Yeovil Town *v* Queens Park Rangers	0-3				9717			
Coventry City *v* Torquay United	2-0				16967			
Sheffield Wednesday *v* Everton	1-1				33304			
Everton *v* Sheffield Wednesday		1-1				32976		
Everton *v* Sheffield Wednesday			1-1				37520	
Sheffield Wednesday *v* Everton				0-5				38953
Huddersfield Town *v* Manchester City	2-2				18102			
Manchester City *v* Huddersfield Town		0-0				24565		
Huddersfield Town *v* Manchester City			0-3				21510	
Arsenal *v* Millwall	2-0				42082			
Derby County *v* Chelsea	1-3				18864			
Wimbledon *v* West Bromwich Albion	4-1				7253			
Reading *v* Southampton	0-1				11319			
Stoke City *v* Liverpool	0-0				31979			
Liverpool *v* Stoke City		1-0				39147		
Hartlepool United *v* Luton Town	1-2				6127			
Ipswich Town *v* Manchester United	1-2				23126			
Port Vale *v* Macclesfield Town	1-0				10808			
Sheffield United *v* Maidstone United	1-0				8907			
Watford *v* Hull City	1-1				12761			
Hull City *v* Watford		2-2				13681		
Watford *v* Hull City			1-0				15261	
Plymouth Argyle *v* Colchester United	2-0				10351			
Blackburn Rovers *v* Portsmouth	1-2				10352			
Halifax Town *v* Nottingham Forest	0-4				4013			
Oldham Athletic *v* Tottenham Hotspur	2-4				16931			
Brighton & Hove Albion *v* AFC Bournemouth	2-0				14372			
Swindon Town *v* Norwich City	0-0				12807			
Norwich City *v* Swindon Town		0-2				12682		
Stockport County *v* Leyton Orient	1-2				4410			
Oxford United *v* Leicester City	2-0				7557			

Fourth Round Proper	Result				Attendance			
Saturday 30th January 1988	*1st Tie*	*1st Rep*	*2nd Rep*	*3rd Rep*	*1st Tie*	*1st Rep*	*2nd Rep*	*3rd Rep*
Coventry City *v* Watford	0-1				22366			
Luton Town *v* Southampton	2-1				10009			
Portsmouth *v* Sheffield United	2-1				13388			
Barnsley *v* Birmingham City	0-2				13219			
Everton *v* Middlesbrough	1-1				36504			

	1st Tie	1st Rep	2nd Rep	3rd Rep	1st Tie	1st Rep	2nd Rep	3rd Rep
Middlesbrough v Everton	2-2				25235			
Everton v Middlesbrough		2-1				32272		
Bradford City v Oxford United	4-2				13653			
Plymouth Argyle v Shrewsbury Town	1-0				12749			
Newcastle United v Swindon Town	5-0				28737			
Port Vale v Tottenham Hotspur	2-1				20045			
Aston Villa v Liverpool	0-2				46324			
Leyton Orient v Nottingham Forest	1-2				19212			
Queens Park Rangers v West Ham United	3-1				23651			
Mansfield Town v Wimbledon	1-2				10892			
Blackpool v Manchester City	1-1				10992			
Manchester City v Blackpool		2-1				26503		
Manchester United v Chelsea	2-0				50962			
Brighton & Hove Albion v Arsenal	1-2				26420			

Fifth Round Proper	Result				Attendance			
Saturday 20th February 1988	1st Tie	1st Rep	2nd Rep	3rd Rep	1st Tie	1st Rep	2nd Rep	3rd Rep
Queens Park Rangers v Luton Town	1-1				15856			
Luton Town v Queens Park Rangers		1-0				10854		
Newcastle United v Wimbledon	1-3				28880			
Port Vale v Watford	0-0				22483			
Watford v Port Vale		2-0				18539		
Portsmouth v Bradford City	3-0				19324			
Arsenal v Manchester United	2-1				54163			
Everton v Liverpool	0-1				47205			
Manchester City v Plymouth Argyle	3-1				29663			
Birmingham City v Nottingham Forest	0-1				34494			

Sixth Round Proper	Result				Attendance			
Saturday 12th March 1988	1st Tie	1st Rep	2nd Rep	3rd Rep	1st Tie	1st Rep	2nd Rep	3rd Rep
Arsenal v Nottingham Forest	1-2				50083			
Wimbledon v Watford	2-1				12326			
Manchester City v Liverpool	0-4				44047			
Luton Town v Portsmouth	3-1				12857			

Semi-Final

Saturday 9th April 1988

Wimbledon v Luton Town 2-1   25963
at Tottenham Hotspur FC

Nottingham Forest v Liverpool 1-2   51627
at Sheffield Wednesday FC

Final

Saturday 14th May 1988

Wimbledon v Liverpool 1-0   98203
at Wembley Stadium

Steve Ogrizoric fists clear from Dave Watson during the Shield match. (*Bob Thomas*)

Wayne Clarke is on target to win the Shield for Everton. (*Bob Thomas*)

Imagine...

...a company that designs, builds and sells complex, sophisticated products, and does it from scratch

Case in point: AC's advanced Mass Airflow Sensor. Just two years from concept to finished product. Each unit virtually custom-made, with lasers making individual adjustments on each and every assembly. The Mass Airflow Sensor is only one example of AC's Advanced Systems capability. With its extensive engineering resources, AC can and does handle the total job.

Design components that exceed existing technology for worldwide systems applications.

Build components that meet world-class production standards, possible only with state-of-the-art manufacturing processes in plants around the world.

Sell components that significantly improve performance and reliability, and which only the most stringent testing and quality standards can assure.

The AC Advanced System approach. The world seems to agree it's the only way to go. And that's not just our imagination.

In a league of its own.

Glenn Hoddle slides in to dispossess Vanenburg. (*Bob Thomas*)

Frank Rijkaard attempts to intercept Beardsley's pass to Lineker. (*Bob Thomas*)

Gary Stevens leaps to clear, watched by Rats of U.S.S.R. (*Bob Thomas*)

OUTSTANDING PROSPECT. QUICK OFF THE MARK. GOOD AT PASSING. REASONABLE TRANSFER FEE.

VAUXHALL. ONCE DRIVEN, FOREVER SMITTEN.

Wimbledon's Vinny Jones (right) with Liverpool's John Aldridge and Nigel Spackman.

Liverpool's Steve McMahon in possession, shadowed by Jones.

F.A. Challenge Cup Competition 1988-89

Exemptions

44 Clubs to the Third Round Proper

Arsenal
Aston Villa
Barnsley
Birmingham City
Blackburn Rovers
AFC Bournemouth
Bradford City
Brighton & Hove Albion
Charlton Athletic
Chelsea
Coventry City
Crystal Palace
Derby County
Everton
Hull City

Ipswich Town
Leeds United
Leicester City
Liverpool
Luton Town
Manchester City
Manchester United
Middlesbrough
Millwall
Newcastle United
Norwich City
Nottingham Forest
Oldham Athletic
Oxford United
Plymouth Argyle

Portsmouth
Queen's Park Rangers
Sheffield Wednesday
Shrewsbury Town
Southampton
Stoke City
Sunderland
Swindon Town
Tottenham Hotspur
Walsall
Watford
West Bromwich Albion
West Ham United
Wimbledon

52 Clubs to the First Round Proper

Aldershot
Bath City*
Blackpool
Bolton Wanderers
Brentford
Bristol City
Bristol Rovers
Burnley
Bury
Cambridge United
Cardiff City
Carlisle United
Chester City
Chesterfield
Colchester United
Crewe Alexandra
Darlington
Doncaster Rovers

Enfield†
Exeter City
Fulham
Gillingham
Grimsby Town
Halifax Town
Hartlepool United
Hereford United
Huddersfield Town
Leyton Orient
Lincoln City
Maidstone United*
Mansfield Town
Northampton Town
Notts County
Peterborough United
Port Vale
Preston North End

Reading
Rochdale
Rotherham United
Scarborough
Scunthorpe United
Sheffield United
Southend United
Stockport County
Swansea City
Telford United†
Torquay United
Tranmere Rovers
Wigan Athletic
Wolverhampton Wanderers
Wrexham
York City

20 Clubs to the Fourth Round Qualifying

Altrincham
Aylesbury United
Bognor Regis Town
Burton Albion
Caernarfon Town
Chelmsford City
Chorley

Dagenham
Farnborough Town
Halesowen Town
Kidderminster Harriers
Macclesfield Town
Newport County
Runcorn

Slough Town
Sutton United
V.S. Rugby
Welling United
Whitby Town
Yeovil Town

† Trophy Finalists
* Two Clubs outside the Football League considered most appropriate

F.A. Cup Final Dates
1872-1988

Year	Date	Year	Date	Year	Date
1872	16th March	1908	25th April	1954	1st May
1873	29th March	1909	26th April	1955	7th May
1874	14th March	1910	23rd (28th) April	1956	5th May
1875	13th (16th) March	1911	22nd (26th) April	1957	4th May
1876	11th (18th) March	1912	20th (24th) April	1958	3rd May
1877	24th March	1913	19th April	1959	2nd May
1878	23rd March	1914	25th April	1960	7th May
1879	29th March	1915	24th April	1961	6th May
1880	10th April	1920	24th April	1962	5th May
1881	9th April	1921	23rd April	1963	25th May
1882	25th March	1922	29th April	1964	2nd May
1883	31st March	1923	28th April	1965	1st May
1884	29th March	1924	26th April	1966	14th May
1885	4th April	1925	25th April	1967	20th May
1886	3rd (10th) April	1926	24th April	1968	18th May
1887	2nd April	1927	23rd April	1969	26th April
1888	24th March	1928	21st April	1970	11th (29th) April
1889	30th March	1929	27th April	1971	8th May
1890	29th March	1930	26th April	1972	6th May
1891	25th March	1931	25th April	1973	5th May
1892	19th March	1932	23rd April	1974	4th May
1893	26th March	1933	29th April	1975	3rd May
1894	31st March	1934	28th April	1976	1st May
1895	20th April	1935	27th April	1977	21st May
1896	18th April	1936	25th April	1978	6th May
1897	10th April	1937	1st May	1979	12th May
1898	16th April	1938	30th April	1980	10th May
1899	15th April	1939	29th April	1981	9th (14th) May
1900	21st April	1946	27th April	1982	22nd (27th) May
1901	20th (27th) April	1947	26th April	1983	21st (26th) May
1902	19th (26th) April	1948	24th April	1984	19th May
1903	18th April	1949	30th April	1985	18th May
1904	23rd April	1950	29th April	1986	10th May
1905	15th April	1951	28th April	1987	16th May
1906	21st April	1952	3rd May	1988	14th May
1907	20th April	1953	2nd May		

Replay dates in brackets

F.A. Challenge Trophy – Final Tie 1988

Enfield 3   Telford United 2
(after a 0-0 draw)

Having suffered two heavy defeats by their Wembley opponents Telford in the GM Vauxhall Conference, Enfield had more reason to feel satisfied with a 0-0 draw in the original match (the third Trophy Final draw in the last five years), but they would have been disappointed that they failed to capitalise on their superiority in the first hour.

That they failed to do so was in large measure due to the excellence of Kevin Charlton in the Telford goal and the central defensive partnership of Steve Nelson and Trevor Storton. The fact that two hours' play had produced no goals had not been a reflection of a lack of commitment to attack, and with both teams playing incisive, flowing football, it was only heroics in both defences which kept the scoresheet blank.

The match had been sporting in the extreme, and the player's spontaneous reaction to climb the Royal Box steps together at the finish to be presented to the chief guest, Gordon Banks, typified the spirit in which it had been played.

The replay, played five days later on the ground of West Bromwich Albion FC, produced another match of fast, attacking football, this time on a saturated surface. It also produced a Trophy winner in Enfield, who had just finished the season seven Conference places behind beaten Telford.

Telford lost Mayman, injured early on, but substitute Cunningham made an immediate contribution by creating Telford's opening goal for Steve Biggins after 14 minutes. Enfield, not in the least dispirited, equalised nine minutes later when Dave Howell's header from Keen's free-kick drifted beyond Charlton's considerable reach.

Enfield took a fortunate lead just before half-time, when Paul Furlong's centre deceived Charlton and dropped over the line, and Telford then countered with a series of attacks which produced several near-misses until a Steve Norris penalty, awarded for hands, levelled the scores on 76 minutes.

But Enfield were not to be denied, and with eight minutes left of a match again contested at a punishing pace, Steve King – the only survivor from the team which had won the Trophy in 1982 – centred from the left and Furlong was on hand to notch the winner.

Enfield: Pape, Cooper, Sparrow (Hayzelden), Howell, Keen, Francis, Lewis (Edmonds), Cottington, Furlong, Harding, King.

Telford United: Charlton, McGinty, Wiggins, Mayman, Nelson, Storton, Joseph, Biggins, Norris, Sankey, Stringer (Griffiths).

Edmonds substituted for Keen (Enfield) in the replay.

Cunningham substituted for Mayman and was himself substituted by Hancock, and Griffiths replaced Stringer (Telford) in the replay.

Referee: Dilkes (Mossley).

Attendances: 20,161 and 6,916

Enfield's Nicky Francis tries a shot at Wembley with Telford's Wiggins out of tackling range.

Enfield's match-winner in the replay, Paul Furlong, finds the going tougher at Wembley.

F.A. Challenge Trophy Competition 1987-88

First Round Qualifying	Result				Attendance			
Saturday 3rd October 1987	*1st Tie*	*1st Rep*	*2nd Rep*	*3rd Rep*	*1st Tie*	*1st Rep*	*2nd Rep*	*3rd Rep*
Alfreton Town *v* Gretna	1-1				202			
Gretna *v* Alfreton Town		2-4				112		
Goole Town *v* Mossley	0-4				221			
Workington *v* Brandon United	0-3				191			
Crook Town *v* Shildon	2-0				122			
Horwich RMI *v* South Liverpool	1-2				173			
Ferryhill Athletic *v* North Shields	1-4				54			
Penrith *v* Worksop Town	0-2				152			
Radcliffe Borough *v* Tow Law Town	1-4				184			
Billingham Synthonia *v* Ryhope CA	3-1				72			
Easington Colliery *v* Stalybridge Celtic	0-0				82			
Stalybridge Celtic *v* Easington Colliery		2-0				245		
Netherfield *v* Consett	0-0				125			
Consett *v* Netherfield		1-1				118		
Consett *v* Netherfield			1-0				100	
Bedlington Terriers *v* Guisborough Town	1-2				104			
Peterlee Newtown *v* Accrington Stanley	2-3				43			
Chester-le-Street Town *v* Chorley	0-1				186			
Bedworth United *v* Hednesford Town	0-0				177			
Hednesford Town *v* Bedworth United		1-0				403		
Sutton Coldfield Town *v* Congleton Town	4-2				203			
Winsford United *v* Witton Albion	2-2				370			
Witton Albion *v* Winsford United		2-1				460		
Dudley Town *v* Matlock Town	0-2				194			
Wolverton Town *v* Buxton	0-5				135			
Moor Green *v* Halesowen Town	2-0				833			
Grantham *v* Alvechurch	1-2				361			
Eastwood Town *v* Colwyn Bay	4-1				196			
Willenhall Town *v* Sutton Town	3-1				192			
Shepshed Charterhouse *v* Redditch United	0-1				258			
Stourbridge *v* Coventry Sporting	0-0				202			
Coventry Sporting *v* Stourbridge		1-3				49		
Leamington *v* Leicester United	0-1				206			
VS Rugby *v* Chatham Town	2-0				422			
Kings Lynn *v* Leyton-Wingate	1-1				544			
Leyton-Wingate *v* Kings Lynn		1-0				147		
Wellingborough Town *v* Billericay Town	1-2				121			
Burnham *v* Hampton	0-1				116			
Kingstonian *v* Uxbridge	3-0				201			
Carshalton Athletic *v* Dunstable	5-3				178			
Stevenage Borough *v* Wembley	2-0				273			
Tilbury *v* Hayes	3-1				81			
Basildon United *v* Gravesend & Northfleet	1-2				146			
Cambridge City *v* Walthamstow Avenue	3-0				400			
St Albans City *v* Bromley	0-2				378			
Banbury United *v* Chesham United	3-1				195			
Finchley *v* Hitchin Town	1-1				77			
Hitchin Town *v* Finchley		2-0				165		
Boreham Wood *v* Kingsbury Town	2-4				102			
Basingstoke Town *v* Folkestone	0-0				358			
Folkestone *v* Basingstoke Town		2-3				242		
Southwick *v* Canterbury City	3-1				142			
Tonbridge AFC *v* Tooting & Mitcham United	2-2				323			
Tooting & Mitcham United *v* Tonbridge AFC		3-1				133		
Dover Athletic *v* Leytonstone Ilford	1-1				295			
Leytonstone Ilford *v* Dover Athletic		4-3				109		
Woking *v* Bognor Regis Town	2-1				337			
Walton & Hersham *v* Farnborough Town	0-0				306			
Farnborough Town *v* Walton & Hersham		0-0				494		

	Result				Attendance			
Walton & Hersham v Farnborough Town.........	1-1				345			
Farnborough Town v Walton & Hersham.........		4-1				270		
Erith & Belvedere v Ashford Town.................	0-1				154			
Epsom & Ewell v Bracknell Town	0-0				106			
Bracknell Town v Epsom & Ewell		0-2				100		
Thanet United v Staines Town	1-0				252			
Marlow v Maidenhead United	4-1				202			
Sheppey United v Croydon	0-0				181			
Croydon v Sheppey United		1-0				187		
Leatherhead v Lewes	4-2				129			
Barry Town v Llanelli..................................	6-0				209			
Taunton Town v Cwmbran Town	1-4				199			
Waterlooville v Weston-super-Mare	4-1				211			
Forest Green Rovers v Minehead	3-0				144			
Worcester City v Bideford	2-0				887			
Witney Town v Gosport Borough	2-0				157			
Gloucester City v Andover	3-0				362			
Frome Town v Clandown	0-1				112			
Trowbridge Town v Ton Pentre	2-2				248			
Ton Pentre v Trowbridge Town		2-3				363		
Poole Town v Oxford City	1-0				212			
Salisbury v Dorchester Town........................	1-0				228			
Maesteg Park v Melksham Town	2-2				29			
Melksham Town v Maesteg Park		4-0				100		

Second Round Qualifying	Result				Attendance			
Saturday 31st October 1987	1st Tie	1st Rep	2nd Rep	3rd Rep	1st Tie	1st Rep	2nd Rep	3rd Rep
Worksop Town v South Liverpool	0-0				296			
South Liverpool v Worksop Town		4-1				158		
Stalybridge Celtic v Consett	3-0				358			
Chorley v Brandon United.............................	2-3				420			
Crook Town v Billingham Synthonia..............	3-7				88			
North Shields v Accrington Stanley................	3-1				178			
Guisborough Town v Tow Law Town	4-1				273			
Alfreton Town v Mossley	3-0				196			
Redditch United v Willenhall Town	2-0				150			
Witton Albion v Eastwood Town	5-0				308			
Leicester United v Alvechurch	0-4				135			
Buxton v Hednesford Town	3-1				301			
Stourbridge v Moor Green.............................	1-0				290			
Sutton Coldfield Town v Matlock Town	1-1				238			
Matlock Town v Sutton Coldfield Town		2-2				353		
Matlock Town v Sutton Coldfield Town			1-0				471	
Stevenage Borough v Kingstonian	2-0				187			
Cambridge City v Bromley	6-2				424			
Kingsbury Town v Billericay Town	3-1				50			
Hampton v Gravesend & Northfleet	2-2				184			
Gravesend & Northfleet v Hampton		1-2				252		
Carshalton Athletic v Hitchin Town................	1-2				189			
Banbury United v Tilbury.............................	0-0				170			
Tilbury v Banbury United.............................		1-2				131		
VS Rugby v Leyton-Wingate.........................	2-3				467			
Marlow v Thanet United	0-0				163			
Thanet United v Marlow		0-1				277		
Tooting & Mitcham United v Epsom & Ewell....	1-0				146			
Leatherhead v Ashford Town........................	0-1				182			
Woking v Basingstoke Town	2-1				301			
Croydon v Farnborough Town........................	1-3				169			
Southwick v Leytonstone Ilford	0-4				162			
Poole Town v Trowbridge Town	3-0				163			
Waterlooville v Clandown	3-1				146			
Melksham Town v Gloucester City	0-2				210			
Worcester City v Barry Town	2-1				806			
Salisbury v Witney Town.............................	1-2				255			
Cwmbran Town v Forest Green Rovers	1-2				67			

103

Third Round Qualifying	Result				Attendance			
Saturday 21st November 1987	*1st Tie*	*1st Rep*	*2nd Rep*	*3rd Rep*	*1st Tie*	*1st Rep*	*2nd Rep*	*3rd Rep*
Spennymoor United *v* Whitley Bay	0-0				260			
Whitley Bay *v* Spennymoor United		1-1				303		
Whitley Bay *v* Spennymoor United			1-3				431	
Whitby Town *v* North Shields	7-1				326			
Newcastle Blue Star *v* Billingham Synthonia	2-0				156			
South Bank *v* Guisborough Town	2-1				236			
Southport *v* Gateshead	0-2				311			
Brandon United *v* South Liverpool	1-2				220			
Morecambe *v* Barrow	2-4				615			
Stalybridge Celtic *v* Frickley Athletic	0-1				585			
Witton Albion *v* Matlock Town	2-0				402			
Stourbridge *v* Rhyl	1-2				346			
Leek Town *v* Hyde United	0-1				365			
Redditch United *v* Northwich Victoria	1-1				313			
Northwich Victoria *v* Redditch United		4-1				625		
Caernarfon Town *v* Alfreton Town	1-0				161			
Buxton *v* Gainsborough Trinity	4-1				246			
Leyton-Wingate *v* Leytonstone Ilford	3-1				254			
Farnborough Town *v* Hitchin Town	3-1				359			
Cambridge City *v* Stevenage Borough	2-1				454			
Hampton *v* Crawley Town	1-2				289			
Grays Athletic *v* Welling United	0-2				395			
Worthing *v* Chelmsford City	2-0				311			
Hendon *v* Worthing	3-1				238			
Marlow *v* Alvechurch	1-0				296			
Dulwich Hamlet *v* Harrow Borough	1-2				102			
Banbury United *v* Barking	3-2				223			
Tooting & Mitcham United *v* Kingsbury Town	4-0				141			
Ashford Town *v* Aylesbury United	1-2				284			
Gloucester City *v* Forest Green Rovers	4-0				628			
Witney Town *v* Wokingham Town	2-4				153			
Slough Town *v* Saltash United	3-3				458			
Saltash United *v* Slough Town		2-5				514		
Waterlooville *v* Windsor & Eton	0-2				259			
Bridgend Town *v* Poole Town	0-6				63			
Worcester City *v* Merthyr Tydfil	0-1				1200			

First Round Proper	Result				Attendance			
Saturday 19th December 1987	*1st Tie*	*1st Rep*	*2nd Rep*	*3rd Rep*	*1st Tie*	*1st Rep*	*2nd Rep*	*3rd Rep*
Kidderminster Harriers *v* Frickley Athletic	1-1				764			
Frickley Athletic *v* Kidderminster Harriers		1-3				732		
Bromsgrove Rovers *v* Blyth Spartans	2-2				727			
Blyth Spartans *v* Bromsgrove Rovers		2-2				1118		
Bromsgrove Rovers *v* Blyth Spartans			3-2				880	
Newcastle Blue Star *v* Rhyl	0-3				253			
South Liverpool *v* Lincoln City	1-1				309			
Lincoln City *v* South Liverpool		2-2				1847		
Lincoln City *v* South Liverpool			3-1				1848	
Gateshead *v* Corby Town	0-0				148			
Corby Town *v* Gateshead		0-2				201		
Burton Albion *v* Barrow	0-0				1021			
Barrow *v* Burton Albion		3-0				971		
Nuneaton Borough *v* Marine	1-1				461			
Marine *v* Nuneaton Borough		2-1				302		
Bangor City *v* Boston United	2-2				450			
Boston United *v* Bangor City		0-0				1558		
Boston United *v* Bangor City			2-1				1891	
Caernarfon Town *v* Stafford Rangers	1-1				251			
Stafford Rangers *v* Caernarfon Town		1-0				669		

	Result		Attendance	
Hyde United v Altrincham	0-1		918	
Buxton v Telford United	2-4		778	
Witton Albion v Whitby Town.......................	2-1		374	
Runcorn v Northwich Victoria......................	2-0		922	
South Bank v Spennymoor United..................	0-0		165	
Spennymoor United v South Bank..................		1-0		244
Macclesfield Town v Bishop Auckland	2-1		805	
Welling United v Leyton-Wingate	1-6		510	
Fareham Town v Hendon	0-2		233	
Fisher Athletic v Marlow	2-0		210	
Enfield v Worthing	4-2		609	
Slough Town v Dagenham	3-1		647	
Windsor & Eton v Barnet	1-1		544	
Barnet v Windsor & Eton		2-1		860
Gloucester City v Yeovil Town	1-3		747	
Farnborough Town v Crawley Town	0-2		377	
Sutton United v Bishop's Stortford	0-2		806	
Cambridge City v Poole Town	2-1		387	
Aylesbury United v Kettering Town	1-1		1222	
Kettering Town v Aylesbury United		5-1		1239
Banbury United v Wealdstone......................	2-2		402	
Wealdstone v Banbury United......................		1-0		448
Wokingham Town v Tooting & Mitcham United	4-0		377	
Bath City v Merthyr Tydfil	2-1		869	
Harrow Borough v Weymouth.......................	1-1		598	
Weymouth v Harrow Borough.......................		1-2		1232
Maidstone United v Dartford	5-1		1091	
Wycombe Wanderers v Cheltenham Town	2-3		1469	

Second Round Proper	Result				Attendance			
Saturday 23rd January 1988	1st Tie	1st Rep	2nd Rep	3rd Rep	1st Tie	1st Rep	2nd Rep	3rd Rep
Kidderminster Harriers v Runcorn	0-2				1439			
Lincon City v Cambridge City.......................	2-1				2566			
Rhyl v Macclesfield Town.............................	0-2				901			
Cheltenham Town v Crawley Town	2-0				1265			
Hendon v Barrow	1-1				455			
Barrow v Hendon		2-1				1799		
Fisher Athletic v Slough Town	2-1				310			
Spennymoor United v Harrow Borough...........	1-0				361			
Gateshead v Wokingham Town	0-4				165			
Enfield v Bishops Stortford	3-1				1064			
Leyton-Wingate v Boston United...................	5-2				454			
Witton Albion v Yeovil Town........................	3-1				1020			
Bath City v Stafford Rangers	0-2				521			
Marine v Maidstone United	0-4				322			
Wealdstone v Telford United	0-3				705			
Barnet v Bromsgrove Rovers	0-0				1049			
Bromsgrove Rovers v Barnet		3-1				1509		
Altrincham v Kettering Town.......................	1-1				881			
Kettering Town v Altrincham.......................		2-3				1021		

Third Round Proper	Result				Attendance			
Saturday 13th February 1988	1st Tie	1st Rep	2nd Rep	3rd Rep	1st Tie	1st Rep	2nd Rep	3rd Rep
Wokingham Town v Spennymoor United.........	3-0				1183			
Altrincham v Fisher Athletic	1-1				809			
Fisher Athletic v Altrincham		0-0				318		
Fisher Athletic v Altrincham			1-1				728	
Altrincham v Fisher Athletic				1-0				929
Runcorn v Barrow	0-1				1004			
Cheltenham Town v Bromsgrove Rovers	2-1				2544			

	Result					Attendance			
Leyton-Wingate v Macclesfield Town..............	1-2					572			
Lincoln City v Maidstone United....................	2-1					2452			
Witton Albion v Enfield	1-2					814			
Telford United v Stafford Rangers.................	1-1					2273			
Stafford Rangers v Telford United.................		2-3						2349	

Fourth Round Proper	Result				Attendance			
Saturday 5th March 1988	*1st Tie*	*1st Rep*	*2nd Rep*	*3rd Rep*	*1st Tie*	*1st Rep*	*2nd Rep*	*3rd Rep*
Enfield v Lincoln City.................................	1-0				2239			
Wokingham Town v Macclesfield Town...........	2-0				1719			
Cheltenham Town v Telford United...............	2-4				3157			
Altrincham v Barrow.................................	0-0				1864			
Barrow v Altrincham.................................		2-1				5121		

Semi-Final
First Leg – Saturday 2nd April 1988

Telford United v Wokingham Town................	2-0		3022
Barrow v Enfield	1-2		6002

Second Leg – Saturday 9th April 1988

Wokingham Town v Telford United................	0-1		2115
Enfield v Barrow	0-1		2445

Telford United won on aggregate 3-0
Barrow drew with Enfield on aggregate 2-2

Replay – Wednesday 13th April 1988

Barrow v Enfield	1-1		1362
at Kidderminster Harriers FC			

Second Replay – Monday 18th April 1988

Enfield v Barrow	1-0		1469
at Stafford Rangers FC			

Final
Saturday 7th May 1988

Enfield v Telford United	0-0		20161
at Wembley Stadium			

Replay – Thursday 12th May 1988

Enfield v Telford United	3-2		6916
at West Bromwich Albion FC			

F.A. Challenge Trophy Winners 1970-88

Year	Winners		Runners-up		Venue
1970	Macclesfield Town	2	Telford United	0	Wembley
1971	Telford United	3	Hillingdon Borough	2	Wembley
1972	Stafford Rangers	3	Barnet	0	Wembley
1973	*Scarborough	2	Wigan Athletic	1	Wembley
1974	Morecambe	2	Dartford	1	Wembley
1975	Matlock Town	4	Scarborough	0	Wembley
1976	*Scarborough	3	Stafford Rangers	2	Wembley
1977	Scarborough	2	Dagenham	1	Wembley
1978	Altrincham	3	Leatherhead	1	Wembley
1979	Stafford Rangers	2	Kettering Town	0	Wembley
1980	Dagenham	2	Mossley	1	Wembley
1981	Bishop's Stortford	1	Sutton United	0	Wembley
1982	*Enfield	1	Altrincham	0	Wembley
1983	Telford United	2	Northwich Victoria	1	Wembley
1984	†Northwich Victoria	2	Bangor City	1	Stoke
1985	Wealdstone	2	Boston United	1	Wembley
1986	Altrincham	1	Runcorn	0	Wembley
1987	§Kidderminster Harriers	2	Burton Albion	1	West Bromwich
1988	§Enfield	3	Telford United	2	West Bromwich

*After extra time   †After 1-1 draw at Wembley   §After 0-0 draw at Wembley

F.A. Challenge Trophy Competition 1988-89

Exemptions

32 Clubs to the First Round Proper

Altrincham	Chorley	Newcastle Blue Star
Aylesbury United	Dartford	Newport County
Barnet	Enfield	Runcorn
Barrow	Fareham Town	Stafford Rangers
Bath City	Fisher Athletic	Sutton United
Blyth Spartans	Hyde United	Telford United
Boston United	Kettering Town	Wealdstone
Bromley	Kidderminster Harriers	Weymouth
Bromsgrove Rovers	Macclesfield Town	Wokingham Town
Burton Albion	Maidstone United	Yeovil Town
Cheltenham Town	Marine	

32 Clubs to the Third Round Qualifying

Bangor City	Harrow Borough	South Bank
Billingham Synthonia	Hendon	Spennymoor United
Bishop Auckland	Leytonstone Ilford	Tooting & Mitcham United
Bishops Stortford	Leyton-Wingate	Welling United
Caernarfon Town	Merthyr Tydfil	Whitby Town
Cambridge City	Morecambe	Whitley Bay
Corby Town	Northwich Victoria	Windsor & Eton
Crawley Town	Nuneaton Borough	Witton Albion
Dagenham	Rhyl	Worthing
Frickley Athletic	Saltash United	Wycombe Wanderers
Gateshead	Slough Town	

107

F.A. Challenge Vase – Final Tie 1988

Colne Dynamoes 1   Emley 0
(after extra time)

Colne Dynamoes, formed as a school old boys team near Burnley in 1963 by Graham White, 44, their manager, fielded the greater number of former professionals at Wembley, and key defender Westwell, once of Preston North End, rarely put a foot wrong as they secured the Vase for the first time.

Stuart Anderson, a paint-sprayer, scored the winner seven minutes into extra time with a crisp half-volley from Burke's cross, but Colne had made fewer incursions into the penalty-area during the match as a whole than their opponents Emley. The Huddersfield team, suffering fresh disappointment after their semi-final defeat in the previous season, had the outstanding forward on view in John Francis, but their finishing was never as sharp as the powerful Francis runs and they were left to rue two unfortunate missed chances which would have taken the Vase to Yorkshire.

Emley manager, Gerry Quinn, 32, was sure that his charges had scored in the first half, when Mason, the Colne goalkeeper on a run of nine consecutive clean sheets, dropped an awkward corner from Paul Gartland and the ball appeared to several Emley players to have gone a yard over the line. (Another Gartland corner kick on the hour had slapped against the bar.)

The match was in injury-time when Mick Green tricked his way past two tired Colne defenders and pulled back a perfect centre from the byline. Centre-back Steve Codd, unmarked six yards out, had the goal at his mercy but his first-time volley flew high and wide of the target. Almost immediately the final whistle blew and Codd collapsed to the ground in despair, his and Emley's frustration more or less complete. It had been the first clear opening engineered by a side which had rattled up no fewer than 24 goals on the way to Wembley.

Geoff Hurst was the chief guest at the Final, so it was fitting that Colne's winner had come in extra time and at the end where Hurst had completed his World Cup hat-trick 22 years earlier.

Colne Dynamoes: Mason, McFadyen, Dunn, Westwell, Bentley, Whitehead (Burke), Roscoe, Anderson, Wood (Coates), Rodaway, Diamond.

Emley: Dennis, Hirst (Burrows), Fielding, Mellor, Codd, Green, Bramald, Francis, Devine, Carmody, Gartland (Cook).

Referee: Seville (Birmingham).

Attendance: 15,146

Steve Codd clears Emley's lines in the Wembley sunshine.

Colne Dynamoes – F.A. Vase Winners.

F.A. Challenge Vase Competition 1987-88

Extra Preliminary Round	Result			Attendance		
Saturday 5th September 1987	*1st Tie*	*1st Rep*	*2nd Rep*	*1st Tie*	*1st Rep*	*2nd Rep*
Rowntree Mackintosh *v* Billingham Town	3-1			46		
Harrogate Railway *v* Eppleton CW	3-0			100		
Dormans Athletic *v* Seaham Red Star	1-0			45		
Tadcaster Albion *v* Great Harwood Town	1-1			25		
Great Harwood Town *v* Tadcaster Albion		5-2			28	
Northallerton Town *v* Norton & Stockton Anc	0-3			36		
Evenwood Town *v* Stockton	1-0			25		
Ponteland United *v* Prudhoe East End	1-5			21		
Horden CW *v* Alnwick Town	1-3			30		
Yorkshire Amateur *v* Bridlington Town	1-3			80		
Maghull *v* Bootle	0-2			63		
Flixton *v* Darwen	0-1			104		
Curzon Ashton *v* Maine Road	1-1			99		
Maine Road *v* Curzon Ashton............................		2-1			71	
Vauxhall Motors (Cheshire) *v* Uniasco ....(walkover for Uniasco)						
Kirkby Town *v* Lancaster City	2-2			33		
Lancaster City *v* Kirkby Town		2-3			59	
(Tie awarded to Lancaster City as Kirkby Town played an ineligible player)						
Eastwood Hanley *v* Oldham Town.......................	2-0			49		
Leyland Motors *v* Linotype	4-1			57		
Formby *v* Ashton United..................................	1-4			70		
Bradley Rangers *v* Burscough...........................	0-1			16		
Mickleover RBL *v* Belper Town	0-1			82		
Harworth CI *v* Gainsborough Town	3-1			76		
Frecheville Community *v* North Ferriby United	1-4			47		
Worsboro Bridge MW *v* Thackley........................	2-2			80		
Thackley *v* Worsboro Bridge MW.......................		1-0			178	
Kiveton Park *v* Liversedge	1-1			20		
Liversedge *v* Kiveton Park		2-0			35	
Hallam *v* Pontefract Collieries	2-0			128		
Louth United *v* Maltby MW	0-1			120		
Heanor Town *v* Armthorpe Welfare	0-3			80		
Boston *v* Brigg Town	2-2			83		
Brigg Town *v* Boston		0-1			55	
Tividale *v* Northfield	0-0			32		
Northfield *v* Tividale		2-2			70	
Northfield *v* Tividale			0-1			87
Halesowen Harriers *v* Brereton Social	1-3			34		
Spalding United *v* Evesham United.....................	3-1			135		
Northampton Spencer *v* Knypersley Victoria	2-2			38		
Knypersley Victoria *v* Northampton Spencer		2-2			80	
Knypersley Victoria *v* Northampton Spencer			1-2			86
Wigston Fields *v* Ashtree Highfield	1-1			42		
Ashtree Highfield *v* Wigston Fields		2-2			42	
Wigston Fields *v* Ashtree Highfield			2-1			29
GKN Sankey *v* Thringstone	4-2			20		
Armitage *v* Chasetown.....................................(walkover for Chasetown)						
Boldmere St Michaels *v* Oldswinford...................	4-0			35		
Paget Rangers *v* Racing Club Warwick	1-2			33		
Bilston Town *v* Ansty Nomads	1-0			85		
Rothwell Town *v* Walsall-Wood..........................	2-1			47		
Malvern Town *v* Hinckley Athletic	1-3			53		
Felixstowe Town *v* Letchworth GC	1-3			52		
Bowers United *v* Diss Town	3-2			71		
Histon *v* Hadleigh United	4-1			80		
Newmarket Town *v* Downham Town	5-2			72		
March Town United *v* Leiston	5-0			82		
St Neots Town *v* Baker Perkins	2-0			76		
Coalite Yaxley *v* London Colney	1-0			50		
Hertford Town *v* Clacton Town..........................	5-1			55		
Aveley *v* Brightlingsea United	4-2			60		

Lowestoft Town v Maldon Town	6-0		160
Wroxham v Chatteris Town	1-2		100
Stowmarket Town v LBC Ortonians	0-2		130
Sandridge Rovers v Rayners Lane	1-0		40
Feltham v Chalfont St Peter	2-3		43
Winslow United v Brimsdown Rovers	0-2		25
Newport Pagnell Town v Clapton	1-0		14
Beckton United v Wingate (Herts)	1-3		15
Ware v The 61 (Luton)	3-1		54
Selby v Bicester Town	3-4		30
Viking Sports v Stotfold	1-3		60
Mount Grace (Potters Bar) v Totternhoe	1-1		38
Totternhoe v Mount Grace (Potters Bar)		3-0	64
Burnham Ramblers v Pennant	4-1		79
Hanwell Town v Ampthill Town	(Tie awarded to Hanwell Town)		
Ruislip Manor v Potton United	4-2		65
Crown & Manor v Biggleswade Town	1-3		20
Ford United (London) v Cheshunt	3-1		28
Arlesey Town v Hemel Hempstead	2-0		30
East Thurrock United v Leavesden Hospital	4-0		71
J-M Sports v Southgate Athletic	0-2		35
Nat West Bank v Hailsham Town	0-3		57
Dorking v Metropolitan Police (Hayes)	8-0		104
Shoreham v Ringmer	3-2		56
Wick v Chobham	6-0		38
Southwark Sports v Chipstead	3-1		28
Beckenham Town v Sittingbourne	0-1		92
Cray Wanderers v West Wickham	2-3		100
Chertsey Town v Tunbridge Wells	3-3		119
Tunbridge Wells v Chertsey Town		0-1	162
Pagham v Danson (Bexley Boro)	(walkover for Pagham)		
Horsham YMCA v Faversham Town	0-5		28
Darenth Heathside v Herne Bay	6-2		35
Cove v Redhill	0-2		54
Merstham v Ash United	2-2		54
Ash United v Merstham		0-2	47
Lancing v Eastbourne United	1-0		87
Brockenhurst v Clanfield	3-1		66
Supermarine v Wallingford Town	3-1		30
Portsmouth RN v East Cowes Victoria Athletic	2-1		Nil
Bridport v Bournemouth	3-2		128
Yate Town v Radstock Town	3-2		118
Barnstaple Town v Tiverton Town	2-3		171
St Austell v Welton Rovers	2-1		85
Brislington v Truro City	1-2		104

Preliminary Round	Result			Attendance		
Saturday 19th September 1987	1st Tie	1st Rep	2nd Rep	1st Tie	1st Rep	2nd Rep
Durham City v Tees Components	4-0			56		
Prudhoe East End v Marske United	3-1			93		
Bridlington Trinity v Seaton Delaval ST	0-2			40		
Harrogate Town v Rowntree Mackintosh	1-0			232		
Dormans Athletic v Coundon TT	0-2			16		
Sporting Club Vaux v Langley Park Welfare	6-3			80		
Ashington v Norton & Stockton Ancients	2-1			37		
Harrogate Railway v Willington	0-1			50		
Gosforth St Nicholas v Wren Rovers	1-1			120		
Wren Rovers v Gosforth St Nicholas		1-0			52	
Bridlington Town v Washington	3-0			68		
Dawdon CW v Marchon Social	0-0			30		
Marchon Social v Dawdon CW		1-3			50	
Evenwood Town v Esh Winning	2-2			53		
Esh Winning v Evenwood Town		1-3			104	
West Auckland Town v Newton Aycliffe	3-1			57		
Annfield Plain v Boldon CA	2-1			43		
Darlington CB v Alnwick Town	1-2			57		
Shotton Comrades v Great Harwood Town	0-3			40		

South Shields *v* Cleator Moor Celtic	1-3	130	
Daisy Hill *v* Poulton Victoria	1-0	35	
Leyland Motors *v* Heswall	0-3	60	
Chadderton *v* Merseyside Police	1-2	100	
Ford Motors (Liverpool) *v* Bootle	1-3	18	
Maine Road *v* Christleton	1-2	21	
Skelmersdale United *v* General Chemicals	0-1	46	
Atherton LR *v* Lancaster City	0-0	50	
Lancaster City *v* Atherton LR	3-2		104
Darwen *v* St Dominics	5-2	177	
Ellesmere Port & Neston *v* Waterloo Dock	1-3	40	
Burscough *v* Prescot Cables	2-0	30	
Colne Dynamoes *v* Glossop	5-4	168	
Eastwood Hanley *v* Droylsden	2-1	49	
Rylands *v* Irlam Town	1-3	30	
Atherton Collieries *v* Burnley Belvedere	3-2	40	
Clitheroe *v* Ashton United	0-2	187	
Nelson *v* Uniasco	1-2	25	
Newton *v* Cheadle Town	2-4	17	
Fryston CW *v* Radford	0-2	28	
Maltby MW *v* Immingham Town	1-1	50	
Immingham Town *v* Maltby MW	1-2		54
Clipstone Welfare *v* Oakham United	3-2	102	
Hatfield Main *v* Belper Town	0-0	107	
Belper Town *v* Hatfield Main	1-1		160
Hatfield Main *v* Belper Town		3-2	74
North Ferriby United *v* Denaby United	2-1	35	
Stapenhill *v* Hinckley Town	2-3	96	
Arnold Kingswell *v* Liversedge	1-0	20	
Harworth CI *v* Skegness Town	4-0	50	
Hall Road Rangers *v* Woolley MW	2-3	46	
Boston *v* Rossington Main	2-2	60	
Rossington Main *v* Boston	1-4		50
Farsley Celtic *v* Ilkeston Town	3-0	147	
Hallam *v* Grimethorpe MW	1-0	93	
Sheffield *v* Kimberley Town	1-0	18	
Arnold *v* Bentley	(walkover for Arnold)		
Derby Prims *v* Armthorpe Welfare	0-1	34	
Ossett Albion *v* Thackley	0-3	98	
Ossett Town *v* Collingham	2-1	55	
West Mids Police *v* Mile Oak Rovers & Youth	1-2	62	
Northampton Spencer *v* Kirkby Muxloe	3-2	27	
Rushall Olympic *v* Stratford Town	3-1	47	
Friar Lane OB *v* Rushden Town	2-1	71	
Westfields *v* Spalding United	0-1	41	
Boldmere St Michaels *v* Raunds United	4-1	58	
Highgate United *v* Desborough Town	0-2	20	
Harrisons *v* Pegasus Juniors	4-2	12	
Lye Town *v* Bloxwich	2-0	106	
Hinckley Athletic *v* Tividale	2-3	120	
Wednesfield Social *v* GKN Sankey	0-0	45	
GKN Sankey *v* Wednesfield Social	1-5		35
Rothwell Town *v* Wigston Fields	3-0	128	
Holbeach United *v* Brereton Social	2-2	49	
Brereton Social *v* Holbeach United	6-3		69
Mirrless Blackstone *v* Solihull Borough	2-1	64	
Chasetown *v* Bourne Town	5-0	81	
Racing Club Warwick *v* Oldbury United	3-2	41	
Long Eaton United *v* Long Buckby	4-0	20	
Redgate United *v* Hanley Town	0-2	80	
Brackley Town *v* Bilston Town	2-0	85	
Huntingdon United *v* Ely City	1-5	72	
Great Yarmouth Town *v* St Neots Town	3-1	140	
St Margaretsbury *v* Brantham Athletic	5-2	32	
Coalite Yaxley *v* St Ives Town	4-2	50	
Eynesbury Rangers *v* Royston Town	3-1	57	
Chatteris Town *v* Ramsey Town	2-0	80	
Hertford Town *v* Letchworth GC	1-2	71	
LBC Ortonians *v* Eton Manor	3-2	46	

112

Harlow Town v Soham Town Rangers	1-0			53		
Halstead Town v Lowestoft Town	1-2			67		
Sawbridgeworth Town v Watton United	3-1			50		
RSSC Ransomes v Eaton Bray United	(walkover for RSSC Ransomes)					
Wivenhoe Town v Somersham Town	6-2			89		
Canvey Island v Histon	1-1			75		
Histon v Canvey Island		2-2			200	
Canvey Island v Histon			3-2			60
Great Shelford v Thetford Town	3-3			84		
Thetford Town v Great Shelford		2-3			178	
Waltham Abbey v Saffron Walden Town	1-2			40		
Harwich & Parkeston v Bowers United	1-0			93		
Newmarket Town v Pirton	1-3			76		
March Town United v Aveley	4-3			136		
Tiptree United v Purfleet	2-2			50		
Purfleet v Tiptree United		2-2			30	
Tiptree United v Purfleet			2-4			63
Burnham Ramblers v Kempston Rovers	1-1			74		
Kempston Rovers v Burnham Ramblers		1-2			80	
Hounslow v Electrolux	6-1			62		
Amersham Town v Beaconsfield United	0-3			45		
Barkingside v Totternhoe	1-0			36		
Newport Pagnell Town v Southgate Athletic	0-1			16		
Molesey v Brimsdown Rovers	2-1			28		
Milton Keynes Borough v Edgware	0-1			40		
Ruislip Manor v Flackwell Heath	1-1			68		
Flackwell Heath v Ruislip Manor		0-2			80	
East Thurrock United v Welwyn GC	4-0			92		
Abingdon United v Wingate (Herts)	3-3			20		
Wingate (Herts) v Abingdon United		1-2			50	
Bicester Town v Hoddesdon Town	2-3			12		
Haringey Borough v Hanwell Town	3-1			46		
Tring Town v Wootton Blue Cross	1-2			30		
Arlesey Town v Park Street	2-0			26		
Metropolitan Police v Ware	0-1			41		
Chalfont St Peter v Norsemen	5-2			57		
Cockfosters v Shillington	0-1			44		
Ford United (London) v Leighton Town	1-3			70		
Biggleswade Town v Northwood	0-2			125		
Ruislip v Berkhamsted Town	1-3			19		
Stotfold v Hornchurch	2-3			77		
Sandridge Rovers v Rainham Town	2-2			46		
Rainham Town v Sandridge Rovers		2-3			23	
Portfield v Ramsgate	0-5			42		
Whitehawk v East Grinstead	1-2			71		
Darenth Heathside v Eastbourne Town	1-5			70		
Dorking v Thames Polytechnic	2-1			138		
Corinthian-Casuals v West Wickham	0-2			62		
Wick v Hastings Town	0-1			85		
Greenwich Borough v Farnham Town	4-3			57		
Old Salesians v Egham Town	1-2			30		
Slade Green v Godalming Town	0-2			37		
Littlehampton Town v Redhill	1-2			81		
Hythe Town v Chertsey Town	1-2			130		
Arundel v Faversham Town	1-3			56		
Horley Town v Lancing	0-0			67		
Lancing v Horley Town		1-3			125	
Burgess Hill Town v Bosham	1-1			61		
Bosham v Burgess Hill Town		0-4			37	
Sittingbourne v Shoreham	0-1			118		
Midland Bank v Cobham	0-1			45		
Corinthian v Pagham	2-1			18		
Banstead Athletic v Peacehaven & Telscombe	1-2			18		
Haywards Heath v Farleigh Rovers	2-3			32		
Merstham v Southwark Sports	2-0			55		
Hailsham Town v Malden Vale	2-2			89		
Malden Vale v Hailsham Town		2-1			73	
Bridport v Portsmouth RN	4-0			138		
Brockenhurst v Vale Recreation	2-2			47		

	1st Tie	1st Rep	2nd Rep	1st Tie	1st Rep	2nd Rep
Vale Recreation v Brockenhurst	4-4			187		
Vale Recreation v Brockenhurst		9-1			318	
Newbury Town v Bashley	1-1			77		
Bashley v Newbury Town		5-0			130	
Flight Refuelling v Supermarine	1-1			21		
Supermarine v Flight Refuelling		1-0			28	
Calne Town v Didcot Town	2-1			69		
Horndean v Swanage Town & Herston	1-2			72		
Petersfield United v Eastleigh	0-1			100		
Wantage Town v Warminster Town	0-0			53		
Warminster Town v Wantage Town		2-3			70	
Devizes Town v Chichester City	3-2			42		
Thame United v First Tower United	5-1			80		
Sherborne Town v Romsey Town	1-5			61		
Westlands Sports v Patchway	4-1			76		
Ilfracombe Town v Almondsbury 85	3-2			103		
Westbury United v Tiverton Town	5-0			57		
Bristol Manor Farm v Robinsons DRG	1-0			60		
Fairford Town v Chard Town	2-0			80		
Shortwood United v St Blazey	2-0			80		
Harrow Hill v Cinderford Town	2-3			45		
Backwell United v Ottery St Mary	2-1			40		
Wimborne Town v Glastonbury	2-1			102		
Portway Bristol v Keynsham Town .... (walkover for Keynsham Town)						
Truro City v Yate Town	0-3			109		
Highworth Town v Moreton Town	1-2			60		
Port of Bristol v St Austell	1-2			50		
Hengrove Athletic v Wotton Rovers	3-2			26		
Larkhall Athletic v Paulton Rovers	6-3			50		
Wellington v Portishead	2-1			65		

First Round   Result   Attendance

Saturday 17th October 1987	1st Tie	1st Rep	2nd Rep	1st Tie	1st Rep	2nd Rep
Murton v Ashington	1-2			40		
Prudhoe East End v Whickham	1-1			220		
Whickham v Prudhoe East End		2-3			240	
Bridlington Town v Annfield Plain	4-0			109		
Wren Rovers v Evenwood Town	2-0			72		
West Allotment Celtic v Sporting Club Vaux	2-3			120		
Durham City v Alnwick Town	2-0			100		
Harrogate Town v Coundon TT	2-3			301		
West Auckland Town v Cleator Moor Celtic	3-0			62		
Willington v Dawdon CW	2-1			53		
Seaton Delaval ST v Great Harwood Town	1-1			75		
Great Harwood Town v Seaton Delaval ST		2-1			40	
Rossendale United v Lancaster City	2-0			363		
Heswall v Rochester	2-1			140		
Burscough v Atherton Collieries	3-2			120		
Waterloo Dock v Eastwood Hanley	2-3			75		
Bridgnorth Town v General Chemicals	3-0			85		
Daisy Hill v Ashton United	2-0			61		
Bootle v Christleton	4-3			80		
Irlam Town v Cheadle Town	3-0			84		
Darwen v Colne Dynamoes	1-4			314		
Merseyside Police v Uniasco	0-2			100		
Lincoln United v Staveley Works	3-2			89		
Borrowash Victoria v Arnold	2-4			81		
Harworth CI v Gresley Rovers	0-1			128		
Hinckley Town v Guiseley	0-2			79		
Radford v Clipstone Welfare	1-2			40		
Arnold Kingswell v Hallam	1-0			40		
Woolley MW v Hatfield Main	2-2			50		
Hatfield Main v Woolley Main		0-0			40	
Woolley MW v Hatfield Main			0-2			40
Armthorpe Welfare v Thackley	2-4			73		
Maltby MW v Ossett Town	2-2			60		
Ossett Town v Maltby MW		1-5			125	

Sheffield v North Ferriby United	1-3	58	
Farsley Celtic v Boston	4-0	197	
Irthlingborough Diamonds v Lye Town	3-0	143	
Friar Lane OB v Northampton Spencer	1-2	117	
Rothwell Town v Racing Club Warwick	3-1	76	
Wednesfield Social v Mirrlees Blackstone	3-1	56	
Mile Oak Rovers & Youth v Harrisons	4-1	101	
Rushall Olympic v Long Eaton United	3-1	67	
Boldmere St Michaels v Desborough Town	1-3	96	
Chasetown v Brackley Town	0-1	174	
Tividale v Brereton Social	3-0	53	
Spalding United v Hanley Town	2-1	157	
Stamford United v Chatteris Town	2-1	129	
Harlow Town v Letchworth GC	0-3	67	
Wivenhoe Town v Bury Town	2-3	231	
Sawbridgeworth Town v Harwich & Parkeston	1-2	48	
Great Shelford v Ely City	4-0	118	
Saffron Walden Town v Pirton	3-1	121	
Gorleston v Great Yarmouth Town	2-2	387	
Great Yarmouth Town v Gorleston		3-1	410
Canvey Island v Eynesbury Rovers	2-0		
RSSC Ransomes v Purfleet	2-1	87	
St Margaretsbury v Stansted	3-3	80	
Stansted v St Margaretsbury		2-3	130
Coalite Yaxley v Lowestoft Town	1-2	120	
LBC Ortonians v March Town United	0-2	129	
Molesey v Burnham Ramblers	2-0	37	
Vauxhall Motors v Southgate Athletic	1-2	48	
Hoddesdon Town v Beaconsfield United	5-0	51	
Arlesey Town v Hounslow	1-2	60	
Sandridge Rovers v Haringey Borough	3-5	65	
Yeading v Edgware	4-1	110	
Hornchurch v Witham Town	0-2	146	
Shillington v Baldock Town	1-0	112	
Woodford Town v Leighton Town	1-0	62	
Berkhamsted Town v Barkingside	3-0	92	
Barton Rovers v Wootton Blue Cross	4-0	102	
Abingdon United v Ware	0-2	43	
Ruislip Manor v Chalfont St Peter	0-3	90	
East Thurrock United v Northwood	3-1	92	
Faversham Town v Shoreham	4-0	71	
Merstham v Chertsey Town	2-2	68	
Chertsey Town v Merstham		3-2	92
Horsham v Crockenhill	4-0	61	
Corinthian v Hastings Town	3-2	83	
Ramsgate v Three Bridges	3-0	167	
Egham Town v Dorking	2-4	134	
Thatcham Town v Farleigh Rovers	3-0	65	
Eastbourne Town v Cobham	4-1	205	
West Wickham v Horley Town	2-0	74	
Peacehaven & Telscombe v Greenwich Borough	2-3	93	
Burgess Hill Town v Alma Swanley	4-0	76	
Malden Vale v Godalming Town	1-2	50	
Redhill v East Grinstead	7-4	156	
Vale Recreation v Thame United	5-2	242	
Supermarine v Eastleigh	3-3	34	
Eastleigh v Supermarine		2-1	122
Romsey Town v Swanage Town & Herston	3-4	50	
Bridport v Devizes Town	3-2	192	
AFC Totton v Bashley	1-1	181	
Bashley v AFC Totton		1-0	120
Calne Town v Wantage Town	2-2	85	
Wantage Town v Calne Town		3-1	76
Chippenham Town v Hungerford Town	0-1	191	
Yate Town v Westland Sports	6-0	120	
Fairford Town v Westbury United	1-2	80	
Cinderford Town v Ilfracombe Town	2-0	63	
Wimborne Town v Moreton Town	1-3	102	
St Austell v Hengrove Athletic	1-1	120	

	2-3		74
Hengrove Athletic v St Austell............................		2-3		74
Larkhall Athletic v Clevedon Town	2-3		62	
Bristol Manor Farm v Shortwood United..............	1-2		81	
Keynsham Town v Backwell United.....................	2-2		40	
Backwell United v Keynsham Town.....................		1-0		82
Wellington v Mangotsfield United	0-1		60	

Second Round	Result			Attendance		
Saturday 7th November 1987	*1st Tie*	*1st Rep*	*2nd Rep*	*1st Tie*	*1st Rep*	*2nd Rep*
Bridlington Town v Wren Rovers	2-2			85		
Wren Rovers v Bridlington Town		3-2			110	
Prudhoe East End v Fleetwood Town	1-3			275		
Maltby MW v Willington	6-1			80		
Thackley v Ashington	6-0			151		
Hatfield Main v Great Harwood Town	5-0			33		
Coundon TT v Colne Dynamoes	0-1			51		
Sporting Club Vaux v Garforth Town	2-0			60		
Durham City v Rossendale United.......................	4-0			219		
West Auckland Town v Guiseley	0-1			52		
Rainworth MW v St Helens Town	1-1			258		
St Helens Town v Rainworth MW........................		0-2			122	
Hucknall Town v North Ferriby United................	0-0			140		
North Ferriby United v Hucknall Town................		2-1			88	
Clipstone Welfare v Eastwood Hanley.................	0-2			75		
Arnold Kingswell v Emley	2-6			130		
Lincoln United v Daisy Hill...............................	2-0			90		
Heswall v Irlam Town	2-1			109		
Warrington Town v Farsley Celtic.......................	2-3			170		
Wythenshawe Amateurs v Bootle........................	2-0			80		
Burscough v Uniasco	0-2			56		
Wisbech Town v Bridgnorth Town.......................	0-1			488		
Tamworth v Arnold	4-0			854		
Gresley Rovers v Mile Oak Rovers & Youth	3-0			508		
Stamford v Atherstone United............................	0-4			260		
Spalding United v Rushall Olympic......................	3-2			149		
Rothwell Town v Brackley Town.........................	1-1			109		
Brackley Town v Rothwell Town		1-1			86	
Rothwell Town v Brackley Town.........................			0-5			165
Irthlingborough Diamonds v Buckingham Town.....	4-0			275		
Northampton Spencer v Desborough Town	4-2			41		
Wednesfield Social v Tividale	2-3			44		
Hounslow v March Town United.........................	3-2			135		
Greay Yarmouth Town v Haverhill Rovers............	0-1			141		
Great Shelford v Witham Town..........................	2-5			320		
Braintree Town v Woodford Town	5-1			208		
Chalfont St Peter v Ware	6-0			79		
Letchworth GC v Bury Town..............................	1-2			120		
Lowestoft Town v Sudbury Town	1-3			246		
St Margaretsbury v Harwich & Parkeston..............	2-3			85		
Hoddesdon Town v Canvey Island......................	3-2			122		
Heybridge Swifts v Berkhamsted Town................	1-2			142		
RSSC Ransomes v Saffron Walden Town	3-2			76		
Shillington v Barton Rovers	1-0			190		
Dorking v Greenwich Borough	2-1			148		
Harefield United v Burgess Hill Town	2-0			68		
Camberley Town v Chertsey Town	3-5			54		
Corinthian v Redhill...	1-1			48		
Redhill v Corinthian...			0-4			304
West Wickham v Godalming Town	2-0			79		
Faversham Town v Southgate Athletic..................	1-3			90		
Ramsgate v Whyteleafe......................................	0-2			138		
East Thurrock United v Eastbourne United	1-0			137		
Collier Row v Molesey	0-2			126		
Southall v Horsham..	2-3			44		
Haringey Borough v Yeading	2-0			60		
Vale Recreation v Westbury United....................	4-3			303		

	1st Tie	1st Rep	2nd Rep	1st Tie	1st Rep	2nd Rep
Abingdon Town v Newport IOW	1-2			123		
Thatcham Town v Eastleigh	3-1			87		
Sholing Sports v Wantage Town	3-1			150		
Havant Town v Bashley	0-2			215		
Hungerford Town v Steyning Town	8-1			108		
Shortwood United v Moreton Town	4-1			80		
Falmouth Town v Sharpness	3-2			292		
Cinderford Town v Bridport	0-3			63		
St Austell v Swanage Town & Herston	4-2			145		
Mangotsfield United v Exmouth Town	1-0			233		
Yate Town v Clevedon Town	1-3			135		
Backwell United v Old Georgians	1-2			84		
Torrington v Dawlish Town	1-1			80		
Dawlish Town v Torrington		2-0			100	

Third Round

	Result			Attendance		
Saturday 12th December 1987	1st Tie	1st Rep	2nd Rep	1st Tie	1st Rep	2nd Rep
Fleetwood Town v Rainworth MW	2-0			411		
Guiseley v Emley	1-2			448		
Colne Dynamoes v Heswall	2-0			201		
Thackley v Maltby MW	4-1			129		
Sporting Club Vaux v Wren Rovers	2-4			60		
Durham City v Uniasco	2-2			200		
Uniasco v Durham City		1-1			100	
Durham City v Uniasco			1-0			327
Farsley Celtic v Eastwood Hanley	5-1			155		
North Ferriby United v Wythenshawe Amateurs	3-2			105		
Lincoln United v Hatfield Main	0-3			100		
Braintree Town v Spalding United	1-0			261		
Tividale v Haringey Borough	1-1			74		
Haringey Borough v Tividale		2-1			62	
Bury Town v Atherstone United	2-3			436		
Hoddesdon Town v Harwich & Parkeston	0-2			96		
Southgate Athletic v Northampton Spencer	4-4			84		
Northampton Spencer v Southgate Athletic		3-1			88	
Chalfont St Peter v East Thurrock United	2-1			231		
Irthlingborough Diamonds v Brackley Town	2-1			192		
Haverhill Rovers v Berkhamsted Town	2-1			119		
RSSC Ransomes v Gresley Rovers	0-0			320		
Gresley Rovers v RSSC Ransomes		2-1			497	
Sudbury Town v Shillington	2-0			288		
Tamworth v Harefield United	2-0			702		
Witham Town v Bridgnorth Town	0-4			195		
Vale Recreation v Sholing Sports	3-1			234		
Hounslow v Molesey	4-2			81		
Whyteleafe v Hungerford Town	0-0			141		
Hungerford Town v Whyteleafe		3-2			98	
Newport IOW v Thatcham Town	2-3			171		
Bashley v Dorking	1-0			300		
Chertsey Town v Horsham	3-0			149		
Corinthian v West Wickham	3-1			63		
Bridport v Dawlish Town	2-1			246		
Old Georgians v Clevedon Town	1-2			105		
St Austell v Shortwood United	0-0			162		
Shortwood United v St Austell		3-2			131	
Mangotsfield United v Falmouth Town	0-2			364		

Fourth Round

	Result			Attendance		
Saturday 16th January 1988	1st Tie	1st Rep	2nd Rep	1st Tie	1st Rep	2nd Rep
North Ferriby United v Wren Rovers	2-1			170		
Farsley Celtic v Hatfield Main	1-1			229		
Hatfield Main v Farsley Celtic		0-3			80	
Bridgnorth Town v Emley	3-3			450		
Emley v Bridgnorth Town		6-0			553	

117

	1st Tie	1st Rep	2nd Rep	1st Tie	1st Rep	2nd Rep
Thackley v Durham City	2-2			451		
Durham City v Thackley		2-0			676	
Colne Dynamoes v Fleetwood Town	2-1			802		
Tamworth v Haringey Borough	3-1			902		
Haverhill Rovers v Atherstone United	0-4			334		
Sudbury Town v Irthlingborough Diamonds	5-3			550		
Gresley Rovers v Northampton Spencer	2-1			815		
Hungerford Town v Braintree Town	0-2			232		
Corinthian v Harwich & Parkeston	3-0			96		
Thatcham Town v Chertsey Town	0-2			194		
Hounslow v Chalfont St Peter	1-0			176		
Shortwood United v Falmouth Town	2-3			210		
Bashley v Vale Recreation	5-1			600		
Bridport v Clevedon Town	1-3			374		

Fifth Round

	Result			Attendance		
Saturday 6th February 1988	1st Tie	1st Rep	2nd Rep	1st Tie	1st Rep	2nd Rep
Gresley Rovers v Emley	0-1			1139		
Durham City v Tamworth	4-2			724		
Atherstone United v Colne Dynamoes	1-2			997		
North Ferriby United v Farsley Celtic	1-2			520		
Clevedon Town v Corinthian	2-1			361		
Chertsey Town v Falmouth Town	0-0			741		
Falmouth Town v Chertsey Town		1-2			1059	
Bashley v Hounslow	2-0			795		
Sudbury Town v Braintree Town	1-0			1195		

Sixth Round

	Result			Attendance		
Saturday 27th February 1988	1st Tie	1st Rep	2nd Rep	1st Tie	1st Rep	2nd Rep
Durham City v Emley	2-4			1010		
Colne Dynamoes v Farsley Celtic	2-0			1022		
Sudbury Town v Clevedon Town	2-0			1400		
Chertsey Town v Bashley	1-3			1102		

Semi-Final

	Result	Attendance
First Leg – Saturday 19th March 1988		
Bashley v Emley	1-1	3260
Sudbury Town v Colne Dynamoes	1-1	2661
Second Leg – Saturday 26th March 1988		
Emley v Bashley	1-0	2630
Colne Dynamoes v Sudbury Town	2-0	1500

Emley won on aggregate 2-1
Colne Dynamoes won on aggregate 3-1

Final

	Result	Attendance
Saturday 23rd April 1988		
Colne Dynamoes v Emley	1-0	15146
at Wembley Stadium		

F.A. Challenge Vase Winners 1975-88

Year	Winners		Runners-up		Venue
1975	Hoddesdon Town	2	Epsom & Ewell	1	Wembley
1976	*Billericay Town	1	Stamford	0	Wembley
1977	Billericay Town	2	Sheffield	1	Nottingham
			After 1-1 draw at Wembley		
1978	Blue Star	2	Barton Rovers	1	Wembley
1979	Billericay Town	4	Almondsbury Greenway	1	Wembley
1980	Stamford	2	Guisborough Town	0	Wembley
1981	*Whickham	3	Willenhall Town	2	Wembley
1982	Forest Green Rovers	3	Rainworth Miners' Welfare	0	Wembley
1983	V. S. Rugby	1	Halesowen Town	0	Wembley
1984	Stansted	3	Stamford	2	Wembley
1985	Halesowen Town	3	Fleetwood Town	1	Wembley
1986	Halesowen Town	3	Southall	0	Wembley
1987	St. Helens Town	3	Warrington Town	2	Wembley
1988	*Colne Dynamoes	1	Emley	0	Wembley

* After extra time

F.A. Challenge Vase Competition 1988-89

Exemptions

32 Clubs Exempt to the Second Round

Abingdon Town
Bashley
Braintree Town
Bridgnorth Town
Chertsey Town
Clevedon Town
Colne Dynamoes
Corinthian
Dawlish Town
Emley
Falmouth Town

Farsley Celtic
Garforth Town
Gresley Rovers
Harefield United
Havant Town
Haverhill Rovers
Horsham
Hungerford Town
Mangotsfield United
Newport (IOW)
Old Georgians

Rainworth Miners Welfare
St Helens Town
Sholing Sports
Sudbury Town
Tamworth
Warrington Town
Whyteleafe
Wisbech Town
Witham Town
Wythenshawe Amateurs

32 Clubs Exempt to the First Round

Barton Rovers
Borrowash Victoria
Bridport
Buckingham Town
Bury Town
Camberley Town
Dorking
Exmouth Town
Guiseley
Harwich & Parkeston
Hatfield Main

Heybridge Swifts
Hounslow
Hucknall Town
Irthlingborough D
Lincoln United
Murton
Northampton Spencer
North Ferriby United
Rocester
Rossendale United
Sharpness

Shortwood United
Stamford
Steyning Town
Thackley
Thatcham Town
Torrington
Vauxhall Motors (Beds)
West Allotment Celtic
Whickham
Yeading

119

FA/GM National School
International Youth Caps 1987-88

Under-15/Under-16

	Sweden	Finland	Norway	Sweden	Denmark	Sweden	Sweden	Scotland	Brazil	Israel	Israel
I. Walker (Tottenham Hotspur)	1	1	1	1	1	1	1	1		1	1
P. Mitchell (Bournemouth)	2	*8	2	*2		*3	2	2		2	2
M. Alexander (Wimbledon)	3	2	3	3	3	2	3	3		*11	*11
W. Seymour (Coventry City)	4		*4	*4	*2	4	*6	4		6	6
J. Kavanagh (Birmingham City)	5	5	5	5	5	5	5	5		9	
P. Williams (Manchester City)	6	8	8	6	*9	*7	*7	*8		*7	7
S. Houghton (Tottenham Hotspur)	7	7	7	9	7	7	7	7		7	*7
S. Walters (Crewe Alexandra)	8	6	6	7	6	6	4	6		4	4
H. Dang (Tottenham Hotspur)	9	9	9	10	8	8	8	8		8	8
M. Turner (Portsmouth)	10	10	10	8	10	10	10	10		10	10
B. Small (Aston Villa)	11	11	11	11	11	11	*11	*11		11	11
J. Stanger (Manchester United)	*1	*1	*1		1*		*1		1		*1
P. Towler (Watford)	*4	4	4	4	4	*4	6	*4		5	5
S. Charlton (Huddersfield Town)	*6	3	*2	2	2	3	11	11		3	3
O. Morah (Tottenham Hotspur)	*9	*2	*8	*6	9				9		
T. Sinclair (Backpool)	*11	*7	*7		*7				7		
D. Hancock (West Ham United)					*11				*2		
A. Cole (Arsenal)						9	9	9		*9	9
A. Fuller (Watford)									2		
K. Fowler (Arsenal)									3		
S. Clements (Arsenal)									4		
C. Gaunt									5		
P. Reed (West Ham United)									6		
C. Makin (Oldham Athletic)									8		
M. Joseph (Arsenal)									10		
M. Flatts (Arsenal)									11		
S. Sheppard (Watford)									*1		
D. Schonberger (Queens Park Rangers)									*3		
R. Price (Oldham Athletic)									*5		
G. Flitcroft (Manchester City)									*7		

*Substitute

FA/GM National School
International Matches 1987-88

Under-15

30.3.88	England	1	Brazil	0	Brentford

Under-16

24.7.87	Sweden	1	England	2	Ronneby
25.7.87	Finland	0	England	3	Ronneby
27.7.87	Norway	0	England	2	Ronneby
28.7.87	Sweden	3	England	1	Ronneby
8.8.87	England	2	Denmark	1	Wembley
9.3.88	England	0	Sweden	2	Aston Villa
11.3.88	England	2	Sweden	0	Fulham
26.3.88	England	2	Scotland	2	Shrewsbury
3.4.88	Israel	1	England	0	Tel Aviv
5.4.88	Israel	1	England	2	Tel Aviv

F.A. Youth Challenge Cup Winners 1953-88

(AGGREGATE SCORES)

Year	Winners		Runners-up	
1953	Manchester United	9	Wolverhampton W	3
1954	Manchester United	5	Wolverhampton W	4
1955	Manchester United	7	West Bromwich Albion	1
1956	Manchester United	4	Chesterfield	3
1957	Manchester United	8	West Ham United	2
1958	Wolverhampton W	7	Chelsea	6
1959	Blackburn Rovers	2	West Ham United	1
1960	Chelsea	5	Preston North End	2
1961	Chelsea	5	Everton	3
1962	Newcastle United	2	Wolverhampton W	1
1963	West Ham United	6	Liverpool	5
1964	Manchester United	5	Swindon Town	2
1965	Everton	3	Arsenal	2
1966	Arsenal	5	Sunderland	3
1967	Sunderland	2	Birmingham City	0
1968	Burnley	3	Coventry City	2
1969	Sunderland	6	West Bromwich Albion	3
1970	Tottenham Hotspur	4	Coventry City	3
1971	Arsenal	2	Cardiff City	0
1972	Aston Villa	5	Liverpool	2
1973	Ipswich Town	4	Bristol City	1
1974	Tottenham Hotspur	2	Huddersfield Town	1
1975	Ipswich Town	5	West Ham United	1
1976	West Bromwich Albion	5	Wolverhampton W	0
1977	Crystal Palace	1	Everton	0
1978*	Crystal Palace	1	Aston Villa	0
1979	Millwall	2	Manchester City	0
1980	Aston Villa	3	Manchester City	2
1981	West Ham United	2	Tottenham Hotspur	1
1982	Watford	7	Manchester United	6
1983†	Norwich City	6	Everton	5
1984	Everton	4	Stoke City	2
1985	Newcastle United	4	Watford	1
1986	Manchester City	3	Manchester United	1
1987	Coventry City	2	Charlton Athletic	1
1988	Arsenal	6	Doncaster Rovers	1

*One leg only   †After a replay

F.A. County Youth Challenge Cup Winners 1945-88

(AGGREGATE SCORES)

Year	Winners		Runners-up	
1945	Staffordshire	3	Wiltshire	2
1946	Berks. & Bucks.	4	Durham	3
1947	Durham	4	Essex	2
1948	Essex	5	Liverpool	3
1949	Liverpool	4	Middlesex	3
1950	Essex	4	Middlesex	3
1951	Middlesex	3	Leics. & Rutland	1
1952	Sussex	3	Liverpool	1
1953	Sheffield & Hallam	5	Hampshire	3
1954	Liverpool	4	Gloucestershire	1
1955	Bedfordshire	2	Sheffield & Hallam	0
1956	Middlesex	3	Staffordshire	2
1957	Hampshire	4	Cheshire	3
1958	Staffordshire	8	London	0
1959	Birmingham	7	London	5
1960	London	6	Birmingham	4
1961	Lancashire	6	Nottinghamshire	3
1962	Middlesex	6	Nottinghamshire	3
1963	Durham	3	Essex	2
1964	Sheffield & Hallam	1	Birmingham	0
1965	Northumberland	7	Middlesex	4
1966	Leics. & Rutland	6	London	5
1967	Northamptonshire	5	Hertfordshire	4
1968	North Riding	7	Devon	4
1969	Northumberland	1	Sussex	0
1970*	Hertfordshire	2	Cheshire	1
1971*	Lancashire	2	Gloucestershire	0
1972*	Middlesex	2	Liverpool	0
1973*	Hertfordshire	3	Northumberland	0
1974*	Nottinghamshire	2	London	0
1975*	Durham	2	Bedfordshire	1
1976*	Northamptonshire	7	Surrey	1
1977*	Liverpool	3	Surrey	0
1978*	Liverpool	3	Kent	1
1979*	Hertfordshire	4	Liverpool	1
1980*	Liverpool	2	Lancashire	0
1981*	Lancashire	3	East Riding	2
1982*†	Devon	3	Kent	2
1983*	London	3	Gloucestershire	0
1984*	Cheshire	2	Manchester	1
1985*	East Riding	2	Middlesex	1
1986*	Hertfordshire	4	Manchester	0
1987*	North Riding	3	Gloucestershire	1
1988*‡	East Riding	5	Middlesex	3

*One leg only   †After a 0-0 draw   ‡After a 1-1 draw

F.A. Youth Challenge Cup Competition 1987-88

Preliminary Round	Result			Attendance		
On or before 5th September 1987	*1st Tie*	*1st Rep*	*2nd Rep*	*1st Tie*	*1st Rep*	*2nd Rep*
Chester-le-Street Town *v* Darlington....................	0-2			29		
Dormans Athletic *v* Billingham Synthonia.............	1-10			Nil		
Billingham Town *v* Stockton	2-0			40		
Marske United *v* Spennymoor United	2-0			35		
Rochdale *v* Tranmere Rovers	0-2			62		
Crewe Alexandra *v* Atherton Collieries	4-1			129		
Marine *v* Formby.......................................	3-0			Nil		
Kirkby Town *v* Chadderton..............................	8-0			15		
Halifax Town *v* Preston North End	0-0			52		
Preston North End *v* Halifax Town		1-0			103	
Atherton LR *v* Rhyl	1-1			26		
Rhyl *v* Atherton LR		8-0			25	
Hinckley Athletic *v* Winsford United	1-1			30		
Winsford United *v* Hinckley Athletic		0-1			73	
Peterborough United *v* Lincoln City....................	2-2			67		
(Tie awarded to Peterborough United as Lincoln City played two over age players)						
Scunthorpe United *v* Boston	4-1			Nil		
Rothwell Town *v* Oldswinford	4-0			48		
Rushall Olympic *v* Bilston Town	3-0			60		
Nuneaton Borough *v* VS Rugby	2-0			20		
Wellingborough Town *v* Rushden Town	1-0			40		
Dunstable *v* Alvechurch	0-0			47		
Alvechurch *v* Dunstable		2-2			60	
Alvechurch *v* Dunstable			1-0			82
Chesham United *v* Enfield	0-0			27		
Enfield *v* Chesham United		5-0			36	
Letchworth GC *v* Saffron Walden Town...............	3-3			20		
Saffron Walden Town *v* Letchworth GC...............		4-1			39	
Wootton Blue Cross *v* Hounslow	5-1			20		
Hendon *v* Hanwell Town	13-0			59		
Uxbridge *v* Welwyn GC	8-2			80		
Royston Town *v* Northwood	3-0			36		
Hornchurch *v* Loughton BC	1-2			83		
Billericay Town *v* Canvey Island........................	3-1			159		
Clapton *v* Danson (Bexley Boro).......................(walkover for Clapton)						
Hastings Town *v* Eastbourne United	1-1			26		
Eastbourne United *v* Hastings Town		4-2			12	
Thanet United *v* Hailsham Town	2-3			24		
Gravesend & Northfleet *v* Ringmer......................	3-0			19		
Steyning Town *v* Southwick ....(walkover for Southwick)						
Welling United *v* Tooting & Mitcham United ....(walkover for Welling United)						
Shoreham *v* Worthing.......................................	1-1			21		
Worthing *v* Shoreham.....................................		2-4			37	
Slough Town *v* Walton & Hersham	2-1			Nil		
Horley Town *v* Haywards Heath	3-3			25		
Haywards Heath *v* Horley Town		2-0			27	
Banstead Athletic *v* Wokingham Town	1-1			15		
Wokingham Town *v* Banstead Athletic		2-1			19	
Ferring *v* Bognor Regis Town	1-0			57		
Maidenhead United *v* Aldershot	1-4			28		
Basingstoke Town *v* Gosport Borough..................	2-0			75		
Weymouth *v* Reading	0-15			150		
Romsey Town *v* Wimborne Town........................	3-2			50		
Poole Town *v* Newbury Town	1-1			29		
Newbury Town *v* Poole Town		3-2			30	
Hungerford Town *v* Hereford United	1-4			60		
Wotton Rovers *v* Cheltenham Town	0-4			33		
Dorchester Town *v* Taunton Town.......................	5-0			34		
Mangotsfield United *v* Torquay United.................	1-1			40		
Torquay United *v* Mangotsfield United.................		1-0			48	

First Round Qualifying	Result			Attendance		
On or before 26th September 1987	*1st Tie*	*1st Rep*	*2nd Rep*	*1st Tie*	*1st Rep*	*2nd Rep*
ICI (Wilton) *v* Darlington	0-11			100		
Billingham Synthonia *v* Yorkshire Amateur	4-2			18		
Carlisle United *v* Billingham Town	3-2			50		
Marske United *v* Custom House Junior	(walkover for Marske United)					
Marine *v* Tranmere Rovers	0-2			50		
Crewe Alexandra *v* Bury	7-0			148		
South Liverpool *v* Kirkby Town	1-2			50		
Preston North End *v* Garforth Town	12-0			102		
Burton Albion *v* Rhyl	3-1			106		
Hinckley Athletic *v* Hillcroft	2-0			40		
Radford *v* Peterborough United	1-8			6		
Scunthorpe United *v* Wisbech Town	5-0			Nil		
Nuneaton Borough *v* Rothwell Town	5-0			41		
Rushall Olympic *v* Banbury United	6-2			42		
Vauxhall Motors *v* Wellingborough Town	1-1			50		
Wellingborough Town *v* Vauxhall Motors		2-0			40	
Alvechurch *v* Abingdon United	2-0			86		
Wootton Blue Cross *v* Enfield	0-2			59		
Saffron Walden Town *v* St Albans City	2-5			30		
Royston Town *v* Hendon	1-5			56		
Uxbridge *v* Ruislip Manor	1-3			105		
Clapton *v* Loughton BC	3-1			37		
Billericay Town *v* Dulwich Hamlet	1-4			110		
Gravesend & Northfleet *v* Eastbourne United	1-1			29		
Eastbourne United *v* Gravesend & Northfleet		2-8			5	
Hailsham Town *v* Whyteleafe	1-6			38		
Shoreham *v* Southwick	2-1			80		
Welling United *v* Sutton United	1-1			70		
Sutton United *v* Welling United		2-0			63	
Wokingham Town *v* Slough Town	2-0			40		
Haywards Heath *v* Marlow	3-2			29		
Basingstoke Town *v* Ferring	1-1			80		
Ferring *v* Basingstoke Town		2-1			70	
Aldershot *v* Horndean	1-1			100		
Horndean *v* Aldershot		3-1			85	
Newbury Town *v* Reading	1-1			57		
Reading *v* Newbury Town		6-1			58	
Romsey Town *v* Oxford City	3-2			17		
Worcester City *v* Hereford United	0-3			64		
Cheltenham Town *v* Yate Town	6-1			29		
Bristol City *v* Dorchester Town	2-0			86		
Torquay United *v* Cwmbran Town	4-1			71		

Second Round Qualifying	Result			Attendance		
On or before 17th October 1987	*1st Tie*	*1st Rep*	*2nd Rep*	*1st Tie*	*1st Rep*	*2nd Rep*
Darlington *v* Billingham Synthonia	0-1			125		
Carlisle United *v* Marske United	2-1			50		
Tranmere Rovers *v* Crewe Alexandra	1-2			124		
Kirkby Town *v* Preston North End	3-3			70		
Preston North End *v* Kirkby Town		7-1			207	
Burton Albion *v* Hinckley Town	2-2			105		
Hinckley Town *v* Burton Albion		3-1			48	
Peterborough United *v* Scunthorpe United	2-1			69		
Nuneaton Borough *v* Rushall Olympic	1-1			41		
Rushall Olympic *v* Nuneaton Borough		0-1			85	
Wellingborough Town *v* Alvechurch	2-0			34		
Enfield *v* St Albans City	2-0			34		
Hendon *v* Ruislip Manor	4-1			48		
Clapton *v* Dulwich Hamlet	0-4			83		
Gravesend & Northfleet *v* Whyteleafe	2-1			40		

	Result			Attendance		
	1st Tie	1st Rep	2nd Rep	1st Tie	1st Rep	2nd Rep
Shoreham v Sutton United	1-1			63		
Sutton United v Shoreham		2-1			58	
Wokingham Town v Haywards Heath	7-1			39		
Ferring v Horndean	2-2			80		
Horndean v Ferring		2-0			103	
Reading v Romsey Town	1-1			29		
Romsey Town v Reading		0-2			102	
Hereford United v Cheltenham Town	1-6			200		
Bristol City v Torquay United	1-0			51		

First Round Proper	Result			Attendance		
On or before 14th November 1987	1st Tie	1st Rep	2nd Rep	1st Tie	1st Rep	2nd Rep
Preston North End v Doncaster Rovers	1-4			223		
Bolton Wanderers v Hull City	0-1			176		
Hartlepool United v Rotherham United	2-0			38		
Huddersfield Town v Everton	0-5			218		
Liverpool v Bradford City	2-0			170		
Wigan Athletic v Carlisle United	5-0			69		
York City v Burnley	1-2			89		
Sunderland v Oldham Athletic	2-1			349		
Blackburn Rovers v Middlesbrough	0-1			142		
Billingham Synthonia v Barnsley	1-6			74		
Peterborough United v Aston Villa	1-1			130		
Aston Villa v Peterborough United		2-2			171	
Peterborough United v Aston Villa			0-2			157
Shrewsbury Town v Kidderminster Harriers	0-0			93		
Kidderminster Harriers v Shrewsbury Town		1-1			80	
Shrewsbury Town v Kidderminster Harriers			5-2			96
Wolverhampton Wanderers v Hednesford Town	6-0			246		
Chester City v Derby County	0-3			158		
Hinckley Athletic v Crewe Alexandra	1-3			64		
West Bromwich Albion v Wrexham	1-1			320		
Wrexham v West Bromwich Albion		1-3			159	
Chesterfield v Northampton Town	2-3			95		
Nuneaton Borough v Walsall	1-5			154		
Grimsby Town v Wellingborough Town	1-0			129		
Dulwich Hamlet v Wokingham Town	3-1			83		
Erith & Belvedere v Queens Park Rangers	0-2			120		
Colchester United v Gillingham	1-0			101		
Brighton & Hove Albion v Croydon	2-0			132		
Hendon v Enfield	3-2			62		
Leyton Orient v Epsom & Ewell	4-0			115		
Cambridge United v Norwich City	2-0			40		
Gravesend & Northfleet v Staines Town	0-2			36		
Horndean v Sutton United	2-0			122		
Portsmouth v Plymouth Argyle	0-2			398		
Cardiff City v AFC Bournemouth	0-1			65		
Reading v Oxford United	4-0			52		
Bristol City v Exeter City	2-0			65		
Cheltenham Town v Swansea City	0-4			202		
Swindon Town v Newport County	3-0			102		

Second Round Proper	Result			Attendance		
On or before 12th December 1987	1st Tie	1st Rep	2nd Rep	1st Tie	1st Rep	2nd Rep
Sheffield United v Stoke City	0-3			274		
Everton v Barnsley	2-0			264		
Wigan Athletic v Leeds United	2-1			238		
Blackpool v Sheffield Wednesday	1-4			76		
Hull City v Liverpool	0-2			197		
Hartlepool United v Middlesbrough	2-3			98		

	Result			Attendance		
Manchester United v Mansfield Town	1-2			561		
Newcastle United v Burnley	2-0			424		
Doncaster Rovers v Port Vale	1-0			135		
Manchester City v Sunderland	5-1			562		
Coventry City v Wolverhampton Wanderers	3-2			576		
Ipswich Town v Notts County	0-2			253		
Nottingham Forest v Birmingham City	3-1			155		
Leicester City v Shrewsbury Town	1-1			214		
Shrewsbury Town v Leicester City		0-1			86	
West Bromwich Albion v Colchester United	4-1			247		
Crewe Alexandra v Aston Villa	2-1			599		
Walsall v Cambridge United...............................	4-2			199		
Grimsby Town v Northampton Town	0-4			72		
Luton Town v Derby County	1-4			77		
Leyton Orient v Fulham	1-0			125		
West Ham United v Chelsea...............................	0-2			284		
Swansea City v Southampton..............................	2-5			259		
Dulwich Hamlet v Queens Park Rangers	0-0			125		
Queens Park Rangers v Dulwich Hamlet		6-0			165	
Plymouth Argyle v Hendon................................	3-0			262		
Brighton & Hove Albion v Staines Town	2-1			93		
Tottenham Hotspur v Bristol Rovers...................	8-0			125		
Watford v AFC Bournemouth	2-1			332		
Horndean v Reading	1-1			162		
Reading v Horndean		5-1			85	
Wimbledon v Crystal Palace	1-0			253		
Swindon Town v Charlton Athletic	1-1			65		
Charlton Athletic v Swindon Town		5-0				
Bristol City v Southend United	2-4			45		
Millwall v Arsenal...	1-5			190		

Third Round Proper

On or before 16th January 1988

	Result			Attendance		
	1st Tie	1st Rep	2nd Rep	1st Tie	1st Rep	2nd Rep
Middlesbrough v Mansfield Town.......................	2-0			109		
Everton v Newcastle United..............................	4-2			423		
West Bromwich Albion v Manchester City............	0-1			462		
Coventry City v Liverpool	1-3			1097		
Crewe Alexandra v Wigan Athletic	0-0			1033		
Wigan Athletic v Crewe Alexandra		0-2			568	
Doncaster Rovers v Sheffield Wednesday.............	2-1			376		
Leicester City v Derby County	1-2			354		
Nottingham Forest v Stoke City	3-0			402		
Southampton v Queens Park Rangers..................	3-0			452		
Walsall v Plymouth Argyle................................	0-1			371		
Charlton Athletic v Tottenham Hotspur...............	2-2			71		
Tottenham Hotspur v Charlton Athletic...............		1-1			103	
Charlton Athletic v Tottenham Hotspur...............			0-1			80
Watford v Chelsea	2-3			387		
Southend United v Northampton Town	0-0			172		
Northampton Town v Southend United		2-3			137	
Brighton & Hove Albion v Leyton Orient..............	2-3			105		
Wimbledon v Arsenal......................................	1-2			351		
Reading v Notts County	2-1			110		

Fourth Round Proper

On or before 13th February 1988

	Result			Attendance		
	1st Tie	1st Rep	2nd Rep	1st Tie	1st Rep	2nd Rep
Southampton v Arsenal.....................................	1-2			755		
Leyton Orient v Manchester City........................	0-1			288		
Nottingham Forest v Everton	1-1			748		
Everton v Nottingham Forest		3-3			509	
Nottingham Forest v Everton			2-1			983

	Result			Attendance		
Southend United v Reading	0-3			330		
Crewe Alexandra v Middlesbrough......................	0-0			1711		
Middlesbrough v Crewe Alexandra......................		0-0			396	
Crewe Alexandra v Middlesbrough......................			3-2			1170
Plymouth Argyle v Doncaster Rovers..................	3-6			1173		
Liverpool v Derby County	1-0			290		
Tottenham Hotspur v Chelsea	6-0			282		

Fifth Round Proper	Result			Attendance		
On or before 5th March 1988	*1st Tie*	*1st Rep*	*2nd Rep*	*1st Tie*	*1st Rep*	*2nd Rep*
Liverpool v Nottingham Forest	3-3			695		
Nottingham Forest v Liverpool		3-0			2072	
Reading v Tottenham Hotspur............................	0-0			378		
Tottenham Hotspur v Reading............................		2-1			261	
Crewe Alexandra v Arsenal	1-1			3886		
Arsenal v Crewe Alexandra		5-1			1151	
Doncaster Rovers v Manchester City....................	2-1			2310		

Semi-Final

Two Legs to be played on or before 2nd April 1988

1st Leg

Doncaster Rovers v Tottenham Hotspur	2-1		5264
Arsenal v Nottingham Forest.............................	1-1		2000

2nd Leg

Tottenham Hotspur v Doncaster Rovers	1-1		1033
Nottingham Forest v Arsenal.............................	0-3		6000

Doncaster Rovers won on aggregate 3-2
Arsenal won on aggregate 4-1

Final

Two Legs to be played on or before 30th April 1988

1st Leg

Doncaster Rovers v Arsenal	0-5		5264

2nd Leg

Arsenal v Doncaster Rovers	1-1		4843

Arsenal won on aggregate 6-1

F.A. County Youth Challenge Cup Competition 1987-88

First Round	1st Tie	1st Rep	2nd Rep
Durham v Cumberland	5-0		
West Riding v East Riding	1-2		
Liverpool v Lancashire	1-2		
Shropshire v Cheshire	2-3		
Nottinghamshire v Derbyshire	1-3		
Huntingdonshire v Lincolnshire	0-3		
Worcestershire v Birmingham	3-3		
Birmingham v Worcestershire		4-0	
Suffolk v Norfolk	3-2		
Bedfordshire v Hertfordshire	2-1		
Middlesex v Essex	5-3		
Royal Navy v Sussex	0-2		
Somerset & Avon (Sth) v Berks & Bucks	1-2		
Cornwall v Dorset	4-0		

Second Round	1st Tie	1st Rep	2nd Rep
North Riding v Northumberland	1-2		
Durham v Westmorland	3-1		
East Riding v Sheffield & Hallamshire	4-1		
Lancashire v Manchester	2-0		
Cheshire v Staffordshire	3-1		
Derbyshire v Leicestershire & Rutland	4-1		
Lincolnshire v Northamptonshire	4-3		
Birmingham v Oxfordshire	0-2		
Gloucestershire v Herefordshire	2-1		
Suffolk v Cambridgeshire	2-1		
Bedfordshire v London	4-1		
Middlesex v Kent	1-0		
Surrey v Hampshire	0-2		
Sussex v Army	1-1		
Army v Sussex		1-5	
Berks & Bucks v Wiltshire	1-2		
Cornwall v Devon	1-2		

Third Round	1st Tie	1st Rep	2nd Rep
Lancashire v East Riding	1-2		
Northumberland v Durham	1-3		
Gloucestershire v Oxfordshire	2-1		
Cheshire v Derbyshire	2-1		
Middlesex v Bedfordshire	2-1		
Lincolnshire v Suffolk	2-2		
Suffolk v Lincolnshire		0-0	
Lincolnshire v Suffolk			1-2
Devon v Wiltshire	6-1		
Hampshire v Sussex	0-1		

Fourth Round	1st Tie	1st Rep	2nd Rep
Cheshire v Durham	3-3		
Durham v Cheshire		3-2	
East Riding v Suffolk	1-0		
Devon v Middlesex	2-2		
Middlesex v Devon		4-2	
Gloucestershire v Sussex	2-1		

Semi-Final

Durham v East Riding 0-3   Gloucestershire v Middlesex 1-2

Final

East Riding v Middlesex 5-3   (after a 1-1 draw)

England Youth Caps 1987-88

	Holland	Rep. of Ireland	Sweden	Belgium	German Dem. Rep.	France
A. Marriott (Arsenal)	1	1				
P. Garland (Tottenham Hotspur)	2	2	2	2	2	2
J. Hall (Tottenham Hotspur)....................	3					
P. Wratten (Manchester United)...............	4	4	4	4		
J. Soloman (Watford)............................	5	5	6	6	5	5
M. Blake (Aston Villa)	6	6			4	4
L. Cormack (Southampton)....................	7					
R. Thomas (Watford)............................	8	8	8	8	8	8
G. Stuart (Chelsea)	9		*7	*7	7	7
S. Murray (Tottenham Hotspur)	10	10	10	10	10	10
M. Parrott (Aston Villa)	11					
J. Bond (Coventry City)..........................	*2					
D. Duffy (Aston Villa)	*5		5	5	6	6
P. Masters (Southampton)	*7	*11	*11	11		*11
G. McKeown (Arsenal)	*11				11	11
J. Drysdale (Watford)		3	3	3	3	3
P. Quinlan (Everton)		7	7	7		*8
A. Shearer (Southampton)		9	9	9	9	9
M. Wallace (Manchester City)..................		11				
D. Kiely (Coventry City)..........................			1	1	1	1
M. Gayle (Brentford).............................			11			

*Substitute

129

Youth International Matches 1947-88

wyc **World Youth Championship**
iyt **International Youth Tournament**
*Qualifying Competition †Professionals ‡Abandoned

ENGLAND v. ALGERIA

| | | | Goals | |
Year	Date	Venue	Eng	Alg
†1984	April 22	Cannes	3	0

ENGLAND v. ARGENTINA

			Eng	Arg
†wyc1981	Oct. 5	Sydney	1	1

ENGLAND v. AUSTRALIA

			Eng	Aus
†wyc1981	Oct. 8	Sydney	1	1

ENGLAND v. AUSTRIA

			Eng	Aust
iyt1949	April 19	Zeist	4	2
iyt1952	April 17	Barcelona	5	5
iyt1957	April 16	Barcelona	0	3
1958	Mar. 4	Highbury	3	2
1958	June 1	Graz	4	3
iyt1960	April 20	Vienna	0	1
†iyt1964	April 1	Rotterdam	2	1
†1980	Sep. 6	Pazin	0	1
†iyt1981	May 29	Bonn	7	0
†1981	Sep. 3	Umag	3	0
†1984	Sep. 6	Izola	2	2

ENGLAND v. BELGIUM

			Eng	Belg
iyt1948	April 16	West Ham	3	1
iyt1951	Mar. 22	Cannes	1	1
iyt1953	Mar. 31	Brussels	2	0
‡1958	Nov. 7	Brussels	3	2
1957	Nov. 3	Sheffield	2	0
†iyt1965	April 15	Ludwigshafen	3	0
*iyt1969	Mar. 11	West Ham	1	0
*iyt1972	May 13	Palma	0	0
†iyt1973	June 4	Viareggio	0	0
†iyt1977	May 19	Lokeren	1	0
†1979	Jan 17	Brussels	4	0
†1980	Sep. 8	Labin	6	1
†1983	April 13	Birmingham	1	1
†1988	May 20	Chatel	0	0

ENGLAND v. BRAZIL

			Eng	Bra
†1986	Mar. 29	Cannes	0	0
†1986	May 13	Peking	1	2
†1987	June 2	Niteroi	0	2

ENGLAND v. BULGARIA

			Eng	Bulg
iyt1956	Mar. 28	Salgotarjan	1	2
iyt1960	April 16	Graz	0	1
iyt1962	April 24	Ploesti	0	0
†1968	April 7	Nimes	0	0
†iyt1969	Mar. 26	Waregem	2	0
†iyt1972	May 13	Palma	0	0
†iyt1979	May 31	Vienna	0	1

ENGLAND v. CAMEROON

			Eng	Cam
†wyc1981	Oct. 3	Sydney	2	0
†1985	June 1	Toulon	1	0

ENGLAND v. CHINA

			Eng	China
†1983	Mar. 31	Cannes	5	1
†wyc1985	Aug. 26	Baku	0	2
†1986	May 5	Peking	1	0

ENGLAND v. CZECHOSLOVAKIA

| | | | Goals | |
Year	Date	Venue	Eng	Czech
iyt1955	April 7	Lucca	0	1
†iyt1966	May 21	Rijeka	2	3
†iyt1969	May 20	Leipzig	3	1
iyt1979	May 24	Bischofshofen	3	0
†1979	Sep. 8	Pula	1	2
†1982	April 11	Cannes	0	1
†iyt1983	May 20	Highbury	1	1

ENGLAND v. DENMARK

			Eng	Den
†1955	Oct. 1	Plymouth	9	2
1956	May 20	Esbjerg	2	1
*†iyt1979	Oct. 31	Esbjerg	3	1
*iyt1980	Mar. 26	Coventry	4	0
†1982	July 15	Stjordal	5	2
†1983	July 16	Holbeck	0	1
†1987	Feb. 16	Manchester	2	1

ENGLAND v. EGYPT

			Eng	Egypt
†wyc1981	Oct. 11	Sydney	4	2

ENGLAND v. FINLAND

			Eng	Fin
†iyt1975	May 19	Berne	1	0

ENGLAND v. FRANCE

			Eng	France
1957	Mar. 24	Fontainbleau	1	0
1958	Mar. 22	Eastbourne	0	1
†iyt1966	May 23	Rijeka	1	2
†iyt1967	May 11	Istanbul	2	0
†1968	Jan. 25	Paris	0	1
*iyt1978	Feb. 8	Crystal Palace	3	1
*iyt1978	Mar. 1	Paris	0	0
†iyt1979	June 2	Vienna	0	0
†1982	April 12	Cannes	0	1
†1983	April 2	Cannes	0	2
†1984	April 23	Cannes	1	2
†1985	June 7	Toulon	1	3
†1986	Mar. 31	Cannes	1	2
†1986	May 11	Peking	1	1
†1988	May 22	Monthey	1	2

ENGLAND v. GERMANY D.R.

			Eng	GDR
iyt1958	April 7	Neunkirchen	1	0
1959	Mar. 8	Zwickau	3	4
1960	April 2	Portsmouth	1	1
†iyt1965	April 25	Essen	2	3
†iyt1969	May 22	Magdeburg	0	4
†iyt1973	June 10	Florence	3	2
†iyt1984	May 25	Moscow	1	1
†1988	May 21	Monthey	1	0

ENGLAND v. GERMANY F.R.

			Eng	GFR
iyt1953	April 4	Boom	3	1
iyt1954	April 15	Gelsenkirchen	2	2
iyt1956	April 1	Sztalinvaros	2	1
1957	Mar. 31	Oberhausen	4	1
1958	Mar. 12	Bolton	1	2
1961	Mar. 12	Flensberg	0	2
†1962	Mar. 31	Northampton	1	0
†1967	Feb. 14	Moenchengladbach	1	0
†iyt1972	May 22	Barcelona	2	0
†1975	Jan. 25	Las Palmas	4	2

			Eng	
†1976	Nov. 14	Monte Carlo	1	1
†IYT1979	May 28	Salzburg	2	0
†1979	Sep. 1	Pula	1	1
†1983	Sep. 5	Pazin	2	0

ENGLAND v. GREECE

			Goals	
Year	Date	Venue	Eng	Greece
IYT1957	April 18	Barcelona	2	3
IYT1959	April 2	Dimitrovo	4	0
†IYT1977	May 23	Beveren	1	1
†1983	May 23	Puspokladany	1	0

ENGLAND v. HUNGARY

			Eng	Hung
IYT1954	April 11	Dusseldorf	1	3
IYT1956	Mar. 31	Tatabanya	2	4
†1956	Oct. 23	Tottenham	2	1
†1956	Oct. 25	Sunderland	2	1
†IYT1965	April 21	Wuppertal	5	0
†IYT1975	May 16	Olten	3	1
†1977	Oct. 16	Las Palmas	3	0
†1979	Sep. 5	Pula	2	0
†1980	Sep. 11	Pula	1	2
†1981	Sep. 7	Porec	4	0
†1983	July 29	Debrecen	1	2
†1983	Sep. 3	Umag	3	2
†1986	Mar. 30	Cannes	2	0

ENGLAND v. ICELAND

			Eng	Ice
†IYT1973	May 31	Viareggio	2	0
†IYT1977	May 21	Turnhout	0	0
*†IYT1983	Oct. 12	Reykjavik	3	0
*†IYT1983	Nov. 1	Crystal Palace	3	0
*†IYT1984	Oct. 16	Manchester	5	3
*†IYT1985	Sep. 11	Reykjavik	5	0

ENGLAND v. IRELAND

			Eng	Ire
1948	May 15	Belfast	2	2
IYT1949	April 18	Haarlem	3	3
1949	May 14	Hull	4	2
1950	May 6	Belfast	0	1
1951	May 5	Liverpool	5	2
1952	April 19	Belfast	0	2
1953	April 11	Wolverhampton	0	0
IYT1954	April 10	Bruehl	5	0
1954	May 8	Newtonards	2	2
1955	May 14	Watford	3	0
1956	May 12	Belfast	0	1
1957	May 11	Leyton	6	2
1958	May 10	Bangor	2	4
1959	May 9	Liverpool	5	0
1960	May 14	Belfast	5	2
1961	May 13	Manchester	2	0
1962	May 12	Londonderry	1	2
†IYT1963	April 23	Wembley	4	0
1963	May 11	Oldham	1	1
1964	Jan. 25	Belfast	3	1
1965	Jan. 22	Birkenhead	2	3
1966	Feb. 26	Belfast	4	0
1967	Feb. 25	Stockport	3	0
1968	Feb. 23	Belfast	0	2
1969	Feb. 28	Birkenhead	0	2
1970	Feb. 28	Lurgan	1	3
1971	Mar. 6	Blackpool	1	1
1972	Mar. 11	Chester	1	1
1973	Mar. 24	Wellington	3	0
1974	April 19	Birkenhead	1	2
†IYT1975	May 13	Kriens	3	0
†IYT1983	May 16	Arnstadt	1	0
*†IYT1981	Feb. 11	Walsall	1	0
*†IYT1981	Mar. 11	Belfast	3	0

ENGLAND v. REP. OF IRELAND

			Goals	Rep.
Year	Date	Venue	Eng	of Ire
IYT1953	April 5	Leuven	2	0
†IYT1964	Mar. 30	Middleburg	6	0
*†IYT1968	Feb. 7	Dublin	0	0
*†IYT1968	Feb. 28	Portsmouth	4	1
*†IYT1970	Jan. 14	Dublin	4	1
*†IYT1970	Feb. 4	Luton	10	0
†IYT1972	May 15	Sabadell	4	0
†IYT1975	May 9	Brunnen	1	0
*†IYT1985	Feb. 26	Dublin	0	1
*†IYT1986	Feb. 25	Leeds	2	0
†1988	Feb. 17	Stoke	2	0

ENGLAND v. ISRAEL

			Eng	Israel
†1962	May 20	Tel Aviv	3	1
†1962	May 22	Haifa	1	2

ENGLAND v. ITALY

			Eng	Italy
IYT1958	April 13	Luxembourg	0	1
IYT1959	Mar. 25	Sofia	1	3
IYT1961	April 4	Braga	2	3
†IYT1965	April 23	Marl-Huels	3	1
†IYT1966	May 25	Rijeka	1	1
†IYT1967	May 5	Izmir	1	0
†1973	Feb. 14	Cava Dei Tirreni	0	1
†1973	Mar. 14	Highbury	1	0
†IYT1973	June 7	Viareggio	1	0
†1978	Nov. 19	Monte Carlo	1	2
*†1979	Feb. 28	Rome	1	0
*†IYT1979	April 4	Birmingham	2	0
†IYT1983	May 22	Watford	1	1
†1984	April 20	Cannes	1	0
†1985	April 5	Cannes	2	2

ENGLAND v. LUXEMBOURG

			Eng	Lux
IYT1950	May 25	Vienna	1	2
IYT1954	April 17	Bad Neuenahr	0	2
1957	Feb. 2	West Ham	7	1
1957	Nov. 17	Luxembourg	3	0
IYT1958	April 9	Eschsalzett	5	0
†IYT1984	May 29	Moscow	2	0

ENGLAND v. MALTA

			Eng	Malta
†IYT1969	May 18	Wolfen	6	0
†IYT1979	May 26	Salzburg	3	0

ENGLAND v. MEXICO

			Eng	Mex
†1984	April 18	Cannes	4	0
†1985	June 5	Toulon	2	0
†WYC1985	Aug. 29	Baku	0	1

ENGLAND v. HOLLAND

			Eng	Hol
IYT1948	April 17	Tottenham	3	2
IYT1951	Mar. 26	Cannes	2	1
†1954	Nov. 21	Arnhem	2	3
†1955	Nov. 5	Norwich	3	1
1957	Mar. 2	Brentford	5	5
IYT1957	April 14	Barcelona	1	2
1957	Oct. 2	Amsterdam	3	2
1961	Mar. 9	Utrecht	0	1
†1962	Jan. 31	Brighton	4	3
IYT1962	April 22	Ploesti	0	3
IYT1963	April 13	Wimbledon	5	0
IYT1968	April 9	Nimes	1	0

ENGLAND v. HOLLAND (contd)

Year	Date	Venue	Eng	Hol
*†IYT1974	Feb. 13	West Bromwich	1	1
*†IYT1974	Feb. 27	The Hague	1	0
†IYT1980	May 23	Halle	1	0
†1982	April 9	Cannes	1	0
†1985	April 7	Cannes	1	3
†1987	Aug. 1	Wembley	3	1

ENGLAND v. NORWAY

Year	Date	Venue	Eng	Nor
†1982	July. 13	Levanger	1	4
†1983	July 14	Korsor	1	0

ENGLAND v. PARAGUAY

			Eng	Par
†WYC1985	Aug. 24	Baku	2	2

ENGLAND v. POLAND

			Eng	Pol
IYT1960	April 18	Graz	4	2
†IYT1964	Mar. 26	Breda	1	1
†IYT1971	May 26	Presnov	0	0
†IYT1972	May 20	Valencia	1	0
†1975	Jan. 21	Las Palmas	1	1
IYT1978	May 9	Chorzow	0	2
†1979	Sept. 3	Porec	0	1

ENGLAND v. POLAND (contd)

Year	Date	Venue	Eng	Pol
†IYT1980	May 25	Leipzig	2	1
†1982	July 17	Steinkjer	3	2
†1983	July 12	Siagelse	1	0

ENGLAND v. PORTUGAL

			Eng	Port
IYT1954	April 18	Bonn	0	2
IYT1961	April 2	Lisbon	0	4
†IYT1964	April 3	The Hague	4	0
†IYT1971	May 30	Prague	3	0
†1978	Nov. 15	Monte Carlo	2	0
†IYT1980	May 18	Rosslau	1	1
†1982	April 7	Cannes	3	0

ENGLAND v. QATAR

			Eng	Qat
†WYC1981	Oct. 14	Sydney	1	2
†1983	April 4	Cannes	1	1

ENGLAND v. RUMANIA

			Eng	Rum
1957	Oct. 15	Tottenham	4	2
IYT1958	April 11	Luxembourg	1	0
IYT1959	Mar. 31	Pazardijc	1	2
†IYT1963	April 15	Highbury	3	0
†WYC1981	Oct. 17	Adelaide	0	1

ENGLAND v. SAAR

			Eng	Saar
IYT1954	April 13	Dortmund	1	1
IYT1955	April 9	Prato	3	1

ENGLAND v. SCOTLAND

			Eng	Sco
1947	Oct. 25	Doncaster	4	2
1948	Oct. 30	Aberdeen	1	3
IYT1949	April 21	Ultrecht	0	1
1950	Feb. 4	Carlisle	7	1
1951	Feb. 3	Kilmarnock	6	1
1952	Mar. 15	Sunderland	3	1

ENGLAND v. SCOTLAND (contd)

Year	Date	Venue	Eng	Sco
1953	Feb. 7	Glasgow	4	3
1954	Feb. 6	Middlesbrough	2	1
1955	Mar. 5	Kilmarnock	3	4
1956	Mar. 3	Preston	2	2
1957	Mar. 9	Aberdeen	3	1
1958	Mar. 1	Hull	2	0
1959	Feb. 28	Aberdeen	1	1
1960	Feb. 27	Newcastle	1	1
1961	Feb. 25	Elgin	3	2
1962	Feb. 24	Peterborough	4	2
†IYT1963	April 19	White City	1	0
1963	May 18	Dumfries	3	1
1964	Feb. 22	Middlesbrough	1	1
1965	Feb. 27	Inverness	1	2
1966	Feb. 5	Hereford	5	3
1967	Feb. 4	Aberdeen	0	1
*†IYT1967	Mar. 1	Southampton	1	0
*†IYT1967	Mar. 15	Dundee	0	0
1968	Feb. 3	Walsall	0	5
1969	Feb. 1	Stranraer	1	0
1979	Jan. 31	Derby	1	2
1971	Jan. 30	Greenock	1	2
1972	Jan. 29	Bournemouth	2	0
1973	Jan. 20	Kilmarnock	3	2
1974	Jan. 26	Brighton	2	2
†IYT1981	May 27	Aachen	0	1
*†IYT1982	Feb. 23	Glasgow	0	1
*†IYT1982	Mar. 23	Coventry	2	2
†IYT1983	May 15	Birmingham	3	0
*†IYT1984	Nov. 27	Fulham	1	2
*1985	April 8	Cannes	1	0
*†IYT1986	Mar. 25	Aberdeen	1	4

ENGLAND v. SPAIN

			Eng	Spain
IYT1952	April 15	Barcelona	1	4
1957	Sept. 26	Birmingham	4	4
IYT1958	April 5	Saarbruecken	2	2
†1958	Oct. 8	Madrid	4	2
IYT1961	Mar. 30	Lisbon	0	0
†1964	Feb. 27	Murcia	2	1
†IYT1964	April 5	Amsterdam	4	0
†IYT1965	April 17	Heilbronn	0	0
†1966	Mar. 30	Swindon	3	0
†IYT1967	May 7	Manisa	2	1
†1971	Mar. 31	Pamplona	2	3
†1971	April 20	Luton	1	1
†1972	Feb. 9	Alicante	0	0
*†IYT1972	Mar. 15	Sheffield	4	1
*†IYT1975	Feb. 25	Bristol	1	1
*†IYT1975	Mar. 18	Madrid	1	0
†1976	Nov. 12	Monte Carlo	3	0
†IYT1978	May 7	Bukowas	1	0
†1978	Nov. 17	Monte Carlo	1	1
†IYT1981	May 25	Siegen	1	2
†IYT1983	May 13	Stoke	1	0

ENGLAND v. SWEDEN

			Eng	Swe
†IYT1971	May 24	Poprad	1	0
†1981	Sep. 5	Pazin	3	2
†1984	Sep. 10	Rovinj	1	1
†1986	Nov. 10	West Bromwich	3	3
†1988	May 19	Sion	2	0

ENGLAND v. SWITZERLAND

			Eng	Swit
IYT1950	May 26	Stockerau	2	1
IYT1951	Mar. 27	Nice	3	1
IYT1952	April 13	Barcelona	4	0
IYT1955	April 11	Florence	0	0
1956	Mar. 11	Schaffhausen	2	0
1956	Oct. 13	Brighton	2	2
1958	May 26	Zurich	3	0
†1960	Oct. 8	Leyton	4	3
*1962	Nov. 22	Coventry	1	0

ENGLAND v. SWITZERLAND (contd)

Year	Date		Venue	Goals Eng	Swit
†1963	Mar.	21	Bienne	7	1
†IYT1973	June	2	Forte Dei Marmi	2	0
†IYT1975	May	11	Buochs	4	0
†1980	Sep.	4	Rovinj	3	0
†1982	Sep.	6	Porec	2	0
†1983	July	26	Hajduboszormeny	4	0
†1983	Sep.	1	Porec	4	2

ENGLAND v. THAILAND

Year	Date		Venue	Eng	Thai
†1986	May	7	Peking	1	2

ENGLAND v. TURKEY

Year	Date		Venue	Goals Eng	Tur
IYT1959	Mar.	29	Dimitrovo	1	1
†IYT1978	May	5	Wodzislaw	1	1

ENGLAND v. U.S.S.R.

Year	Date		Venue	Eng	USSR
†IYT1963	April	17	Tottenham	2	0
†IYT1967	May	13	Istanbul	0	1
†IYT1968	April	11	Nimes	1	1
†IYT1971	May	28	Prague	1	1
†1978	Oct.	10	Las Palmas	1	0
†1982	Sep.	4	Umag	1	0
†1983	Mar.	29	Cannes	0	0
†IYT1983	May	17	Aston Villa	0	2
†IYT1984	May	27	Moscow	1	1
†1984	Sep.	8	Porec	1	0
†1985	April	3	Cannes	2	1
†1985	June	3	Toulon	0	2

ENGLAND v. URUGUAY

Year	Date		Venue	Eng	Uru
†1977	Oct.	9	Las Palmas	1	1
†1987	June	10	Montevideo	2	2

ENGLAND v. WALES

Year	Date		Venue	Eng	Wales
1948	Feb.	28	High Wycombe	4	3
IYT1948	April	15	London	4	0
1949	Feb.	26	Swansea	0	0
1950	Feb.	25	Worcester	1	0
1951	Feb.	17	Wrexham	1	1
1952	Feb.	23	Plymouth	6	0

ENGLAND v. WALES (contd)

Year	Date		Venue	Goals Eng	Wales
1953	Feb.	21	Swansea	4	2
1954	Feb.	20	Derby	2	1
1955	Feb.	19	Milford Haven	7	2
1956	Feb.	18	Shrewsbury	5	1
1957	Feb.	9	Cardiff	7	1
1958	Feb.	15	Reading	8	2
1959	Feb.	14	Portmadoc	3	0
1960	Mar.	19	Canterbury	1	1
1961	Mar.	18	Newtown	4	0
1962	Mar.	17	Swindon	4	0
1963	Mar.	16	Haverfordwest	1	0
1964	Mar.	14	Leeds	2	1
1965	Mar.	20	Newport	2	2
1966	Mar.	19	Northampton	4	1
1967	Mar.	18	Cwmbran	3	3
1968	Mar.	16	Watford	2	3
1969	Mar.	15	Haverfordwest	3	1
*†IYT1970	Feb.	25	Newport	0	0
*†IYT1970	Mar.	18	Leyton	1	2
1970	April	20	Reading	0	0
1971	Feb.	20	Aberystwyth	1	2
1972	Feb.	19	Swindon	4	0
1973	Feb.	24	Portmadoc	4	1
*†IYT1974	Jan.	9	West Bromwich	1	0
1974	Mar.	2	Shrewsbury	2	1
*†IYT1974	Mar.	13	Cardiff	0	1
*†IYT1976	Feb.	11	Cardiff	1	0
*†IYT1976	Mar.	3	Manchester	2	3
*†IYT1977	Mar.	9	West Bromwich	1	0
*†IYT1977	Mar.	23	Cardiff	1	1

ENGLAND v. YUGOSLAVIA

Year	Date		Venue	Eng	Yugo
IYT1953	April	2	Liege	1	1
1958	Feb.	4	Chelsea	2	2
IYT1962	April	20	Ploesti	0	5
†IYT1967	May	9	Izmir	1	1
†IYT1971	May	22	Bardejov	1	0
†IYT1972	May	17	Barcelona	1	0
†1976	Nov.	16	Monte Carlo	0	3
†1978	May	20	Altenberg	2	0
†1981	Sep.	10	Pula	5	0
†1982	Sep.	9	Pula	1	0
†1983	July	25	Debrechen	4	4
†1983	Sep.	8	Pula	2	2
†1984	Sep.	12	Buje	1	4

Review of the Barclays League Season 1987-88

A Liverpool team without Ian Rush but reinforced with the likes of Peter Beardsley, Ray Houghton and "Footballer of the Year" John Barnes, swept all before them to register their 17th Championship win all told and their seventh in the last 10 years. They finished nine points ahead of their nearest challengers, Manchester United, and clinched the title on 23rd April, when Beardsley's goal beat Tottenham before the Anfield faithful.

With the Championship issue apparently cut and dried early in the New Year, most of the end-of-season drama concerned the respective struggles to preserve and attain First Division status.

Troubled Watford, who actually had three different managers for one F.A. Cup tie in January, went down with Oxford United, whose manager Mark Lawrenson still finished the season with a Championship medal, having played in the requisite number of matches for Liverpool(!) Portsmouth joined them, having completed just one First Division season after a 28-year wait, as a 2-1 home defeat by Newcastle United in the penultimate fixture sealed their fate.

Chelsea, with a solitary League victory in their last 26 matches, failed to beat fellow strugglers Charlton Athletic at home on the last Saturday (1-1) and had to face the anguish of the play-offs.

John Docherty's Millwall achieved promotion to the top flight for the first time in the club's 103-year history amid scenes of delirium at Hull on 2nd May, and the Second Division Championship was theirs by four points from Aston Villa, promoted by the old-fashioned maxim of

scoring five more goals than Middlesbrough during the season.

Paradoxically, Villa only managed a goalless draw at Swindon in their last match, but it sufficed because Middlesbrough had an attack of promotion jitters in front of a 27,000 crowd at Ayresome Park and lost 2-1 to 13th-placed Leicester City, a team with only three away wins to their credit all season. The north-east club were to be joined in the play-offs by Bradford City and Blackburn Rovers, the latter wrecking Millwall's celebration party at The Den by winning 4-1 and thereby claiming fifth spot in the table. Crystal Palace missed the play-offs by two points for the second season running.

At the foot of the Second Division Reading, the Simod Cup winners, scrambled a goalless home draw with Hull City in their last match when three points would have given them a chance of avoiding automatic relegation. They went down with Huddersfield Town, who never seemed to recover from that 10-1 drubbing at Maine Road back in November, and Sheffield United survived to make the play-offs.

Sunderland, relegated last season, were clear winners of the Third Division by nine points, but any one of six other clubs could have claimed the other automatic promotion place as the season moved into its final fortnight. Apparently out of contention for much of the season, Brighton & Hove Albion stole up on the blind side of a group of established promotion candidates and pipped them all by beating Bristol Rovers 2-1, urged on by a partisan crowd of nearly 20,000 at the Goldstone.

A 1-0 win against doomed Doncaster Rovers enabled Joe Jordan's Bristol City to leapfrog over Northampton Town and grab a play-off place along with Notts County and Walsall, while at the other end Southend United achieved safety by swamping fellow seasiders Blackpool 4-0 at home in their final match and consigned Rotherham United to the play-offs. Grimsby Town sank into the Fourth Division, their second demotion in successive seasons, although their points total was 17 more than York and Doncaster.

Wolverhampton Wanderers were aggrieved to have lost out to Aldershot in last year's play-offs despite finishing nine points ahead of them in the table, but they made no mistake this time and won the Fourth Division by five points from Welsh Cup finalists Cardiff City. Bolton Wanderers secured the last promotion place by winning 1-0 at Wrexham, and two clubs who faced each other on the last Saturday, Torquay United and Scunthorpe United, finished a point behind to join Swansea City in the play-off bracket. It had been quite an achievement for the Devon club, considering that they had been a few seconds from dropping into the GM Vauxhall Conference a year earlier.

Newport County bowed out of the League in ignominious fashion, losing 1-0 at home to Rochdale in front of a crowd boosted by a thousand souvenir programme-hunters. The Welsh club ended the season 19 points adrift of 23rd-placed Carlisle United and now make way for Conference champions Lincoln City, back in the fold after just one year's absence.

Attendances showed an increase over the previous season of well over half a million. Goalscoring was also on the increase.

Barclays League Play-Offs

Division 1 (relegation)/Division 2 (promotion)
Semi-Finals
Blackburn Rovers v Chelsea 0-2,1-4
Bradford City v Middlesbrough 2-1, 0-2
Final
Middlesbrough v Chelsea 2-0, 0-1

Division 2 (relegation)/Division 3 (promotion)
Semi-Finals
Bristol City v Sheffield United 1-0, 1-1
Notts County v Walsall 1-3, 1-1
Final
Bristol City v Walsall 1-3, 2-0, 0-4 (replay)

Division 3 (relegation)/Division 4 (promotion)
Semi-Finals
Swansea City v Rotherham United 1-0, 1-1
Torquay United v Scunthorpe United 2-1, 1-1
Final
Swansea City v Torquay United 2-1, 3-3

First Division Results 1987-88

Home team (rows) × Away team (columns). Column abbreviations: ARS = Arsenal, CHA = Charlton Athletic, CHE = Chelsea, COV = Coventry City, DER = Derby County, EVE = Everton, LIV = Liverpool, LUT = Luton Town, MUN = Manchester United, NEW = Newcastle United, NOR = Norwich City, NOF = Nottingham Forest, OXF = Oxford United, POR = Portsmouth, QPR = Queens Park Rangers, SHW = Sheffield Wednesday, SOU = Southampton, TOT = Tottenham Hotspur, WAT = Watford, WHU = West Ham United, WIM = Wimbledon.

Home \ Away	ARS	CHA	CHE	COV	DER	EVE	LIV	LUT	MUN	NEW	NOR	NOF	OXF	POR	QPR	SHW	SOU	TOT	WAT	WHU	WIM
Arsenal	—	4-0	3-1	1-1	2-1	1-1	1-2	2-1	1-2	1-1	2-0	0-2	2-0	6-0	0-1	3-1	0-1	2-1	0-1	1-0	3-0
Charlton Athletic	0-3	—	2-2	3-0	1-0	1-1	0-1	1-0	0-0	2-1	3-1	2-2	1-0	1-0	1-0	2-0	2-0	1-1	1-0	3-0	1-1
Chelsea	1-1	1-1	—	3-3	1-3	0-0	0-0	3-0	1-2	1-1	1-0	2-2	1-3	1-0	1-1	1-1	1-0	0-2	1-1	1-1	1-1
Coventry City	0-0	0-1	3-3	—	0-3	2-1	0-1	0-1	0-1	2-2	0-1	0-1	1-0	0-0	2-2	1-2	2-1	1-1	1-1	0-0	3-1
Derby County	0-0	1-1	4-1	0-1	—	0-1	0-1	0-0	2-1	1-0	1-2	2-1	2-1	0-0	2-1	2-1	1-2	0-0	1-1	1-1	2-1
Everton	1-2	3-2	4-1	2-1	2-0	—	1-0	2-1	2-1	1-1	3-0	0-0	2-1	1-0	2-0	4-0	4-0	1-1	2-0	3-1	2-2
Liverpool	2-1	1-0	3-0	4-0	4-0	0-1	—	1-0	3-3	4-0	2-0	5-0	2-0	4-0	4-0	1-0	1-0	2-0	4-1	0-0	2-1
Luton Town	1-1	0-0	3-0	1-0	1-0	2-0	1-0	—	0-0	4-1	2-1	1-1	7-4	4-1	2-1	2-2	1-0	1-2	2-0	3-1	2-0
Manchester United	0-0	2-1	2-1	0-1	4-1	2-1	1-1	3-0	—	0-1	2-1	2-0	3-1	2-0	2-0	4-2	0-2	1-0	2-0	3-1	2-1
Newcastle United	0-1	2-0	3-1	2-2	0-0	1-1	1-4	4-0	0-0	—	1-3	2-2	1-1	1-1	1-1	1-1	2-2	2-0	3-0	2-1	1-2
Norwich City	2-4	2-0	3-2	1-2	2-1	0-1	0-0	0-2	1-0	2-0	—	1-2	2-0	1-0	2-0	3-0	3-0	2-1	1-0	0-0	0-1
Nottingham Forest	0-1	2-1	4-4	0-1	2-1	0-0	1-2	2-2	0-2	1-2	3-0	—	0-2	4-1	1-1	0-3	3-3	3-0	1-1	1-2	0-0
Oxford United	0-0	1-1	0-3	2-0	1-2	0-1	0-3	2-5	0-0	0-1	3-0	1-1	—	5-2	1-0	0-3	0-0	0-0	0-0	1-2	2-5
Portsmouth	1-1	1-1	3-1	1-0	1-0	0-1	0-2	1-2	1-1	0-1	1-3	2-1	2-2	—	0-0	1-0	2-0	1-0	2-3	0-1	2-1
Queens Park Rangers	2-0	2-0	1-3	2-1	2-1	2-0	0-1	2-1	2-0	1-1	1-0	3-1	4-0	2-0	—	1-0	2-1	0-3	1-0	2-1	1-0
Sheffield Wednesday	3-3	3-1	1-1	3-0	2-1	4-2	0-5	3-0	4-1	1-1	4-0	2-0	3-1	5-0	0-1	—	3-2	2-1	2-1	2-1	2-2
Southampton	4-2	0-1	1-0	3-0	3-2	0-1	0-2	4-1	2-2	0-2	2-0	0-0	3-0	2-1	2-0	1-2	—	2-1	1-0	2-1	0-3
Tottenham Hotspur	1-2	1-1	0-2	2-1	1-2	0-0	2-0	1-0	2-0	2-1	2-1	3-0	0-0	2-0	0-3	2-1	2-1	—	1-1	0-1	3-0
Watford	0-1	1-0	1-1	1-1	2-0	4-0	4-1	2-0	3-0	0-0	1-0	1-1	0-0	2-3	1-0	2-1	1-0	2-1	—	1-0	1-2
West Ham United	0-1	1-1	1-1	0-1	1-1	1-0	0-0	1-1	1-1	3-1	2-0	3-2	0-1	1-1	0-1	2-0	3-1	1-1	2-1	—	1-2
Wimbledon	3-1	4-1	2-2	1-2	2-1	1-1	1-1	2-0	2-1	0-0	1-0	1-1	1-1	2-2	1-2	1-1	2-0	3-0	1-2	1-1	—

First Division Final Positions 1987-88

			Home				Away					
	P	W	D	L	F	A	W	D	L	F	A	GD	Pts
1. Liverpool	40	15	5	0	49	9	11	7	2	38	15	+63	90
2. Manchester United	40	14	5	1	41	17	9	7	4	30	21	+33	81
3. Nottingham Forest	40	11	7	2	40	17	9	6	5	27	22	+28	73
4. Everton	40	14	4	2	34	11	5	9	6	19	16	+26	70
5. Queens Park Rangers	40	12	4	4	30	14	7	6	7	18	24	+10	67
6. Arsenal	40	11	4	5	35	16	7	8	5	23	23	+19	66
7. Wimbledon	40	8	9	3	32	20	6	6	8	26	27	+11	57
8. Newcastle United	40	9	6	5	32	23	5	8	7	23	30	+2	56
9. Luton Town	40	11	6	3	40	21	3	5	12	17	37	−1	53
10. Coventry City	40	6	8	6	23	25	7	6	6	23	28	−7	53
11. Sheffield Wednesday	40	10	2	8	27	30	5	6	9	25	36	−14	53
12. Southampton	40	6	8	6	27	26	6	6	8	22	27	−4	50
13. Tottenham Hotspur	40	9	5	6	26	23	3	6	11	12	25	−10	47
14. Norwich City	40	7	5	8	26	26	5	4	11	14	26	−12	45
15. Derby County	40	6	7	7	18	17	4	6	10	17	28	−10	43
16. West Ham United	40	6	9	5	23	21	3	6	11	17	31	−12	42
17. Charlton Athletic	40	7	7	6	23	21	2	8	10	15	31	−4	42
18. Chelsea	40	7	11	2	24	17	2	4	14	26	51	−18	42
19. Portsmouth	40	4	8	8	21	27	3	6	11	15	39	−30	35
20. Watford	40	4	5	11	15	24	3	6	11	12	27	−24	32
21. Oxford United	40	5	7	8	24	34	1	6	13	20	46	−36	31

Liverpool – First Division Champions. (*Harry Ormesher*)

137

Second Division Results 1987-88

	Aston Villa	Barnsley	Birmingham City	Blackburn Rovers	Bournemouth	Bradford City	Crystal Palace	Huddersfield Town	Hull City	Ipswich Town	Leeds United	Leicester City	Manchester City	Middlesbrough	Millwall	Oldham Athletic	Plymouth Argyle	Reading	Sheffield United	Shrewsbury Town	Stoke City	Swindon Town	West Bromwich Albion
Aston Villa	—	1-3	1-2	3-2	1-2	2-4	1-1	0-1	2-1	1-3	1-1	0-2	0-2	2-1	1-1	0-1	1-3	0-2	1-1	1-2	0-0	0-0	0-2
Barnsley	0-0	—	2-0	0-1	1-2	3-2	1-2	1-0	1-0	0-2	1-1	0-0	2-0	1-0	0-1	2-1	1-1	1-1	3-1	3-0	2-2	1-0	2-2
Birmingham City	0-2	2-2	—	2-0	4-2	3-0	2-2	2-0	1-0	4-1	2-0	3-0	1-1	1-2	1-1	1-1	0-2	0-0	3-1	0-2	3-1	2-0	0-0
Blackburn Rovers	1-1	1-0	1-0	—	1-1	2-1	1-2	2-2	0-2	1-2	1-1	1-4	4-2	3-0	0-0	3-1	1-2	2-1	2-1	2-2	2-1	1-0	0-1
Bournemouth	1-1	2-1	1-1	3-1	—	2-0	3-0	2-1	2-1	1-2	3-2	0-1	2-0	3-0	0-0	2-1	1-0	2-0	1-0	4-2	3-0	0-2	0-1
Bradford City	1-0	3-0	1-1	1-1	2-0	—	1-2	1-2	0-0	4-0	2-0	0-2	2-2	1-2	0-1	0-2	2-1	1-1	1-2	2-2	2-2	2-2	0-1
Crystal Palace	4-1	1-1	0-6	2-3	2-3	2-0	—	2-2	2-3	1-0	4-4	1-3	1-1	1-0	2-3	1-1	2-0	1-1	1-1	2-2	1-1	1-0	1-0
Huddersfield Town	1-1	1-0	2-0	2-2	0-2	0-1	1-1	—	4-0	3-0	4-0	3-0	10-1	4-1	3-2	6-1	3-2	2-1	3-1	1-1	4-1	3-2	1-1
Hull City	5-0	1-3	1-1	1-1	6-2	2-0	0-0	0-2	—	2-0	0-2	2-1	2-0	1-0	2-0	1-2	3-1	0-0	2-2	1-0	0-0	1-1	1-1
Ipswich Town	1-0	2-3	1-0	1-1	2-3	2-2	1-2	1-0	1-0	—	1-1	2-0	3-1	0-0	1-1	4-1	0-0	1-1	1-2	4-2	2-2	2-2	1-0
Leeds United	1-2	1-1	0-1	1-0	0-0	0-0	3-0	3-1	1-0	1-0	—	3-2	1-2	3-1	1-1	6-3	2-2	1-0	2-1	2-2	1-4	4-2	1-0
Leicester City	2-1	1-1	2-2	3-3	4-1	2-1	1-0	2-2	0-2	1-0	4-2	—	1-2	1-0	2-0	4-2	1-2	2-1	0-0	2-1	3-2	1-1	1-1
Manchester City	1-1	1-1	0-3	2-1	0-2	2-4	0-0	3-1	3-0	2-0	1-0	1-0	—	2-1	1-1	3-2	2-0	1-2	0-0	1-0	1-3	4-1	1-1
Middlesbrough	0-0	0-3	0-2	0-2	0-0	2-1	3-1	1-4	0-0	4-1	2-0	0-1	1-1	—	2-1	1-1	1-0	0-2	0-1	1-1	1-0	0-0	0-0
Millwall	2-1	4-1	1-0	1-2	1-2	1-0	2-1	0-1	1-2	1-0	4-1	1-1	0-0	1-2	—	0-0	1-2	2-3	1-2	0-0	1-2	1-1	1-4
Oldham Athletic	2-1	1-1	1-3	1-0	2-2	5-3	3-1	2-2	1-0	2-1	1-1	1-2	1-0	1-1	1-1	—	1-0	3-0	0-5	2-3	2-2	0-0	0-0
Plymouth Argyle	5-2	2-1	1-0	2-2	3-1	5-1	1-1	1-2	1-0	4-0	2-1	3-2	0-1	2-1	1-0	2-0	—	1-0	2-1	1-0	1-0	1-0	1-0
Reading	2-1	5-2	2-1	1-0	3-0	3-0	0-2	2-2	2-1	0-0	1-0	2-0	0-0	4-2	1-3	1-1	4-4	—	4-1	4-1	4-2	0-1	0-1
Sheffield United	1-1	1-2	0-1	4-1	1-2	2-0	2-1	0-2	1-2	1-0	5-0	1-3	3-1	3-2	2-1	1-1	0-0	2-1	—	2-0	1-0	2-0	4-0
Shrewsbury Town	1-2	2-1	0-0	2-2	2-0	1-1	1-2	0-1	1-1	2-1	0-1	1-3	4-0	4-1	2-2	2-0	1-0	0-1	0-1	—	1-1	1-1	2-1
Stoke City	0-1	5-2	2-0	0-0	0-0	1-4	2-0	0-3	0-0	2-0	0-0	1-1	3-0	2-0	5-1	3-0	0-0	0-3	0-0	3-1	—	3-0	2-0
Swindon Town	2-1	0-1	1-1	1-0	2-0	2-0	2-1	1-4	3-2	4-2	3-2	1-1	2-3	2-2	4-3	1-0	0-1	1-0	2-1	1-0	1-0	—	1-2
West Bromwich Albion	0-0	3-1	0-1	3-1	3-2	4-1	4-1	1-3	1-0	1-1	0-0	4-2	2-1	2-0	2-1	3-3	1-2	0-0	3-0	0-1	3-0	2-0	—

Second Division Final Positions 1987-88

		Home					Away						
	P	W	D	L	F	A	W	D	L	F	A	GD	Pts
1. Millwall	44	15	3	4	45	23	10	4	8	27	29	+20	82
2. Aston Villa	44	9	7	6	31	21	13	5	4	37	20	+27	78
3. Middlesbrough	44	15	4	3	44	16	7	8	7	19	20	+27	78
4. Bradford City	44	14	3	5	49	26	8	8	6	25	28	+20	77
5. Blackburn Rovers	44	12	8	2	38	22	9	6	7	30	30	+16	77
6. Crystal Palace	44	16	3	3	50	21	6	6	10	36	38	+27	75
7. Leeds United	44	14	4	4	37	18	5	8	9	24	33	+10	69
8. Ipswich Town	44	14	3	5	38	17	5	6	11	23	35	+9	66
9. Manchester City	44	11	4	7	50	28	8	4	10	30	32	+20	65
10. Oldham Athletic	44	13	4	5	43	27	5	7	10	29	37	+8	65
11. Stoke City	44	12	6	4	34	22	5	5	12	16	35	−7	62
12. Swindon Town	44	10	7	5	43	25	6	4	12	30	35	+13	59
13. Leicester City	44	12	5	5	35	20	4	6	12	27	41	+1	59
14. Barnsley	44	11	4	7	42	32	4	8	10	19	30	−1	57
15. Hull City	44	10	8	4	32	22	4	7	11	22	38	−6	57
16. Plymouth Argyle	44	12	4	6	44	26	4	4	14	21	41	−2	56
17. Bournemouth	44	7	7	8	36	30	6	3	13	20	38	−12	49
18. Shrewsbury Town	44	7	8	7	23	22	4	8	10	19	32	−12	49
19. Birmingham City	44	7	9	6	20	24	4	6	12	21	42	−15	48
20. West Bromwich Albion	44	8	7	7	29	26	4	4	14	21	43	−19	47
21. Sheffield United	44	8	6	8	27	28	5	1	16	18	46	−29	46
22. Reading	44	5	7	10	20	25	5	5	12	24	45	−26	42
23. Huddersfield Town	44	4	6	12	20	38	2	4	16	21	62	−59	28

Millwall – Second Division Champions.

Third Division Results 1987-88

	Aldershot	Blackpool	Brentford	Brighton & Hove Alb.	Bristol City	Bristol Rovers	Bury	Chester City	Chesterfield	Doncaster Rovers	Fulham	Gillingham	Grimsby Town	Mansfield Town	Northampton Town	Notts County	Port Vale	Preston North End	Rotherham United	Southend United	Sunderland	Walsall	Wigan Athletic	York City
Aldershot	—	0-0	4-1	1-4	2-1	3-0	0-2	4-1	2-0	2-1	0-3	6-0	3-2	3-0	4-1	0-2	3-0	0-0	1-3	0-1	3-2	0-1	3-2	1-2
Blackpool	3-2	—	0-1	1-3	4-2	3-1	5-1	0-1	1-0	4-2	2-1	3-3	3-0	2-0	3-1	1-1	1-2	3-0	3-1	1-1	0-2	1-2	0-0	2-1
Brentford	3-0	2-1	—	1-1	0-2	1-1	0-3	1-0	2-0	1-2	2-0	2-2	0-2	2-1	0-1	1-1	1-0	3-0	1-1	0-3	3-1	0-0	2-1	1-0
Brighton & Hove Alb.	1-1	1-3	2-3	—	3-2	3-3	3-2	1-0	2-2	1-0	4-0	3-3	0-1	1-2	2-2	2-1	1-0	3-1	1-1	3-2	3-1	0-0	1-0	3-2
Bristol City	2-0	1-3	0-0	5-2	—	0-0	3-2	2-2	2-0	0-1	4-1	2-1	1-1	1-2	2-2	2-1	1-0	1-0	2-0	3-2	0-0	3-0	4-1	2-1
Bristol Rovers	3-1	2-0	2-2	1-2	1-0	—	0-0	2-1	2-0	4-1	3-1	2-1	4-2	2-1	0-5	1-1	1-0	4-0	3-2	0-2	4-3	3-0	0-1	0-1
Bury	1-0	3-1	1-1	2-2	1-0	4-1	—	0-4	2-1	1-1	4-4	2-1	0-2	1-0	0-2	1-2	1-3	0-0	3-2	2-1	1-2	2-2	0-1	1-0
Chester City	1-0	1-1	1-1	1-1	2-2	0-1	0-0	—	1-0	1-1	0-0	1-1	1-0	0-2	0-2	1-1	1-3	0-0	0-2	1-1	0-2	2-1	1-2	2-1
Chesterfield	1-0	2-1	0-1	0-2	2-0	2-0	1-0	1-0	—	1-0	2-0	1-1	0-0	0-2	0-5	3-0	0-1	0-0	1-1	1-1	1-3	2-1	0-1	2-0
Doncaster Rovers	0-0	3-1	2-1	0-2	1-1	2-0	1-0	2-0	1-0	—	4-0	2-0	5-0	2-3	3-1	0-1	0-0	3-2	0-0	1-3	0-2	2-1	1-1	3-1
Fulham	1-2	2-1	3-0	4-0	3-1	1-1	2-0	2-2	1-0	3-2	—	2-2	1-1	0-0	3-1	0-2	0-1	4-1	1-1	1-1	2-1	2-0	0-1	5-1
Gillingham	2-1	0-0	2-2	3-3	2-1	2-1	1-4	4-2	1-0	2-0	2-2	—	5-0	0-0	2-2	0-1	0-0	4-2	1-2	1-3	2-1	0-0	1-1	0-2
Grimsby Town	1-1	2-1	3-0	1-1	4-2	0-2	1-0	0-3	1-0	5-0	1-1	1-0	—	1-0	0-0	2-3	0-0	0-0	1-3	0-0	0-2	1-2	0-1	0-2
Mansfield Town	1-0	2-3	1-2	5-2	1-2	2-1	1-0	0-2	3-1	0-0	0-0	2-1	1-0	—	2-0	1-0	1-0	2-1	2-1	4-1	2-1	4-1	3-2	2-2
Northampton Town	1-0	1-1	3-0	1-2	2-1	0-2	1-1	2-0	0-5	0-1	2-1	0-0	3-0	3-1	—	3-1	1-1	0-0	2-2	1-1	1-0	2-1	2-2	2-2
Notts County	2-1	2-1	2-0	2-1	2-1	1-1	1-2	1-1	3-0	0-1	0-2	0-1	0-0	2-1	3-1	—	1-3	1-2	1-2	1-2	1-1	2-1	3-5	3-1
Port Vale	4-2	4-0	2-3	1-0	1-0	1-0	1-3	2-2	0-1	0-0	0-1	0-0	0-0	1-1	1-1	1-3	—	2-0	2-1	1-0	3-3	2-1	2-0	4-2
Preston North End	0-2	2-1	4-2	3-1	1-0	4-0	0-0	0-0	0-0	3-2	4-1	4-2	0-0	2-1	0-0	1-2	4-2	—	2-2	1-2	1-1	1-0	2-0	1-1
Rotherham United	1-0	3-0	1-1	1-1	2-0	3-2	3-2	0-2	1-1	1-0	0-2	1-1	0-0	4-0	0-0	1-2	2-1	3-0	—	1-1	3-0	5-2	1-1	1-2
Southend United	0-1	4-0	1-1	0-2	3-2	0-1	2-1	1-1	1-1	8-1	3-0	0-2	4-2	1-1	1-1	1-1	0-1	4-2	1-1	—	7-0	1-0	1-1	0-3
Sunderland	3-2	0-2	1-1	3-1	0-1	4-0	1-2	0-2	0-0	0-1	0-2	2-1	1-0	2-2	1-4	2-1	1-1	2-2	0-1	7-0	—	2-2	2-2	2-1
Walsall	0-1	1-2	0-0	0-0	3-0	2-2	1-2	2-1	0-4	2-0	1-1	0-2	1-3	2-1	2-1	2-0	0-1	1-1	1-1	1-1	1-1	—	3-1	1-3
Wigan Athletic	3-2	0-0	2-1	1-0	4-1	2-3	0-2	1-1	1-1	1-0	3-4	2-1	4-4	2-1	0-1	1-1	3-2	4-1	1-1	3-2	4-1	1-2	—	3-1
York City	2-2	1-3	1-0	0-2	2-1	0-1	1-1	2-1	2-0	3-1	5-1	0-0	0-2	2-2	2-2	3-1	2-3	1-1	1-2	0-3	2-1	1-3	3-1	—

Third Division Final Positions 1987-88

			Home				Away						
	P	W	D	L	F	A	W	D	L	F	A	GD	Pts
1. Sunderland	46	14	7	2	51	22	13	5	5	41	26	+44	93
2. Brighton & Hove Albion	46	15	7	1	37	16	8	8	7	32	31	+22	84
3. Walsall	46	15	6	2	39	22	8	7	8	29	28	+18	82
4. Notts County	46	14	4	5	53	24	9	8	6	29	25	+33	81
5. Bristol City	46	14	6	3	51	30	7	6	10	26	32	+15	75
6. Northampton Town	46	12	8	3	36	18	6	11	6	34	33	+19	73
7. Wigan Athletic	46	11	8	4	36	23	9	4	10	34	38	+9	72
8. Bristol Rovers	46	14	5	4	43	19	4	7	12	25	37	+12	66
9. Fulham	46	10	5	8	36	24	9	4	10	33	36	+9	66
10. Blackpool	46	13	4	6	45	27	4	10	9	26	35	+9	65
11. Port Vale	46	12	8	3	36	19	6	3	14	22	37	+2	65
12. Brentford	46	9	8	6	27	23	7	6	10	26	36	−6	62
13. Gillingham	46	8	9	6	45	21	6	8	9	32	40	+16	59
14. Bury	46	9	7	7	33	26	6	7	10	25	31	+1	59
15. Chester City	46	9	8	6	29	30	5	8	10	22	32	−11	58
16. Preston North End	46	10	6	7	30	23	5	7	11	18	36	−11	58
17. Southend United	46	10	6	7	42	33	4	7	12	23	50	−18	55
18. Chesterfield	46	10	5	8	25	28	5	5	13	16	42	−29	55
19. Mansfield Town	46	10	6	7	25	21	4	6	13	23	38	−11	54
20. Aldershot	46	12	3	8	45	32	3	5	15	19	42	−10	53
21. Rotherham United	46	8	8	7	28	25	4	8	11	22	41	−16	52
22. Grimsby Town	46	6	7	10	25	29	6	7	10	23	29	−10	50
23. York City	46	4	7	12	27	45	4	2	17	21	46	−43	33
24. Doncaster Rovers	46	6	5	12	25	36	2	4	17	15	48	−44	33

Sunderland – Third Division Champions.

Fourth Division Results 1987-88

	Bolton Wanderers	Burnley	Cambridge United	Cardiff City	Carlisle United	Colchester United	Crewe Alexandra	Darlington	Exeter City	Halifax Town	Hartlepool United	Hereford United	Leyton Orient	Newport County	Peterborough United	Rochdale	Scarborough	Scunthorpe United	Stockport County	Swansea City	Torquay United	Tranmere Rovers	Wolverhampton Wanderers	Wrexham
Bolton Wanderers	—	2-1	2-2	2-0	5-0	4-0	1-1	1-2	1-0	2-0	0-0	1-0	1-2	6-0	2-0	0-0	3-1	0-1	2-1	1-1	1-2	2-0	1-0	2-0
Burnley	2-1	—	0-2	1-2	4-3	0-3	0-1	2-1	3-1	3-1	0-0	0-1	2-0	2-0	1-2	4-1	1-0	1-1	1-1	1-0	1-0	1-1	0-3	0-1
Cambridge United	2-2	2-1	—	0-0	1-2	0-1	4-1	3-1	2-1	1-1	0-0	1-1	1-2	4-1	1-3	2-1	1-0	3-1	0-0	0-3	0-1	1-1	1-1	0-1
Cardiff City	1-0	2-1	4-0	—	4-2	4-0	1-0	3-1	3-2	0-1	1-1	3-1	1-2	4-1	0-2	2-0	0-0	3-1	0-0	1-0	3-3	3-0	3-2	1-1
Carlisle United	0-2	3-4	2-1	0-0	—	4-0	0-1	3-3	0-2	0-1	3-1	3-1	0-0	3-1	4-1	2-0	4-3	3-1	0-0	1-2	3-3	3-2	0-1	1-4
Colchester United	3-0	0-1	0-0	0-1	1-0	—	1-4	3-1	0-2	2-1	1-0	1-0	0-0	3-1	1-1	0-1	1-1	0-3	0-1	2-2	1-1	0-0	0-1	1-2
Crewe Alexandra	2-1	0-1	0-0	0-0	4-1	0-0	—	2-1	2-1	0-1	1-1	0-3	3-3	0-5	1-1	0-1	1-0	2-1	3-1	2-2	1-3	0-0	2-4	1-2
Darlington	1-0	4-2	0-0	0-2	1-1	0-2	1-0	—	2-0	4-2	1-0	2-1	2-3	3-0	1-1	1-1	1-0	1-2	2-1	3-1	0-3	0-1	2-4	2-1
Exeter City	1-1	1-2	1-0	0-1	1-1	0-2	1-0	4-1	—	4-2	1-0	2-2	2-3	3-0	1-1	1-1	1-9	1-1	2-1	3-1	0-1	2-1	2-4	2-1
Halifax Town	0-0	2-1	3-0	0-0	1-1	3-1	1-0	2-2	2-0	—	3-1	2-1	1-0	3-1	0-0	1-1	2-2	1-1	2-0	1-1	2-0	1-2	2-1	2-0
Hartlepool United	0-0	2-1	0-1	0-1	0-0	0-2	1-1	2-5	2-0	2-1	—	1-2	2-2	4-2	0-1	1-1	0-1	1-1	0-1	0-2	0-0	2-1	2-1	2-1
Hereford United	0-3	2-1	1-1	1-2	4-1	3-1	1-1	1-3	3-1	4-1	3-1	—	0-3	3-1	0-1	0-0	3-1	1-1	1-1	2-3	0-1	3-1	1-3	3-1
Leyton Orient	1-2	4-1	0-2	4-1	4-1	0-0	1-1	4-3	0-0	0-0	1-0	2-0	—	4-1	2-0	0-0	4-1	2-3	1-0	3-0	0-0	1-2	0-2	2-1
Newport County	0-1	0-1	0-0	1-2	1-2	0-1	0-4	2-1	0-2	0-1	1-0	0-1	0-3	—	0-1	8-0	0-1	2-3	0-1	3-0	0-2	1-2	0-3	0-2
Peterborough United	0-4	5-0	3-2	4-3	4-1	0-2	2-2	2-1	0-1	0-1	1-2	4-0	0-2	3-0	—	0-1	1-1	2-0	0-0	0-1	0-2	2-0	0-2	0-2
Rochdale	2-2	0-1	2-2	2-1	1-2	0-2	1-1	1-3	0-1	0-1	2-3	0-2	3-1	2-4	0-1	—	2-1	0-0	0-1	3-0	0-0	0-0	0-2	3-1
Scarborough	4-0	1-0	1-0	4-1	3-1	3-1	1-0	1-0	1-0	1-0	1-1	3-1	1-0	3-1	1-1	2-1	—	1-1	0-0	2-0	3-1	2-0	2-2	2-1
Scunthorpe United	1-1	1-1	3-2	1-0	1-0	2-2	1-0	1-1	1-0	1-1	3-0	2-1	3-2	5-1	5-0	1-1	3-0	—	0-0	1-2	2-3	3-0	2-2	3-1
Stockport County	1-2	2-0	0-2	2-1	0-1	1-4	2-2	1-3	1-1	1-1	1-0	2-1	5-1	1-2	2-1	0-3	0-0	0-1	—	1-2	2-1	1-2	0-2	1-1
Swansea City	1-0	0-1	1-1	2-2	3-1	1-2	1-1	3-0	1-1	1-0	3-1	2-1	3-0	1-2	2-1	5-0	1-0	1-1	0-1	—	2-1	1-2	0-2	1-2
Torquay United	2-1	1-3	0-1	0-1	1-0	0-2	1-0	0-0	1-1	2-0	1-1	1-0	1-1	6-1	3-1	6-1	3-0	1-1	1-1	1-0	—	1-0	0-0	3-1
Tranmere Rovers	2-0	0-1	0-1	1-4	3-1	2-0	2-2	2-1	0-1	0-1	0-1	2-0	2-1	4-0	0-2	2-0	1-0	4-1	3-0	0-1	1-0	—	3-0	1-0
Wolverhampton Wdrs	4-0	3-0	3-0	3-0	4-0	0-1	2-1	5-3	3-0	0-1	2-1	0-0	2-0	2-1	3-1	2-3	1-0	4-1	4-0	2-0	1-2	3-0	—	0-2
Wrexham	0-1	1-3	3-0	3-0	4-0	0-1	2-1	0-1	3-0	2-2	2-1	0-0	2-2	4-1	3-1	2-3	1-0	2-1	1-2	1-2	2-3	3-0	4-2	—

142

Fourth Division Final Positions 1987-88

		Home				Away						
	P	W	D	L	F	A	W	D	L	F	A	GD	Pts
1. Wolverhampton Wanderers	46	15	3	5	47	19	12	6	5	35	24	+39	90
2. Cardiff City................................	46	15	6	2	39	14	9	7	7	27	27	+25	85
3. Bolton Wanderers	46	15	6	2	42	12	7	6	10	24	30	+24	78
4. Scunthorpe United	46	14	5	4	42	20	6	12	5	34	31	+25	77
5. Torquay United..........................	46	10	7	6	34	16	11	7	5	32	25	+25	77
6. Swansea City	46	9	7	7	35	28	11	3	9	27	28	+6	70*
7. Peterborough United	46	10	5	8	28	26	10	5	8	24	27	−1	70
8. Leyton Orient............................	46	13	4	6	55	27	6	8	9	30	36	+22	69
9. Colchester United	46	10	5	8	23	22	9	5	9	24	29	−4	67
10. Burnley....................................	46	12	5	6	31	22	8	2	13	26	40	−5	67
11. Wrexham..................................	46	13	3	7	46	26	7	3	13	23	32	+11	66
12. Scarborough.............................	46	12	8	3	38	19	5	6	12	18	29	+8	65
13. Darlington	46	13	6	4	39	25	5	5	13	32	44	+2	65
14. Tranmere Rovers.......................	46	14	2	7	43	20	5	7	11	18	33	+8	64**
15. Cambridge United.....................	46	10	6	7	32	24	6	7	10	18	29	−2	61
16. Hartlepool United	46	9	7	7	25	25	6	7	10	25	32	−7	59
17. Crewe Alexandra	46	7	11	5	25	19	6	8	9	32	34	+4	58
18. Halifax Town.............................	46	11	7	5	37	25	3	7	13	17	34	−5	55†
19. Hereford United	46	8	7	8	25	27	6	5	12	16	32	−18	54
20. Stockport County	46	7	7	9	26	26	5	8	10	18	32	−14	51
21. Rochdale	46	5	9	9	28	34	6	6	11	19	42	−29	48
22. Exeter City	46	8	6	9	33	29	3	7	13	20	39	−15	46
23. Carlisle United	46	9	5	9	38	33	3	3	17	19	53	−29	44
24. Newport County	46	4	5	14	19	36	2	2	19	16	69	−70	25

*Promoted after play-offs
**Two points deducted for failing to meet a fixture
†One point deducted for fielding an unregistered player

Wolverhampton Wanderers – Fourth Division Champions.

143

Football League Champions 1888-1988

FIRST DIVISION 1888-1988

Season	Winners	Pts.	Max.	Season	Winners	Pts.	Max.
1888-89	Preston North End	40		1937-38	Arsenal	52	
1889-90	Preston North End	33	44	1938-39	Everton	59	
1890-91	Everton	29		1946-47	Liverpool	57	
1891-92	Sunderland	42	52	1947-48	Arsenal	59	
1892-93	Sunderland	48		1948-49	Portsmouth	58	
1893-94	Aston Villa	44		1949-50	*Portsmouth	53	
1894-95	Sunderland	47	60	1950-51	Tottenham Hotspur	60	
1895-96	Aston Villa	45		1951-52	Manchester United	57	
1896-97	Aston Villa	47		1952-53	*Arsenal	54	
1897-98	Sheffield United	42		1953-54	Wolverhampton Wanderers	57	
1898-99	Aston Villa	45		1954-55	Chelsea	52	
1899-1900	Aston Villa	50		1955-56	Manchester United	60	
1900-01	Liverpool	45		1956-57	Manchester United	64	
1901-02	Sunderland	44	68	1957-58	Wolverhampton Wanderers	64	
1902-03	Sheffield Wednesday	42		1958-59	Wolverhampton Wanderers	61	
1903-04	Sheffield Wednesday	47		1959-60	Burnley	55	
1904-05	Newcastle United	48		1960-61	Tottenham Hotspur	66	
1905-06	Liverpool	51		1961-62	Ipswich Town	56	84
1906-07	Newcastle United	51		1962-63	Everton	61	
1907-08	Manchester United	52		1963-64	Liverpool	57	
1908-09	Newcastle United	53		1964-65	*Manchester United	61	
1909-10	Aston Villa	53	76	1965-66	Liverpool	61	
1910-11	Manchester United	52		1966-67	Manchester United	60	
1911-12	Blackburn Rovers	49		1967-68	Manchester City	58	
1912-13	Sunderland	54		1968-69	Leeds United	67	
1913-14	Blackburn Rovers	51		1969-70	Everton	66	
1914-15	Everton	46		1970-71	Arsenal	65	
1919-20	West Bromwich Albion	60		1971-72	Derby County	58	
1920-21	Burnley	59		1972-73	Liverpool	60	
1921-22	Liverpool	57		1973-74	Leeds United	62	
1922-23	Liverpool	60		1974-75	Derby County	53	
1923-24	*Huddersfield Town	57		1975-76	Liverpool	60	
1924-25	Huddersfield Town	58		1976-77	Liverpool	57	
1925-26	Huddersfield Town	57		1977-78	Nottingham Forest	64	
1926-27	Newcastle United	56		1978-79	Liverpool	68	
1927-28	Everton	53	84	1979-80	Liverpool	60	
1928-29	Sheffield Wednesday	52		1980-81	Aston Villa	60	
1929-30	Sheffield Wednesday	60		1981-82	Liverpool	87	
1930-31	Arsenal	66		1982-83	Liverpool	82	
1931-32	Everton	56		1983-84	Liverpool	80	
1932-33	Arsenal	58		1984-85	Everton	90	126
1933-34	Arsenal	59		1985-86	Liverpool	88	
1934-35	Arsenal	58		1986-87	Everton	86	
1935-36	Sunderland	56		1987-88	Liverpool	90	
1936-37	Manchester City	57					

SECOND DIVISION 1892-1988

Season	Winners	Pts.	Max.	Season	Winners	Pts.	Max.
1892-93	Small Heath	36	44	1913-14	Notts County	53	76
1893-94	Liverpool	50	56	1914-15	Derby County	53	
1894-95	Bury	48		1919-20	Tottenham Hotspur	70	
1895-96	*Liverpool	46	60	1920-21	Birmingham	58	
1896-97	Notts. County	42		1921-22	Nottingham Forest	56	
1897-98	Burnley	48		1922-23	Notts County	53	
1898-99	Manchester City	52		1923-24	Leeds United	54	
1899-1900	Sheffield Wednesday	54		1924-25	Leicester City	59	
1900-01	Grimsby Town	49		1925-26	Sheffield Wednesday	60	
1901-02	West Bromwich Albion	55	68	1926-27	Middlesbrough	62	
1902-03	Manchester City	54		1927-28	Manchester City	59	
1903-04	Preston North End	50		1928-29	Middlesbrough	55	
1904-05	Liverpool	58		1929-30	Blackpool	58	
1905-06	Bristol City	66		1930-31	Everton	61	
1906-07	Nottingham Forest	60		1931-32	Wolverhampton Wanderers	56	
1907-08	Bradford City	54		1932-33	Stoke City	56	
1908-09	Bolton Wanderers	52		1933-34	Grimsby Town	59	
1909-10	Manchester City	54	76	1934-35	Brentford	61	
1910-11	West Bromwich Albion	53		1935-36	Manchester United	56	
1911-12	Derby County	54		1936-37	Leicester City	56	
1012-13	Preston North End	53		1937-38	Aston Villa	57	

*Won on goal average/difference

No competition 1915-18 and 1939-46

Season	Winners	Pts.	Max.	Season	Winners	Pts.	Max.
1938-39	Blackburn Rovers	55		1967-68	Ipswich Town	59	
1946-47	Manchester City	62		1968-69	Derby County	63	84
1947-48	Birmingham City	59	84	1969-70	Huddersfield Town	60	
1948-49	Fulham	57		1970-71	Leicester City	59	
1949-50	Tottenham Hotspur	61		1971-72	Norwich City	57	
1950-51	Preston North End	57		1972-73	Burnley	62	
1951-52	Sheffield Wednesday	53		1973-74	Middlesbrough	65	
1952-53	Sheffield United	60		1974-75	Manchester United	61	
1953-54	*Leicester City	56		1975-76	Sunderland	56	
1954-55	*Birmingham City	54		1976-77	Wolverhampton Wanderers	57	
1955-56	Sheffield Wednesday	55		1977-78	Bolton Wanderers	58	84
1956-57	Leicester City	61		1978-79	Crystal Palace	57	
1957-58	West Ham United	57		1979-80	Leicester City	55	
1958-59	Sheffield Wednesday	62		1980-81	West Ham United	66	
1959-60	Aston Villa	59		1981-82	Luton Town	88	
1960-61	Ipswich Town	59		1982-83	Queen's Park Rangers	85	
1961-62	Liverpool	62		1983-84	*Chelsea	88	
1962-63	Stoke City	53		1984-85	Oxford United	84	126
1963-64	Leeds United	63		1985-86	Norwich City	84	
1964-65	Newcastle United	57		1986-87	Derby County	84	
1965-66	Manchester City	59		1987-88	Millwall	82	
1966-67	Coventry City	59					

THIRD DIVISION (S) 1920-58

Season	Winners	Pts.	Max.	Season	Winners	Pts.	Max.
1920-21	Crystal Palace	59		1936-37	Luton Town	58	
1921-22	*Southampton	61		1937-38	Millwall	56	
1922-23	Bristol City	59		1938-39	Newport County	55	
1923-24	Portsmouth	59		1946-47	Cardiff City	66	84
1924-25	Swansea Town	57		1947-48	Queen's Park Rangers	61	
1925-26	Reading	57		1948-49	Swansea Town	62	
1926-27	Bristol City	62		1949-50	Notts County	58	
1927-28	Millwall	65		1950-51	Nottingham Forest	70	
1928-29	*Charlton Athletic	54	84	1951-52	Plymouth Argyle	66	
1929-30	Plymouth Argyle	68		1952-53	Bristol Rovers	64	
1930-31	Notts County	59		1953-54	Ipswich Town	64	
1931-32	Fulham	57		1954-55	Bristol City	70	92
1932-33	Brentford	62		1955-56	Leyton Orient	66	
1933-34	Norwich City	61		1956-57	*Ipswich Town	59	
1934-35	Charlton Athletic	61		1957-58	Brighton and Hove Albion	60	
1935-36	Coventry City	57					

THIRD DIVISION (N) 1921-58

Season	Winners	Pts.	Max.	Season	Winners	Pts.	Max.
1921-22	Stockport County	56	76	1936-37	Stockport County	60	
1922-23	Nelson	51		1937-38	Tranmere Rovers	56	
1923-24	Wolverhampton Wanderers	63		1938-39	Barnsley	67	
1924-25	Darlington	58		1946-47	Doncaster Rovers	72	84
1925-26	Grimsby Town	61		1947-48	Lincoln City	60	
1926-27	Stoke City	63		1948-49	Hull City	65	
1927-28	Bradford	63	84	1949-50	Doncaster Rovers	55	
1928-29	Bradford City	63		1950-51	Rotherham United	71	
1929-30	Port Vale	67		1951-52	Lincoln City	69	
1930-31	Chesterfield	58		1952-53	Oldham Athletic	59	
1931-32	*Lincoln City	57	80	1953-54	Port Vale	69	92
1932-33	Hull City	59		1954-55	Barnsley	65	
1933-34	Barnsley	62		1955-56	Grimsby Town	68	
1934-35	Doncaster Rovers	57	84	1956-57	Derby County	63	
1935-36	Chesterfield	60		1957-58	Scunthorpe United	66	

THIRD DIVISION 1958-88

Season	Winners	Pts.	Max.	Season	Winners	Pts.	Max.
1958-59	Plymouth Argyle	62		1962-63	Northampton Town	62	
1959-60	Southampton	61		1963-64	*Coventry City	60	
1960-61	Bury	68		1964-65	Carlisle United	60	
1961-62	Portsmouth	65		1965-66	Hull City	69	

*Won on goal average   No competition 1939-46

Season	Winners	Pts.	Max.	Season	Winners	Pts.	Max.
1966-67	Queen's Park Rangers	67		1977-78	Wrexham	61	
1967-68	Oxford United	57		1978-79	Shrewsbury Town	61	
1968-69	*Watford	64	92	1979-80	Grimsby Town	62	
1969-70	Orient	62		1980-81	Rotherham United	61	
1970-71	Preston North End	61		1981-82	Burnley	80	
1971-72	Aston Villa	70		1982-83	Portsmouth	91	
1972-73	Bolton Wanderers	61		1983-84	Oxford United	95	
1973-74	Oldham Athletic	62		1984-85	Bradford City	94	138
1974-75	Blackburn Rovers	60		1985-86	Reading	94	
1975-76	Hereford United	63		1986-87	AFC Bournemouth	97	
1976-77	Mansfield Town	64		1987-88	Sunderland	93	

FOURTH DIVISION 1958-88

Season	Winners	Pts.	Max.	Season	Winners	Pts.	Max.
1958-59	Port Vale	64		1973-74	Peterborough United	65	
1958-60	Walsall	65	92	1974-75	Mansfield Town	68	
1960-61	Peterborough United	66		1975-76	Lincoln City	74	
1961-62	Millwall	56	88	1976-77	Cambridge United	65	
1962-63	Brentford	62		1977-78	Watford	71	
1963-64	*Gillingham	60		1978-79	Reading	65	
1964-65	Brighton and Hove Albion	63		1979-80	Huddersfield Town	66	
1965-66	Doncaster Rovers	59		1980-81	Southend United	67	
1966-67	Stockport County	64		1981-82	Sheffield United	96	
1967-68	Luton Town	66		1982-83	Wimbledon	98	
1968-69	Doncaster Rovers	59		1983-84	York City	101	
1969-70	Chesterfield	64		1984-85	Chesterfield	91	138
1970-71	Notts County	69	92	1985-86	Swindon Town	102	
1971-72	Grimsby Town	63		1986-87	Northampton Town	99	
1972-73	Southport	62		1987-88	Wolverhampton Wanderers	90	

The Football Association Opens its Human Performance Department

Over the last four years The Football Association has initiated a number of major technical developments. In September 1984 The Football Association/GM National School was instituted at Lilleshall Hall National Sports Centre. Two years later The Football Association National Rehabilitation and Sports Injury Centre was opened, also at Lilleshall. Both projects have already received acclaim at home and abroad. Now, in 1988, the Rehabilitation Centre has expanded to incorporate a Human Performance Department.

The Rehabilitation and Sports Injury Centre has already become recognised as the National Centre for the rehabilitation and treatment of sports related injuries. There are now many top professional footballers whose rehabilitation following injuries and surgery has been undertaken at the Centre. Their treatment has ensured that they have returned to the highest level of fitness required in the shortest and safest possible time. For some players, this treatment has enabled them to return, when in the past their careers may well have been finished.

Although established with the professional footballer in mind, anyone from sport can attend. The Rehabilitation Centre has become the National Centre for injured jockeys, Rugby League players, international gymnasts and competitors from a variety of sports, including Rugby Union, cricket and hockey. Patients are usually admitted on a Monday and are given a complete medical examination and assessment by the Centre's Physiotherapists and Doctor. On the basis of this assessment, together with the referring Doctor's/Specialist's report, an intensive and individual rehabilitation programme is planned. A typical rehabilitation programme, designed not only to deal with the injury but also to maintain and develop general fitness, would include the following: individual physiotherapy treatment, general gymnasium work, general fitness training and assessments, isokinetic testing and exercising, specific remedial exercise programmes, swimming and cycling, specific sport training and the use of Lilleshall's sporting facilities.

England midfielder Neil Webb under scrutiny.

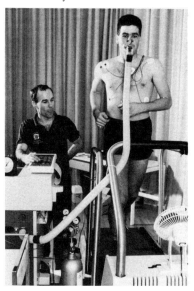

Aware that many injuries and physical problems can be prevented, the Rehabilitation Centre has now been expanded to include a Human Performance and Physiological Assessment Department. This means that The Football Association now has a Centre that can assess, treat, rehabilitate and educate professional footballers on injury prevention and training programmes.

In sport, fitness can play a decisive part in determining success or failure. The aim of the Department, therefore, is to assess the fitness of sportspeople and provide guidance on appropriate training requirements. Objective evaluation will then allow for areas of weakness to be identified and appropriate training methods prescribed, for progress to be monitored, for recovery after illness or injury to be assessed and for advice on diet, nutrition and exercise to be given.

The Department contains the most comprehensive and modern equipment available for the evaluation of physical fitness and exercise physiology, including respiratory fitness, muscle strength and endurance, lung functions, fully computerised exercise testing equipment to measure cardio-respiratory fitness, muscle strength and endurance, lung functions, body fats and endurance, speed and recovery.

The Department is staffed by a resident sports scientist and visiting specialists from the Department of Physical Education and Sports Science at Loughborough University. These specialists provide the Department with access to the latest scientific research information within the field of sports science. The residential staff have been working with The Football Association in the physiological assessments of professional footballers at all levels, as well as elite competitors from a variety of other sports.

Lilleshall Hall National Sports Centre, Nr. Newport, Shropshire, TF10 9AT. Telephone: 0952 605828.

*The Rehabilitation Centre and Human Performance Department are recognised by Health First, Private Patients Plan, BUPA, LAMPS and other leading health insurance companies, and are supported by The Football Trust.

Football League/Milk/Littlewoods Cup Winners 1961-88

Year	Winners	Runners-up	Score	Venue
1961	*Aston Villa	Rotherham United	3-2	
1962	*Norwich City	Rochdale	4-0	
1963	*Birmingham City	Aston Villa	3-1	
1964	*Leicester City	Stoke City	4-3	
1965	*Chelsea	Leicester City	3-2	
1966	*West Bromwich Albion	West Ham United	5-3	
1967	Queen's Park Rangers	West Bromwich Albion	3-2	Wembley
1968	Leeds United	Arsenal	1-0	Wembley
1969	†Swindon Town	Arsenal	3-1	Wembley
1970	†Manchester City	West Bromwich Albion	2-1	Wembley
1971	Tottenham Hotspur	Aston Villa	2-0	Wembley
1972	Stoke City	Chelsea	2-1	Wembley
1973	Tottenham Hotspur	Norwich City	1-0	Wembley
1974	Wolverhampton Wanderers	Manchester City	2-1	Wembley
1975	Aston Villa	Norwich City	1-0	Wembley
1976	Manchester City	Newcastle United	2-1	Wembley
1977	‡Aston Villa	Everton	3-2	Wembley
1978	¶Nottingham Forest	Liverpool	1-0	Manchester
1979	Nottingham Forest	Southampton	3-2	Wembley
1980	Wolverhampton Wanderers	Nottingham Forest	1-0	Wembley
1981	§Liverpool	West Ham United	2-1	Birmingham
1982	†Liverpool	Tottenham Hotspur	3-1	Wembley
1983	†Liverpool	Manchester United	2-1	Wembley
1984	¶Liverpool	Everton	1-0	Manchester
1985	Norwich City	Sunderland	1-0	Wembley
1986	Oxford United	Queen's Park Rangers	3-0	Wembley
1987	Arsenal	Liverpool	2-1	Wembley
1988	Luton Town	Arsenal	3-2	Wembley

*Aggregate score
†After extra time
‡After 0-0 and 1-1 draws at Wembley and Sheffield
¶After 0-0 draw at Wembley
§After 1-1 draw at Wembley

Littlewoods Challenge Cup 1987-88

First Round (Two Legs)

Blackpool	2:0	Chester City	0:1
Bournemouth	1:3	Exeter City	1:1
Brentford	2:2	Southend United	1:4
Bristol Rovers	1:0	Hereford United	0:2
Bury	2:3	Preston North End	2:2
Cambridge United	1:4	Aldershot	1:1
Chesterfield	2:0	Peterborough United	1:2
Crewe Alexandra	3:1	Shrewsbury Town	3:4
Fulham	3:2	Colchester United	1:0
Gillingham	1:0*	Brighton & Hove Albion	0:1
Grimsby Town	3:1	Darlington	2:2†
Halifax Town	1:0	York City	1:1
Leyton Orient	1:0	Millwall	1:1
Mansfield Town	2:1	Birmingham City	2:0
Newport County	2:2	Cardiff City	1:2
Port Vale	0:0	Northampton Town	1:4
Rochdale	3:0	Tranmere Rovers	1:1
Rotherham United	4:3	Huddersfield Town	4:1
Scarborough	1:1	Doncaster Rovers	0:3
Scunthorpe United	3:1	Hartlepool United	1:0
Stockport County	0:0	Carlisle United	1:3
Sunderland	1:0	Middlesbrough	0:2
Swindon Town	3:2	Bristol City	0:3
Torquay United	2:1	Swansea City	1:1
West Bromwich Albion	2:0	Walsall	3:0
Wigan Athletic	2:3	Bolton Wanderers	3:1
Wolverhampton Wanderers	3:2	Notts County	0:1
Wrexham	1:0	Burnley	0:3

* Won on penalty-kicks
† Won on away goals

Littlewoods Challenge Cup Competition 1987-88

2nd Round (2 Legs)	3rd Round	4th Round	5th Round	Semi-Final (2 Legs)	Final

Luton Town 1:4	*Luton Town 3				
Wigan Athletic 0:2		Luton Town 1			
Cambridge United 0:1	Coventry City 1		*Luton Town 2		
Coventry City 1:2					
Ipswich Town 1:4	*Ipswich Town 1				
Northampton Town 1:2		*Ipswich Town 0			
Southend United 1:0	Southend United 0				
Derby County 0:0				Luton Town 1:2	
Peterborough United 4:1	*Peterborough United 0:0				
Plymouth Argyle 1:1		*Reading 0:0			
Reading 3:2	Reading 0:1		Bradford City 0		
Chelsea 1:3					
Charlton Athletic 3:0	*Charlton Athletic 0				
Walsall 0:2		Bradford City 0:1		First leg at Oxford	
Fulham 1:1	Bradford City 1			Second leg at Luton	
Bradford City 5:2					Luton Town 3
Oxford United 1:2	*Oxford United 0:3				
Mansfield Town 1:0		*Oxford United 2			
Leicester City 2:2	Leicester City 0:2		*Oxford United 2		
Scunthorpe United 1:1					
Rochdale 1:1	*Wimbledon 2				
Wimbledon 1:2		Wimbledon 1			
Blackpool 1:1	Newcastle United 1				
Newcastle United 0:4				Oxford United 1:0	
Bury 2:1	*Bury 1				
Sheffield United 1:1		*Bury 1			
Queens Park Rangers 2:0	Queens Park Rangers 0		Manchester United 0		
Millwall 1:0					
Manchester United 5:1	*Manchester United 2				
Hull City 0:0		Manchester United 2			
Crystal Palace 4:2	Crystal Palace 1				
Newport County 0:0				At Wembley	
Blackburn Rovers 1:0	*Liverpool 0				
Liverpool 1:1		*Everton 2			
Everton 3:0	Everton 1		*Everton 2		
Rotherham United 2:0					
Leeds United 1:4	*Leeds United 2:2				
York City 1:0		Oldham Athletic 1			
Carlisle United 4:1	Oldham Athletic 2:4				
Oldham Athletic 3:4				Everton 0:1	
Manchester City 1:2	*Manchester City 3				
Wolverhampton Wand. 2:0		*Manchester City 3			
Nottingham Forest 5:1	Nottingham Forest 0		Manchester City 0		
Hereford United 0:1					
Swindon Town 3:3	*Swindon Town 1:2				
Portsmouth 1:1		Watford 1			
Darlington 0:0	Watford 1:4			First leg at Everton	
Watford 3:8				Second leg at Arsenal	
Middlesbrough 0:0	*Aston Villa 2				Arsenal 2
Aston Villa 1:1		*Aston Villa 1			
Torquay United 1:0	Tottenham Hotspur 1		*Sheffield Wednesday 0		
Tottenham Hotspur 0:3					
Barnsley 0:5	*Barnsley 1				
West Ham United 0:2		Sheffield Wednesday 2			
Shrewsbury Town 1:1	Sheffield Wednesday 2				
Sheffield Wednesday 1:2				Arsenal 1:3	
Stoke City 2:1	*Stoke City 2				
Gillingham 0:0		Stoke City 0			
Burnley 1:0	Norwich City 1		Arsenal 1		
Norwich City 1:1					
Bournemouth 1:2	Bournemouth 0				
Southampton 0:2		*Arsenal 3			
Doncaster Rovers 0:0	*Arsenal 3				
Arsenal 3:1					

*Denotes home club   † Won on away goals rule

Sherpa Van Trophy Competition 1987-88

Preliminary Round

Bolton Wanderers	0	Preston North End	0
Preston North End	5	Stockport County	2
Stockport County	1	Bolton Wanderers	3
Carlisle United	2	Chester City	1
Chester City	2	Blackpool	1
Blackpool	0	Carlisle United	1
Doncaster Rovers	0	Mansfield Town	1
Mansfield Town	3	Hartlepool United	2
Hartlepool United	1	Doncaster Rovers	0
Rochdale	0	Tranmere Rovers	0
Tranmere Rovers	1	Burnley	2
Burnley	3	Rochdale	2
Rotherham United	1	Scarborough	0
Scarborough	0	Sunderland	3
Sunderland	7	Rotherham United	1
Scunthorpe United	2	Grimsby Town	0
Grimsby Town	2	Halifax Town	1
Halifax Town	3	Scunthorpe United	0
Wigan Athletic	2	Crewe Alexandra	2
Bury	5	Wigan Athletic	2
Crewe Alexandra	0	Bury	0
York City	3	Darlington	4
Darlington	2	Chesterfield	1
Chesterfield	2	York City	0
Bristol City	2	Swansea City	0
Swansea City	1	Wolverhampton Wanderers	1
Wolverhampton Wanderers	3	Bristol City	1
Cardiff City	3	Wrexham	2
Wrexham	2	Walsall	2
Walsall	3	Cardiff City	1
Colchester United	3	Peterborough United	2
Cambridge United	0	Colchester United	0
Peterborough United	3	Cambridge United	0
Newport County	2	Port Vale	0
Port Vale	2	Exeter City	0
Exeter City	0	Newport County	1
Notts County	1	Northampton Town	0
Northampton Town	1	Brentford	0
Brentford	3	Notts County	2
Southend United	1	Fulham	0
Fulham	1	Brighton & Hove Albion	6
Brighton & Hove Albion	3	Southend United	2
Torquay United	2	Bristol Rovers	0
Bristol Rovers	0	Hereford United	2
Hereford United	0	Torquay United	2
Gillingham	2	Leyton Orient	2
Leyton Orient	2	Aldershot	2
Aldershot	3	Gillingham	1

First Round

Northern Section:

Burnley	1	Chester City	0
Bury	1	Bolton Wanderers	0
Carlisle United	0	Hartlepool United	2
Darlington	3	Rotherham United	2

Halifax Town	2	Chesterfield	1
Mansfield Town	1	Scunthorpe United	0
Preston North End	3	Rochdale	1
Sunderland	1	Crewe Alexandra	0

Southern Section:

Aldershot	1	Bristol City	0
Brighton & Hove Albion	4	Southend United	2
Colchester United	1*	Leyton Orient	1
Newport County	2	Hereford United	3
Notts County	2	Cardiff City	0
Torquay United	1	Port Vale	0
Walsall	1	Peterborough United	2
Wolverhampton Wanderers	4	Brentford	0

Quarter-Final

Northern Section:

Bury	0	Burnley	1
Darlington	1	Halifax Town	2
Preston North End	2	Mansfield Town	1
Sunderland	0	Hartlepool United	1

Southern Section:

Aldershot	0	Torquay United	1
Colchester United	2	Notts County	3
Hereford United	0	Brighton & Hove Albion	1
Wolverhampton Wanderers	4	Peterborough United	0

Semi-Final

Northern Section:

Burnley	0*	Halifax Town	0
Hartlepool United	0	Preston North End	2

Southern Section:

Brighton & Hove Albion	1	Notts County	5
Wolverhampton Wanderers	1	Torquay United	0

Final

Northern Section
First Leg:

Burnley	0	Preston North End	0

Second Leg:

Preston North End	1	Burnley	3

Southern Section
First Leg:

Notts County	1	Wolverhampton Wanderers	1

Second Leg:

Wolverhampton Wanderers	3	Notts County	0

Play-Off Final (at Wembley Stadium)

Wolverhampton Wanderers	2	Burnley	0

*Won on penalty-kicks

Wolverhampton Wanderers – Sherpa Van Trophy Winners.

Freight Rover/Sherpa Van Trophy Winners 1985-88

Year	Winners		Runners-up		Venue
1985	Wigan Athletic	3	Brentford	1	Wembley
1986	Bristol City	3	Bolton Wanderers	0	Wembley
1987	Mansfield Town	1*	Bristol City	1	Wembley
1988	Wolverhampton Wanderers	2	Burnley	0	Wembley

*Won on penalty-kicks

Full Members'/Simod Cup Winners 1986-88

Year	Winners		Runners-up		Venue
1986	Chelsea	5	Manchester City	4	Wembley
1987	Blackburn Rovers	1	Charlton Athletic	0	Wembley
1988	Reading	4	Luton Town	1	Wembley

Simod Cup Competition 1987-88

First Round

Aston Villa	0	Bradford City	5
Blackburn Rovers	1	Swindon Town	2
Charlton Athletic	1*	Hull City	1
Chelsea	2	Barnsley	1
Derby County	3	Birmingham City	1
Ipswich Town	1	Middlesbrough	0
Leeds United	3	Sheffield United	0
Leicester City	1	Huddersfield Town	0
Manchester City	6	Plymouth Argyle	2
Newcastle United	2	Shrewsbury Town	1
Oldham Athletic	0	West Bromwich Albion	3
Oxford United	1	Crystal Palace	0
Portsmouth	0	Stoke City	3
Queen's Park Rangers	1	Reading	3
Sheffield Wednesday	2	Bournemouth	0
West Ham United	1	Millwall	2

Second Round

Bradford City	2	Newcastle United	1
Charlton Athletic	1	Leicester City	2
Ipswich Town	2	West Bromwich Albion	1
Manchester City	0	Chelsea	2
Millwall	2	Leeds United	0
Reading	1	Oxford United	0
Sheffield Wednesday	0	Stoke City	1
Swindon Town	2	Derby County	1

Third Round

Bradford City	1	Southampton	0
Coventry City	2	Wimbledon	1
Everton	1	Luton Town	2
Ipswich Town	5	Watford	2
Leicester City	0	Stoke City	0*
Millwall	2	Norwich City	3
Reading	2	Nottingham Forest	1
Swindon Town	4	Chelsea	0

Quarter-Final

Coventry City	2	Ipswich Town	0
Luton Town	4	Stoke City	1
Reading	2	Bradford City	1
Swindon Town	2	Norwich City	0

Semi-Final

Luton Town	2	Swindon Town	1
Reading	1*	Coventry City	1

Final

Reading	4	Luton Town	1
(at Wembley Stadium)			

*Won on penalty-kicks

F.A. Sunday Cup Winners 1965-88

Year	Winners		Runners-up		Venue
1965	*London	6	Staffordshire	2	
1966	Unique United	1	Aldridge Fabrications	0	Dudley
1967	Carlton United	2	Stoke Works	0	Hendon
1968	Drovers	2	Brook United	0	Cambridge
1969	Leigh Park	3	Loke United	1	Romford
1970	Vention United	1	Unique United	0	Corby
1971	Beacontree Rovers	2	Saltley United	0	Leamington
1972	Newtown Unity	4	Springfield Colts	0	Dudley
1973	†Carlton United	2	Wear Valley	1	Spennymoor
1974	Newtown Unity	3	Brentford East	0	Birmingham
1975	Fareham Town Centipedes	1	Players Ath Engineers	0	High Wycombe
1976	Brandon United	2	Evergreen	1	Spennymoor
1977	Langley Park R.H.	2	Newtown Unity	0	Spennymoor
1978	Arras	2	Lion Rangers	1	Bishop's Stortford
	(After 2-2 draw at Nuneaton)				
1979	Lobster	3	Carlton United	2	Southport
1980	Fantail	1	Twin Foxes	0	Letchworth
1981	Fantail	1	Mackintosh	0	Birkenhead
1982	Dingle Rail	2	Twin Foxes	1	Hitchin
1983	Eagle	2	Lee Chapel North	1	Walthamstow
1984	†Lee Chapel North	4	Eagle	3	Dagenham
	(After 1-1 draw at Runcorn)				
1985	Hobbies	2	Avenue	1	Nuneaton
	(After 1-1 draw at Norwich and 2-2 draw at Birkenhead)				
1986	Avenue	1	Glenn Sports	0	Birkenhead
1987	†Lodge Cottrell	1	Avenue	0	Birmingham
1988	Nexday	2	Sunderland Humb. Plains	0	Newcastle

*Aggregate score
†After extra time

F.A. Sunday Cup Competition 1987-88

	First Round	Result			Attendance		
Sunday 4th October 1987		1st Tie	1st Rep	2nd Rep	1st Tie	1st Rep	2nd Rep
Croxteth & Gillmoss RBL *v* Iron Bridge		3-2			90		
Whetley Lane *v* Carlisle United Supporters		2-1			85		
Carnforth *v* Britannia		1-2			301		
Hermy *v* Victoria Lodge	(walkover for Victoria Lodge)						
Cleator Moor WMC *v* Morrison Sports		1-3			40		
Central Eight *v* Blackhall WMC		0-3			123		
Gardeners Moston *v* Horton Three Horse Shoes	(walkover for Horton Three Horse Shoes)						
East & West Toxteth *v* Hoval Farrar		4-2			200		
Nenthead *v* Northwood		2-0			114		
Dudley & Weetslade *v* Woodpecker		1-3			150		
Overpool United *v* Blyth Waterloo SC		4-0			100		
Sartan United *v* Brereton Town		2-3			60		
Polesworth Bull *v* Kettering Odyssey	(walkover for Kettering Odyssey)						
Birmingham Celtic *v* Broad Plain House		1-3			60		
Lion Rangers *v* Beaufort		1-0			40		
Rose United *v* Bulmers		3-2			61		
Taylor Brothers *v* Cork & Bottle	(walkover for Cork & Bottle)						
Cabot Towers *v* Hallen Sunday		2-0			40		
Nexday *v* Port of Bristol		4-0			156		

Jubilee Inn *v* Biddestone	3-1			81		
Hawkesbury Upton *v* Sandwell	1-1			9		
Sandwell *v* Hawkesbury Upton		5-0			10	
Rutland Rovers *v* Whitecross Rangers	3-2			20		
Gamlingay OB *v* Brimsdown Rovers	0-2			80		
Oxford Road Social *v* St Josephs........................	1-2			100		
St Joseph's (S Oxhey) *v* Dereham Hobbies Utd	0-2			108		
Sheffield House Rangers *v* Sanco	1-2			51		
Taverners *v* Essex Sports	0-3			24		
Bedford Athletic *v* Artois United	0-2			100		
Horndean *v* Evergreen.....................................	0-0			70		
Evergreen *v* Horndean......................................		0-1			85	
Sheerness East *v* Victoria.................................	5-0			100		
Verulam Arms Athletic *v* Ford Basildon	1-5			75		
Dee Roof Vikings *v* Watford Labour Club	4-2			60		
Bushey Mead OB *v* Scott	0-2			30		

Second Round	Result			Attendance		
Sunday 1st November 1987	1st	1st	2nd	1st	1st	2nd
	Tie	Rep	Rep	Tie	Rep	Rep
Eagle *v* Hartlepool Lion Hotel	2-1			27		
Nenthead *v* Overpool United	0-1			147		
Sunderland Humb Plains *v*						
Croxteth & Gillmoss RBL	1-0			300		
Blackhall WMC *v* Marchon...............................	3-2			134		
Boundary *v* Fantail	0-1			40		
Nicosia *v* Whetley Lane....................................	4-0			30		
Gorton Albion *v* Avenue	2-3			140		
Almethik *v* Britannia..	3-1			60		
Morrison Sports *v* Deborah United	2-1			120		
Woodpecker *v* Horton Three Horse Shoes.............	3-0			50		
Framwellgate Moor & Pity Me *v*						
East & West Toxteth	0-2			110		
Cork & Bottle *v* Olympic Star	0-2			Nil		
Nirvana *v* Brereton Town	2-3			70		
Slade Celtic *v* Halesowen Harriers	4-0			36		
Broad Plain House *v* Kettering Odyssey	3-0			76		
Cabot Towers *v* Acorn	4-2			30		
Newey Goodman *v* Sandwell	1-0			29		
St Josephs *v* Jubilee Inn	4-0			142		
Leggatts Athletic *v* Rose United.........................	1-3			65		
Lodge Cottrell *v* Rutland Rovers	3-1			53		
AD Bulwell *v* Nexday	2-3			39		
Horndean *v* Trinity	1-2			51		
Leyton Argyle *v* Dereham Hobbies United	6-3			50		
Brimsdown Rovers *v* Glenn Sports......................	3-1			32		
Essex Sports *v* Sanco	1-5			20		
Sheerness East *v* St Peters.................................	0-2			100		
Lee Chapel North FC *v* Scott ....(Aband.)				78		
(Tie awarded to Lee Chapel North FC)						
Lion Rangers *v* Dee Roof Vikings.......................	4-0			52		
Inter Volante *v* Artois United	1-2			20		
Ranelagh Sports *v* Girton Eagles	6-1			40		
Featherby Sports *v* Ford Basildon	0-4			17		

Third Round	Result			Attendance		
Sunday 6th December 1987	1st	1st	2nd	1st	1st	2nd
	Tie	Rep	Rep	Tie	Rep	Rep
Avenue *v* Blackhall WMC	1-0			48		
Almethik *v* East & West Toxteth	1-0			360		
Olympic Star *v* Eagle	5-1			96		
Newey Goodman *v* Victoria Lodge	3-2			49		
Brereton Town *v* Lodge Cottrell..........................	1-0			100		

	Result			Attendance		
	1st Tie	1st Rep	2nd Rep	1st Tie	1st Rep	2nd Rep
Nicosia v Overpool United	1-0			42		
Morrison Sports v Sunderland Humb Plains	0-1			100		
Woodpecker v Fantail	2-1			150		
Trinity v Nexday	0-4			56		
Leyton Argyle v St Peters	0-0			16		
St Peters v Leyton Argyle		0-2			25	
Lee Chapel North v Slade Celtic	3-1			94		
Ranelagh Sports v Ford Basildon	1-1			80		
Ford Basildon v Ranelagh Sports		2-1			60	
Lion Rangers v Artois United	3-2			13		
Rose United v Broad Plain House	0-3			84		
Brimsdown Rovers v Cabot Towers	1-1			20		
Cabot Towers v Brimsdown Rovers		3-2			40	
Sanco v St Josephs	3-2			42		

Fourth Round

Sunday 3rd January 1988	Result			Attendance		
	1st Tie	1st Rep	2nd Rep	1st Tie	1st Rep	2nd Rep
Avenue v Woodpecker	4-3			50		
Almethik v Sunderland Humb Plains	1-4			104		
Olympic Star v Newey Goodman	1-0			68		
Brereton Town v Nicosia	1-2			150		
Broad Plain House v Ford Basildon	1-3			80		
Leyton Argyle v Lion Rangers	1-4			21		
Nexday v St Josephs	5-0			225		
Cabot Towers v Lee Chapel North	4-5			30		

Fifth Round

Sunday 31st January 1988	Result			Attendance		
	1st Tie	1st Rep	2nd Rep	1st Tie	1st Rep	2nd Rep
Nicosia v Avenue	2-2			260		
Avenue v Nicosia		2-2			134	
Avenue v Nicosia			3-0			30
Sunderland Humb Plains v Olympic Star	3-1			231		
Lion Rangers v Ford Basildon	1-0			37		
Nexday v Lee Chapel North	3-0			241		

Semi-Final

Sunday 13th March 1988

	1st Tie	1st Rep
Nexday v Lion Rangers	2-2	
at Kettering Town FC		
Lion Rangers v Nexday		0-2
at VS Rugby FC		
Sunderland Humb Plains v Avenue	2-1	
at Spennymoor United FC		

Final

Sunday 1st May 1988

Nexday v Sunderland Humb Plains	2-0
at Newcastle United FC	

157

Other Leagues' Tables 1987-88

GM VAUXHALL CONFERENCE

	P	W	D	L	Goals F	A	Pts
Lincoln City	42	24	10	8	86	48	82
Barnet	42	23	11	8	93	45	80
Kettering Town	42	22	9	11	68	48	75
Runcorn	42	21	11	10	68	47	74
Telford United	42	20	10	12	65	50	70
Stafford Rangers	42	20	9	13	79	58	69
Kidderminster Harriers	42	18	15	9	75	66	69
Sutton United	42	16	18	8	77	54	66
Maidstone United	42	18	9	15	79	64	63
Weymouth	42	18	9	15	53	43	63
Macclesfield Town	42	18	9	15	64	62	63
Enfield	42	15	10	17	68	78	55
Cheltenham Town	42	11	20	11	64	67	53
Altrincham	42	14	10	18	59	59	52
Fisher Athletic	42	13	13	16	58	61	52
Boston United	42	14	7	21	60	75	49
Northwich Victoria	42	10	17	15	46	57	47
Wycombe Wanderers	42	11	13	18	50	76	46
Welling United	42	11	9	22	50	72	42
Bath City	42	9	10	23	48	76	37
Wealdstone	42	5	17	20	39	76	32
Dagenham	42	5	6	31	37	104	21

THE NORTHERN PREMIER FOOTBALL LEAGUE

	P	W	D	L	Goals F	A	Pts
Chorley	42	26	10	6	78	35	88
Hyde United	42	25	10	7	91	52	85
Caernarfon Town	42	22	10	10	56	34	76
Morecambe	42	19	15	8	61	41	72
Barrow	42	21	8	13	70	41	71
Worksop Town	42	20	11	11	74	55	71
Bangor City	42	20	10	12	72	55	70
Rhyl	42	18	13	11	70	42	67
Marine	42	19	10	13	67	45	67
Frickley Athletic	42	18	11	13	61	55	65
Witton Albion	42	16	12	14	61	47	60
Goole Town	42	17	9	16	71	61	60
Horwich	42	17	9	16	46	42	60
Southport	42	15	12	15	43	48	57
South Liverpool	42	10	19	13	56	64	49
Buxton	42	11	14	17	72	76	47
Mossley	42	11	11	20	54	75	44
Gateshead	42	11	7	24	52	71	40
Matlock Town	42	10	8	24	58	89	38
Gainsborough Trinity	42	8	10	24	38	81	34
Oswestry Town	42	6	10	26	44	101	28
Workington	42	6	3	33	28	113	21

*One point deducted.

BEAZER HOMES LEAGUE

Premier Division

	P	W	D	L	Goals F	A	Pts
Aylesbury United	42	27	8	7	79	35	89
Dartford	42	27	8	7	79	39	89
Cambridge City	42	24	8	10	84	43	80
Bromsgrove Rovers	42	22	11	9	65	39	77
Worcester City	42	22	6	14	58	48	72
Crawley Town	42	17	14	11	73	63	65
Alvechurch	42	17	13	12	54	52	64
Leicester United	42	15	14	13	68	59	59

	P	W	D	L	Goals F	A	Pts
Fareham Town	42	16	11	15	51	59	59
Corby Town	42	16	8	18	61	64	56
Dorchester Town	42	14	14	14	51	57	56
Ashford Town	42	12	16	14	45	54	52
Shepshed Charterhouse	42	13	11	18	53	62	50
Bedworth United	42	12	14	16	49	64	50
Gosport Borough	42	10	17	15	39	49	47
Burton Albion	42	11	14	17	62	74	47
V.S. Rugby	42	10	16	16	52	57	46
Redditch United	42	10	13	19	55	63	43
Chelmsford City	42	11	10	21	60	75	43
Willenhall Town	42	9	12	21	39	76	39
Nuneaton Borough	42	8	13	21	58	77	37
Witney Town	42	8	11	23	45	71	35

Midland Division

	P	W	D	L	Goals F	A	Pts
Merthyr Tydfil	42	30	4	8	102	40	94
Moor Green	42	26	8	8	91	49	86
Grantham Town	42	27	4	11	97	53	85
Atherstone United	42	22	10	10	93	56	76
Sutton Coldfield Town	42	22	6	14	71	47	72
Halesowen Town	42	18	15	9	75	59	69
Gloucester City	42	18	14	10	86	62	68
Dudley Town	42	20	5	17	64	55	65
Forest Green Rovers	42	14	16	12	67	54	58
Banbury United	42	17	7	18	48	46	58
Bridgnorth Town	42	16	7	19	59	75	55
Buckingham Town	42	15	9	18	74	75	54
King's Lynn	42	16	6	20	53	63	54
Wellingborough Town	42	14	10	18	67	70	52
Rushden Town	42	14	9	19	69	85	51
Trowbridge Town	42	14	3	25	53	82	45
Bilston Town	42	12	8	22	52	87	44
Hednesford Town	42	11	10	21	50	81	43
Mile Oak Rovers	42	9	14	19	43	65	41
Coventry Sporting	42	11	8	23	46	83	41
Stourbridge	42	10	10	22	46	79	40
Paget Rangers	42	10	9	23	49	89	39

Southern Division

	P	W	D	L	Goals F	A	Pts
Dover Athletic	40	28	10	2	81	28	94
Waterlooville	40	27	10	3	88	33	91
Salisbury	40	24	11	5	71	33	83
Gravesend & Northfleet	40	20	12	8	60	32	72
Thanet United	40	17	13	10	60	38	64
Andover	40	17	13	10	64	58	64
Dunstable	40	17	12	11	78	56	63
Burnham	40	17	10	13	61	45	61
Bury Town	40	17	7	16	80	67	58
Erith & Belvedere	40	16	9	15	52	56	57
Sheppey United	40	14	10	16	58	52	52
Hastings Town	40	14	10	16	62	70	52
Tonbridge A.F.C.	40	14	8	18	51	56	50
Poole Town	40	13	10	17	67	70	49
Baldock Town	40	12	12	16	44	53	48
Hounslow	40	11	8	21	41	76	41
Folkestone	40	9	11	20	47	76	38
Corinthian	40	9	10	21	49	67	37
Ruislip	40	5	13	22	33	88	28
Canterbury City	40	7	6	27	33	87	27
Chatham Town	40	7	5	28	39	88	26

VAUXHALL-OPEL LEAGUE

Premier Division

	P	W	D	L	F	A	Pts
Yeovil Town	42	24	9	9	66	34	81
Bromley	42	23	7	12	68	40	76
Slough Town	42	21	9	12	67	41	72
Leytonstone/Ilford	42	20	11	11	59	43	71
Wokingham Town	42	21	7	14	62	52	70
Hayes	42	20	9	13	62	48	69
Windsor & Eton	42	16	17	9	59	43	65
Farnborough Town	42	17	11	14	63	60	62
Carshalton Athletic	42	16	13	13	49	41	61
Hendon	42	16	12	14	62	58	60
Tooting & Mitcham Utd	42	15	14	13	57	59	59
Harrow Borough	42	15	11	16	53	58	56
Bishop's Stortford	42	15	10	17	55	58	55
Kingstonian	42	14	12	16	47	53	54
St. Albans City	42	15	6	21	60	69	51
Bognor Regis Town	42	14	9	19	41	57	51
Leyton-Wingate	42	14	8	20	58	64	50
Croydon	42	11	13	18	40	52	46
Barking	42	11	12	19	44	57	45
Dulwich Hamlet	42	10	11	21	46	64	41
Hitchin Town	42	10	8	24	46	79	38
Basingstoke Town	42	6	17	19	37	71	35

Division One

	P	W	D	L	F	A	Pts
Marlow	42	32	5	5	100	44	101
Grays Athletic	42	30	10	2	74	25	100
Woking	42	25	7	10	91	52	82
Boreham Wood	42	21	9	12	65	45	72
Staines Town	42	19	11	12	71	48	68
Wembley	42	18	11	13	54	46	65
Basildon United	42	18	9	15	65	58	63
Walton & Hersham	42	15	16	11	53	44	61
Hampton	42	17	10	15	59	54	61
Leatherhead	42	16	11	15	64	53	59
Southwick	42	13	12	17	59	63	51
Oxford City	42	13	12	17	70	77	51
Worthing	42	14	8	20	67	73	50
Kingsbury Town	42	11	17	14	62	69	50
Walthamstow Avenue	42	13	11	18	53	63	50
Lewes	42	12	13	17	83	77	49
Uxbridge	42	11	16	15	41	47	49
Chesham United	42	12	10	20	69	77	46
Bracknell Town	42	12	9	21	54	80	45
Billericay Town	42	11	11	20	58	88	44
Stevenage Borough	42	11	9	22	36	64	42
Wolverton Town (MK)	42	3	3	36	23	124	12

Division Two North

	P	W	D	L	F	A	Pts
Wivenhoe Town	42	26	10	6	105	42	88
Collier Row	42	22	13	7	71	39	79
Tilbury	42	18	15	9	61	40	69
Berkhamsted Town	42	19	12	11	71	53	69
Harlow Town	42	17	16	9	67	36	67
Ware	42	17	15	10	63	58	66
Witham Town	42	17	14	11	69	47	65
Vauxhall Motors	42	16	17	9	56	42	65
Heybridge Swifts	42	17	13	12	56	50	64
Tring Town	42	18	6	18	69	67	60
Letchworth Garden City	42	18	5	19	59	64	59
Finchley	42	16	10	16	67	54	58
Clapton	42	14	15	13	50	62	57
Hornchurch	42	13	15	14	56	65	54
Barton Rovers	42	13	10	19	43	60	49
Rainham Town	42	12	12	18	63	66	48
Royston Town	42	13	8	21	49	70	47
Saffron Walden Town	42	13	7	22	34	67	46
Hemel Hempstead	42	11	12	19	38	71	45
Haringey Borough	42	11	8	23	54	78	41
Aveley	42	8	13	21	42	65	37
Hertford Town	42	8	4	30	45	92	28

Division Two South

	P	W	D	L	F	A	Pts
Chalfont St. Peter	42	26	9	7	81	35	87
Metropolitan Police	42	23	17	2	80	32	86
Dorking	42	25	11	6	86	39	86
Feltham	42	21	12	9	74	41	75
Epsom & Ewell	42	21	11	10	71	49	74
Chertsey Town	42	22	7	13	63	47	73
Whyteleafe	42	20	11	11	84	55	71
Hungerford Town	42	21	7	14	66	54	70
Ruislip Manor	42	21	5	16	74	57	68
Yeading	42	19	10	13	83	56	67
Maidenhead United	42	18	12	12	69	54	66
Eastbourne United	42	18	10	14	67	57	64
Harefield United	42	18	6	18	59	60	60
Egham Town	42	12	12	18	45	55	48
Horsham	42	12	10	20	45	66	46
Southall	42	11	11	20	42	63	44
Molesey	42	11	11	20	42	63	44
Newbury Town	42	8	13	21	40	81	37
Camberley Town	42	9	9	24	51	94	36
Flackwell Heath	42	6	8	28	42	96	26
Banstead Athletic	42	6	7	29	34	81	25
Petersfield United	42	6	7	29	45	102	25

Attendances at Football League Matches

Season	Matches Played	Total (Millions)	Div. 1	Div. 2	Div. 3 (S)	Div. 3 (N)
1946-47	1848	35·6	15·0	11·1	5·7	3·9
1947-48	1848	40·3	16·7	12·3	6·7	4·6
1948-49	1848	41·3	17·9	11·4	7·0	5·0
1949-50	1848	40·5	17·3	11·7	7·1	4·4
1950-51	2028	39·6	16·7	10·8	7·4	4·8
1951-52	2028	39·0	16·1	11·1	7·0	4·9
1952-53	2028	37·1	16·1	9·7	6·7	4·7
1953-54	2028	36·2	16·2	9·5	6·3	4·2
1954-55	2028	34·1	15·1	9·0	6·0	4·1
1955-56	2028	33·2	14·1	9·1	5·7	4·3
1956-57	2028	32·7	13·8	8·7	5·6	4·6
1957-58	2028	33·6	14·5	8·7	6·1	4·3
1958-59	2028	33·6	14·7	8·6	5·9	4·3
1959-60	2028	32·5	14·4	8·4	5·7	4·0
1960-61	2028	28·6	12·9	7·0	4·8	3·9
1961-62	2015	28·0	12·1	7·5	5·2	3·3
1962-63	2028	28·9	12·5	7·8	5·3	3·3
1963-64	2028	28·5	12·5	7·6	5·4	3·0
1964-65	2028	27·6	12·7	7·0	4·4	3·5
1965-66	2028	27·2	12·5	6·9	4·8	3·0
1966-67	2028	28·9	14·2	7·3	4·4	3·0
1967-68	2028	30·1	15·3	7·5	4·0	3·4
1968-69	2028	29·4	14·6	7·4	4·3	3·1
1969-70	2028	29·6	14·9	7·6	4·2	2·9
1970-71	2028	28·2	14·0	7·1	4·4	2·8
1971-72	2028	28·7	14·5	6·8	4·7	2·7
1972-73	2028	25·4	14·0	5·6	3·7	2·1
1973-74	2027	25·0	13·1	6·3	3·4	2·2
1974-75	2028	25·6	12·6	7·0	4·1	2·0
1975-76	2028	24·9	13·1	5·8	3·9	2·1
1976-77	2028	26·2	13·6	6·3	4·2	2·1
1977-78	2028	25·4	13·3	6·5	3·3	2·3
1978-79	2028	24·5	12·7	6·2	3·4	2·3
1979-80	2028	24·6	12·2	6·1	4·0	2·3
1980-81	2028	21·9	11·4	5·2	3·6	1·7
1981-82	2028	20·0	10·4	4·8	2·8	2·0
1982-83	2028	18·8	9·3	5·0	2·9	1·6
1983-84	2028	18·3	8·7	5·3	2·7	1·5
1984-85	2028	17·8	9·8	4·0	2·7	1·4
1985-86	2028	16·5	9·0	3·6	2·5	1·4
1986-87	2028	17·4	9·1	4·2	2·4	1·7
1987-88	2030	18·0	8·1	5·3	2·8	1·8

NOTE: *From Season 1958-1959 onwards for Div. 3 (S) read Div. 3 and for Div. 3 (N) read Div. 4.*

F.A. Cup Attendances 1966-88

	1st Round	2nd Round	3rd Round	4th Round	5th Round
1987-88	204,411	104,561	720,121	443,133	281,461
1986-87	209,290	146,769	593,520	349,342	263,550
1985-86	171,142	130,034	486,838	495,526	311,833
1984-85	174,604	137,078	616,229	320,772	269,232
1983-84	192,276	151,647	625,965	417,298	181,832
1982-83	191,312	150,046	670,503	452,688	260,069
1981-82	236,220	127,300	513,185	356,987	203,334
1980-81	246,824	194,502	832,578	534,402	320,530
1979-80	267,121	204,759	804,701	507,725	364,039
1978-79	243,773	185,343	880,345	537,748	243,683
1977-78	258,248	178,930	881,406	540,164	400,751
1976-77	379,230	192,159	942,523	631,265	373,330
1975-76	255,533	178,099	867,880	573,843	471,925
1974-75	283,956	170,466	914,994	646,434	393,323
1973-74	214,236	125,295	840,142	747,909	346,012
1972-73	259,432	169,114	938,741	735,825	357,386
1971-72	277,726	236,127	986,094	711,399	486,378
1970-71	329,687	230,942	956,683	757,852	360,687
1969-70	345,229	195,102	925,930	651,374	319,893
1968-69	331,858	252,710	1,094,043	883,675	464,915
1967-68	322,121	236,195	1,229,519	771,284	563,779
1966-67	390,292	295,112	1,288,341	921,303	602,111

	6th Round	Semi-Finals & Final	Total	No. of matches	Average per match
1987-88	119,313	177,585	2,050,585	155	13,229
1986-87	119,396	195,533	1,877,400	165	11,378
1985-86	184,262	192,316	1,971,951	168	11,738
1984-85	148,690	242,754	1,909,359	157	12,162
1983-84	185,382	187,000	1,941,400	166	11,695
1982-83	193,845	291,162	2,209,625	154	14,348
1981-82	124,308	279,621	1,840,955	160	11,506
1980-81	288,714	339,250	2,756,800	169	16,312
1979-80	157,530	355,541	2,661,416	163	16,328
1978-79	263,213	249,897	2,604,002	166	15,687
1977-78	137,059	198,020	2,594,578	160	16,216
1976-77	205,379	258,216	2,982,102	174	17,139
1975-76	206,851	205,810	2,759,941	161	17,142
1974-75	268,361	291,369	2,968,903	172	17,261
1973-74	233,307	273,051	2,779,952	167	16,646
1972-73	241,934	226,543	2,928,975	160	18,306
1971-72	230,292	248,546	3,158,562	160	19,741
1970-71	304,937	279,644	3,220,432	162	19,879
1969-70	198,537	390,700	3,026,765	170	17,805
1968-69	188,121	216,232	3,431,554	157	21,857
1967-68	240,095	223,831	3,586,824	160	22,418
1966-67	252,672	217,378	3,967,209	169	23,475

The Football Association Fixture Programme
1988-89

AUGUST 1988
Sat 20   England v Israel (U-16)
          F.A. Charity Shield
Sat 27   Opening of Football League Season
Wed 31   Littlewoods Cup (1) 1st Leg

SEPTEMBER 1988
Sat 3   F.A. Cup (P)
Wed 7   Littlewoods Cup (1) 2nd Leg
          European Cups (1) 1st Leg
Sat 10   F.A. Vase (EP)
          F.A. Youth Cup (P)*
Tues 13   England v Denmark (U-21)
Wed 14   England v Denmark (F)
          Norway v Scotland (WC)
          N. Ireland v Republic of Ireland
          (WC)
          Holland v Wales (WC)
Sat 17   F.A. Cup (IQ)
Tues 20   Republic of Ireland v England (U-17)
Sat 24   F.A. Trophy (1Q)
Wed 28   Littlewoods Cup (2) 1st Leg

OCTOBER 1988
Sat 1   F.A. Cup (2Q)
          F.A. Youth Cup (1Q)*
Wed 5   European Cups (1) 2nd Leg
Sat 8   F.A. Vase (P)
Sun 9   F.A. Sunday Cup (1)
Wed 12   Littlewoods Cup (2) 2nd Leg
Sat 15   F.A. Cup (3Q)
Tues 18   England v Sweden (U-21)
Wed 19   England v Sweden (WC)
          Scotland v Yugoslavia (WC)
          Hungary v N. Ireland (WC)
          Wales v Finland (WC)
Sat 22   F.A. Trophy (2Q)
          F.A. Youth Cup (2Q)*
          F.A. County Youth Cup (1)*
Wed 26   European Cups (2) 1st Leg
          England v Greece (EYC)
Sat 29   F.A. Cup (4Q)

NOVEMBER 1988
Wed 2   Littlewoods Cup (3)
          F.A. XI v Northern Premier League
          (prov)
Sat 5   F.A. Vase (1)
Wed 9   European Cups (2) 2nd Leg
Sun 13   F.A. Sunday Cup (2)
Tues 15   England v France (EYC)
Sat 19   F.A. Cup (1P)
          F.A. Youth Cup (1P)*

Wed 23   U.E.F.A. Cup (3) 1st Leg
          F.A. XI v Northern League
Sat 26   F.A. Vase (2)
Wed 30   Littlewoods Cup (4)

DECEMBER 1988
Sat 3   F.A. Trophy (3Q)
          F.A. County Youth Cup (2)*
Wed 7   U.E.F.A. Cup (3) 2nd Leg
          F.A. XI v Vauxhall-Opel League
Sat 10   F.A. Cup (2P)
Sat 17   F.A. Vase (3)
          F.A. Youth Cup (2P)*
Sun 18   F.A. Sunday Cup (3)
Wed 21   Spain v N. Ireland (WC)

JANUARY 1989
Sat 7   F.A. Cup (3)
Sat 14   F.A. Trophy (1P)
          F.A. Youth Cup (3P)*
Wed 18   Littlewoods Cup (5)
Sat 21   F.A. Vase (4)
          F.A. County Youth Cup (3)*
Sun 22   F.A. Sunday Cup (4)
Sat 28   F.A. Cup (4P)

FEBRUARY 1989
Sat 4   F.A. Trophy (2P)
Tues 7   Greece v England (U-21)
Wed 8   Greece v England (F)
          Cyprus v Scotland (WC)
          N. Ireland v Spain (WC)
Sat 11   F.A. Vase (5)
          F.A. Youth Cup (4P)*
Wed 15   Littlewoods Cup (SF) 1st Leg
Sat 18   F.A. Cup (5P)
Sun 19   F.A. Sunday Cup (5)
Wed 22   Littlewoods Cup (SF) 2nd Leg
Sat 25   F.A. Trophy (3P)
          F.A. County Youth Cup (4)*

MARCH 1989
Wed 1   European Cups (QF) 1st Leg
Sat 4   F.A. Vase (6)
          F.A. Youth Cup (5P)*
Tues 7   Albania v England (U-21)
Wed 8   Albania v England (WC)
          Scotland v France (WC)
          Greece v England (EYC)
Sat 11   F.A. Trophy (4P)
          England v Belgium (Schoolboys)
Wed 15   European Cups (QF) 2nd Leg

162

Sat 18	F.A. Cup (6P)
Sun 19	F.A. Sunday Cup (SF)
Sat 25	F.A. Vase (SF) 1st Leg
	F.A. County Youth Cup (SF)*

APRIL 1989

Sat 1	F.A. Vase (SF) 2nd Leg
	F.A. Youth Cup (SF)*
Wed 5	European Cups (SF) 1st Leg
Sat 8	F.A. Trophy (SF) 1st Leg
Sat 9	Littlewoods Cup Final
Sat 15	F.A. Cup (SF)
	F.A. Trophy (SF) 2nd Leg
Wed 19	European Cups (SF) 2nd Leg
Tues 25	Scotland v Cyprus (WC)
	England v Albania (U-21)
Wed 26	England v Albania (WC)
	Malta v N. Ireland (WC)
	Czechoslovakia v England (EYC)
Sat 29	F.A. County Youth Cup Final
Sun 30	F.A. Sunday Cup Final

MAY 1989

Wed 3	U.E.F.A. Cup Final 1st Leg
Sat 6	F.A. Vase Final
	F.A. Youth Cup Final*
Wed 10	European Cup Winners' Cup Final
Sat 13	F.A. Trophy Final
Wed 17	U.E.F.A. Cup Final 2nd Leg
Sat 20	F.A. Cup Final
Wed 24	European Champion Clubs' Cup Final
Sat 27	England v West Germany (Schoolboys)
Wed 31	Wales v West Germany (WC)

JUNE 1989

Fri 2	England v Poland (U-21)
Sat 3	England v Poland (WC)
Wed 7	Denmark v England (F)

P = Preliminary Round   EP = Extra Preliminary Round   1Q = First Qualifying Round
1P = First Round Proper   F = Friendly International   WC = World Cup
EYC = European Youth Championship   QF = Quarter-Final   SF = Semi-Final
* = Closing date for round

Barclays League
FIXTURE LIST

Season 1988-89
© The Football League Limited 1988 (Licence No.P105-1)

Sat. 27th August

FIRST DIVISION
Aston Villa v Millwall ....
Charlton Athletic v Liverpool..
Derby County v Middlesbrough ....
Everton v Newcastle United..
Manchester United v Queens Park Rangers......................
Norwich City v Nottingham Forest ....
Sheffield Wednesday v Luton Town ....
Southampton v West Ham United ....
Tottenham Hotspur v Coventry City ....
Wimbledon v Arsenal ....

SECOND DIVISION
Brighton & Hove Albion v Bradford City ....
Chelsea v Blackburn Rovers..
Hull City v Manchester City ....
Leeds United v Oxford United...
Leicester City v West Bromwich Albion ....
Oldham Athletic v Barnsley ....
Shrewsbury Town v Portsmouth......................................
Stoke City v Ipswich Town ....
Sunderland v A.F.C. Bournemouth..................................
Swindon Town v Crystal Palace.......................................
Walsall v Plymouth Argyle ....
Watford v Birmingham City ....

THIRD DIVISION
Brentford v Huddersfield Town ....
Bristol Rovers v Wigan Athletic......................................
Bury v Wolverhampton Wanderers...................................
Cardiff City v Fulham ....
Chester City v Blackpool ....
Chesterfield v Aldershot..
Gillingham v Swansea City ....
Mansfield Town v Northampton Town ....
Notts County v Bristol City ....
Preston North End v Port Vale ....
Reading v Sheffield United ....
Southend United v Bolton Wanderers..............................

FOURTH DIVISION
Burnley v Rochdale ....
Cambridge United v Grimsby Town ....
Carlisle United v Peterborough United.............................
Colchester United v York City...
Darlington v Stockport County ....
Exeter City v Wrexham ....
Leyton Orient v Crewe Alexandra....................................
Lincoln City v Hartlepool United ....
Rotherham United v Doncaster Rovers.............................
Scarborough v Tranmere Rovers.....................................
Scunthorpe United v Hereford United ....
Torquay United v Halifax Town.......................................

Mon. 29th August

SECOND DIVISION
Barnsley v Swindon Town...
Bradford City v Stoke City ....
Manchester City v Oldham Athletic..................................

Oxford United v Hull City ....
Portsmouth v Leicester City ....
West Bromwich Albion v Watford....................................

Tues. 30th August

SECOND DIVISION
Crystal Palace v Chelsea ....

Fri. 2nd September

FOURTH DIVISION
Tranmere Rovers v Colchester United ....

Sat. 3rd September

FIRST DIVISION
Arsenal v Aston Villa...
Coventry City v Everton ....
Liverpool v Manchester United ....
Luton Town v Wimbledon ....
Middlesbrough v Norwich City ....
Millwall v Derby County ....
Newcastle United v Tottenham Hotspur ....
Nottingham Forest v Sheffield Wednesday ....
Queens Park Rangers v Southampton ....
West Ham United v Charlton Athletic...............................

SECOND DIVISION
A.F.C. Bournemouth v Chelsea..
Barnsley v Stoke City ....
Birmingham City v Leicester City....................................
Blackburn Rovers v Oldham Athletic................................
Bradford City v Shrewsbury Town...................................
Crystal Palace v Watford ....
Ipswich Town v Sunderland ....
Manchester City v Walsall...
Oxford United v Brighton & Hove Albion ....
Plymouth Argyle v Hull City ....
Portsmouth v Leeds United...
West Bromwich Albion v Swindon Town ....

THIRD DIVISION
Aldershot v Gillingham ....
Blackpool v Notts County ....
Bolton Wanderers v Cardiff City ....
Bristol City v Chesterfield ....
Fulham v Southend United ....
Huddersfield Town v Preston North End ....
Northampton Town v Brentford ....
Port Vale v Chester City ....
Sheffield United v Bristol Rovers ....
Swansea City v Bury ....
Wigan Athletic v Mansfield Town ....
Wolverhampton Wanderers v Reading..............................

FOURTH DIVISION
Crewe Alexandra v Scunthorpe United ....
Doncaster Rovers v Exeter City ....

Grimsby Town v Torquay United ....
Halifax Town v Burnley ....
Hartlepool United v Darlington ....
Hereford United v Cambridge United ....
Peterborough United v Scarborough ....
Rochdale v Rotherham United ....
Stockport County v Leyton Orient ....
Wrexham v Lincoln City ....
York City v Carlisle United ....

Fri. 9th September

THIRD DIVISION
Southend United v Swansea City ....

FOURTH DIVISION
Colchester United v Doncaster Rovers ....

Sat. 10th September

FIRST DIVISION
Aston Villa v Liverpool ....
Charlton Athletic v Millwall ....
Derby County v Newcastle United ....
Everton v Nottingham Forest ....
Manchester United v Middlesbrough ....
Norwich City v Queens Park Rangers ....
Sheffield Wednesday v Coventry City ....
Southampton v Luton Town ....
Tottenham Hotspur v Arsenal ....
Wimbledon v West Ham United ....

SECOND DIVISION
Brighton & Hove Albion v A.F.C. Bournemouth ....
Chelsea v Oxford United ....
Hull City v Barnsley ....
Leeds United v Manchester City ....
Leicester City v Ipswich Town ....
Oldham Athletic v Birmingham City ....
Shrewsbury Town v West Bromwich Albion ....
Stoke City v Blackburn Rovers ....
Sunderland v Bradford City ....
Walsall v Crystal Palace ....
Watford v Plymouth Argyle ....

THIRD DIVISION
Brentford v Wigan Athletic ....
Bristol Rovers v Aldershot ....
Bury v Port Vale ....
Cardiff City v Huddersfield Town ....
Chester City v Bristol City ....
Chesterfield v Wolverhampton Wanderers ....
Gillingham v Sheffield United ....
Mansfield Town v Fulham ....
Notts County v Northampton Town ....
Preston North End v Blackpool ....
Reading v Bolton Wanderers ....

FOURTH DIVISION
Burnley v York City ....
Cambridge United v Stockport County ....
Carlisle United v Tranmere Rovers ....
Darlington v Peterborough United ....
Exeter City v Halifax Town ....
Leyton Orient v Hereford United ....
Lincoln City v Crewe Alexandra ....
Rotherham United v Wrexham ....
Scarborough v Rochdale ....
Scunthorpe United v Grimsby Town ....
Torquay United v Hartlepool United ....

Sun. 11th September

SECOND DIVISION
Swindon Town v Portsmouth ....

Fri. 16th September

FOURTH DIVISION
Halifax Town v Carlisle United ....
Stockport County v Burnley ....
Tranmere Rovers v Cambridge United ....
Wrexham v Colchester United ....

Sat. 17th September

FIRST DIVISION
Arsenal v Southampton ....
Coventry City v Charlton Athletic ....
Liverpool v Tottenham Hotspur ....
Luton Town v Manchester United ....
Middlesbrough v Wimbledon ....
Millwall v Everton ....
Newcastle United v Norwich City ....
Nottingham Forest v Derby County ....
Queens Park Rangers v Sheffield Wednesday ....
West Ham United v Aston Villa ....

SECOND DIVISION
A.F.C. Bournemouth v Leeds United ....
Barnsley v Chelsea ....
Birmingham City v Sunderland ....
Blackburn Rovers v Swindon Town ....
Bradford City v Oldham Athletic ....
Crystal Palace v Shrewsbury Town ....
Ipswich Town v Watford ....
Manchester City v Brighton & Hove Albion ....
Oxford United v Leicester City ....
Plymouth Argyle v Stoke City ....
Portsmouth v Hull City ....
West Bromwich Albion v Walsall ....

THIRD DIVISION
Aldershot v Southend United ....
Blackpool v Mansfield Town ....
Bolton Wanderers v Bristol Rovers ....
Bristol City v Preston North End ....
Fulham v Bury ....
Huddersfield Town v Gillingham ....
Northampton Town v Chesterfield ....
Port Vale v Cardiff City ....
Sheffield United v Chester City ....
Swansea City v Brentford ....
Wigan Athletic v Reading ....
Wolverhampton Wanderers v Notts County ....

FOURTH DIVISION
Crewe Alexandra v Darlington ....
Doncaster Rovers v Torquay United ....
Grimsby Town v Rotherham United ....
Hartlepool United v Leyton Orient ....
Hereford United v Scarborough ....
Peterborough United v Lincoln City ....
Rochdale v Exeter City ....
York City v Scunthorpe United ....

Mon. 19th September

THIRD DIVISION
Port Vale v Chesterfield ....

FOURTH DIVISION
Stockport County v Halifax Town ....
Tranmere Rovers v Peterborough United ....

Tues. 20th September

SECOND DIVISION
Chelsea v Manchester City ....
Hull City v Blackburn Rovers ....

Oldham Athletic v Oxford United ....
Shrewsbury Town v Ipswich Town ....
Stoke City v Portsmouth ....
Sunderland v Crystal Palace ....
Swindon Town v A.F.C. Bournemouth ....
Walsall v Birmingham City ....
Watford v Bradford City ....

Blackpool v Bristol City ....
Bolton Wanderers v Fulham ....
Cardiff City v Bury ....
Huddersfield Town v Notts County ....
Mansfield Town v Gillingham ....
Preston North End v Chester City ....
Sheffield United v Northampton Town ....
Wigan Athletic v Swansea City ....
Wolverhampton Wanderers v Aldershot ....

Cambridge United v Lincoln City ....
Colchester United v Scarborough ....
Darlington v Exeter City ....
Rochdale v Doncaster Rovers ....
Rotherham United v Leyton Orient ....
Scunthorpe United v Carlisle United ....
Torquay United v Burnley ....
Wrexham v Grimsby Town ....
York City v Hartlepool United ....

Wed. 21st September

SECOND DIVISION
Brighton & Hove Albion v West Bromwich Albion ....
Leeds United v Barnsley ....
Leicester City v Plymouth Argyle ....

THIRD DIVISION
Bristol Rovers v Brentford ....
Reading v Southend United ....

FOURTH DIVISION
Hereford United v Crewe Alexandra ....

Fri. 23rd September

FOURTH DIVISION
Crewe Alexandra v Stockport County ....
Halifax Town v Tranmere Rovers ....
Leyton Orient v Darlington ....

Sat. 24th September

FIRST DIVISION
Aston Villa v Nottingham Forest ....
Charlton Athletic v Newcastle United ....
Derby County v Queens Park Rangers ....
Everton v Luton Town ....
Manchester United v West Ham United ....
Norwich City v Millwall ....
Sheffield Wednesday v Arsenal ....
Southampton v Liverpool ....
Tottenham Hotspur v Middlesbrough ....
Wimbledon v Coventry City ....

SECOND DIVISION
A.F.C. Bournemouth v Oxford United ....
Barnsley v Manchester City ....
Blackburn Rovers v Birmingham City ....
Ipswich Town v Bradford City ....
Leeds United v Chelsea ....
Leicester City v Watford ....
Oldham Athletic v Hull City ....
Plymouth Argyle v West Bromwich Albion ....

Portsmouth v Crystal Palace ....
Shrewsbury Town v Sunderland ....
Swindon Town v Brighton & Hove Albion ....
Walsall v Stoke City ....

Aldershot v Bolton Wanderers ....
Brentford v Sheffield United ....
Bristol City v Port Vale ....
Bury v Mansfield Town ....
Chester City v Huddersfield Town ....
Chesterfield v Blackpool ....
Fulham v Wigan Athletic ....
Gillingham v Reading ....
Northampton Town v Bristol Rovers ....
Notts County v Preston North End ....
Southend United v Cardiff City ....
Swansea City v Wolverhampton Wanderers ....

Burnley v Colchester United ....
Carlisle United v Rotherham United ....
Doncaster Rovers v Wrexham ....
Exeter City v Scunthorpe United ....
Grimsby Town v Rochdale ....
Hartlepool United v Cambridge United ....
Lincoln City v Hereford United ....
Peterborough United v York City ....
Scarborough v Torquay United ....

Fri. 30th September

THIRD DIVISION
Wigan Athletic v Blackpool ....

FOURTH DIVISION
Cambridge United v Carlisle United ....
Tranmere Rovers v Hartlepool United ....

Sat. 1st October

FIRST DIVISION
Coventry City v Middlesbrough ....
Liverpool v Newcastle United ....
Millwall v Queens Park Rangers ....
Norwich City v Charlton Athletic ....
Nottingham Forest v Luton Town ....
Sheffield Wednesday v Aston Villa ....
Southampton v Derby County ....
Tottenham Hotspur v Manchester United ....
West Ham United v Arsenal ....
Wimbledon v Everton ....

SECOND DIVISION
Birmingham City v Barnsley ....
Bradford City v Portsmouth ....
Brighton & Hove Albion v Leeds United ....
Chelsea v Leicester City ....
Crystal Palace v Plymouth Argyle ....
Hull City v Walsall ....
Manchester City v Blackburn Rovers ....
Oxford United v Shrewsbury Town ....
Stoke City v A.F.C. Bournemouth ....
Sunderland v Oldham Athletic ....
Watford v Swindon Town ....
West Bromwich Albion v Ipswich Town ....

THIRD DIVISION
Bolton Wanderers v Sheffield United ....
Brentford v Gillingham ....
Bristol City v Swansea City ....
Cardiff City v Bristol Rovers ....
Chesterfield v Bury ....
Huddersfield Town v Fulham ....
Mansfield Town v Notts County ....
Northampton Town v Aldershot ....

Preston North End v Southend United ....
Reading v Chester City ....
Wolverhampton Wanderers v Port Vale ....

FOURTH DIVISION
Colchester United v Lincoln City ....
Darlington v Burnley ....
Hereford United v Grimsby Town ....
Rochdale v Crewe Alexandra ....
Rotherham United v Exeter City....................................
Scunthorpe United v Scarborough ....
Stockport County v Doncaster Rovers............................
Torquay United v Leyton Orient...................................
Wrexham v Peterborough United..................................
York City v Halifax town ....

Mon. 3rd October

THIRD DIVISION
Port Vale v Huddersfield Town ....

Tues. 4th October

SECOND DIVISION
Birmingham City v Plymouth Argyle ....
Chelsea v Walsall ....
Crystal Palace v Ipswich Town ....
Hull City v Leicester City...
Stoke City v Shrewsbury Town ....
Sunderland v Leeds United ....
Watford v Oldham Athletic..

THIRD DIVISION
Aldershot v Wigan Athletic...
Blackpool v Northampton Town ....
Bury v Reading ....
Gillingham v Bristol City ....
Notts County v Chesterfield ....
Southend United v Mansfield Town ....
Swansea City v Bolton Wanderers ....

FOURTH DIVISION
Burnley v Rotherham United ....
Carlisle United v Colchester United...............................
Crewe Alexandra v Cambridge United............................
Doncaster Rovers v Hereford United..............................
Grimsby Town v Tranmere Rovers ....
Halifax Town v Wrexham ....
Hartlepool United v Rochdale ....
Leyton Orient v York City ....

Wed. 5th October

SECOND DIVISION
Bradford City v Blackburn Rovers..................................
Brighton & Hove Albion v Barnsley ....
Manchester City v Portsmouth......................................
Oxford United v Swindon Town.....................................
West Bromwich Albion v A.F.C. Bournemouth.................

THIRD DIVISION
Bristol Rovers v Preston North End ....
Chester City v Brentford ....
Fulham v Wolverhampton Wanderers ....

FOURTH DIVISION
Exeter City v Torquay United.......................................
Lincoln City v Scunthorpe United ....
Peterborough United v Stockport County ....
Scarborough v Darlington..

Fri. 7th October

FOURTH DIVISION
Tranmere Rovers v York City..

Sat. 8th October

FIRST DIVISION
Arsenal v Millwall ....
Aston Villa v Wimbledon ....
Charlton Athletic v Tottenham Hotspur ....
Derby County v Norwich City.......................................
Everton v Southampton ....
Luton Town v Liverpool...
Manchester United v Sheffield Wednesday......................
Middlesbrough v West Ham United ....
Newcastle United v Coventry City ....
Queens Park Rangers v Nottingham Forest ....

SECOND DIVISION
A.F.C. Bournemouth v Birmingham City ....
Barnsley v West Bromwich Albion ....
Blackburn Rovers v Crystal Palace ....
Ipswich Town v Manchester City....................................
Leeds United v Watford ....
Leicester City v Brighton & Hove Albion ....
Oldham Athletic v Stoke City ....
Plymouth Argyle v Bradford City ....
Portsmouth v Oxford United ....
Shrewsbury Town v Hull City ....
Walsall v Sunderland ....

THIRD DIVISION
Bolton Wanderers v Blackpool ....
Bristol City v Fulham ....
Cardiff City v Reading ....
Gillingham v Chesterfield ....
Mansfield Town v Bristol Rovers...................................
Northampton Town v Huddersfield Town ....
Preston North End v Bury...
Sheffield United v Wolverhampton Wanderers ....
Wigan Athletic v Port Vale ....

FOURTH DIVISION
Burnley v Exeter City ....
Cambridge United v Halifax Town ....
Colchester United v Scunthorpe United...........................
Darlington v Rotherham United ....
Doncaster Rovers v Hartlepool United............................
Grimsby Town v Peterborough United ....
Hereford United v Carlisle United..................................
Rochdale v Stockport County ....
Scarborough v Leyton Orient ....
Torquay United v Lincoln City ....
Wrexham v Crewe Alexandra.......................................

Sun. 9th October

SECOND DIVISION
Swindon Town v Chelsea ....

THIRD DIVISION
Aldershot v Swansea City ....
Brentford v Southend United ....
Notts County v Chester City...

Fri. 14th October

FOURTH DIVISION
Halifax Town v Rochdale ....

Sat. 15th October

FIRST DIVISION
Charlton Athletic v Aston Villa.....................................
Coventry City v Millwall..
Everton v Derby County ....
Luton Town v Arsenal ....
Manchester United v Norwich City...............................
Newcastle United v Middlesbrough ....
Nottingham Forest v Liverpool.....................................
Queens Park Rangers v West Ham United ....
Sheffield Wednesday v Wimbledon................................
Tottenham Hotspur v Southampton...............................

SECOND DIVISION
Birmingham City v West Bromwich Albion......................
Blackburn Rovers v Barnsley ....
Bradford City v Crystal Palace ....
Hull City v Sunderland ....
Ipswich Town v Oxford United......................................
Leicester City v Stoke City ....
Oldham Athletic v Chelsea ....
Plymouth Argyle v Manchester City ....
Portsmouth v A.F.C. Bournemouth ....
Shrewsbury Town v Walsall ....
Watford v Brighton & Hove Albion.................................

THIRD DIVISION
Blackpool v Sheffield United ....
Bristol Rovers v Notts County ....
Bury v Brentford..
Chester City v Cardiff City ....
Chesterfield v Preston North End ....
Fulham v Aldershot..
Huddersfield Town v Bristol City ....
Port Vale v Bolton Wanderers ....
Reading v Mansfield Town...
Southend United v Gillingham......................................
Swansea City v Northampton Town ....
Wolverhampton Wanderers v Wigan Athletic....................

FOURTH DIVISION
Carlisle United v Torquay United...................................
Crewe Alexandra v Doncaster Rovers.............................
Exeter City v Grimsby Town ....
Hartlepool United v Wrexham.......................................
Leyton Orient v Colchester United ....
Lincoln City v Scarborough ....
Peterborough United v Burnley ....
Rotherham United v Tranmere Rovers ....
Scunthorpe United v Cambridge United ....
Stockport County v Hereford United ....
York City v Darlington ....

Sun. 16th October

SECOND DIVISION
Swindon Town v Leeds United ....

Fri. 21st October

FOURTH DIVISION
Colchester United v Cambridge United ....
Doncaster United v Halifax Town ....

Sat. 22nd October

FIRST DIVISION
Arsenal v Queens Park Rangers....................................
Aston Villa v Everton ....
Derby County v Charlton Athletic...................................
Liverpool v Coventry City..
Middlesbrough v Luton Town..

Millwall v Nottingham Forest ....
Norwich City v Tottenham Hotspur ....
Southampton v Sheffield Wednesday ....
West Ham United v Newcastle United ....
Wimbledon v Manchester United....................................

SECOND DIVISION
A.F.C. Bournemouth v Shrewsbury Town ....
Barnsley v Ipswich Town ....
Brighton & Hove Albion v Oldham Athletic.......................
Chelsea v Plymouth Argyle ....
Crystal Palace v Hull City ....
Leeds United v Leicester City.......................................
Manchester City v Birmingham City ....
Oxford United v Blackburn Rovers ....
Stoke City v Watford ....
Sunderland v Swindon Town ....
Walsall v Portsmouth ....
West Bromwich Albion v Bradford City ....

THIRD DIVISION
Aldershot v Huddersfield Town ....
Blackpool v Port Vale ....
Bolton Wanderers v Wolverhampton Wanderers ....
Brentford v Preston North End......................................
Bristol Rovers v Chester City ....
Gillingham v Bury...
Mansfield Town v Cardiff City ....
Northampton Town v Bristol City ....
Notts County v Reading ....
Sheffield United v Wigan Athletic ....
Southend United v Chesterfield ....
Swansea City v Fulham ....

FOURTH DIVISION
Burnley v Leyton Orient...
Exeter City v Carlisle United...
Grimsby Town v York City ....
Hartlepool United v Crewe Alexandra ....
Lincoln City v Darlington ....
Peterborough United v Hereford United ....
Rochdale v Scunthorpe United ....
Scarborough v Stockport County....................................
Torquay United v Rotherham United ....
Wrexham v Tranmere Rovers..

Mon. 24th October

THIRD DIVISION
Port Vale v Sheffield United..

FOURTH DIVISION
Stockport County v Hartlepool United..............................
Tranmere Rovers v Lincoln City ....

Tues. 25th October

SECOND DIVISION
Birmingham City v Stoke City ....
Crystal Palace v Oxford United......................................
Hull City v Chelsea ....
Ipswich Town v Portsmouth ....
Oldham Athletic v A.F.C. Bournemouth............................
Plymouth Argyle v Shrewsbury Town...............................
Sunderland v Blackburn Rovers.....................................
Watford v Barnsley ....

THIRD DIVISION
Bristol City v Aldershot...
Bury v Southend United ....
Cardiff City v Notts County...
Chesterfield v Brentford ....
Fulham v Northampton Town...
Huddersfield Town v Swansea City ....
Preston North End v Gillingham.....................................
Wigan Athletic v Bolton Wanderers ....
Wolverhampton Wanderers v Blackpool ....

Cambridge United v Scarborough ....
Carlisle United v Burnley ....
Crewe Alexandra v Grimsby Town ....
Darlington v Torquay United ....
Halifax Town v Peterborough United.............................
Leyton Orient v Exeter City ....
Rotherham United v Colchester United...........................
Scunthorpe United v Wrexham ....
York City v Doncaster Rovers ....

Wed. 26th October

SECOND DIVISION

Bradford City v Leeds United..
Brighton & Hove Albion v Walsall ....
Leicester City v Swindon Town ....
West Bromwich Albion v Manchester City ....

THIRD DIVISION

Chester City v Mansfield Town ....
Reading v Bristol Rovers ....

FOURTH DIVISION

Hereford United v Rochdale ....

Fri. 28th October

THIRD DIVISION

Southend United v Wigan Athletic ....

FOURTH DIVISION

Colchester United v Stockport County ....

Sat. 29th October

FIRST DIVISION

Arsenal v Coventry City ....
Aston Villa v Tottenham Hotspur ....
Charlton Athletic v Sheffield Wednesday ....
Derby County v Wimbledon ....
Everton v Manchester United..
Luton Town v Queens Park Rangers ....
Middlesbrough v Millwall ....
Newcastle United v Nottingham Forest ....
Norwich City v Southampton..
West Ham United v Liverpool ....

SECOND DIVISION

A.F.C. Bournemouth v Ipswich Town.............................
Barnsley v Plymouth Argyle...
Blackburn Rovers v West Bromwich Albion.....................
Chelsea v Brighton & Hove Albion................................
Leeds United v Hull City ....
Manchester City v Sunderland ....
Oxford United v Bradford City ....
Portsmouth v Oldham Athletic ....
Shrewsbury Town v Leicester City.................................
Stoke City v Crystal Palace...
Swindon Town v Birmingham City ....
Walsall v Watford ....

THIRD DIVISION

Aldershot v Chester City ....
Blackpool v Cardiff City ....
Bolton Wanderers v Chesterfield....................................
Brentford v Port Vale ....
Bristol Rovers v Huddersfield Town ....
Gillingham v Wolverhampton Wanderers ....
Mansfield Town v Bristol City......................................
Northampton Town v Reading.......................................
Notts County v Fulham ....
Sheffield United v Bury ....
Swansea City v Preston North End ....

FOURTH DIVISION

Burnley v Cambridge United...
Doncaster Rovers v Leyton Orient ....
Exeter City v Crewe Alexandra.....................................
Grimsby Town v Halifax Town ....
Hartlepool United v Hereford United ....
Lincoln City v Carlisle United.......................................
Peterborough United v Scunthorpe United ....
Rochdale v Darlington ....
Scarborough v Rotherham United ....
Torquay United v Tranmere Rovers ....
Wrexham v York City ....

Tues. 1st November

THIRD DIVISION

Sheffield United v Cardiff City......................................

Wed. 2nd November

SECOND DIVISION

Oxford United v Sunderland ....

Fri. 4th November

FOURTH DIVISION

Cambridge United v Exeter City ....
Crewe Alexandra v Colchester United ....
Halifax Town v Hartlepool United ....
Tranmere Rovers v Rochdale ....

Sat. 5th November

FIRST DIVISION

Coventry City v West Ham United ....
Liverpool v Middlesbrough ....
Manchester United v Aston Villa ....
Millwall v Luton Town ....
Nottingham Forest v Arsenal...
Queens Park Rangers v Newcastle United.........................
Sheffield Wednesday v Everton ....
Southampton v Charlton Athletic....................................
Tottenham Hotspur v Derby County................................
Wimbledon v Norwich City ....

SECOND DIVISION

Birmingham City v Portsmouth......................................
Bradford City v A.F.C. Bournemouth..............................
Brighton & Hove Albion v Shrewsbury Town ....
Crystal Palace v Barnsley...
Hull City v Swindon Town ....
Ipswich Town v Leeds United ....
Leicester City v Manchester City ....
Oldham Athletic v Walsall ....
Plymouth Argyle v Blackburn Rovers ....
Sunderland v Stoke City ....
Watford v Chelsea ....
West Bromwich Albion v Oxford United ....

THIRD DIVISION

Bristol City v Bolton Wanderers ....
Bury v Notts County ....
Cardiff City v Gillingham..
Chester City v Swansea City ....
Chesterfield v Bristol Rovers ....
Fulham v Blackpool...
Huddersfield Town v Sheffield United ....
Port Vale v Aldershot ....
Preston North End v Mansfield Town...............................
Reading v Brentford ....
Wigan Athletic v Northampton Town ....
Wolverhampton Wanderers v Southend United ....

FOURTH DIVISION

Carlisle United v Scarborough ....
Darlington v Doncaster Rovers.....................................
Hereford United v Wrexham..
Leyton Orient v Peterborough United.............................
Rotherham United v Lincoln City ....
Scunthorpe United v Burnley ....
Stockport County v Grimsby Town.................................
York City v Torquay United...

Mon. 7th November

FOURTH DIVISION

Tranmere Rovers v Hereford United ....

Tues. 8th November

SECOND DIVISION

Ipswich Town v Walsall ....

THIRD DIVISION

Aldershot v Sheffield United ....
Brentford v Notts County ....
Bristol City v Wolverhampton Wanderers........................
Bury v Chester City ....
Chesterfield v Cardiff City ....
Fulham v Reading...
Gillingham v Blackpool...
Huddersfield Town v Bolton Wanderers ....
Northampton Town v Port Vale ....
Preston North End v Wigan Athletic...............................
Southend United v Bristol Rovers ....
Swansea City v Mansfield Town ....

FOURTH DIVISION

Burnley v Lincoln City ....
Darlington v Cambridge United......................................
Grimsby Town v Doncaster Rovers ....
Halifax Town v Colchester United...................................
Leyton Orient v Carlisle United ....
Rotherham United v Scunthorpe United ....
Torquay United v Rochdale ....
Wrexham v Stockport County...
York City v Crewe Alexandra...

Wed. 9th November

FOURTH DIVISION

Exeter City v Scarborough ....
Peterborough United v Hartlepool United ....

Fri. 11th November

SECOND DIVISION

Shrewsbury Town v Oldham Athletic...............................

FOURTH DIVISION

Colchester United v Torquay United ....
Stockport County v York City ....

Sat. 12th November

FIRST DIVISION

Charlton Athletic v Everton ....
Coventry City v Luton Town ....
Derby County v Manchester United ....
Liverpool v Millwall ....
Middlesbrough v Queens Park Rangers ....
Newcastle United v Arsenal ....
Norwich City v Sheffield Wednesday...............................

Southampton v Aston Villa ....
Tottenham Hotspur v Wimbledon ....
West Ham United v Nottingham Forest ....

SECOND DIVISION

A.F.C. Bournemouth v Crystal Palace ....
Barnsley v Bradford City ....
Blackburn Rovers v Brighton & Hove Albion...................
Chelsea v Sunderland..
Leeds United v West Bromwich Albion ....
Manchester City v Watford ....
Oxford United v Birmingham City...................................
Portsmouth v Plymouth Argyle ....
Swindon Town v Ipswich Town ....
Walsall v Leicester City ....

THIRD DIVISION

Blackpool v Aldershot ....
Bolton Wanderers v Bury ....
Bristol Rovers v Gillingham ....
Cardiff City v Northampton Town ....
Chester City v Chesterfield..
Mansfield Town v Brentford ....
Notts County v Southend United ....
Port Vale v Swansea City ....
Reading v Preston North End ....
Sheffield United v Fulham ....
Wigan Athletic v Bristol City ....
Wolverhampton Wanderers v Huddersfield Town ....

FOURTH DIVISION

Cambridge United v Rotherham United ....
Carlisle United v Darlington ....
Crewe Alexandra v Tranmere Rovers ....
Doncaster Rovers v Peterborough United.........................
Hartlepool United v Grimsby Town.................................
Hereford United v Halifax Town.....................................
Lincoln City v Exeter City...
Rochdale v Wrexham..
Scarborough v Burnley..
Scunthorpe United v Leyton Orient.................................

Sun. 13th November

SECOND DIVISION

Stoke City v Hull City ....

Sat. 19th November

FIRST DIVISION

Arsenal v Middlesbrough..
Aston Villa v Derby County ....
Everton v Nowich City ....
Luton Town v West Ham United.....................................
Manchester United v Southampton..................................
Millwall v Newcastle United ....
Nottingham Forest v Coventry City ....
Queens Park Rangers v Liverpool ....
Sheffield Wednesday v Tottenham Hotspur.......................
Wimbledon v Charlton Athletic ....

SECOND DIVISION

A.F.C. Bournemouth v Manchester City ....
Bradford City v Chelsea ....
Crystal Palace v Leicester City ....
Hull City v Birmingham City ....
Ipswich Town v Brighton & Hove Albion ....
Oldham Athletic v Leeds United ....
Oxford United v Plymouth Argyle ....
Portsmouth v Barnsley ....
Shrewsbury Town v Watford ....
Stoke City v Swindon Town ....
Sunderland v West Bromwich Albion...............................
Walsall v Blackburn Rovers ....

Tues. 22nd November

SECOND DIVISION
Birmingham City v Leeds United ....
Blackburn Rovers v Shrewsbury Town ....

Fri. 25th November

FOURTH DIVISION
Colchester United v Darlington ....
Crewe Alexandra v Peterborough United ....
Stockport County v Tranmere Rovers ....

Sat. 26th November

FIRST DIVISION
Charlton Athletic v Nottingham Forest...........................
Coventry City v Aston Villa ....
Derby County v Arsenal ....
Liverpool v Wimbledon...
Middlesbrough v Sheffield Wednesday ....
Newcastle United v Manchester United...........................
Norwich City v Luton Town ....
Southampton v Millwall ....
Tottenham Hotspur v Queens Park Rangers.....................
West Ham United v Everton ....

SECOND DIVISION
Barnsley v A.F.C. Bournemouth ....
Birmingham City v Ipswich Town..................................
Blackburn Rovers v Portsmouth ....
Brighton & Hove Albion v Sunderland............................
Chelsea v Shrewsbury Town ....
Leeds United v Stoke City ....
Leicester City v Bradford City ....
Manchester City v Oxford United...................................
Plymouth Argyle v Oldham Athletic ....
Swindon Town v Walsall...
Watford v Hull City ....
West Bromwich Albion v Crystal Palace ....

THIRD DIVISION
Blackpool v Swansea City...
Bolton Wanderers v Northampton Town ....
Bristol Rovers v Bury..
Cardiff City v Brentford ....
Chester City v Southend United.....................................
Mansfield Town v Aldershot ....
Notts County v Gillingham...
Port Vale v Fulham...
Reading v Chesterfield ....
Sheffield United v Bristol City ....
Wigan Athletic v Huddersfield Town ....
Wolverhampton Wanderers v Preston North End...............

FOURTH DIVISION
Cambridge United v Leyton Orient ....
Carlisle United v Grimsby Town ....
Doncaster Rovers v Burnley..
Hartlepool United v Exeter City ....
Hereford United v Rotherham United ....
Lincoln City v Halifax Town...
Rochdale v York City ....
Scarborough v Wrexham ....
Scunthorpe United v Torquay United ....

Fri. 2nd December

THIRD DIVISION
Southend United v Port Vale...

FOURTH DIVISION
Halifax Town v Crewe Alexandra...................................

Torquay United v Cambridge United ....
Tranmere Rovers v Doncaster Rovers.............................

Sat. 3rd December

FIRST DIVISION
Arsenal v Liverpool...
Aston Villa v Norwich City ....
Everton v Tottenham Hotspur ....
Luton Town v Newcastle United ....
Manchester United v Charlton Athletic ....
Millwall v West Ham United ....
Nottingham Forest v Middlesbrough...............................
Queens Park Rangers v Coventry City.............................
Sheffield Wednesday v Derby County ....
Wimbledon v Southampton..

SECOND DIVISION
A.F.C. Bournemouth v Blackburn Rovers ....
Bradford City v Birmingham City...................................
Crystal Palace v Manchester City...................................
Hull City v Brighton & Hove Albion ....
Ipswich Town v Plymouth Argyle ....
Oldham Athletic v Leicester City ....
Oxford United v Barnsley ....
Portsmouth v West Bromwich Albtion ....
Shrewsbury Town v Swindon Town ....
Stoke City v Chelsea ....
Sunderland v Watford...
Walsall v Leeds United ....

THIRD DIVISION
Aldershot v Notts County ....
Brentford v Bolton Wanderers.......................................
Bristol City v Reading..
Bury v Wigan Athletic..
Chesterfield v Mansfield Town.......................................
Fulham v Bristol Rovers ....
Gillingham v Chester City...
Huddersfield Town v Blackpool ....
Preston North End v Cardiff City ....
Swansea City v Sheffield United.....................................

FOURTH DIVISION
Burnley v Hartlepool United ....
Darlington v Scunthorpe United ....
Exeter City v Colchester United.....................................
Grimsby Town v Scarborough ....
Leyton Orient v Lincoln City ....
Peterborough United v Rochdale ....
Rotherham United v Stockport County ....
Wrexham v Carlisle United ....
York City v Hereford United..

Sun. 4th December

THIRD DIVISION
Northampton Town v Wolverhampton Wanderers ....

Tues. 6th December

SECOND DIVISION
Plymouth Argyle v Brighton & Hove Albion ....

Sat. 10th December

FIRST DIVISION
Charlton Athletic v Queens Park Rangers.........................
Coventry City v Manchester United.................................
Derby County v Luton Town ....
Liverpool v Everton ....
Middlesbrough v Aston Villa..

Newcastle United v Wimbledon ....
Norwich City v Arsenal ....
Southampton v Nottingham Forest ....
Tottenham Hotspur v Millwall ....
West Ham United v Sheffield Wednesday ....

SECOND DIVISION

Barnsley v Walsall ....
Birmingham City v Crystal Palace ....
Blackburn Rovers v Ipswich Town.....................................
Brighton & Hove Albion v Stoke City ....
Chelsea v Portsmouth ....
Leeds United v Shrewsbury Town ....
Leicester City v Sunderland ....
Manchester City v Bradford City.......................................
Plymouth Argyle v A.F.C. Bournemouth ....
Swindon Town v Oldham Athletic......................................
Watford v Oxford United ....
West Bromwich Albion v Hull City....................................

Fri. 16th December

SECOND DIVISION

Birmingham City v Chelsea..
Ipswich Town v Oldham Athletic ....

FOURTH DIVISION

Crewe Alexandra v Torquay United ....
Halifax Town v Scarborough ....
Rochdale v Colchester United ....
Tranmere Rovers v Darlington ....
Wrexham v Cambridge United ....
York City v Rotherham United...

Sat. 17th December

FIRST DIVISION

Arsenal v Manchester United ....
Coventry City v Derby County...
Liverpool v Norwich City...
Luton Town v Aston Villa...
Middlesbrough v Charlton Athletic....................................
Millwall v Sheffield Wednesday ....
Newcastle United v Southampton......................................
Queens Park Rangers v Everton ....
West Ham United v Tottenham Hotspur............................

SECOND DIVISION

A.F.C. Bournemouth v Walsall ....
Barnsley v Leicester City ....
Blackburn Rovers v Watford ....
Bradford City v Swindon Town ....
Crystal Palace v Leeds United ....
Portsmouth v Brighton & Hove Albion ....

THIRD DIVISION

Blackpool v Bristol Rovers...
Bolton Wanderers v Chester City ....
Bristol City v Cardiff City ....
Fulham v Preston North End ....
Huddersfield Town v Bury ....
Port Vale v Reading ....
Sheffield United v Southend United...................................
Swansea City v Chesterfield ....
Wolverhampton Wanderers v Mansfield Town...................

FOURTH DIVISION

Doncaster Rovers v Scunthorpe United.............................
Grimsby Town v Leyton Orient ....
Hartlepool United v Carlisle United ....
Hereford United v Burnley ....
Peterborough United v Exeter City....................................
Stockport County v Lincoln City ....

Sun. 18th December

FIRST DIVISION

Nottingham Forest v Wimbledon ....

SECOND DIVISION

Manchester City v Shrewsbury Town ....
Plymouth Argyle v Sunderland ....
West Bromwich Albion v Stoke City ....

THIRD DIVISION

Aldershot v Brentford...
Northampton Town v Gillingham.......................................
Wigan Athletic v Notts County ....

Mon. 26th December

FIRST DIVISION

Aston Villa v Queens Park Rangers ....
Charlton Athletic v Arsenal ....
Derby County v Liverpool ....
Everton v Middlesbrough ....
Manchester United v Nottingham Forest ....
Norwich City v West Ham United ....
Sheffield Wednesday v Newcastle United..........................
Southampton v Coventry City..
Tottenham Hotspur v Luton Town ....
Wimbledon v Millwall..

SECOND DIVISION

Brighton & Hove Albion v Crystal Palace ....
Chelsea v Ipswich Town ....
Hull City v Bradford City...
Leeds United v Blackburn Rovers ....
Leicester City v A.F.C. Bournemouth.................................
Oldham Athletic v West Bromwich Albion ....
Shrewsbury Town v Birmingham City ....
Stoke City v Manchester City ....
Sunderland v Barnsley ....
Swindon Town v Plymouth Argyle.....................................
Walsall v Oxford United...
Watford v Portsmouth..

THIRD DIVISION

Brentford v Blackpool...
Bristol Rovers v Wolverhampton Wanderers.....................
Bury v Bristol City..
Cardiff City v Swansea City ....
Chester City v Wigan Athletic ....
Chesterfield v Huddersfield Town ....
Gillingham v Fulham ....
Mansfield Town v Port Vale ....
Notts County v Sheffield United..
Preston North End v Bolton Wanderers.............................
Reading v Aldershot...
Southend United v Northampton Town ....

FOURTH DIVISION

Burnley v Wrexham..
Cambridge United v Doncaster Rovers ....
Carlisle United v Rochdale ....
Colchester United v Peterborough United ....
Darlington v Halifax Town...
Exeter City v Hereford United..
Leyton Orient v Tranmere Rovers......................................
Lincoln City v Grimsby Town ....
Rotherham United v Crewe Alexandra ....
Scarborough v York City ....
Scunthorpe United v Hartlepool United ....
Torquay United v Stockport County ....

Wed. 28th December

FOURTH DIVISION

Lincoln City v Doncaster Rovers..

Fri. 30th December

SECOND DIVISION
Oldham Athletic v Crystal Palace ....

THIRD DIVISION
Cardiff City v Wigan Athletic ....
Gillingham v Port Vale...
Reading v Blackpool...

FOURTH DIVISION
Cambridge United v Rochdale...
Colchester United v Hartlepool United ....

Sat. 31st December

FIRST DIVISION
Aston Villa v Arsenal..
Charlton Athletic v West Ham United...............................
Derby County v Millwall ....
Everton v Coventry City ....
Manchester United v Liverpool ....
Norwich City v Middlesbrough ....
Sheffield Wednesday v Nottingham Forest ....
Southampton v Queens Park Rangers ....
Tottenham Hotspur v Newcastle United ....
Wimbledon v Luton Town ....

SECOND DIVISION
Brighton & Hove Albion v Birmingham City ....
Chelsea v West Bromwich Albion ....
Hull City v Ipswich Town...
Leeds United v Plymouth Argyle ....
Leicester City v Blackburn Rovers....................................
Shrewsbury Town v Barnsley...
Stoke City v Oxford United...
Sunderland v Portsmouth ....
Swindon Town v Manchester City ....
Walsall v Bradford City ....
Watford v A.F.C. Bournemouth ....

THIRD DIVISION
Brentford v Wolverhampton Wanderers.............................
Bristol Rovers v Swansea City ....
Bury v Aldershot ....
Chester City v Northampton Town ....
Chesterfield v Fulham ....
Mansfield Town v Huddersfield Town ....
Notts County v Bolton Wanderers ....
Preston North End v Sheffield United ....
Southend United v Bristol City ....

FOURTH DIVISION
Burnley v Grimsby Town...
Carlisle United v Stockport County ....
Darlington v Hereford United ....
Exeter City v York City...
Leyton Orient v Wrexham ....
Rotherham United v Halifax Town.....................................
Scarborough v Crewe Alexandra..
Scunthorpe United v Tranmere Rovers ....
Torquay United v Peterborough United ....

Mon. 2nd January

FIRST DIVISION
Arsenal v Tottenham Hotspur ....
Coventry City v Sheffield Wednesday...............................
Liverpool v Aston Villa...
Luton Town v Southampton...
Middlesbrough v Manchester United ....
Millwall v Charlton Athletic..
Newcastle United v Derby County.....................................
Nottingham Forest v Everton ....
Queens Park Rangers v Norwich City...............................
West Ham United v Wimbledon ....

SECOND DIVISION
A.F.C. Bournemouth v Brighton & Hove Albion...............
Barnsley v Hull City ....
Birmingham City v Oldham Athletic................................
Blackburn Rovers v Stoke City ....
Bradford City v Sunderland ....
Crystal Palace v Walsall..
Ipswich Town v Leicester City ....
Manchester City v Leeds United ....
Oxford United v Chelsea ....
Plymouth Argyle v Watford ....
Portsmouth v Swindon Town..
West Bromwich Albion v Shrewsbury Town ....

THIRD DIVISION
Aldershot v Cardiff City ....
Blackpool v Bury ....
Bolton Wanderers v Mansfield Town ....
Bristol City v Bristol Rovers ....
Fulham v Brentford ....
Huddersfield Town v Southend United.............................
Northampton Town v Preston North End ....
Port Vale v Notts County..
Sheffield United v Chesterfield ....
Swansea City v Reading ....
Wigan Athletic v Gillingham ....
Wolverhampton Wanderers v Chester City ....

FOURTH DIVISION
Crewe Alexandra v Carlisle United...................................
Doncaster Rovers v Scarborough ....
Grimsby Town v Colchester United ....
Halifax Town v Scunthorpe United ....
Hartlepool United v Rotherham United ....
Hereford United v Torquay United ....
Peterborough United v Cambridge United ....
Rochdale v Leyton Orient...
Stockport County v Exeter City ....
Tranmere Rovers v Burnley ....
Wrexham v Darlington..
York City v Lincoln City...

Fri. 6th January

FOURTH DIVISION
Tranmere Rovers v Exeter City..
Wrexham v Torquay United..

Sat. 7th January

THIRD DIVISION
Aldershot v Preston North End...
Blackpool v Southend United ....
Bolton Wanderers v Gillingham ....
Bristol City v Brentford..
Fulham v Chester City..
Huddersfield Town v Reading ....
Northampton Town v Bury ....
Port Vale v Bristol Rovers ....
Sheffield United v Mansfield Town ....
Swansea City v Notts County ....
Wigan Athletic v Chesterfield...
Wolverhampton Wanderers v Cardiff City ....

FOURTH DIVISION
Crewe Alexandra v Burnley ....
Doncaster Rovers v Carlisle United ....
Grimsby Town v Darlington..
Halifax Town v Leyton Orient ....
Hartlepool United v Scarborough.....................................
Hereford United v Colchester United ....
Peterborough United v Rotherham United ....
Rochdale v Lincoln City ....
Stockport County v Scunthorpe United ....
York City v Cambridge United ....

Fri. 13th January

THIRD DIVISION
Southend United v Fulham ....

FOURTH DIVISION
Colchester United v Tranmere Rovers ....

Sat. 14th January

FIRST DIVISION
Aston Villa v Newcastle United ....
Charlton Athletic v Luton Town ....
Derby County v West Ham United ....
Everton v Arsenal ....
Manchester United v Millwall ....
Norwich City v Coventry City ....
Sheffield Wednesday v Liverpool ....
Southampton v Middlesbrough ....
Tottenham Hotspur v Nottingham Forest ....
Wimbledon v Queens Park Rangers ....

SECOND DIVISION
Brighton & Hove Albion v Plymouth Argyle ....
Chelsea v Crystal Palace ....
Hull City v A.F.C. Bournemouth ....
Leeds United v Birmingham City ....
Leicester City v Portsmouth ....
Oldham Athletic v Manchester City ....
Shrewsbury Town v Blackburn Rovers ....
Stoke City v Bradford City ....
Sunderland v Oxford United ....
Swindon Town v Barnsley ....
Walsall v Ipswich Town ....
Watford v West Bromwich Albion ....

THIRD DIVISION
Brentford v Northampton Town ....
Bristol Rovers v Sheffield United ....
Bury v Swansea City ....
Cardiff City v Bolton Wanderers ....
Chester City v Port Vale ....
Chesterfield v Bristol City ....
Gillingham v Aldershot ....
Mansfield Town v Wigan Athletic....................................
Notts County v Blackpool ....
Preston North End v Huddersfield Town ....
Reading v Wolverhampton Wanderers ....

FOURTH DIVISION
Burnley v Halifax Town ....
Cambridge United v Hereford United ....
Carlisle United v York City ....
Darlington v Hartlepool United ....
Exeter City v Doncaster Rovers ....
Leyton Orient v Stockport County....................................
Lincoln City v Wrexham ....
Rotherham United v Rochdale ....
Scarborough v Peterborough United ....
Scunthorpe United v Crewe Alexandra ....
Torquay United v Grimsby Town ....

Fri. 20th January

FOURTH DIVISION
Halifax Town v Torquay United.......................................
Stockport County v Darlington ....

Sat. 21st January

FIRST DIVISION
Arsenal v Sheffield Wednesday ....
Coventry City v Wimbledon ....

Liverpool v Southampton ....
Luton Town v Everton ....
Middlesbrough v Tottenham Hotspur ....
Millwall v Norwich City ....
Newcastle United v Charlton Athletic ....
Nottingham Forest v Aston Villa ....
Queens Park Rangers v Derby County ....
West Ham United v Manchester United ....

SECOND DIVISION
A.F.C. Bournemouth v Sunderland...................................
Barnsley v Oldham Athletic ....
Birmingham City v Watford ....
Blackburn Rovers v Chelsea...
Bradford City v Brighton & Hove Albion ....
Crystal Palace v Swindon Town.......................................
Ipswich Town v Stoke City ....
Manchester City v Hull City ....
Oxford United v Leeds United...
Plymouth Argyle v Walsall...
Portsmouth v Shrewsbury Town ....
West Bromwich Albion v Leicester City ....

THIRD DIVISION
Aldershot v Bristol Rovers...
Blackpool v Preston North End..
Bolton Wanderers v Reading...
Bristol City v Chester City ....
Fulham v Mansfield Town..
Huddersfield Town v Cardiff City.....................................
Northampton Town v Notts County...................................
Port Vale v Bury ....
Sheffield United v Gillingham...
Swansea City v Southend United......................................
Wigan Athletic v Brentford ....
Wolverhampton Wanderers v Chesterfield..........................

FOURTH DIVISION
Crewe Alexandra v Leyton Orient....................................
Doncaster Rovers v Rotherham United..............................
Grimsby Town v Cambridge United ....
Hartlepool United v Lincoln City ....
Hereford United v Scunthorpe United ....
Peterborough United v Carlisle United...............................
Rochdale v Burnley ....
Tranmere Rovers v Scarborough......................................
Wrexham v Exeter City...
York City v Colchester United...

Fri. 27th January

FOURTH DIVISION
Colchester United v Wrexham ....

Sat. 28th January

THIRD DIVISION
Brentford v Swansea City ....
Bristol Rovers v Bolton Wanderers...................................
Bury v Fulham..
Cardiff City v Port Vale ....
Chester City v Sheffield United ....
Chesterfield v Northampton Town.....................................
Gillingham v Huddersfield Town......................................
Mansfield Town v Blackpool ....
Notts County v Wolverhampton Wanderers ....
Preston North End v Bristol City......................................
Reading v Wigan Athletic ....
Southend United v Aldershot ....

FOURTH DIVISION
Burnley v Stockport County ....
Cambridge United v Tranmere Rovers...............................
Carlisle United v Halifax Town..
Darlington v Crewe Alexandra ....
Exeter City v Rochdale ....

174

Leyton Orient v Hartlepool United...............................
Lincoln City v Peterborough United ....
Rotherham United v Grimsby Town ....
Scarborough v Hereford United...............................
Scunthorpe United v York City...............................
Torquay United v Doncaster Rovers...............................

Fri. 3rd February

THIRD DIVISION
Southend United v Preston North End ....
Swansea City v Bristol City ....

Sat. 4th February

FIRST DIVISION
Arsenal v West Ham United...............................
Aston Villa v Sheffield Wednesday ....
Charlton Athletic v Norwich City ....
Derby County v Southampton ....
Everton v Wimbledon ....
Luton Town v Nottingham Forest...............................
Manchester United v Tottenham Hotspur ....
Middlesbrough v Coventry City ....
Newcastle United v Liverpool...............................
Queens Park Rangers v Millwall ....

SECOND DIVISION
A.F.C. Bournemouth v West Bromwich Albion.................
Barnsley v Brighton & Hove Albion ....
Blackburn Rovers v Bradford City...............................
Ipswich Town v Crystal Palace ....
Leeds United v Sunderland ....
Leicester City v Hull City...............................
Oldham Athletic v Watford...............................
Plymouth Argyle v Birmingham City ....
Portsmouth v Manchester City...............................
Shrewsbury Town v Stoke City ....
Walsall v Chelsea ....

THIRD DIVISION
Aldershot v Northampton Town ....
Blackpool v Wigan Athletic ....
Bristol Rovers v Cardiff City ....
Bury v Chesterfield...............................
Chester City v Reading ....
Fulham v Huddersfield Town ....
Gillingham v Brentford ....
Port Vale v Wolverhampton Wanderers ....
Sheffield United v Bolton Wanderers ....

FOURTH DIVISION
Burnley v Torquay United ....
Carlisle United v Scunthorpe United...............................
Crewe Alexandra v Hereford United ....
Doncaster Rovers v Rochdale...............................
Exeter City v Darlington ....
Grimsby Town v Wrexham ....
Halifax Town v Stockport County ....
Hartlepool United v York City ....
Leyton Orient v Rotherham United...............................
Lincoln City v Cambridge United ....
Peterborough United v Tranmere Rovers ....
Scarborough v Colchester United ....

Sun. 5th February

SECOND DIVISION
Swindon Town v Oxford United...............................

THIRD DIVISION
Notts County v Mansfield Town ....

Fri. 10th February

FOURTH DIVISION
Colchester United v Burnley ....
Stockport County v Crewe Alexandra ....
Tranmere Rovers v Halifax Town...............................

Sat. 11th February

FIRST DIVISION
Coventry City v Newcastle United...............................
Liverpool v Luton Town...............................
Millwall v Arsenal ....
Norwich City v Derby County...............................
Nottingham Forest v Queens Park Rangers ....
Sheffield Wednesday v Manchester United......................
Southampton v Everton ....
Tottenham Hotspur v Charlton Athletic ....
West Ham United v Middlesbrough ....
Wimbledon v Aston Villa ....

SECOND DIVISION
Birmingham City v A.F.C. Bournemouth ....
Bradford City v Plymouth Argyle ....
Brighton & Hove Albion v Leicester City ....
Chelsea v Swindon Town ....
Crystal Palace v Blackburn Rovers ....
Hull City v Shrewsbury Town ....
Manchester City v Ipswich Town...............................
Oxford United v Portsmouth ....
Stoke City v Oldham Athletic ....
Sunderland v Walsall ....
Watford v Leeds United ....
West Bromwich Albion v Barnsley ....

THIRD DIVISION
Bolton Wanderers v Swansea City ....
Brentford v Chester City ....
Bristol City v Gillingham ....
Cardiff City v Sheffield United...............................
Chesterfield v Notts County ....
Huddersfield Town v Port Vale ....
Mansfield Town v Southend United ....
Northampton Town v Blackpool ....
Preston North End v Bristol Rovers ....
Reading v Bury ....
Wigan Athletic v Aldershot...............................
Wolverhampton Wanderers v Fulham ....

FOURTH DIVISION
Cambridge United v Hartlepool United...............................
Darlington v Leyton Orient...............................
Hereford United v Lincoln City ....
Rochdale v Grimsby Town...............................
Rotherham United v Carlisle United...............................
Scunthorpe United v Exeter City...............................
Torquay United v Scarborough...............................
Wrexham v Doncaster Rovers ....
York City v Peterborough United...............................

Tues. 14th February

SECOND DIVISION
A.F.C. Bournemouth v Hull City...............................

Fri. 17th February

THIRD DIVISION
Southend United v Brentford ....

FOURTH DIVISION
Crewe Alexandra v Wrexham...............................
Halifax Town v Cambridge United ....
Stockport County v Rochdale...............................

Sat. 18th February

Charlton Athletic v Derby County ....
Coventry City v Liverpool...
Everton v Aston Villa ....
Luton Town v Middlesbrough..
Manchester United v Wimbledon ....
Newcastle United v West Ham United ....
Nottingham Forest v Millwall ....
Queens Park Rangers v Arsenal.....................................
Sheffield Wednesday v Southampton ....
Tottenham Hotspur v Norwich City ....

SECOND DIVISION
Birmingham City v Manchester City ....
Blackburn Rovers v Oxford United ....
Bradford City v West Bromwich Albion ....
Hull City v Crystal Palace ....
Ipswich Town v Barnsley ....
Leicester City v Leeds United..
Oldham Athletic v Brighton & Hove Albion.....................
Plymouth Argyle v Chelsea ....
Portsmouth v Walsall ....
Shrewsbury Town v A.F.C. Bournemouth ....
Swindon Town v Sunderland ....
Watford v Stoke City ....

THIRD DIVISION
Blackpool v Bolton Wanderers ....
Bristol Rovers v Mansfield Town....................................
Bury v Preston North End...
Chester City v Notts County ....
Chesterfield v Gillingham ....
Fulham v Bristol City ....
Huddersfield Town v Northampton Town ....
Port Vale v Wigan Athletic ....
Reading v Cardiff City ....
Wolverhampton Wanderers v Sheffield United ....

FOURTH DIVISION
Carlisle United v Hereford United...................................
Exeter City v Burnley ....
Hartlepool United v Doncaster Rovers............................
Leyton Orient v Scarborough ....
Lincoln City v Torquay United ....
Peterborough United v Grimsby Town ....
Rotherham United v Darlington ....
Scunthorpe United v Colchester United............................
York City v Tranmere Rovers..

Sun. 19th February

THIRD DIVISION
Swansea City v Aldershot ....

Fri. 24th February

THIRD DIVISION
Wigan Athletic v Wolverhampton Wanderers....................

FOURTH DIVISION
Colchester United v Leyton Orient ....
Darlington v York City ....
Doncaster Rovers v Crewe Alexandra..............................

Sat. 25th February

FIRST DIVISION
Arsenal v Luton Town ....
Aston Villa v Charlton Athletic......................................
Derby County v Everton ....
Liverpool v Nottingham Forest ....

Millwall v Coventry City...
Norwich City v Manchester United..................................
Southampton v Tottenham Hotspur................................
West Ham United v Queens Park Rangers ....
Wimbledon v Sheffield Wednesday..................................

SECOND DIVISION
A.F.C. Bournemouth v Portsmouth ....
Barnsley v Blackburn Rovers ....
Brighton & Hove Albion v Watford ....
Chelsea v Oldham Athletic ....
Crystal Palace v Bradford City ....
Leeds United v Swindon Town ....
Manchester City v Plymouth Argyle ....
Oxford United v Ipswich Town ....
Stoke City v Leicester City ....
Sunderland v Hull City...
Walsall v Shrewsbury Town ....
West Bromwich Albion v Birmingham City......................

THIRD DIVISION
Aldershot v Fulham...
Bolton Wanderers v Port Vale ....
Brentford v Bury ....
Bristol City v Huddersfield Town ....
Cardiff City v Chester City ....
Gillingham v Southend United..
Mansfield Town v Reading ....
Northampton Town v Swansea City ....
Notts County v Bristol Rovers ....
Preston North End v Chesterfield ....
Sheffield United v Blackpool ....

FOURTH DIVISION
Burnley v Peterborough United ....
Cambridge United v Scunthorpe United ....
Grimsby Town v Exeter City ....
Hereford United v Stockport County ....
Rochdale v Halifax Town ....
Scarborough v Lincoln City ....
Torquay United v Carlisle United....................................
Tranmere Rovers v Rotherham United ....
Wrexham v Hartlepool United..

Sun. 26th February

FIRST DIVISION
Middlesbrough v Newcastle United ....

Tues. 28th February

SECOND DIVISION
A.F.C. Bournemouth v Oldham Athletic...........................
Barnsley v Watford ....
Blackburn Rovers v Sunderland......................................
Chelsea v Hull City...
Portsmouth v Ipswich Town ....
Shrewsbury Town v Plymouth Argyle ....
Stoke City v Birmingham City ....
Swindon Town v Leicester City ....
Walsall v Brighton & Hove Albion ....

THIRD DIVISION
Aldershot v Bristol City..
Blackpool v Wolverhampton Wanderers ....
Bolton Wanderers v Wigan Athletic ....
Brentford v Chesterfield ....
Gillingham v Preston North End ....
Mansfield Town v Chester City ....
Northampton Town v Fulham...
Notts County v Cardiff City...
Sheffield United v Port Vale..
Southend United v Bury ....
Swansea City v Huddersfield Town ....

176

Burnley v Carlisle United ....
Colchester United v Rotherham United...........................
Doncaster Rovers v York City ....
Grimsby Town v Crewe Alexandra ....
Hartlepool United v Stockport County ....
Rochdale v Hereford United ....
Torquay United v Darlington ....
Wrexham v Scunthorpe United ....

Carlisle United v Exeter City ....
Crewe Alexandra v Hartlepool United ....
Darlington v Lincoln City ....
Hereford United v Peterborough United ....
Leyton Orient v Burnley...
Rotherham United v Torquay United ....
Scunthorpe United v Rochdale ....
Stockport County v Scarborough...................................
York City v Grimsby Town ....

Wed. 1st March

SECOND DIVISION
Leeds United v Bradford City.......................................
Manchester City v West Bromwich Albion ....
Oxford United v Crystal Palace.....................................

THIRD DIVISION
Bristol Rovers v Reading ....

FOURTH DIVISION
Exeter City v Leyton Orient ....
Lincoln City v Tranmere Rovers ....
Peterborough United v Halifax Town...............................
Scarborough v Cambridge United ....

Fri. 3rd March

SECOND DIVISION
Oldham Athletic v Shrewsbury Town...............................

FOURTH DIVISION
Halifx Town v Doncaster Rovers....................................
Tranmere Rovers v Wrexham..

Sat. 4th March

FIRST DIVISION
Coventry City v Arsenal ....
Liverpool v West Ham United ....
Manchester United v Everton..
Millwall v Middlesbrough ....
Nottingham Forest v Newcastle United ....
Queens Park Rangers v Luton Town ....
Sheffield Wednesday v Charlton Athletic.........................
Southampton v Norwich City..
Tottenham Hotspur v Aston Villa ....
Wimbledon v Derby County..

SECOND DIVISION
Birmingham City v Oxford United...................................
Bradford City v Barnsley ....
Brighton & Hove Albion v Blackburn Rovers....................
Crystal Palace v A.F.C. Bournemouth ....
Hull City v Stoke City ....
Ipswich Town v Swindon Town ....
Leicester City v Walsall ....
Plymouth Argyle v Portsmouth......................................
Sunderland v Chelsea..
Watford v Manchester City ....

THIRD DIVISION
Bristol City v Northampton Town ....
Bury v Gillingham ....
Cardiff City v Mansfield Town ....
Chester City v Bristol Rovers ....
Chesterfield v Southend United ....
Fulham v Swansea City ....
Huddersfield Town v Aldershot ....
Port Vale v Blackpool ....
Preston North End v Brentford......................................
Reading v Notts County ....
Wigan Athletic v Sheffield United ....
Wolverhampton Wanderers v Bolton Wanderers ....

Sun. 5th March

SECOND DIVISION
West Bromwich Albion v Leeds United ....

FOURTH DIVISION
Cambridge United v Colchester United ....

Fri. 10th March

THIRD DIVISION
Southend United v Wolverhampton Wanderers ....

FOURTH DIVISION
Colchester United v Crewe Alexandra ....
Doncaster Rovers v Darlington......................................
Torquay United v York City..

Sat. 11th March

FIRST DIVISION
Arsenal v Nottingham Forest...
Aston Villa v Manchester United ....
Charlton Athletic v Southampton ....
Derby County v Tottenham Hotspur................................
Everton v Sheffield Wednesday ....
Luton Town v Millwall ....
Middlesbrough v Liverpool ....
Newcastle United v Queens Park Rangers........................
Norwich City v Wimbledon ....
West Ham United v Coventry City ....

SECOND DIVISION
A.F.C. Bournemouth v Bradford City..............................
Barnsley v Crystal Palace ....
Blackburn Rovers v Plymouth Argyle ....
Chelsea v Watford ....
Leeds United v Ipswich Town..
Manchester City v Leicester City....................................
Oxford United v West Bromwich Albion ....
Portsmouth v Birmingham City......................................
Shrewsbury Town v Brighton & Hove Albion ....
Stoke City v Sunderland ....
Swindon Town v Hull City ....
Walsall v Oldham Athletic ....

THIRD DIVISION
Aldershot v Port Vale ....
Blackpool v Fulham..
Bolton Wanderers v Bristol City ....
Brentford v Reading ....
Bristol Rovers v Chesterfield ....
Gillingham v Cardiff City...
Mansfield Town v Preston North End..............................
Northampton Town v Wigan Athletic ....
Notts County v Bury ....
Sheffield United v Huddersfield Town.............................
Swansea City v Chester City ....

FOURTH DIVISION
Burnley v Scunthorpe United ....
Exeter City v Cambridge United ....
Grimsby Town v Stockport County..................................

Hartlepool United v Halifax Town ....
Lincoln City v Rotherham United ....
Peterborough United v Leyton Orient ....
Rochdale v Tranmere Rovers ....
Scarborough v Carlisle United ....
Wrexham v Hereford United ....

Mon. 13th March

THIRD DIVISION
Port Vale v Brentford ....

FOURTH DIVISION
Stockport County v Colchester United ....
Tranmere Rovers v Torquay United ....

Tues. 14th March

SECOND DIVISION
Birmingham City v Swindon Town ....
Crystal Palace v Stoke City...
Hull City v Leeds United ....
Ipswich Town v A.F.C. Bournemouth............................
Oldham Athletic v Portsmouth ....
Plymouth Argyle v Barnsley ....
Sunderland v Manchester City ....
Watford v Walsall ....

THIRD DIVISION
Bristol City v Mansfield Town..
Bury v Sheffield United ....
Cardiff City v Blackpool ....
Chesterfield v Bolton Wanderers...................................
Fulham v Notts County ....
Huddersfield Town v Bristol Rovers ....
Preston North End v Swansea City ....
Wigan Athletic v Southend United ....
Wolverhampton Wanderers v Gillingham ....

FOURTH DIVISION
Cambridge United v Burnley...
Carlisle United v Lincoln City..
Crewe Alexandra v Exeter City......................................
Darlington v Rochdale ....
Halifax Town v Grimsby Town ....
Leyton Orient v Doncaster Rovers ....
Rotherham United v Scarborough ....
Scunthorpe United v Peterborough United ....
York City v Wrexham ....

Wed. 15th March

SECOND DIVISION
Bradford City v Oxford United ....
Brighton & Hove Albion v Chelsea.................................
Leicester City v Shrewsbury Town.................................
West Bromwich Albion v Blackburn Rovers.....................

THIRD DIVISION
Chester City v Aldershot ....
Reading v Northampton Town...

FOURTH DIVISION
Hereford United v Hartlepool United ....

Fri. 17th March

FOURTH DIVISION
Halifax Town v Exeter City..
Stockport County v Cambridge United...........................
Tranmere Rovers v Carlisle United................................

Sat. 18th March

FIRST DIVISION
Arsenal v Wimbledon ....
Coventry City v Tottenham Hotspur ....
Liverpool v Charlton Athletic ....
Luton Town v Sheffield Wednesday...............................
Middlesbrough v Derby County ....
Millwall v Aston Villa ....
Newcastle United v Everton ....
Nottingham Forest v Norwich City ....
Queens Park Rangers v Manchester United.....................
West Ham United v Southampton ....

SECOND DIVISION
A.F.C. Bournemouth v Swindon Town ....
Barnsley v Leeds United..
Birmingham City v Walsall...
Blackburn Rovers v Hull City ....
Bradford City v Watford ....
Crystal Palace v Sunderland ....
Ipswich Town v Shrewsbury Town.................................
Manchester City v Chelsea..
Oxford United v Oldham Athletic ....
Plymouth Argyle v Leicester City ....
Portsmouth v Stoke City...
West Bromwich Albion v Brighton & Hove Albion............

THIRD DIVISION
Aldershot v Chesterfield..
Blackpool v Chester City ....
Bolton Wanderers v Southend United ....
Bristol City v Notts County ....
Fulham v Cardiff City ....
Huddersfield Town v Brentford ....
Northampton Town v Mansfield Town ....
Port Vale v Preston North End ....
Sheffield United v Reading ....
Wigan Athletic v Bristol Rovers.....................................
Wolverhampton Wanderers v Bury.................................

FOURTH DIVISION
Crewe Alexandra v Lincoln City ....
Doncaster Rovers v Colchester United ....
Grimsby Town v Scunthorpe United ....
Hartlepool United v Torquay United ....
Hereford United v Leyton Orient ....
Peterborough United v Darlington ....
Rochdale v Scarborough..
Wrexham v Rotherham United ....
York City v Burnley ....

Sun. 19th March

THIRD DIVISION
Swansea City v Gillingham...

Fri. 24th March

SECOND DIVISION
Oldham Athletic v Blackburn Rovers...............................
Watford v Crystal Palace ....

THIRD DIVISION
Brentford v Fulham ....
Gillingham v Wigan Athletic ....

FOURTH DIVISION
Colchester United v Grimsby Town ....

Sat. 25th March

FIRST DIVISION

Aston Villa v West Ham United......................................
Charlton Athletic v Coventry City ....
Derby County v Nottingham Forest ....
Everton v Millwall..
Manchester United v Luton Town ....
Norwich City v Newcastle United ....
Sheffield Wednesday v Queens Park Rangers ....
Southampton v Arsenal...
Tottenham Hotspur v Liverpool....................................
Wimbledon v Middlesbrough ....

SECOND DIVISION

Brighton & Hove Albion v Oxford United ....
Chelsea v A.F.C. Bournemouth.....................................
Hull City v Plymouth Argyle ....
Leeds United v Portsmouth..
Leicester City v Birmingham City ....
Shrewsbury Town v Bradford City ....
Stoke City v Barnsley...
Sunderland v Ipswich Town ....
Swindon Town v West Bromwich Albion ....
Walsall v Manchester City...

THIRD DIVISION

Bristol Rovers v Bristol City...
Bury v Blackpool..
Cardiff City v Aldershot ....
Chester City v Wolverhampton Wanderers ....
Chesterfield v Sheffield United ....
Mansfield Town v Bolton Wanderers ....
Notts County v Port Vale...
Preston North End v Northampton Town ....
Reading v Swansea City ....
Southend United v Huddersfield Town............................

FOURTH DIVISION

Burnley v Tranmere Rovers ....
Cambridge United v Peterborough United ....
Carlisle United v Crewe Alexandra.................................
Darlington v Wrexham ....
Exeter City v Stockport County ....
Leyton Orient v Rochdale..
Lincoln City v York City...
Rotherham United v Hartlepool United ....
Scarborough v Doncaster Rovers ....
Scunthorpe United v Halifax Town ....
Torquay United v Hereford United ....

Mon. 27th March

FIRST DIVISION

Arsenal v Charlton Athletic ....
Coventry City v Southampton.......................................
Liverpool v Derby County ....
Luton Town v Tottenham Hotspur ....
Middlesbrough v Everton ....
Millwall v Wimbledon ....
Newcastle United v Sheffield Wednesday.........................
Nottingham Forest v Manchester United ....
Queens Park Rangers v Aston Villa ....
West Ham United v Norwich City ....

SECOND DIVISION

A.F.C. Bournemouth v Leicester City..............................
Barnsley v Sunderland ....
Birmingham City v Shrewsbury Town ....
Blackburn Rovers v Leeds United ....
Bradford City v Hull City..
Crystal Palace v Brighton & Hove Albion ....
Manchester City v Stoke City ....
Oxford United v Walsall..
Plymouth Argyle v Swindon Town..................................
Portsmouth v Watford...
West Bromwich Albion v Oldham Athletic ....

THIRD DIVISION

Aldershot v Reading...
Blackpool v Brentford...
Bolton Wanderers v Preston North End...........................
Bristol City v Bury...
Fulham v Gillingham ....
Huddersfield Town v Chesterfield..................................
Northampton Town v Southend United ....
Port Vale v Mansfield Town...
Sheffield United v Notts County....................................
Swansea City v Cardiff City...
Wigan Athletic v Chester City.......................................
Wolverhampton Wanderers v Bristol Rovers....................

FOURTH DIVISION

Crewe Alexandra v Rotherham United ....
Doncaster Rovers v Cambridge United ....
Grimsby Town v Lincoln City ....
Halifax Town v Darlington...
Hartlepool United v Scunthorpe United ....
Hereford United v Exeter City.......................................
Peterborough United v Colchester United ....
Rochdale v Carlisle United ....
Stockport County v Torquay United ....
Tranmere Rovers v Leyton Orient ....
Wrexham v Burnley ....
York City v Scarborough ....

Tues. 28th March

SECOND DIVISION

Ipswich Town v Chelsea ....

Fri. 31st March

THIRD DIVISION

Southend United v Sheffield United................................

FOURTH DIVISION

Cambridge United v Wrexham ....
Colchester United v Rochdale ....
Torquay United v Crewe Alexandra ....

Sat. 1st April

FIRST DIVISION

Aston Villa v Luton Town..
Charlton Athletic v Middlesbrough.................................
Derby County v Coventry City.......................................
Everton v Queens Park Rangers ....
Manchester United v Arsenal ....
Norwich City v Liverpool...
Sheffield Wednesday v Millwall ....
Southampton v Newcastle United...................................
Tottenham Hotspur v West Ham United...........................
Wimbledon v Nottingham Forest ....

SECOND DIVISION

Brighton & Hove Albion v Manchester City ....
Chelsea v Barnsley...
Hull City v Portsmouth...
Leeds United v A.F.C. Bournemouth ....
Leicester City v Oxford United ....
Oldham Athletic v Bradford City ....
Shrewsbury Town v Crystal Palace ....
Stoke City v Plymouth Argyle.......................................
Sunderland v Birmingham City ....
Swindon Town v Blackburn Rovers ....
Walsall v West Bromwich Albion ....
Watford v Ipswich Town..

THIRD DIVISION

Brentford v Aldershot...
Bristol Rovers v Blackpool...

179

Bury v Huddersfield Town ....
Cardiff City v Bristol City ....
Chester City v Bolton Wanderers ....
Chesterfield v Swansea City ....
Gillingham v Northampton Town ....
Mansfield Town v Wolverhampton Wanderers..................
Notts County v Wigan Athletic ....
Preston North End v Fulham ....
Reading v Port Vale ....

FOURTH DIVISION
Burnley v Hereford United ....
Carlisle United v Hartlepool United ....
Darlington v Tranmere Rovers ....
Exeter City v Peterborough United................................
Leyton Orient v Grimsby Town ....
Lincoln City v Stockport County ....
Rotherham United v Halifax Town..................................
Scunthorpe United v Doncaster Rovers...........................

Tues. 4th April

SECOND DIVISION
Chelsea v Birmingham City ....
Hull City v Oxford United ....
Oldham Athletic v Ipswich Town ....
Shrewsbury Town v Manchester City ....
Stoke City v West Bromwich Albion ....
Sunderland v Plymouth Argyle ....
Swindon Town v Bradford City ....
Walsall v A.F.C. Bournemouth ....
Watford v Blackburn Rovers ....

THIRD DIVISION
Brentford v Bristol City...
Bury v Northampton Town ....
Cardiff City v Wolverhampton Wanderers ....
Chesterfield v Wigan Athletic ....
Gillingham v Bolton Wanderers ....
Mansfield Town v Sheffield United ....
Notts County v Swansea City ....
Preston North End v Aldershot......................................
Southend United v Blackpool ....

FOURTH DIVISION
Burnley v Crewe Alexandra ....
Cambridge United v York City ....
Carlisle United v Doncaster Rovers ....
Colchester United v Hereford United ....
Darlington v Grimsby Town ....
Leyton Orient v Halifax Town ....
Rotherham United v Peterborough United ....
Scunthorpe United v Stockport County ....
Torquay United v Wrexham..

Wed. 5th April

SECOND DIVISION
Brighton & Hove Albion v Portsmouth ....
Leeds United v Crystal Palace ....
Leicester City v Barnsley ....

THIRD DIVISION
Bristol Rovers v Port Vale ....
Chester City v Fulham...
Reading v Huddersfield Town ....

FOURTH DIVISION
Exeter City v Tranmere Rovers......................................
Lincoln City v Rochdale ....
Scarborough v Hartlepool United...................................

Fri. 7th April

THIRD DIVISION
Wigan Athletic v Cardiff City ....

FOURTH DIVISION
Halifax Town v Rotherham United..................................
Stockport County v Carlisle United ....

Sat. 8th April

FIRST DIVISION
Arsenal v Everton ....
Coventry City v Norwich City ....
Liverpool v Sheffield Wednesday ....
Luton Town v Charlton Athletic ....
Middlesbrough v Southampton ....
Millwall v Manchester United ....
Newcastle United v Aston Villa ....
Nottingham Forest v Tottenham Hotspur ....
Queens Park Rangers v Wimbledon................................
West Ham United v Derby County ....

SECOND DIVISION
A.F.C. Bournemouth v Watford ....
Barnsley v Shrewsbury Town...
Birmingham City v Brighton & Hove Albion ....
Blackburn Rovers v Leicester City..................................
Bradford City v Walsall ....
Crystal Palace v Oldham Athletic...................................
Ipswich Town v Hull City ....
Manchester City v Swindon Town ....
Oxford United v Stoke City...
Portsmouth v Sunderland ....
West Bromwich Albion v Chelsea ....

THIRD DIVISION
Aldershot v Bury ....
Blackpool v Reading..
Bolton Wanderers v Notts County..................................
Bristol City v Southend United ....
Fulham v Chesterfield ....
Huddersfield Town v Mansfield Town ....
Northampton Town v Chester City ....
Port Vale v Gillingham...
Sheffield United v Preston North End ....
Swansea City v Bristol Rovers ....
Wolverhampton Wanderers v Brentford..........................

FOURTH DIVISION
Crewe Alexandra v Scarborough....................................
Doncaster Rovers v Lincoln City....................................
Grimsby Town v Burnley ....
Hartlepool United v Colchester United ....
Hereford United v Darlington..
Peterborough United v Torquay United ....
Rochdale v Cambridge United ....
Tranmere Rovers v Scunthorpe United ....
Wrexham v Leyton Orient ....
York City v Exeter City..

Sun. 9th April

SECOND DIVISION
Plymouth Argyle v Leeds United ....

Fri. 14th April

THIRD DIVISION
Southend United v Reading ....

FOURTH DIVISION
Crewe Alexandra v Rochdale ....
Halifax Town v York City...

Sat. 15th April

Arsenal v Newcastle United ....
Aston Villa v Southampton ....
Everton v Charlton Athletic ....
Luton Town v Coventry City ....
Manchester United v Derby County ....
Millwall v Liverpool ....
Nottingham Forest v West Ham United..........................
Queens Park Rangers v Middlesbrough ....
Sheffield Wednesday v Norwich City..............................
Wimbledon v Tottenham Hotspur ....

SECOND DIVISION
A.F.C. Bournemouth v Stoke City ....
Barnsley v Birmingham City...
Blackburn Rovers v Manchester City ....
Bradford City v Ipswich Town ....
Crystal Palace v Portsmouth...
Leeds United v Brighton & Hove Albion ....
Leicester City v Chelsea ....
Oldham Athletic v Sunderland..
Shrewsbury Town v Oxford United.................................
Swindon Town v Watford ....
Walsall v Hull City ....
West Bromwich Albion v Plymouth Argyle ....

THIRD DIVISION
Aldershot v Wolverhampton Wanderers..........................
Brentford v Bristol Rovers...
Bristol City v Blackpool ....
Bury v Cardiff City ....
Chesterfield v Port Vale ....
Fulham v Bolton Wanderers...
Gillingham v Mansfield Town ....
Huddersfield Town v Chester City ....
Northampton Town v Sheffield United............................
Preston North End v Notts County ....
Swansea City v Wigan Athletic ....

FOURTH DIVISION
Burnley v Darlington ....
Carlisle United v Cambridge United ....
Doncaster Rovers v Stockport County............................
Exeter City v Rotherham United.....................................
Grimsby Town v Hereford United ....
Hartlepool United v Tranmere Rovers ....
Leyton Orient v Torquay United ....
Lincoln City v Colchester United ....
Peterborough United v Wrexham....................................
Scarborough v Scunthorpe United ....

Tues. 18th April

THIRD DIVISION
Nothampton Town v Bolton Wanderers ....

Fri. 21st April

THIRD DIVISION
Port Vale v Bristol City ....

FOURTH DIVISION
Colchester United v Carlisle United................................
Stockport County v Peterborough United ....
Wrexham v Halifax Town ....

Sat. 22nd April

FIRST DIVISION
Charlton Athletic v Manchester United ....
Coventry City v Queens Park Rangers............................
Derby County v Sheffield Wednesday ....
Liverpool v Arsenal...

Middlesbrough v Nottingham Forest...............................
Newcastle United v Luton Town ....
Norwich City v Aston Villa ....
Southampton v Wimbledon..
Tottenham Hotspur v Everton ....
West Ham United v Millwall ....

SECOND DIVISION
Birmingham City v Blackburn Rovers.............................
Brighton & Hove Albion v Swindon Town ....
Chelsea v Leeds United..
Hull City v Oldham Athletic ....
Ipswich Town v West Bromwich Albion ....
Manchester City v Barnsley..
Oxford United v A.F.C. Bournemouth ....
Plymouth Argyle v Crystal Palace...................................
Portsmouth v Bradford City ....
Stoke City v Walsall...
Sunderland v Shrewsbury Town ....
Watford v Leicester City...

THIRD DIVISION
Blackpool v Chesterfield...
Bolton Wanderers v Aldershot ....
Bristol Rovers v Northampton Town ....
Cardiff City v Southend United ....
Chester City v Preston North End ....
Mansfield Town v Bury ....
Notts County v Huddersfield Town.................................
Reading v Gillingham ....
Sheffield United v Brentford ....
Wigan Athletic v Fulham ....
Wolverhampton Wanderers v Swansea City ....

FOURTH DIVISION
Cambridge United v Crewe Alexandra ....
Darlington v Scarborough..
Hereford United v Doncaster Rovers...............................
Rochdale v Hartlepool United ....
Rotherham United v Burnley ....
Scunthorpe United v Lincoln City ....
Torquay United v Exeter City...
Tranmere Rovers v Grimsby Town ....
York City v Leyton Orient ....

Fri. 28th April

THIRD DIVISION
Gillingham v Bristol Rovers ....
Southend United v Notts County.....................................

FOURTH DIVISION
Torquay United v Scunthorpe United ....
Tranmere Rovers v Stockport County ....

Sat. 29th April

FIRST DIVISION
Arsenal v Norwich City ....
Aston Villa v Middlesbrough..
Everton v Liverpool ....
Luton Town v Derby County ....
Manchester United v Coventry City................................
Millwall v Tottenham Hotspur ....
Nottingham Forest v Southampton ....
Queens Park Rangers v Charlton Athletic........................
Sheffield Wednesday v West Ham United ....
Wimbledon v Newcastle United ....

SECOND DIVISION
A.F.C. Bournemouth v Barnsley ....
Bradford City v Leicester City ....
Crystal Palace v West Bromwich Albion ....
Hull City v Watford ....
Ipswich Town v Birmingham City...................................
Oldham Athletic v Plymouth Argyle ....

Oxford United v Manchester City......................................
Portsmouth v Blackburn Rovers ....
Shrewsbury Town v Chelsea..
Stoke City v Leeds United ....
Sunderland v Brighton & Hove Albion.............................
Walsall v Swindon Town...

Aldershot v Blackpool ....
Brentford v Mansfield Town...
Bristol City v Wigan Athletic ....
Bury v Bolton Wanderers ....
Chesterfield v Chester City..
Fulham v Sheffield United ....
Huddersfield Town v Wolverhampton Wanderers ....
Northampton Town v Cardiff City ....
Preston North End v Reading ....
Swansea City v Port Vale ....

Burnley v Doncaster Rovers..
Darlington v Colchester United ....
Exeter City v Hartlepool United ....
Grimsby Town v Carlisle United ....
Halifax Town v Lincoln City..
Leyton Orient v Cambridge United ....
Peterborough United v Crewe Alexandra ....
Rotherham United v Hereford United ....
Wrexham v Scarborough ....
York City v Rochdale ....

Mon. 1st May

Barnsley v Oxford United..
Birmingham City v Bradford City...................................
Blackburn Rovers v A.F.C. Bournemouth ....
Brighton & Hove Albion v Hull City ....
Chelsea v Stoke City ....
Leeds United v Walsall ....
Leicester City v Oldham Athletic ....
Manchester City v Crystal Palace ....
Plymouth Argyle v Ipswich Town ....
Swindon Town v Shrewsbury Town ....
Watford v Sunderland...
West Bromwich Albion v Portsmouth ....

Blackpool v Gillingham...
Bolton Wanderers v Huddersfield Town ....
Bristol Rovers v Southend United ....
Cardiff City v Chesterfield ....
Chester City v Bury ....
Notts County v Brentford ....
Port Vale v Northampton Town ....
Reading v Fulham ....
Sheffield United v Aldershot ....
Wigan Athletic v Preston North End...............................
Wolverhampton Wanderers v Bristol City........................

Carlisle United v Leyton Orient ....
Colchester United v Halifax Town...................................
Crew Alexandra v York City ....
Doncaster Rovers v Grimsby Town ....
Hartlepool United v Peterborough United ....
Hereford United v Tranmere Rovers ....
Lincoln City v Burnley ....
Rochdale v Torquay United ....
Scarborough v Exeter City ....
Scunthorpe United v Rotherham United ....
Stockport County v Wrexham...

Tues. 2nd May

Mansfield Town v Swansea City ....

Cambridge United v Darlington ....

Fri. 5th May

Colchester United v Exeter City......................................
Crewe Alexandra v Halifax Town....................................

Sat. 6th May

Charlton Athletic v Wimbledon ....
Coventry City v Nottingham Forest ....
Derby County v Aston Villa ....
Liverpool v Queens Park Rangers ....
Middlesbrough v Arsenal...
Newcastle United v Millwall...
Norwich City v Everton...
Southampton v Manchester United..................................
Tottenham Hotspur v Sheffield Wednesday.......................
West Ham United v Luton Town......................................

Barnsley v Portsmouth ....
Birmingham City v Hull City ....
Blackburn Rovers v Walsall ....
Brighton & Hove Albion v Ipswich Town ....
Chelsea v Bradford City ....
Leeds United v Oldham Athletic.....................................
Leicester City v Crystal Place ....
Manchester City v A.F.C. Bournemouth ....
Plymouth Argyle v Oxford United...................................
Swindon Town v Stoke City ....
Watford v Shrewsbury Town ....
West Bromwich Albion v Sunderland...............................

Blackpool v Huddersfield Town ....
Bolton Wanderers v Brentford..
Bristol Rovers v Fulham..
Cardiff City v Preston North End ....
Chester City v Gillingham ....
Mansfield Town v Chesterfield..
Notts County v Aldershot ....
Port Vale v Southend United ....
Reading v Bristol City ....
Sheffield United v Swansea City ....
Wigan Athletic v Bury ....
Wolverhampton Wanderers v Northampton Town ....

Cambridge United v Torquay United................................
Carlisle United v Wrexham ....
Doncaster Rovers v Tranmere Rovers...............................
Hartlepool United v Burnley ....
Hereford United v York City ....
Lincoln City v Leyton Orient ....
Rochdale v Peterborough United ....
Scarborough v Grimsby Town ....
Scunthorpe United v Darlington ....
Stockport County v Rotherham United.............................

Sat. 13th May

Arsenal v Derby County...
Aston Villa v Coventry City ....
Everton v West Ham United ....
Luton Town v Norwich City ....
Manchester United v Newcastle United............................
Millwall v Southampton ....
Nottingham Forest v Charlton Athletic.............................
Queens Park Rangers v Tottenham Hotspur......................

Sheffield Wednesday v Middlesbrough ....
Wimbledon v Liverpool..

SECOND DIVISION
A.F.C. Bournemouth v Plymouth Argyle ....
Bradford City v Manchester City ....
Crystal Palace v Birmingham City ....
Hull City v West Bromwich Albion.................................
Ipswich Town v Blackburn Rovers...................................
Oldham Athletic v Swindon Town ....
Oxford United v Watford ....
Portsmouth v Chelsea ....
Shrewsbury Town v Leeds United ....
Stoke City v Brighton & Hove Albion ....
Sunderland v Leicester City ....
Walsall v Barnsley..

THIRD DIVISION
Aldershot v Mansfield Town ....
Brentford v Cardiff City ....
Bristol City v Sheffield United ....
Bury v Bristol Rovers..

Chesterfield v Reading ....
Fulham v Port Vale ....
Gillingham v Notts County...
Huddersfield Town v Wigan Athletic ....
Preston North End v Wolverhampton Wanderers..............
Southend United v Chester City.....................................
Swansea City v Blackpool ....

FOURTH DIVISION
Burnley v Scarborough...
Darlington v Carlisle United ....
Exeter City v Lincoln City..
Grimsby Town v Hartlepool United.................................
Halifax Town v Hereford United.....................................
Leyton Orient v Scunthorpe United ....
Peterborough United v Doncaster Rovers.........................
Rotherham United v Cambridge United ....
Torquay United v Colchester United ....
Tranmere Rovers v Crewe Alexandra ....
Wrexham v Rochdale...
York City v Stockport County ....

B & Q LEAGUE FIXTURES 1988-89

© Scottish Football League 1988

Sat. 13th August

Celtic v Heart of Midlothian ....
Dundee v Aberdeen ....
Hamilton Academical v Rangers ....
Hibernian v Motherwell ....
St. Mirren v Dundee United ....

FIRST DIVISION
Ayr United v Clydebank ....
Falkirk v Airdrieonians ....
Forfar Athletic v Meadowbank Thistle ....
Morton v Clyde ....
Partick Thistle v Dunfermline Athletic ....
Queen of the South v Kilmarnock ....
St. Johnstone v Raith Rovers...

SECOND DIVISION
Albion Rovers v East Stirlingshire ....
Brechin City v Alloa ....
Cowdenbeath v Montrose ....
Dumbarton v East Fife ....
Queens Park v Berwick Rangers ....
Stirling Albion v Stenhousemuir ....
Stranraer v Arbroath ....

Sat. 20th August

PREMIER DIVISION
Aberdeen v St. Mirren ....
Dundee United v Celtic...
Heart of Midlothian v Hamilton Academical ....
Motherwell v Dundee ....
Rangers v Hibernian..

FIRST DIVISION
Airdrieonians v Morton ....
Clyde v Forfar Athletic ....
Clydebank v Falkirk ....
Dunfermline Athletic v St. Johnstone ....
Kilmarnock v Partick Thistle ....
Meadowbank Thistle v Ayr United ....
Raith Rovers v Queen of the South ....

SECOND DIVISION
Alloa v Cowdenbeath ....
Arbroath v Brechin City ....
Berwick Rangers v Stranraer ....
East Fife v Albion Rovers ....
East Stirlingshire v Queens Park ....
Montrose v Stirling Albion..
Stenhousemuir v Dumbarton..

Sat. 27th August

PREMIER DIVISION
Dundee United v Aberdeen ....
Hamilton Academical v Motherwell ....
Hibernian v Heart of Midlothian ....
Rangers v Celtic..
St. Mirren v Dundee ....

FIRST DIVISION
Airdrieonians v Queen of the South ....
Clyde v Partick Thistle ....
Dunfermline Athletic v Raith Rovers...............................
Forfar Athletic v St. Johnstone ....
Kilmarnock v Ayr United ....
Meadowbank Thistle v Falkirk..
Morton v Clydebank ....

SECOND DIVISION
Arbroath v Alloa ....
Dumbarton v Queens Park...
East Fife v Cowdenbeath ....
Montrose v Brechin City...
Stenhousemuir v East Stirlingshire ....
Stirling Albion v Berwick Rangers...................................
Stranraer v Albion Rovers ....

Sat. 3rd September

PREMIER DIVISION
Aberdeen v Hibernian ....
Celtic v Hamilton Academical ....
Dundee v Dundee United ....
Heart of Midlothian v St. Mirren ....
Motherwell v Rangers..

FIRST DIVISION
Ayr United v Forfar Athletic ....
Clydebank v Kilmarnock ....
Falkirk v Dunfermline Athletic ....
Partick Thistle v Morton...
Queen of the South v Meadowbank Thistle ....
Raith Rovers v Clyde ....
St. Johnstone v Airdrieonians ....

SECOND DIVISION
Albion Rovers v Dumbarton ....
Alloa v Stenhousemuir ....
Berwick Rangers v Arbroath ....
Brechin City v Stirling Albion ....
Cowdenbeath v Stranraer ....
East Stirlingshire v East Fife ....
Queens Park v Montrose ....

Sat. 10th September

FIRST DIVISION
Airdrieonians v Kilmarnock ....
Ayr United v Falkirk ....
Clyde v Clydebank ....
Dunfermline Athletic v Queen of the South.......................
Forfar Athletic v Partick Thistle ....
Meadowbank Thistle v Raith Rovers ....
Morton v St. Johnstone ....

SECOND DIVISION
Albion Rovers v Brechin City...
Dumbarton v Stranraer ....
East Fife v Alloa ....
East Stirlingshire v Berwick Rangers...............................

Montrose v Arbroath ....

Stenhousemuir v Cowdenbeath.....................................

Stirling Albion v Queens Park ....

Sat. 17th September

PREMIER DIVISION

Celtic v Aberdeen ....

Dundee United v Hibernian ....

Hamilton Academical v Dundee ....

Heart of Midlothian v Rangers.......................................

St. Mirren v Motherwell ....

FIRST DIVISION

Clydebank v Dunfermline Athletic ....

Falkirk v Morton...

Kilmarnock v Clyde...

Partick Thistle v Ayr United ....

Queen of the South v Forfar Athletic ....

Raith Rovers v Airdrieonians ....

St. Johnstone v Meadowbank Thistle ....

SECOND DIVISION

Alloa v East Stirlingshire ....

Arbroath v Stenhousemuir...

Berwick Rangers v Montrose..

Brechin City v Dumbarton...

Cowdenbeath v Albion Rovers ....

Queens Park v East Fife ....

Stranraer v Stirling Albion ....

Sat. 24th September

PREMIER DIVISION

Aberdeen v Heart of Midlothian ....

Dundee v Celtic ....

Hibernian v Hamilton Academical ....

Motherwell v Dundee United ....

Rangers v St. Mirren..

FIRST DIVISION

Airdrieonians v Partick Thistle ....

Ayr United v St. Johnstone ....

Clyde v Falkirk ....

Dunfermline Athletic v Kilmarnock.................................

Forfar Athletic v Raith Rovers..

Meadowbank Thistle v Clydebank...................................

Morton v Queen of the South ....

SECOND DIVISION

Albion Rovers v Queens Park...

Dumbarton v Alloa ....

East Fife v Arbroath ....

East Stirlingshire v Brechin City.....................................

Montrose v Stranraer..

Stenhousemuir v Berwick Rangers ....

Stirling Albion v Cowdenbeath ....

Tues. 27th September

PREMIER DIVISION

Dundee United v Rangers..

Hamilton Academical v Aberdeen...................................

Wed. 28th September

PREMIER DIVISION

Celtic v Motherwell ....

Heart of Midlothian v Dundee ....

St. Mirren v Hibernian ....

Sat. 1st October

PREMIER DIVISION

Dundee United v Heart of Midlothian...............................

Hibernian v Celtic ....

Motherwell v Aberdeen ....

Rangers v Dundee...

St. Mirren v Hamilton Academical ....

FIRST DIVISION

Airdrieonians v Meadowbank Thistle...............................

Clyde v Dunfermline Athletic..

Clydebank v Forfar Athletic...

Kilmarnock v Morton ....

Queen of the South v Falkirk ....

Raith Rovers v Ayr United ....

St. Johnstone v Partick Thistle ....

SECOND DIVISION

Alloa v Albion Rovers ....

Arbroath v Stirling Albion ....

Berwick Rangers v Dumbarton.......................................

Cowdenbeath v East Stirlingshire ....

Montrose v Stenhousemuir ....

Queens Park v Brechin City ....

Stranraer v East Fife ....

Sat. 8th October

PREMIER DIVISION

Aberdeen v Rangers...

Celtic v St. Mirren ....

Dundee v Hibernian ....

Hamilton Academical v Dundee United ....

Heart of Midlothian v Motherwell ....

FIRST DIVISION

Ayr United v Queen of the South ....

Dunfermline Athletic v Airdrieonians...............................

Falkirk v St. Johnstone...

Forfar Athletic v Kilmarnock ....

Meadowbank Thistle v Clyde ....

Morton v Raith Rovers ....

Partick Thistle v Clydebank ....

SECOND DIVISION

Albion Rovers v Berwick Rangers ....

Brechin City v Cowdenbeath ....

Dumbarton v Arbroath ....

East Fife v Montrose..

East Stirlingshire v Stranraer ....

Stenhousemuir v Queens Park ....

Stirling Albion v Alloa ....

Tues. 11th October

PREMIER DIVISION

Hamilton Academical v Heart of Midlothian ....

Wed. 12th October

PREMIER DIVISION

Celtic v Dundee United...

Dundee v Motherwell ....

Hibernian v Rangers..

St. Mirren v Aberdeen ....

Sat. 15th October

FIRST DIVISION

Airdrieonians v Clyde...

Ayr United v Dunfermline Athletic ....

Forfar Athletic v Morton ....
Meadowbank Thistle v Kilmarnock ....
Partick Thistle v Falkirk ....
Raith Rovers v Clydebank ....
St. Johnstone v Queen of the South ....

SECOND DIVISION
Albion Rovers v Arbroath ....
Alloa v Berwick Rangers ....
Brechin City v Stranraer ....
Dumbarton v Stirling Albion ....
East Fife v Stenhousemuir ....
East Stirlingshire v Montrose...
Queens Park v Cowdenbeath..

Sat. 22nd October

PREMIER DIVISION
Aberdeen v Dundee ....
Dundee United v St. Mirren...
Heart of Midlothian v Celtic..
Motherwell v Hibernian ....
Rangers v Hamilton Academical ....

FIRST DIVISION
Clyde v St. Johnstone ....
Clydebank v Airdrieonians ....
Dunfermline Athletic v Meadowbank Thistle ....
Falkirk v Forfar Athletic...
Kilmarnock v Raith Rovers..
Morton v Ayr United ....
Queen of the South v Partick Thistle ....

SECOND DIVISION
Arbroath v East Stirlingshire ....
Berwick Rangers v East Fife..
Cowdenbeath v Dumbarton ....
Montrose v Alloa ....
Stenhousemuir v Brechin City ....
Stirling Albion v Albion Rovers ....
Stranraer v Queens Park..

Sat. 29th October

PREMIER DIVISION
Celtic v Dundee..
Dundee United v Motherwell ....
Hamilton Academical v Hibernian ....
Heart of Midlothian v Aberdeen ....
St. Mirren v Rangers...

FIRST DIVISION
Ayr United v Clyde ....
Falkirk v Raith Rovers ....
Forfar Athletic v Airdrieonians......................................
Morton v Dunfermline Athletic......................................
Partick Thistle v Meadowbank Thistle ....
Queen of the South v Clydebank ....
St. Johnstone v Kilmarnock ....

SECOND DIVISION
Albion Rovers v Montrose...
Brechin City v Berwick Rangers....................................
Cowdenbeath v Arbroath ....
Dumbarton v East Stirlingshire......................................
Queens Park v Alloa..
Stirling Albion v East Fife...
Stranraer v Stenhousemuir..

Tues. 1st November

PREMIER DIVISION
Motherwell v St. Mirren ....
Rangers v Heart of Midlothian.......................................

Wed. 2nd November

PREMIER DIVISION
Aberdeen v Celtic ....
Dundee v Hamilton Academical ....
Hibernian v Dundee United..

Sat. 5th November

PREMIER DIVISION
Dundee United v Dundee..
Hamilton Academical v Celtic..
Hibernian v Aberdeen ....
Rangers v Motherwell..
St. Mirren v Heart of Midlothian....................................

FIRST DIVISION
Airdrieonians v Ayr United ....
Clyde v Queen of the South..
Clydebank v St. Johnstone...
Dunfermline Athletic v Forfar Athletic ....
Kilmarnock v Falkirk..
Meadowbank Thistle v Morton ....
Raith Rovers v Partick Thistle ....

SECOND DIVISION
Alloa v Stranraer ....
Arbroath v Queens Park...
Berwick Rangers v Cowdenbeath ....
East Fife v Brechin City...
East Stirlingshire v Stirling Albion.................................
Montrose v Dumbarton ....
Stenhousemuir v Albion Rovers......................................

Sat. 12th November

PREMIER DIVISION
Aberdeen v Dundee United ....
Celtic v Rangers..
Dundee v St. Mirren..
Heart of Midlothian v Hibernian ....
Motherwell v Hamilton Academical ....

FIRST DIVISION
Clydebank v Clyde ....
Falkirk v Ayr United ....
Kilmarnock v Airdrieonians ....
Partick Thistle v Forfar Athletic.....................................
Queen of the South v Dunfermline Athletic......................
Raith Rovers v Meadowbank Thistle ....
St. Johnstone v Morton..

SECOND DIVISION
Albion Rovers v East Fife..
Brechin City v Arbroath ....
Cowdenbeath v Alloa ....
Dumbarton v Stenhousemuir..
Queens Park v East Stirlingshire ....
Stirling Albion v Montrose...
Stranraer v Berwick Rangers..

Sat. 19th November

PREMIER DIVISION
Aberdeen v Motherwell ....
Celtic v Hibernian...
Dundee v Rangers...
Hamilton Academical v St. Mirren ....
Heart of Midlothian v Dundee United..............................

FIRST DIVISION
Airdrieonians v Raith Rovers ....
Ayr United v Partick Thistle...

Clyde v Kilmarnock ....
Dunfermline Athletic v Clydebank ....
Forfar Athletic v Queen of the South ....
Meadowbank Thistle v St. Johnstone ....
Morton v Falkirk ....

SECOND DIVISION
Alloa v Brechin City ....
Arbroath v Stranraer ....
Berwick Rangers v Queens Park ....
East Fife v Dumbarton ....
East Stirlingshire v Albion Rovers ....
Montrose v Cowdenbeath ....
Stenhousemuir v Stirling Albion ....

Sat. 26th November

PREMIER DIVISION
Dundee United v Hamilton Academical ....
Hibernian v Dundee ....
Motherwell v Heart of Midlothian ....
Rangers v Aberdeen ....
St. Mirren v Celtic ....

FIRST DIVISION
Clydebank v Meadowbank Thistle ....
Falkirk v Clyde ....
Kilmarnock v Dunfermline Athletic ....
Partick Thistle v Airdrieonians ....
Queen of the South v Morton ....
Raith Rovers v Forfar Athletic ....
St. Johnstone v Ayr United ....

SECOND DIVISION
Alloa v East Fife ....
Arbroath v Motnrose ....
Berwick Rangers v East Stirlingshire ....
Brechin City v Albion Rovers ....
Cowdenbeath v Stenhousemuir ....
Queens Park v Stirling Albion ....
Stranraer v Dumbarton ....

Sat. 3rd December

PREMIER DIVISION
Aberdeen v Hamilton Academical ....
Dundee v Heart of Midlothian ....
Hibernian v St. Mirren ....
Motherwell v Celtic ....
Dundee v Dundee United ....

FIRST DIVISION
Ayr United v Meadowbank Thistle ....
Falkirk v Clydebank ....
Forfar Athletic v Clyde ....
Morton v Airdrieonians ....
Partick Thistle v Kilmarnock ....
Queen of the South v Raith Rovers ....
St. Johnstone v Dunfermline Athletic ....

Sat. 10th December

PREMIER DIVISION
Celtic v Aberdeen ....
Dundee United v Hibernian ....
Hamilton Academical v Dundee ....
Heart of Midlothian v Rangers ....
St. Mirren v Motherwell ....

FIRST DIVISION
Airdrieonians v Forfar Athletic ....
Clyde v Ayr United ....
Clydebank v Queen of the South ....
Dunfermline Athletic v Morton ....

Kilmarnock v St. Johnstone ....
Meadowbank Thistle v Partick Thistle ....
Raith Rovers v Falkirk ....

SECOND DIVISION
Albion Rovers v Cowdenbeath ....
Dumbarton v Brechin City ....
East Fife v Queens Park ....
East Stirlingshire v Alloa ....
Montrose v Berwick Rangers ....
Stenhousemuir v Arbroath ....
Stirling Albion v Stranraer ....

Sat. 17th December

PREMIER DIVISION
Aberdeen v St. Mirren ....
Dundee United v Celtic ....
Heart of Midlothian v Hamilton Academical ....
Motherwell v Dundee ....
Rangers v Hibernian ....

FIRST DIVISION
Airdrieonians v Clydebank ....
Ayr United v Morton ....
Forfar Athletic v Falkirk ....
Meadowbank Thistle v Dunfermline Athletic ....
Partick Thistle v Queen of the South ....
Raith Rovers v Kilmarnock ....
St. Johnstone v Clyde ....

SECOND DIVISION
Alloa v Dumbarton ....
Arbroath v East Fife ....
Berwick Rangers v Stenhousemuir ....
Brechin City v East Stirlingshire ....
Cowdenbeath v Stirling Albion ....
Queens Park v Albion Rovers ....
Stranraer v Montrose ....

Sat. 24th December

FIRST DIVISION
Clyde v Airdrieonians ....
Clydebank v Raith Rovers ....
Dunfermline Athletic v Ayr United ....
Falkirk v Partick Thistle ....
Kilmarnock v Meadowbank Thistle ....
Morton v Forfar Athletic ....
Queen of the South v St. Johnstone ....

SECOND DIVISION
Albion Rovers v Stenhousemuir ....
Brechin City v East Fife ....
Cowdenbeath v Berwick Rangers ....
Dumbarton v Montrose ....
Queens Park v Arbroath ....
Stirling Albion v East Stirlingshire ....
Stranraer v Alloa ....

Sat. 31st December

PREMIER DIVISION
Celtic v Heart of Midlothian ....
Dundee v Aberdeen ....
Hamilton Academical v Rangers ....
Hibernian v Motherwell ....
St. Mirren v Dundee United ....

FIRST DIVISION
Airdrieonians v St. Johnstone ....
Clyde v Raith Rovers ....
Dunfermline Athletic v Falkirk ....
Forfar Athletic v Ayr United ....

Kilmarnock v Clydebank ....
Meadowbank Thistle v Queen of the South ....
Morton v Partick Thistle ....

SECOND DIVISION
Alloa v Queens Park ....
Arbroath v Cowdenbeath ....
Berwick Rangers v Brechin City ....
East Fife v Stirling Albion ....
East Stirlingshire v Dumbarton ....
Montrose v Albion Rovers ....
Stenhousemuir v Stranraer ....

Tues. 3rd January

PREMIER DIVISION
Dundee United v Aberdeen ....
Hamilton Academical v Motherwell ....
Hibernian v Heart of Midlothian ....
Rangers v Celtic...
St. Mirren v Dundee ....

FIRST DIVISION
Ayr United v Kilmarnock ....
Clydebank v Morton..
Falkirk v Meadowbank Thistle.......................................
Partick Thistle v Clyde ....
Queen of the South v Airdrieonians ....
Raith Rovers v Dunfermline Athletic...............................
St. Johnstone v Forfar Athletic ....

SECOND DIVISION
Albion Rovers v Stranraer ....
Alloa v Arbroath ....
Berwick Rangers v Stirling Albion...................................
Brechin City v Montrose...
Cowdenbeath v East Fife ....
East Stirlingshire v Stenhousemuir ....
Queens Park v Dumbarton...

Sat. 7th January

PREMIER DIVISION
Aberdeen v Hibernian ....
Celtic v Hamilton Academical ....
Dundee v Dundee United ....
Heart of Midlothian v St. Mirren....................................
Motherwell v Rangers..

FIRST DIVISION
Ayr United v Airdrieonians ....
Falkirk v Kilmarnock ....
Forfar Athletic v Dunfermline Athletic ....
Morton v Meadowbank Thistle ....
Partick Thistle v Raith Rovers ....
Queen of the South v Clyde ....
St. Johnstone v Clydebank ....

Sat. 14th January

PREMIER DIVISION
Aberdeen v Rangers..
Celtic v St. Mirren...
Dundee v Hibernian ....
Hamilton Academical v Dundee United ....
Heart of Midlothian v Motherwell ....

FIRST DIVISION
Airdrieonians v Falkirk ....
Clyde v Morton ....
Clydebank v Ayr United..
Dunfermline Athletic v Partick Thistle ....
Kilmarnock v Queen of the South....................................
Meadowbank Thistle v Forfar Athletic ....
Raith Rovers v St. Johnstone...

SECOND DIVISION
Arbroath v Berwick Rangers ....
Dumbarton v Albion Rovers ....
East Fife v East Stirlingshire..
Montrose v Queens Park ....
Stenhousemuir v Alloa...
Stirling Albion v Brechin City ....
Stranraer v Cowdenbeath ....

Sat. 21st January

PREMIER DIVISION
Dundee United v Heart of Midlothian...............................
Hibernian v Celtic..
Motherwell v Aberdeen ....
Rangers v Dundee..
St. Mirren v Hamilton Academical ....

FIRST DIVISION
Airdrieonians v Dunfermline Athletic...............................
Clyde v Meadowbank Thistle ....
Clydebank v Partick Thistle ....
Kilmarnock v Forfar Athletic ....
Queen of the South v Ayr United ....
Raith Rovers v Morton ....
St. Johnstone v Falkirk ....

SECOND DIVISION
Arbroath v Albion Rovers ....
Berwick Rangers v Alloa ....
Cowdenbeath v Queens Park...
Montrose v East Stirlingshire..
Stenhousemuir v East Fife ....
Stirling Albion v Dumbarton ....
Stranraer v Brechin City ....

Sat. 28th January

SECOND DIVISION
Albion Rovers v Stirling Albion ....
Alloa v Montrose ....
Brechin City v Stenhousemuir ....
Dumbarton v Cowdenbeath ....
East Fife v Berwick Rangers..
East Stirlingshire v Arbroath ....
Queens Park v Stranraer..

Sat. 4th February

FIRST DIVISION
Ayr United v Raith Rovers ....
Dunfermline Athletic v Clyde..
Falkirk v Queen of the South ....
Forfar Athletic v Clydebank ....
Meadowbank Thistle v Airdrieonians...............................
Morton v Kilmarnock ....
Partick Thistle v St. Johnstone ....

SECOND DIVISION
Alloa v Stirling Albion ....
Arbroath v Dumbarton ....
Berwick Rangers v Albion Rovers....................................
Cowdenbeath v Brechin City ....
Montrose v East Fife ....
Queens Park v Stenhousemuir ....
Stranraer v East Stirlingshire ....

Sat. 11th February

PREMIER DIVISION
Celtic v Motherwell ....
Dundee United v Rangers...

Hamilton Academical v Aberdeen....................................
Heart of Midlothian v Dundee ....
St. Mirren v Hibernian ....

FIRST DIVISION
Airdrieonians v Forfar Athletic..
Clydebank v Queen of the South ....
Dunfermline Athletic v St. Johnstone ....
Kilmarnock v Clyde..
Meadowbank Thistle v Raith Rovers ....
Morton v Falkirk...
Partick Thistle v Ayr United..

SECOND DIVISION
Albion Rovers v Alloa ....
Brechin City v Queens Park ....
Dumbarton v Berwick Rangers.......................................
East Fife v Stranraer ....
East Stirlingshire v Cowdenbeath ....
Stenhousemuir v Montrose ....
Stirling Albion v Arbroath ....

Sat. 18th February

SECOND DIVISION
Alloa v Arbroath ....
Berwick Rangers v Stirling Albion...................................
Cowdenbeath v Stenhousemuir.......................................
Dumbarton v East Fife ....
East Stirlingshire v Brechin City.....................................
Montrose v Stranraer ....
Queens Park v Albion Rovers...

Sat. 25th February

PREMIER DIVISION
Aberdeen v Heart of Midlothian ....
Dundee v Celtic..
Hibernian v Hamilton Academical ....
Motherwell v Dundee United ....
Rangers v St. Mirren ....

FIRST DIVISION
Ayr United v Meadowbank Thistle ....
Clyde v Clydebank ....
Falkirk v Dunfermline Athletic.......................................
Forfar Athletic v Morton ....
Queen of the South v Partick Thistle ....
Raith Rovers v Airdrieonians ....
St. Johnstone v Kilmarnock ....

SECOND DIVISION
Albion Rovers v Montrose ....
Arbroath v Berwick Rangers..
Brechin City v Alloa ....
East Fife v Cowdenbeath ....
Stenhousemuir v East Stirlingshire ....
Stirling Albion v Queens Park ....
Stranraer v Dumbarton ....

Sat. 4th March

FIRST DIVISION
Clyde v Ayr United ....
Clydebank v Dunfermline Athletic ....
Falkirk v Meadowbank Thistle..
Forfar Athletic v St. Johnstone ....
Kilmarnock v Airdrieonians ....
Morton v Partick Thistle ....
Raith Rovers v Queen of the South...................................

SECOND DIVISION
Albion Rovers v East Fife ....
Alloa v Stenhousemuir...

Berwick Rangers v East Stirlingshire.................................
Brechin City v Arbroath ....
Cowdenbeath v Dumbarton ....
Queens Park v Montrose ....
Stranraer v Stirling Albion ....

Sat. 11th March

PREMIER DIVISION
Aberdeen v Dundee ....
Dundee United v St. Mirren...
Heart of Midlothian v Celtic..
Motherwell v Hibernian ....
Rangers v Hamilton Academical......................................

FIRST DIVISION
Airdrieonians v Clyde ....
Ayr United v Kilmarnock ....
Dunfermline Athletic v Raith Rovers................................
Meadowbank Thistle v Clydebank ....
Partick Thistle v Falkirk ....
Queen of the South v Forfar Athletic ....
St. Johnstone v Morton ....

SECOND DIVISION
Arbroath v Stranraer ....
Dumbarton v Queens Park...
East Fife v Alloa ....
East Stirlingshire v Albion Rovers ....
Montrose v Cowdenbeath ....
Stenhousemuir v Berwick Rangers ....
Stirling Albion v Brechin City...

Sat. 18th March

FIRST DIVISION
Falkirk v Ayr United ....
Kilmarnock v Forfar Athletic ....
Meadowbank Thistle v Clyde ....
Morton v Clydebank...
Partick Thistle v Aidrieonians...
Queen of the South v Dunfermline Athletic.........................
Raith Rovers v St. Johnstone ....

SECOND DIVISION
Albion Rovers v Stranraer ....
Arbroath v East Fife ....
Berwick Rangers v Alloa ....
Brechin City v Stenhousemuir ....
Cowdenbeath v Queens Park..
Dumbarton v Montrose...
Stirling Albion v East Stirlingshire ....

Sat. 25th March

PREMIER DIVISION
Celtic v Dundee United..
Dundee v Motherwell ....
Hamilton Academical v Heart of Midlothian ....
Hibernian v Rangers ....
St. Mirren v Aberdeen ....

FIRST DIVISION
Airdrieonians v Morton...
Ayr United v Raith Rovers ....
Clyde v Partick Thistle ....
Clydebank v Falkirk ....
Dunfermline Athletic v Kilmarnock ....
Forfar Athletic v Meadowbank Thistle ....
St. Johnstone v Queen of the South ....

SECOND DIVISION
Alloa v Cowdenbeath ....
East Fife v Stirling Albion...

East Stirlingshire v Dumbarton ....
Montrose v Brechin City ....
Queens Park v Arbroath ....
Stenhousemuir v Albion Rovers ....
Stranraer v Berwick Rangers ....

Sat. 1st April

PREMIER DIVISION
Aberdeen v Dundee United ....
Celtic v Rangers ....
Dundee v St. Mirren ....
Heart of Midlothian v Hibernian ....
Motherwell v Hamilton Academical ....

FIRST DIVISION
Airdrieonians v Queen of the South ....
Clydebank v St. Johnstone ....
Forfar Athletic v Ayr United ....
Kilmarnock v Falkirk ....
Morton v Meadowbank Thistle ....
Partick Thistle v Dunfermline Athletic ....
Raith Rovers v Clyde ....

SECOND DIVISION
Berwick Rangers v Queens Park ....
Brechin City v Albion Rovers ....
Cowdenbeath v Arbroath ....
East Stirlingshire v East Fife ....
Stenhousemuir v Montrose ....
Stirling Albion v Dumbarton ....
Stranraer v Alloa ....

Sat. 8th April

PREMIER DIVISION
Dundee United v Dundee ....
Hamilton Academical v Celtic ....
Hibernian v Aberdeen ....
Rangers v Motherwell ....
St. Mirren v Heart of Midlothian ....

FIRST DIVISION
Ayr United v Clydebank ....
Clyde v Forfar Athletic ....
Dunfermline Athletic v Airdrieonians ....
Falkirk v Raith Rovers ....
Meadowbank Thistle v Kilmarnock ....
Queen of the South v Morton ....
St. Johnstone v Partick Thistle ....

SECOND DIVISION
Albion Rovers v Cowdenbeath ....
Alloa v Stirling Albion ....
Arbroath v Stenhousemuir ....
Dumbarton v Berwick Rangers ....
East Fife v Stranraer ....
Montrose v East Stirlingshire ....
Queens Park v Brechin City ....

Sat. 15th April

PREMIER DIVISION
Aberdeen v Hamilton Academical ....
Dundee v Heart of Midlothian ....
Hibernian v St. Mirren ....
Motherwell v Celtic ....
Rangers v Dundee United ....

FIRST DIVISION
Airdrieonians v St. Johnstone ....
Dunfermline Athletic v Morton ....
Falkirk v Clyde ....
Forfar Athletic v Clydebank ....
Kilmarnock v Raith Rovers ....
Partick Thistle v Meadowbank Thistle ....
Queen of the South v Ayr United ....

SECOND DIVISION
Berwick Rangers v Cowdenbeath ....
Dumbarton v Brechin City ....
East Fife v Stenhousemuir ....
East Stirlingshire v Alloa ....
Montrose v Arbroath ....
Stirling Albion v Albion Rovers ....
Stranraer v Queens Park ....

Sat. 22nd April

PREMIER DIVISION
Celtic v Dundee ....
Dundee United v Motherwell ....
Hamilton Academical v Hibernian ....
Heart of Midlothian v Aberdeen ....
St. Mirren v Rangers ....

FIRST DIVISION
Ayr United v Dunfermline Athletic ....
Clyde v Queen of the South ....
Clydebank v Partick Thistle ....
Meadowbank Thistle v Airdrieonians ....
Morton v Kilmarnock ....
Raith Rovers v Forfar Athletic ....
St. Johnstone v Falkirk ....

SECOND DIVISION
Albion Rovers v Dumbarton ....
Alloa v Montrose ....
Arbroath v East Stirlingshire ....
Brechin City v Berwick Rangers ....
Cowdenbeath v Stranraer ....
Queens Park v East Fife ....
Stenhousemuir v Stirling Albion ....

Sat. 29th April

PREMIER DIVISION
Aberdeen v Celtic ....
Dundee v Hamilton Academical ....
Hibernian v Dundee United ....
Motherwell v St. Mirren ....
Rangers v Heart of Midlothian ....

FIRST DIVISION
Airdrieonians v Falkirk ....
Clyde v Morton ....
Forfar Athletic v Dunfermline Athletic ....
Kilmarnock v Partick Thistle ....
Queen of the South v Meadowbank Thistle ....
Raith Rovers v Clydebank ....
St. Johnstone v Ayr United ....

SECOND DIVISION
Alloa v Albion Rovers ....
Arbroath v Dumbarton ....
Cowdenbeath v Brechin City ....
East Fife v Berwick Rangers ....
East Stirlingshire v Queens Park ....
Montrose v Stirling Albion ....
Stenhousemuir v Stranraer ....

190

Sat. 6th May

PREMIER DIVISION

Aberdeen v Motherwell ....

Celtic v Hibernian ....

Dundee v Rangers..

Hamilton Academical v St. Mirren ....

Heart of Midlothian v Dundee United............................

FIRST DIVISION

Ayr United v Airdrieonians ....

Clydebank v Kilmarnock...

Dunfermline Athletic v Clyde.......................................

Falkirk v Queen of the South ....

Meadowbank Thistle v St. Johnstone ....

Morton v Raith Rovers ....

Partick Thistle v Forfar Athletic....................................

SECOND DIVISION

Albion Rovers v Arbroath ....

Berwick Rangers v Montrose...

Brechin City v East Fife...

Dumbarton v Stenhousemuir...

Queens Park v Alloa..

Stirling Albion v Cowdenbeath ....

Stranraer v East Stirlingshire ....

Sat. 13th May

PREMIER DIVISION

Dundee United v Hamilton Academical ....

Hibernian v Dundee ....

Motherwell v Heart of Midlothian ....

Rangers v Aberdeen ....

St. Mirren v Celtic ....

FIRST DIVISION

Ayr United v Morton ....

Clyde v St. Johnstone...

Clydebank v Airdrieonians ....

Dunfermline Athletic v Meadowbank Thistle ....

Forfar Athletic v Falkirk...

Queen of the South v Kilmarnock...................................

Raith Rovers v Partick Thistle ....

SECOND DIVISION

Albion Rovers v Berwick Rangers...................................

Arbroath v Stirling Albion ....

Dumbarton v Alloa ....

East Fife v Montrose..

East Stirlingshire v Cowdenbeath ....

Stenhousemuir v Queens Park ....

Stranraer v Brechin City ....